God, Truth,
and Witness

God, Truth, and Witness

Engaging Stanley Hauerwas

L. Gregory Jones,
Reinhard Hütter,
and C. Rosalee Velloso Ewell,
Editors

BrazosPress
Grand Rapids, Michigan

© 2005 by L. Gregory Jones, Reinhard Hütter, and C. Rosalee Velloso Ewell

Published by Brazos Press
a division of Baker Publishing Group
P.O. Box 6287, Grand Rapids, MI 49516-6287
www.brazospress.com

Printed in the United States of America

Library of Congress Cataloging-in-Publication Data
God, truth, and witness : engaging Stanley Hauerwas / L. Gregory Jones, Reinhard Hütter, and C. Rosalee Velloso Ewell, editors.
    p.   cm.
  Includes bibliographical references and index.
  ISBN 1-58743-151-3 (hardcover)
  1. Philosophical theology. I. Hauerwas, Stanley, 1940– II. Jones, L. Gregory. III. Hütter, Reinhard, 1958– IV. Velloso da Silva, C. Rosalee. V. Title.
BT40.G57 2005
230—dc22   2004030657

Contents

Engaging Stanley Hauerwas   7
L. Gregory Jones, Reinhard Hütter, C. Rosalee Velloso Ewell

Part 1 Truthful Witness . . . and the Freedom of Friendship

    1. Sighing for the Love of Truth: Augustine's Quest   13
       Rowan A. Greer

    2. Can We Be Free without a Creator?   35
       David B. Burrell, CSC

    3. The Virtue of Writing Appropriately   53
       Hans S. Reinders

Part 2 Being a Christian . . . and Facing (Post-)Christendom

    4. A Constantinian Bishop: St. Ambrose of Milan   73
       Robert Louis Wilken

    5. The Politics of Diaspora   88
       Arne Rasmusson

    6. God and King   112
       Robert N. Bellah

    7. Hauerwasian Hooks and the Christian Social Imagination   131
       Emmanuel M. Katongole

    8. Christian Civilization   153
       Robert W. Jenson

Part 3 A City on a Hill . . . and the Church(es)

    9. Representing the Absent in the City   167
       Bernd Wannenwetsch

10. The Belligerent Kingdom   193
    H. Tristram Engelhardt, Jr.
11. Ecumenisms in Conflict   212
    George Lindbeck
12. What's Going On in the Church in South Africa?   229
    Neville Richardson

Part 4   Practicing Theology . . . and Learning from the Other

13. "An Immense Darkness" and the Tasks of Theology   257
    Nicholas Lash
14. Learning Made Strange   280
    Harry Huebner
15. Abrahamic Hauerwas   309
    Peter Ochs

Contributors   329
Index   332

Engaging Stanley Hauerwas

L. Gregory Jones, Reinhard Hütter, C. Rosalee Velloso Ewell

Engaging Stanley Hauerwas, dubbed "America's best theologian" by *Time* magazine in 2001, is joyful, frustrating, and transformative. It is joyful because few scholars are more interested in conversation and debate. Students and colleagues testify to Hauerwas's willingness to read drafts of work, promptly offering extensive and often penetratingly insightful comments. He maintains a remarkable correspondence, dictating long, passionately intellectual letters to a wide range of friends and colleagues around the world about everything from the practice of medicine to the reasons the Cubs will win "this year's" World Series (it does not matter which year it is). There are few people who write or read more widely than does Stanley Hauerwas. To become involved with him in conversation or correspondence, to read his work, or to bump into him in the hall is to be invited—and often expected—to explore issues you otherwise would never have imagined.

Engaging Stanley Hauerwas is also frustrating, in part because he is so intellectually gregarious. It is difficult to follow all the threads he finds fascinating and still retain a focus on your own passions. Hauerwas negotiates with great skill the boundary between being a scholar and becoming a dilettante, but those of us without that skill or interest often find ourselves frustrated by his apparent lack of focus or attention to such matters as historical detail and contextual specificity. In addition, engaging Hauerwas is frustrating because he spends far more time writing occasional essays than he does displaying the coherence of his thought in rigorous, book-length exposition. As a result, students and readers and colleagues are left to figure out how, for example, his convictions about the centrality of Jesus for the moral life cohere with his writings on medicine or the professions. Engaging Stanley Hauerwas also can be frustrating because he is a contrarian and a polemicist, drawn to exaggerated pronouncements in the passionate service of compelling others to see things differently—or at least in the interest of stirring up a more lively debate. It is, to say the least, frustrating to be on the receiving end of a Hauerwasian polemic delivered with passionate cleverness, but without sufficient nuance or care for the particularities of a position.

Yet while engaging Stanley Hauerwas can be alternately joyful and frustrating, and sometimes simultaneously so, most people have found this engagement to be transformative. Hauerwas's writings have persuaded many to be more critical of liberal political theory and practice, of Christian attitudes toward war and peace, and of the influence of American culture on the churches. To be transformed by an engagement with Hauerwas is not always to be persuaded, however; his writings have left many readers unconvinced. Yet even such readers have found themselves changed by the encounter because Hauerwas has transformed the character of the debates. He has been at the forefront of major transformations in theology, on topics as diverse as the centrality of Jesus and the church for shaping Christian life; the importance of character, the virtues, and friendship (themes he has retrieved from Aristotle and Aquinas and has emphasized since his dissertation); the wider retrieval of Aquinas's significance for theology and ethics; the use of narrative, both as a conceptual matter and with respect to the relevance of particular narratives; a Christian vision of medicine, especially through engagement with people with "intellectual disabilities"; and the significance of Scripture and "radical traditions."

Perhaps most significant, however, are the ways in which engaging Stanley Hauerwas has been transformative for people who have come to know him personally. He not only writes about friendship; he embodies it. He embraces friends of diverse backgrounds, ages, and commitments. He has friends whom he has met at Durham Bulls games, friends who have been his students and colleagues, friends from his churches, and friends whom he has met largely through correspondence. He befriends children with a disarming simplicity and joy. To be claimed as a friend by Stanley Hauerwas is also to be claimed by the diverse company of his friends. Such friendship is a joyful thing.

Friendship with Stanley Hauerwas is also frustrating, however, because it does not exempt you from challenge and disagreement; indeed, these experiences come with the territory. Hauerwas presses his friends more sharply than he does those with whom he shares less. He also often presumes that those with whom he has much in common ought to share even more. This presumption can be humorous—when, for example, he tries to convince European or African friends of the importance of baseball—but it also can be profoundly important. For example, he is a vigorous evangelist for his local church and has invited even the proprietor of his favorite local restaurant, the Flying Burrito, to come to church with him.

Friendship with Stanley Hauerwas is at its heart transformative because it is easy to be affected by his sheer joy for life, his creativity and depth and breadth as a scholar, and his passionate love for God and the gospel of Jesus Christ. And so, on the occasion of his sixty-fifth birthday, we thought it appropriate to gather, via the written page, some of Hauerwas's scholarly friends and to ask them to engage, once again, with Stanley Hauerwas.

In taking on this task, we were conscious of several major challenges, not the least of which was how to narrow down the extensive list of Hauerwas's scholarly friends. We began with several presumptions that helped us create a manageable list: we would not include any of his current colleagues at Duke,[1] nor any of his former students (ourselves included); we would not include those who contributed to a different collection of essays published in the United Kingdom, *Faithfulness and Fortitude;*[2] we would, where possible, invite Hauerwas's senior colleagues, those with whom he had been in conversation the longest; and we would seek to include friends from a variety of contexts, including diverse areas of the world. Unfortunately, prior commitments kept some potential contributors from being able to engage Stanley Hauerwas in this volume. We are thankful, however, for those who accepted the challenge, and we find it a cause for joy that were the limits of time and publication not upon us, the list of contributors could have included many, many more names.

We invited contributors to write essays that would engage Stanley Hauerwas's work, and we suggested themes of God, Truth, and Witness as foci for consideration. We chose these themes because they figure prominently in Hauerwas's work, especially his Gifford Lectures, published in 2001 as *With the Grain of the Universe.*[3]

---

1. When we invited Emmanuel Katongole to participate, he expected to be teaching full time at Uganda Martyrs University; since that time, he has joined the faculty of Duke Divinity School and so now is a colleague of Stanley Hauerwas.

2. Mark Thiessen Nation and Samuel Wells, eds., *Faithfulness and Fortitude: In Conversation with the Theological Ethics of Stanley Hauerwas* (Edinburgh: T. & T. Clark, 2000).

3. Stanley Hauerwas, *With the Grain of the Universe: The Church's Witness and Natural Theology* (Grand Rapids, Mich.: Brazos Press, 2001).

Indeed, our decision to undertake this book was made with those Gifford Lectures in view. We do not present these essays to Stanley Hauerwas as a valediction, for he is still very much an active scholar. We anticipate that many more essays and books will come from his hand—including responses to the essays in this volume. But we thought that in the wake of Hauerwas's major book-length statement in the Gifford Lectures, it would be appropriate and fruitful to invite senior colleagues to engage him in continuing conversation.

The diverse contributions of these colleagues reflect the joyful, frustrating, and transformative character of engaging Stanley Hauerwas. Several essays probe the adequacy of Hauerwas's work in one way or another, reflecting ongoing disagreements. Other essays use the themes Hauerwas has developed to explore important contemporary issues. Some of the contributors challenge Hauerwas to attend more carefully to either historical or contemporary contexts, and others extend his analysis into areas where—despite his breadth—Hauerwas has offered more intimation than argument. All of the essays, in their own ways, bear witness to their authors' appreciation for the transforming effects of intellectual and personal friendship with Stanley Hauerwas. We have divided the contributions into four sections, each of which touches on a major theme of Hauerwas's work and an area that needs, and warrants, continuing conversation and debate.

We could not have completed this book without the aid of friends and colleagues whose effectiveness and diligence have been remarkable: Paula Gilbert, who helped us conceive the project and offered advice while thoughtfully keeping the project secret from her husband, Stanley; Carol Shoun and Anne Weston, who edited the various essays into publishable form; Amy Turnbull, Carol Rush, and Mary Ann Andrus, who managed the process with great care; and our spouses, Susan Pendleton Jones, Nancy Heitzenrater Hütter, and Samuel E. Ewell, who patiently encouraged us despite the time the project took away from them and our families.

Editing this book has been, for the three of us, a labor of love. Each of us has been privileged to call Stanley Hauerwas a friend as well as a teacher, mentor, and colleague. We have found studying and working with him to be joyful, frustrating, and transformative. We have engaged Stanley Hauerwas and been engaged by him. We are grateful that he has not only claimed us as friends but also invited us to join the company of his friends. And so we offer this book to him—and to you—in appreciation, in friendship, and in the hope that the conversations will continue for many years to come.

Part 1

Truthful Witness . . . and the Freedom of Friendship

1

Sighing for the Love of Truth: Augustine's Quest

Rowan A. Greer

Truth, truth: how in my inmost being the very marrow of my mind sighed for you!

—Augustine, *Confessions*[1]

In the *Confessions*, Augustine the bishop looks back across a quarter century to view himself at the age of nineteen. It was his reading of Cicero's *Hortensius* that had kindled in him a love of wisdom and had led him to the Manichees who "used to say, 'Truth, truth.'" He now sees that the "dishes" of truth they offered him were "splendid hallucinations," "false mythologies," and "empty phantoms." Like the prodigal son, he was filling his belly with the husks the swine ate (*Conf.* 3.6.11). Augustine the prodigal continued to wander in a far country. After his

1. Saint Augustine, *Confessions*, trans. Henry Chadwick (Oxford: Oxford University Press, 1991), 3.6.10. I use Chadwick's translation throughout. Cf. *Util. cred.* 8.20.

13

repudiation of the Manichees he was tempted to embrace the skepticism of the Academics, failing to understand that their conviction that truth lay beyond human capacity was designed to preserve Plato's inklings of ultimate Truth (*Conf.* 5.10.19). Augustine was, of course, right to believe that truth is one way of describing the goal of human life. "The happy life is joy based on the truth" (*Conf.* 10.23.33).[2] But if truth is the prodigal's home, Augustine did not come to himself and begin his return journey until he found himself in the garden at Milan. Augustine the convert, the priest and bishop, remained Augustine the prodigal; however, he was no longer wandering but "struggling to return from this *far country* (Luke 15:13) by the road he has made in the humanity of the divinity of his only Son."[3] Augustine has not discovered truth, but he has embraced the promise that all who ask will receive and can "breathe in his truth . . . more deeply" (*Conf.* 8.7.17).[4]

Truth, then, is one among other keys that can unlock the doors through which Augustine's readers can enter his thought and travel with him on his homeward journey. Much the same judgment can be made about Stanley Hauerwas's writings, though I am quick to say that I do not mean to suggest that Stanley is a new Augustine or that Augustine is a Stanley ahead of time. There are obvious differences, not merely in the times for which their writings are tracts, but also in their understandings of truth. Augustine's insistence upon the great gulf between the Christian life in this world and the destiny awaiting the saints in the age to come is not one of Stanley's emphases. And if the ghost of Plato haunts Augustine, it is Aristotle's that we find in Stanley's writings, perhaps dressed as Thomas. Nevertheless, there are correlations. Both Augustine and Stanley locate truth in the Trinity and the revelation of the triune God in the story of Christ's incarnate life, death, and resurrection and in that of Scripture. Both insist that what God has enabled us to apprehend of truth must find expression in truthful lives that bear witness to Truth. Both articulate their thought in a coherent but not fully systematic way and do so in order to invite the reader into their mutual quest. Both are prolific writers. Diogenes would find his search

2. Cf. his comment on Ps. 4:2 in *Enarrat. Ps.* The verse reads, "Why do you love vanity and seek a lie?" Augustine comments: "Truth alone, from which all things are true, maketh blessed." Unless otherwise noted, all translations of Augustine are from *Nicean and Post-Nicean Fathers*, ed. Philip Schaff, 1st ser., vols. 1–8 (New York: Christian Literature Publishing Company, 1885).

3. Saint Augustine, *The Trinity*, trans. Edmund Hill, OP (Brooklyn, N.Y.: New City Press, 1991), 4.1. For this text I use Hill's translation throughout.

4. Cf. *Conf.* 12.1.1, and Stanley Hauerwas, *Vision and Virtue* (Notre Dame, Ind.: University of Notre Dame Press, 1974), 46: "We adhere to a reality whose depth we do not know, for we cannot comprehend its manifold richness."

rewarded, for both are truth-tellers about themselves and about their worlds. In what follows I wish only to meditate upon Augustine's views of truth with a Hauerwasian framework in mind.

Vision and Virtue

In his *Confessions* Augustine understands his conversion as both prepared and unexpected. His reading of the Platonic books, in all likelihood Latin translations of Plotinus by Marius Victorinus, together with the examples of Victorinus and Antony, paved the way for the intrusion of God's grace and the breaking of his chains. What he found in the Platonic books was the idea of the soul's capacity for movement toward or away from God. In the *Soliloquies* we can discern something of how that insight first appeared to him, since it is one of the four writings Augustine composed at Cassiciacum in the interval between his conversion in 386 and his baptism the next year.

The work is unfinished, but it gives us a clear picture of how Augustine understood the vision of God as one of Truth. After a brief introduction, Book 1 begins with a long prayer addressed to God the Creator who is also "the Truth, in, by and through whom all truths are true." God is also Wisdom, Life, Beatitude, the Good, the Beautiful, and "the Intelligible Light, in, by and through whom all intelligible things are illumined." But buried in the prayer is the story of creation and redemption that finds its focus in the begotten Son, one with his Father, who became for us in the incarnation the Way, the Door, the Bread of Life, the Living Water, and who swallowed up death in victory and leads us into all truth by purifying us in faith, hope, and love. This story within a prayer is faith's answer to Augustine's desire to know himself and God. The inner dialogue between Augustine and his Reason that follows is an attempt to move from faith to understanding, a seeking that does not fully attain its object.[5]

Book 1 focuses upon the moral purification that must precede the vision of God, and Reason "promises to let you see God with your mind as the sun is seen with the eye" (*Solil.* 1.6.12). This vision of God requires that the soul has sound eyes, and so the first stage of seeking

---

5. See *Solil.* 1.2.7: "I have made my prayer to God. *Reason.*—What then do you wish to know? *Augustine.*—All that I have mentioned in my prayer. . . . I desire to know God and the soul." Cf. 1.3.8: "My question is not about what I believe but about what I know. Possibly we may be rightly said to believe everything we know, but not to know what we only believe." Translation from J. H. S. Burleigh, ed., *Augustine: Earlier Writings*, Library of Christian Classics 6 (Philadelphia: Westminster, 1953).

understanding is the healing of the soul's eyes by faith, hope, and love. Only then can the soul look in order to see. In this life, the vision that unites the soul with God also requires faith, hope, and love. In the life to come, love alone suffices, since faith will yield to sight, and hope to its object. Reason interrogates Augustine and asks how far he has been healed and whether he is still disturbed by the passions, "the well-known diseases and perturbations of the mind" (*Solil.* 1.9.16). Augustine has clearly made excellent progress, but Reason points out that a "spent pestilence is a very different thing from one that is merely quiescent." A dung heap does not stink until it is stirred (*Solil.* 1.11.19). Augustine's dream of "imagined fondlings" proves Reason's point and shows "what remains to be cured" (*Solil.* 1.14.25). The book ends when Reason equates Augustine's desire to know the soul and God with wanting to know the truth.

Book 2 then asks how we can know the truth. The question is framed in the context of Augustine's desire to be in order to live and to live in order to know. Moreover, his wish is to be, to live, and to know eternally. Part of the confusion of the book revolves around the tension between the problem of how we can know the truth and the issue of the soul's immortality. The inconclusive conclusion is that truth is eternal and that its presence in the soul and the soul's participation in truth prove the soul's immortality. Augustine repeatedly alerts the reader to the dubious character of Reason's argumentation. It is too quick, too circuitous.[6] Faith seeks understanding but fails to find it. What really explains this peculiarity of Book 2 is that Augustine in a dreamlike way is asking questions about the epistemological issues found, for example, in Cicero's *Academica*.

These issues depend upon Greek philosophy in general and in particular upon Antiochus of Ascalon's revival of a dogmatic Platonism against the skeptical Academics. Epicurus had argued that all knowledge comes from sense impressions and that all sense perceptions are true.[7] Against him, the Academics argued that things seen are false as well as true, that false presentations cannot be said to be perceived, that true and false presentations are indistinguishable to the senses, and, consequently, that "there is no presentation that is capable of being perceived."[8] The

---

6. *Solil.* 2.3.4; 2.4.5; 2.7.13–14; 2.13.24; 2.14.25; 2.20.34.

7. See Cicero, *De natura deorum. Academica*, Loeb Classical Library, Cicero, vol. 19, ed. and trans. H. Rackham (Cambridge, Mass.: Harvard University Press, 1967), 1.5.19; 2.25.79; 2.26.82; 2.46.142. Cf. Augustine, *Solil.* 2.4.5: "If falsity be banished from the universe, that means that all things become true." Also 2.5.8: "Then, if whatever is is true there will be nothing false."

8. Cicero, *Acad.* 2.13.40: "Nullum igitur est visum quod percipi possit."

point is not that we can have no probable knowledge but that the senses are unreliable—the oar that appears broken in the water; twins, seal-impressions, and eggs that are indistinguishable.[9] Antiochus, in his turn, argues that sense impressions *are* reliable, since "the senses contain the highest truth, given that they are sound and healthy and also that all obstacles and hindrances are removed."[10] Nevertheless, he adds that the senses are instruments of the mind, which is the percipient.[11]

Augustine rings the changes on these ideas but in the second part of Book 2 (11.19–20.36) presses beyond them.[12] Knowledge that derives from sense impressions may not be totally unreliable. Nevertheless, since falsity involves both likeness and unlikeness to truth, truth and falsehood are "inevitably intertwined" at this level. "We ought to seek the absolute truth, not that double-faced thing that is partly true and partly false" (*Solil.* 2.10.18). The search, then, moves on to "the art of dialectic" and the school disciplines such as "literary studies." Dialectic informs all the school disciplines, and in this sense "literature as a true discipline is created by the same art as you have just defended against the charge of falsehood." But this means that we must distinguish dialectic as a school discipline from its function as the source of truth in all the disciplines (*Solil.* 2.11.21). This difficulty and others prompt Augustine to complain again about the "circuitous" character of the argument (*Solil.* 2.14.25). Reason finally resorts to an exhortation and advises Augustine to "return to your inward self" where truth dwells, however much it may seem to be forgotten (*Solil.* 2.19.33–2.20.34).

The solution, then, in the final analysis, is Plato's doctrine of reminiscence as found particularly in the *Meno*. In a commonsense way we often bring to memory what we had forgotten. When someone or some thing reminds us in this way "the whole thing suddenly comes back to our memory as if a light had been kindled, and we have no further trouble in recalling it" (*Solil.* 2.20.34). Similarly, in learning truths that transcend the sensible world, we "draw them out from the oblivion that has overwhelmed them, or dig them out as it were." These truths point beyond themselves to "the face of Truth, whose splendour glimmers

9. Cicero, *Acad.* 2.7.19; 2.17.54; 2.18.57; 2.25.79. Cf. Augustine, *Solil.* 2.6.11; 2.7.13; 2.9.17; 2.19.79.

10. Cicero, *Acad.* 2.17.19.

11. Cf. what appears to be Augustine's reductio ad absurdum of the idea in *Solil.* 2.4.5–2.5.7. See John Dillon's discussion of Antiochus's criterion of truth in *The Middle Platonists* (London: Duckworth, 1977), 63–69.

12. See Dillon's discussion of Albinus in *The Middle Platonists*, 273–76. For the way these issues find their way into the thought of Clement of Alexandria, see S. R. C. Lilla, *Clement of Alexandria: A Study in Christian Platonism and Gnosticism* (London: Oxford University Press, 1971), 124–27, 131, 166–69, 173.

even now in these liberal arts." "The face of Truth remains one and immutable" (*Solil.* 2.20.35). The soul's potential access to Truth itself demonstrates its immortality. Augustine will come to see that this way of putting the point might imply Plato's doctrine of the transmigration of souls. In his *Retractions* Augustine refers to the passage just cited and supplies a succinct definition of his doctrine of illumination:[13]

> I do not approve this. When even untrained persons, suitably questioned, are able to return correct answers, a more credible reason is that they have according to their capacity the presence of the light of the Eternal Reason. Hence they catch a glimpse of immutable truth. The reason is not that they once knew it and have forgotten, as Plato and others like him have thought.

Illumination, then, depends not upon the soul's prior existence, but upon its capacity for apprehending—though not comprehending—eternal Truth. And Augustine clearly identifies Truth with God. His prayer at the beginning of the *Soliloquies* implies that he sees no contradiction between his faith and the philosophical themes by which he seeks to understand it.[14]

The vision of truth Augustine describes, of course, echoes Plato's myth of the cave. The philosopher king leaves behind the sensible world of shadows and ascends to the full light of the intelligible world. The ascent, for Augustine as for Plotinus, is at the same time an inward journey, a surer path than using the stepping stones of the visible creation as a means for apprehending God.[15] Moreover, virtue is in one sense the preparatory requirement for vision. The soul's eyes require healing. At the same time, the vision is what enables virtue. The philosopher king is meant to return to the cave in order to explain what the shadows really mean. In his mature thought, Augustine treats the inner ascent as a movement from sense knowledge to the visionary knowledge that

---

13. *Retract.* 1.4.4. Cf. *Trin.* 12.15.24 and *Ep.* 7, where the allusion to the *Meno* is clear.

14. See R. A. Markus, "Augustine: Reason and Illumination," in *The Cambridge History of Later Greek and Early Medieval Philosophy*, ed. A. H. Armstrong (Cambridge: Cambridge University Press, 1970), 362–73.

15. See, e.g., Plotinus, *The Enneads*, abr. with intro. John Dillon, trans. Stephen Mac-Kenna (London: Penguin Books, 1991), 1.6.8–9: "The Fatherland to us is There whence we have come, and there is the Father. What then is our course, what the manner of our flight? This is not a journey for the feet; the feet bring us only from land to land; nor need you think of a coach or ship to carry you away; all this order of things you must set aside and refuse to see: you must close the eyes and call instead upon another vision which is to be waked within you. . . . Withdraw into yourself and look." Cf. Augustine's allusion to this passage, *Conf.* 8.8.19.

transcends the visible world. In direct sense perception, impressions stamp themselves on the mind, but conception revives those impressions in a more inward way. Beyond these two forms of knowing are what he calls "knowledge" and "wisdom." "Knowledge" is primarily moral in character, whereas "wisdom" is the contemplation of God. The inward movement, then, becomes outward as the vision expresses itself in virtue. This pattern informs Augustine's argument in Books 11–14 of *On the Trinity*, and in Book 12 "knowledge" becomes part of the image of God only when it is united with "wisdom." Virtue and vision must be bonded with one another. Something of this view may be found earlier in *On Free Will* in the context of Augustine's argument for the existence of God. The "inner light of which bodily sense knows nothing" (*Lib.* 2.8.23)[16] enables us to know the science of numbers and, consequently, of wisdom. Those who "live partly in the contemplation of truth and partly in laborious duties, which they owe to human society, these think they hold the palm of wisdom" (*Lib.* 2.9.25). What they contemplate is the "rules and guiding lights of the virtues" (*Lib.* 2.10.29). The Platonizing equation of knowledge and virtue dominates Augustine's understanding of vision and virtue. Doing the truth brings knowledge, while knowing the truth enables us to do it.

There would be many ways of elaborating the pattern I am describing. In *On the Trinity*, Book 8, Augustine worries with the large question of how we can know God in order to love him and with the smaller question concerning by what principle we can love one another. Perhaps that principle is an "inner truth present to the mind," a form of justice by which we love justice in ourselves and in others. "Whoever therefore loves men should love them either because they are just or in order that they might be just. This is how he ought to love himself, either because he is just or in order to be just" (*Trin.* 8.9). This love of justice is what it means to love our neighbors as ourselves. The implication of the argument is that the love of self and neighbor depends upon loving the form of justice, and it is possible to argue that this form is one of those guiding lights involved in the contemplation of God. Elsewhere Augustine says that only God can be an ultimate object of love. Consequently, we can "enjoy" loving God; but we must treat all other loves as proximate.[17] Yet all lesser loves are to be ordered under the love of God and so given a value they could not otherwise have. Loving ourselves and others in order that we and they may conform to the inner truth

16. Translations are from *Augustine: Earlier Writings*.

17. The contrast is between enjoyment and "use" (*fruor* and *utor*), but the English translation "use" has misleading connotations. For the ordering of loves, see, e.g., *Conf.* 4.6.11–12.9, *Doctr. chr.* 1.22.20–26.27.

of justice is to see humans in the light of God's love. This is why love of God and love of neighbor are one love. At the human level our loves are appetitive, and we seek union with those we love. But by their right ordering these loves share in God's creative love, and we can desire that those we love *be* and flourish. And so, once more, we find the union of virtue and vision.

To examine Augustine's thought from the perspective of vision and virtue tends to reveal Augustine the Christian Platonist. Indeed, in *Of True Religion* he argues that Christianity is in substance what Plato taught. Suppose, Augustine says, that Plato were asked about his teaching, and one of his disciples had said:

> You have persuaded me that truth is seen not with the bodily eyes but by the pure mind, and that any soul that cleaves to truth is thereby made happy and perfect. Nothing hinders the perception of truth more than a life devoted to lusts, and the false images of sensible things. . . . Therefore the mind has to be healed. . . . Now, if some great and divine man should arise to persuade the peoples that such things were to be at least believed if they could not grasp them with the mind . . . would you not judge that such a man is worthy of divine honours? (*Ver. rel.* 3.3)[18]

Plato's answer is affirmative, and Augustine's point is that what Plato taught unpersuasively to the few is now made available to all because of Christ. Platonism, then, is an unpersuasive and churchless harbinger of Christianity. To be sure, the themes that revolve around vision and virtue are not merely Platonist. Augustine has Christianized them by insisting that God has revealed the vision in Scripture and in the incarnation of his Son and by arguing that this revelation of truth finds its witness in the community of the church. But Augustine not only Christianizes the themes, he also examines them from a perspective that seeks to test the ideal by the actual.[19]

Truthfulness and Tragedy

Let me suggest that Augustine's cold and honest perspective upon his ideal of vision and virtue is not entirely a factor of the emergence of his

18. The translation is from *Augustine: Earlier Writings*.
19. See Martha C. Nussbaum, "The Christian Ascent: Augustine," in *Upheavals of Thought: The Intelligence of Emotions* (Cambridge: Cambridge University Press, 2001), 527–56. Cf. Stanley Hauerwas, *The Peaceable Kingdom* (Notre Dame, Ind.: University of Notre Dame Press, 1983), 30: "Furthermore, we cannot see the world rightly unless we are changed, for as sinners we do not desire to see truthfully."

mature theology, with its doctrines of original sin and operative grace. It is true that by the time he writes the *Questions to Simplicianus* in 396, soon after becoming the bishop of Hippo, Augustine has arrived at his understanding of the two ideas that at the very least transform earlier Christian views and that radically reinterpret the Christian Platonism to which he had been converted. The first of these ideas is that what we inherit from Adam is not merely mortality in its obvious meaning, but also spiritual and eternal death. The second is the correlate of this conclusion, that God's grace must be not merely persuasive but operative and sovereign. Conversion becomes a resurrection from death in the widest possible sense and not merely a healing or an education. Nevertheless, from the beginning Augustine has doubts about his capacity to be healed and about the conventions of Christian Platonism. It is these doubts that plant the seed of his mature view. If he discovers in himself obstacles to moral purification that he can neither understand nor control, where do they come from? His reading of St. Paul leads him to conclude that they are the product of his being Adam's child, and it follows that his utter helplessness requires God's sovereign act in prevenient grace. These convictions by no means replace his ideal of vision and virtue. They simply mean that he finds himself moving away from God and incapable of turning round toward the inner vision without operative grace. In Augustine's development, then, his understanding of truthfulness and tragedy is discontinuous because his mature view sharpens and hardens his sense of the tragic. But it is also continuous because of the lively sense of human sin, including not least his own, that characterizes even his earliest writings.

One way of seeking to establish this conclusion is to examine Augustine's treatment of 1 John 2:16 on either side of the watershed of 396. He wrote *Of True Religion* in 390 or 391 and *Confessions* some time in 397 or shortly after. The earlier work is remarkable because of the absence of Augustine's two mature doctrines. There is no mention of original sin in the later sense. Rather, it is merely the death of the body that "we owe to the primal sin" (*Ver. rel.* 12.25). Although the body became "weak and mortal" because of Adam's sin, "even in this corruptible body it is permitted to us to work towards righteousness" (*Ver. rel.* 15.29). The church is the threshing floor where "every one voluntarily makes himself either corn or chaff" (*Ver. rel.* 6.10). In the incarnation, Christ "did nothing by violence, but everything by persuasion." His life was "an education in morals" (*Ver. rel.* 16.31–32). Thus, the chief argument of the treatise revolves around how with God's help we can find the vision and virtue that will save us. The last section, however, is a discussion of the obstacles we encounter in this enterprise. And it is the text from 1 John 2:16 that supplies the organizing principle for the section: "All that is in the world is lust of the flesh, lust of the eyes, and ambition of this world."[20] There are three classes of people—the lovers of "the lower pleasures," the "curious," and the "proud" (*Ver. rel.* 38.70).

Augustine begins his discussion by correlating the three classes with the three temptations of Christ—in the Lukan order. Turning the stone to bread alludes to the pleasures of the flesh; worshipping Satan, to pride; casting himself down from the pinnacle of the temple, to curiosity (*Ver. rel.* 38.71). This order, of course, reverses the last two of the Johannine themes. Augustine's discussion of bodily pleasure (*Ver. rel.* 29.72–45.83) does include references to eating and drinking and to the ideal of virginity (*Ver. rel.* 44.82), but most of it is concerned with an appeal to turn from the "outward man." "Return within yourself. In the inward man dwells truth." It is there that "the light of reason is kindled" (*Ver. rel.* 39.72). A Cartesian-like argument reinforces the exhortation. Even if someone doubts, he knows the truth that he doubts. But Augustine is quick to add that even this kind of reasoning "does not create truth, but discovers it" (*Ver. rel.* 39.73).[21] Turning from bodily pleasure, then, is the inward journey toward illumination and the discovery of the image of God. Subduing cupidity transforms this vice into the cardinal virtue of temperance (*Ver. rel.* 41.78).

The next stage is the conquest of pride, which perversely imitates God by seeking a false "unity and omnipotence" (*Ver. rel.* 44.84). Though he does not use these expressions, it is clear that Augustine thinks of pride as the ambition and vainglory to be found in the lust for dominion and the love of self. It is the ordering of love that conquers pride. Loving God with all our heart and soul and mind is "the relationship which binds all together." The person who does this need not sorrow for "the death of anyone, for he who loves God with all his mind knows that nothing can perish for him unless it also perish in the sight of God" (*Ver. rel.* 47.91).[22] Finally, just as we must transform cupidity to temperance, so we must turn pride into justice as the proper ordering of all things under God.

---

20. *Concupiscentia carnis, concupiscentia oculorum, ambitio saeculi.*

21. Cf. two other passages that describe the inward ascent. *Ver. rel.* 42.79: "Let us turn to God so that we may deserve to be illumined by his Word, the true light [John 1:9]. . . . We must, then, seek the realm where number exists in complete tranquillity; for there existence is, above all, unity." *Ver. rel.* 44.82: "Man is rightly said to be made in the image and likeness of God. Not otherwise could he behold unchangeable truth with his mind."

22. See the whole of *Ver. rel.* 46.86–47.92. The discussion implies the ideal of virginity and the possibility of a view that would regard sexuality as a product of the fall. In *Retract.* 1.13.8 Augustine says, "I completely disapprove of this notion." He had not yet seen that had they not fallen Adam and Eve would have had sexual relations in paradise before the fall.

The last stage involves overcoming "curiosity," which is a false "joy of knowing things" (*Ver. rel.* 49.94). Augustine is thinking of spectacles, juggling tricks, jests, and games, which are "phantasms" that attack us "like brigands" (*Ver. rel.* 49.95). The antidote, of course, is knowledge of eternal Truth; and there may be the implication that this knowledge is the prudence that transforms curiosity to wisdom.

The three vices mentioned in 1 John 2:16 correlate with three of the four cardinal virtues, and their transformation into virtue removes them as obstacles to illumination and knowledge of truth. Doing so does not appear impossible. The Christian's task, then, is to conquer the bodily passions, then to acquire virtue, and finally to arrive at the contemplation of God as Truth. Virtue leads to vision. But Augustine can also describe the task in reverse order; vision leads to virtue:

> Those who desire these true ends first put off curiosity; for they know that certain knowledge which is within, and they enjoy it as far as they can in this life. Then they put off obstinacy and receive facility in acting. . . . Lastly, they seek bodily tranquillity by abstaining from things that are not necessary for living this life. (*Ver. rel.* 53.103)

Augustine continues by recognizing that we now know only in part (1 Cor. 13:12) and that the task will find its perfection only in the life to come. Nevertheless, the early Augustine has not yet despaired of a present if partial healing; the obstacles can be largely overcome.

The same scriptural text (1 John 2:16) also provides the structure for Augustine's discussion at the end of Book 10 of the *Confessions*. He has examined his memory as though it were a great storehouse. He identifies his memory with his soul, and in it he finds sense impressions and remembered emotions. He points out that we can remember sorrow with joy and joy with sorrow. But *memoria* is not tied to the past, and it also contains the timeless principles of the sciences. He compares himself to the woman in the parable who searches for her lost coin. It is lost, but not so lost that she fails to look for it. Augustine appears to be looking for the lost coin of the image of God within him. It is the "beauty so old and so new" that has called and touched him, summoning him to the search. But the decisive breakthrough of his conversion, to shift the metaphor, has given him not the cure but only the medicine that will effect it. "You are the physician, I am the patient. You are pitiful, I am the object of pity. Is not human life on earth a trial?" (*Conf.* 10.28.39). Already God has commanded him to abstain "from the lust of the flesh and the lust of the eyes and the ambition of the secular world." But not yet has God's medicine enabled him to respond to the commands of 1 John 2:16 in any perfect way (*Conf.* 10.30.41). The "lust of the flesh"

includes sexual temptations, eating and drinking, perfumes, the pleasures of the ear and the eyes—all the senses (*Conf.* 10.30.34). The "lust
of the eyes" is "vain inquisitiveness" and curiosity, and it displays itself
in the fascination with mangled corpses, public spectacles, magic, the
theater, idle tales, and even such sights as a dog chasing a rabbit or a
lizard catching a fly (*Conf.* 10.35). The "ambition of the secular world"
is pride (*Conf.* 10.36). Augustine comes closer to passing the test with
respect to the first two commands, but he confesses his pride in his
pleasure at praise and in his tendency to self-justification in the face
of blame (*Conf.* 10.37.60–61). He is by no means healed, but he has
confidence in Christ the physician (*Conf.* 10.41.69).

What is surprising about Augustine's use of 1 John 2:16 in *Confessions*
10 is not so much the way he applies the text to his own self-examina-
tion, but his reversal of the order of lusts, a reversal that conforms to the
order of the biblical text.[23] Pride rather than curiosity is the climactic
vice. Since pride is opposed to love, and curiosity to knowledge, does
Augustine now see love as more important than knowledge, and is God
better understood as the Good than as Truth? I am reluctant to go that
far, largely because I am unconvinced that Augustine treats the will and
the intellect as separable faculties, and so he does not mean to oppose
love to knowledge.[24] There may be a shift of emphasis, but not one that
would sever love from knowledge.

Another way to explain the peculiarity I have noted is to argue that
Augustine employs two rather different patterns in order to explain the
Christian life. One of them focuses upon the dialectic of contemplation
and action. In this pattern contemplation is both the goal of the active
life of virtue and its enabler. Thus, in *Of True Religion* Augustine treats
the opposite of pride as action and virtue, and the opposite of curiosity as contemplation and vision. Moral purgation leads to illumination
and vice versa. Augustine employs the same pattern in *On the Trinity*
12. But he also uses another pattern in the same treatise that seems to
me to inform his treatment of the Johannine text in *Confessions* 10. It
is possible to argue that beginning with Book 8 of *On the Trinity* Au-

---

23. Cf. his comment on Ps. 8:7–8 (beasts, birds, and fish) in *Enarrat. Ps.* The three
creatures mentioned in the psalm correspond to the three vices in 1 John 2:16, but with
the last two reversed. He goes on to correlate the three vices with Christ's temptation—in
the Lukan order. On the other hand, when he treats the verse in his homilies on 1 John,
he keeps the Johannine order and makes the reference to Christ's temptation in Matthew's
order. Sermon 62 on Luke 14:16ff. (the parable of the banquet) treats the three excuses in
reverse order: marrying a wife is the lust of the flesh; buying five pairs of oxen, the lust
of the eyes; buying a farm, the ambition of life.

24. See my attempt to understand what Augustine means by the will, "Augustine's Transformation of the Free Will Defence," *Faith and Philosophy* 13, no. 4 (1996): 471–86.

gustine, generally speaking, treats the Christian life as one involving three intertwined activities—remembering, knowing, and loving. These activities do not appear arranged hierarchically, and the only reason we distinguish them is because we are still in this life and have not yet found the lost coin of the image of God, a discovery that will coincide with the full coalescence of the three activities, whereby they will cease being activities. The Christian life, then, becomes a movement from the soul's dispersion to its unification by cleaving to God. This second pattern looks a little like a Christianized version of Plotinus's schema of the soul's destiny as a movement from diversity toward the One. From this perspective, we need not arrange curiosity and pride in *Confessions* 10 hierarchically, but can think of them as two dimensions of the failure of the "inner man" to attain truth.

There are ways of illustrating the point I am making. For example, in *On the Trinity* 8 Augustine argues that we must know something before we can love it and, consequently, asks how we can know God in order to love him. The conclusion he reaches is paradoxical. It is our capacity for love that gives us the principle of knowledge by which we can know God in order to love him. Augustine makes the same point in his comments on John 16:12–13:

> For that cannot be loved which is altogether unknown. But when what is known, in however small a measure, is also loved, by the self-same love one is led on to a better and fuller knowledge. If, then, you grow in the love which the Holy Spirit spreads abroad in your hearts (Rom. 5:5), "He will teach you all truth" (John 16:13). (*Tract. ev. Jo.* 96)

Loving and knowing become no more than two ways of speaking of the same thing. Nevertheless, since this pattern describes a movement from the soul's dispersion toward its unification in the recovered image of God, it points toward the tragic character of human life. Even when God's grace through the Spirit "spreads abroad" love in our hearts, we remain no more than convalescent in this life. For this reason, Augustine increasingly relocates vision and illumination in the age to come.[25]

The fact that we can distinguish remembering, knowing, and loving implies that even those people whom God's grace has delivered from original sin have not yet been cured. The tragedy of human life involves

---

25. Even his account of illumination and the Platonic books in *Conf.* 7 underlines the imperfection of his experience. He refers to his weakness of sight in *Conf.* 7.10.16 and 7.16.23. The Ostia "vision" in Book 9 is not really a vision at all but an all too brief transcendence of the multiplicity of speech (*Conf.* 9.10.24). In *Trin.* 4.20 he rebukes the proud "who think that they can purify themselves for contemplating God."

the persistence of the disease after its power has been broken. And it is possible to describe the tragedy as a failure of knowledge. In *Of Free Will* Augustine notes that although all people wish to be happy, none are. The reason for this shortfall rests in the orientation of the soul and the disordered character of its willing. The disorder is the consequence of Adam's fall, and Augustine describes it not so much by appealing to the evil will as by speaking of a penal condition of ignorance and difficulty. We fail to know the truth and are unable to do it. Increasingly, however, Augustine shifts his emphasis to the willing that is the obstacle to knowing. In *On the Spirit and the Letter,* he comments on Romans 1:18–23 and says: "Observe, he [Paul] does not say that they were ignorant of the truth, but that they held down the truth in unrighteousness" (*Spir. et litt.* 19.12). Ignorance of the truth is really a rebellion against it and a form of idolatry. And in the long run the idol is the self. Thus, it is pride as the love of self that triggers Adam's sin. As a result, pride becomes Augustine's preferred way of speaking of original sin, with love of God as its opposite. Ignorance is really pride, while knowledge is really love. This does not mean that we need to deny that truthfulness involves recognizing the tragedy of our own incapacity to become what we are meant to be and to know and love God. Augustine plays upon the double meaning of "confession":

> When I am evil, making confession is simply to be displeased with myself. When I am good, making confession to you is simply to make no claim on my own behalf, for you, Lord "confer blessing on the righteous" (Ps. 5:13) but only after you have first "justified the ungodly" (Rom. 4:5). (*Conf.* 10.2.2)

Truthfulness, then, means not only that we recognize ourselves as finite creatures, but also that we do not confuse the medicine given us by prevenient grace with the cure it will effect. Such truthfulness is possible only for the elect, and it recognizes tragedy even as it is confident of the triumph of the completed cure, which is firmly located in the age to come.

A Community of Character

Thus far in the argument I have tried to suggest that truthfulness is associated with God's prevenient grace as Augustine describes it in the account of his conversion in *Confessions* 8. The breaking of chains is God's freeing of his will from its bondage to sin and is what enables him to see both the truth of his condition and the path that will lead him to the vision of God in the age to come. The healing of his passions becomes possible because his fundamental desire (*voluntas*) has been redirected so that he can begin to live the virtuous life.[26] But Augustine's conversion was not merely a private experience, and it was only complete when he was baptized in Milan.[27] In *Confessions* 9.6.14 he says that "we" were baptized; he is referring to his son Adeodatus and to Alypius, both of whom joined him in the rite. Augustine was moved by the music during the ceremony; its "sounds flowed into my ears and the truth was distilled into my heart." There is, I think, an insoluble puzzle as to how Augustine envisages the relation of prevenient grace and baptism. He can speak of both as operating to free people from original sin.[28] Nevertheless, the church includes tares as well as wheat, the reprobate as well as the elect. If prevenient grace and baptism are identical as the inner and outer meaning of the same thing, then they must be necessary but insufficient for salvation. God's grace, of course, continues to operate; and Augustine can speak of the grace of perseverance. What is unclear is whether the grace that follows baptism is sovereign or not. Do the reprobate fail to attain salvation because they do not honor their baptism or because God's grace abandons them or because of some combination of divine and human action?

Despite these puzzles, Augustine increasingly sees the Christian life in its community setting. In a number of ways he articulates an ecclesiastical as well as a conversion understanding of Christianity. Here it is the church that makes Christians and not Christians that make the church. As early as *Of True Religion* Augustine exhorts Romanianus to hold fast to the Catholic faith, and what he surely refers to is the community that witnesses to true religion. It is in the church that "a wholesome regimen is produced for the faithful . . . whereby the due observance of piety makes the ailing mind well for the perception of unchanging truth" (*Trin.* 1.4). The Catholic faith is not the same as absolute Truth, and so immediately following the passage I have just cited Augustine urges

26. For the breaking of chains (Ps. 115 [116]:16–17), see *Conf.* 8.1.1; 8.5.10; 8.6.13; 8.9.20; 8.11.25; 9.1.1. See also his discussions of the passions in *Civ.* 14.6–10, especially 14.6: "The important factor in those emotions is the character of a man's will. If the will is wrongly directed, the emotions will be wrong; if the will is right, the emotions will be not only blameless but praiseworthy." Translation from St. Augustine, *Concerning the City of God against the Pagans*, trans. Henry Bettenson, Penguin Classics (London: Penguin Books, 1987).

27. Cf. Hauerwas, *Vision and Virtue*, 8: "The development of men of truthful vision and virtue, however, will not come from wider society. Rather such men will come from the communities that have had the confidence in the truth of their images and symbols to use and embody them seriously and without embarrassment."

28. See, e.g., *Civ.* 13.3–4, 14, 23; 14.1, 26.

the readers of *On the Trinity* to join him in seeking God's face always (Ps. 105:4), and "wherever you notice that you have gone wrong come back to me; or that I have, call me back to you" (*Trin.* 1.5).[29] Faith is not the same as sight.[30] Nevertheless, it is the necessary path to truth, and Christians must receive the Catholic faith and make it their own. There is one teaching given to all believers; "but what is believed is one thing, the faith it is believed with is another" (*Trin.* 13.5). The internalization of the church's faith can become the faith that seeks understanding.[31]

It was probably in 399 that Augustine sent a Carthaginian deacon his advice about how to catechize the uninstructed; this treatise gives a clear picture of how Augustine understands the way the Christian community forms the character of Christians. His argument is a response to the deacon's perplexities both about how he should instruct catechumens and about his own frustrations in attempting to do so. Augustine notes the difference between teaching groups of people and private instruction (*Catech.* 15.23), but most of his advice presupposes that the catechist will deal with people seeking baptism at an individual level. For this reason the catechist must inquire into the motives of catechumens. Some of them wish to become Christians because they have "been smitten with some sort of fear of God." For others "the mercy of God comes to be present through the ministry of the catechiser," with the result that the person "wishes to become in reality that which he had made up his mind only to feign" (*Catech.* 5.9). The hope, then, is that prevenient grace will draw people to baptism, but the operation of grace is largely hidden from the catechist. And Augustine leaves room for those destined to become reprobate, "chaff" that the church bears upon its threshing floor "until the period of winnowing" (*Catech.* 17.26). Again, despite the puzzles I

29. Cf. *Fund.* 3.4: "Let neither of us assert that he has found the truth; let us seek it as if it were unknown to us both. For truth can be sought with zeal and unanimity if by no rash presumption it is believed to have been already found and ascertained." Cf. Stanley Hauerwas, *Christian Existence Today: Essays on Church, World, and Living in Between* (1988; repr., Grand Rapids, Mich.: Brazos Press, 2001), 9: "Theological convictions inextricably involve truth-claims that are in principle open to challenge."

30. 2 Cor. 5:7. Augustine cites the verse with some frequency and does not, so far as I can see, oppose faith and works. See, e.g., *Trin.* 8.6, where he also cites 1 Cor. 13:12.

31. One way of understanding *On the Trinity* is to treat Books 1–7 as Augustine's articulation of the Catholic faith and Books 8–15 as a failed quest for understanding. See, e.g., *Trin.* 7.12: "If this [the doctrine of the Trinity] cannot be grasped by understanding, let it be held by faith." Also *Trin.* 8.1: "Let us turn our attention to the things we are going to discuss in a more inward manner than the things that have been discussed above, though in fact they are the same things; but let us all the while still keep to the rule that just because a thing is not yet clear to our understanding, we must not therefore dismiss it from the firm assent of our faith."

noted above, there is a mysterious connection between God's grace and the preparation for baptism.

The theme of love dominates Augustine's treatment of both the instruction and the instructor. The teaching must be primarily a narration of the sacred history of Scripture, which consists of five epochs in the Old Testament that point beyond themselves to the climactic sixth epoch initiated by the incarnate Lord; the sacred story then concludes with the seventh epoch of the age to come.[32] The Old Testament veils the New, and the New Testament reveals the Old. The community, then, is story-formed;[33] but the story finds its focus in the narrative of Christ's life, death, and resurrection. The incarnation reveals God's love in such a way that it kindles the love of God and neighbor in Christians (*Catech.* 4.8). Moreover, the story must be adapted to the special needs of those who hear it; "the same charity is due to all, yet the same medicine is not to be administered to all." There are differences among the catechumens—the educated, the dull, citizens and foreigners, rich and poor, old and young, men and women (*Catech.* 15.23). The love of the catechists accommodates the story to all sorts and conditions of people. And it is their love that makes them cheerful givers (2 Cor. 9:7) and enables them to overcome the various frustrations to which they are subject—the inability to express thoughts in adequate words, the repetitive character of teaching, the argumentative and indifferent responses of the catechumens.

While Augustine's emphasis is upon love as the content of the story and as the defining characteristic of the storyteller, he also speaks of truth. He refers to the "genuine verities which we narrate" and says that "the simple truth of the explanation which we adduce ought to be like the gold which binds together a row of gems" (*Catech.* 6.10).[34] The truth of the scriptural story as a whole finds its focus in the story of Christ. But it also implies the truth of the general resurrection (*Catech.* 7.11), as well as "the truths which are most indispensable on the subject of

32. See *Catech.* 3.6, 17.28, and 22.39. The epochs are those that begin with Adam, Noah, Abraham, David, the Babylonian captivity, Christ, and the end of the world. Cf. *Civ.* 16.24, 43; 17.1. Augustine employs Matthew's genealogy, as well as the ideas of seven days in the week and seven ages of a human being. In *Saeculum: History and Society in the Theology of St. Augustine* (Cambridge: Cambridge University Press, 1970), 18, R. A. Markus notes: "The decisive event of the Incarnation tends to eclipse the sixfold division by casting its shadow backwards." See also Appendix D.

33. Cf. Stanley Hauerwas, "A Story-Formed Community," in *A Community of Character: Toward a Constructive Christian Social Ethic* (Notre Dame, Ind.: University of Notre Dame Press, 1981), 9–35.

34. Cf. Stanley Hauerwas, "A Qualified Ethic: The Narrative Character of Christian Ethics, " in *The Peaceable Kingdom*, 25–26, 29.

the unity of the Catholic Church, on that of temptation, on that of a Christian conversation in view of the future judgment" (*Catech.* 13.18). The absolute Truth that is God reveals itself in a true narrative and particularly in the true story of the incarnate Lord, but it also demands truthfulness in those who receive these stories. The catechist may encounter a catechumen who speaks what is false. But "the very untruth he utters should be made the point from which we start" (*Catech.* 5.9), a basis for winning him to the truth. The catechumen who is a rhetorician must learn "to listen to discourses remarkable for their truth, rather than to those which are notable for their eloquence" (*Catech.* 9.13).[35] If the catechists themselves find that they have said something false, their love and humility ought to enable them to recognize their fault and to correct it (*Catech.* 11.16).

The truth of the story has truthfulness in the community as its correlate; truth must have truthful witnesses.[36] Moreover, if Scripture reveals the truth of God and his revelation in Christ, it must bear true witness. This relationship between the truth of Scripture and truthful witness is Augustine's chief concern in his long epistolary controversy with Jerome regarding the interpretation of Paul's rebuke of Peter for compelling Gentile Christians to live as Jews by observing Jewish rules for table fellowship (Gal. 2:11–14).[37] Jerome's interpretation of the passage assumes that Peter broke a rule of his own devising—a rule that freed all Christians from the law—but that he did so in order to avoid offending the Jewish Christians and driving them away from Christ. Moreover, says Jerome, Paul, like Peter, could employ such an "honorable economy," which is not to be identified with a

---

35. Cf. *Conf.* 7.20.26: "I prattled on as if I were expert, but unless I had sought your way in Christ our Saviour (Titus 1:4), I would have been not expert but expunged" (*non peritus sed periturus;* not skilled in speaking but doomed to perish).

36. Cf. Hauerwas, *Christian Existence Today,* 10: "Christians are people who remain convinced that the truthfulness of their beliefs must be demonstrated in their lives."

37. In 394 or 395 Augustine sent Jerome *Ep.* 28, raising questions about his interpretation of the passage in Galatians. The letter was never delivered, but in 397 Augustine sent Jerome *Ep.* 40, replying to a letter from Jerome that apparently dealt with the controversy over Origen and taking the opportunity to repeat his problems with Jerome's interpretation of Galatians. This letter, too, failed to reach Jerome. In 402 Augustine wrote Jerome *Ep.* 67, disavowing that he had written a treatise against Jerome. The same year Jerome replied (*Ep.* 68), saying he had received Augustine's recent letter (*Ep.* 67), but that he had also seen *Ep.* 40, which he professed to doubt was Augustine's. In 403 Augustine sent Jerome *Ep.* 71 and copies of *Ep.* 28 and 40. In 404 Jerome wrote Augustine a prickly letter (*Ep.* 72), annoyed that Augustine had allowed *Ep.* 40 to circulate. Augustine replied (*Ep.* 73) in what purported to be an irenic mood, but lamenting Jerome's quarrel with Rufinus. The same year Jerome wrote his full response (*Ep.* 75) to *Ep.* 28, 40, and 71. In 405 Jerome wrote a more irenic letter (*Ep.* 81), while Augustine's *Ep.* 82 gave Jerome a full reply to Jerome's *Ep.* 72, 75, and 81.

"pious lie."[38] Paul circumcised Timothy (Acts 16:3), discharged a Nazirite vow in the temple (Acts 21:26), and explicitly said that "he became as a Jew, in order to win Jews" (1 Cor. 9:20). Jerome at least implies that Paul and Peter had agreed with one another and that the incident in Antioch was their joint economy (*Ep.* 75.3.9–11; 4.17). In any case, Jerome claims to be following the interpretation of Origen, Didymus, Apollinaris, and Chrysostom, one that was designed to refute the pagan Porphyry's use of the passage to malign Christians for their childish quarrels and Paul for his presumption in rebuking his superior (*Ep.* 75.3.4, 6, 11). Augustine, of course, disagrees. He argues that for a time Jewish Christians were allowed to continue their observance of the law, but that Gentile Christians were freed from it. Thus, Peter did employ a pious lie, and Paul was right to rebuke him. Augustine's deeper reason for rejecting Jerome's interpretation, however, does not revolve around whether or not it is right to tell a pious lie, but is tied to his conviction that Scripture must always be true.[39] Consequently, if we admit that Paul's narrative in Galatians is false, "the authority of the Holy Scriptures" becomes "wholly uncertain and wavering" (*Ep.* 40.4.4). Indeed, if Paul is lying, however nobly, we might conclude that he is lying when he commends marriage (*Ep.* 28.3.4). The issue of the pious or "dutiful" lie is a "mighty question," but it is not the major issue that divides Augustine from Jerome (*Ep.* 82.2.22).

Augustine addresses the question of lying more directly in his treatise *On Lying,* which was written about the same time he tried to send his first letter to Jerome in 395. He did not publish the work, but it circulated all the same; and in his *Retractions* he allows it to stand despite its obscurity. In the treatise, Augustine defines the liar as the person "who has one thing in his mind and utters another in words, or by signs of whatever kind" (*De mend.* 3). This means that someone who has a false idea does not lie by expressing it. But even if we add to the definition the will to deceive, it remains inadequate. A person can tell the truth in order to deceive or can tell what is false in order to undeceive. And this conundrum is only the beginning of the "dark corners" and "cavern-like windings" encountered in considering what it means to lie. The problem of the noble or medicinal lie has its roots in Plato, and the common view of Christians before Augustine admitted the goodness of a lie meant to benefit others.[40] Augustine's discussion not only examines

---

38. *Ep.* 75.3.11 (*honestam dispensationem . . . officiosum mendacium*).

39. Cf. Hauerwas, *A Community of Character,* 63: "By regarding scripture as an authority Christians mean to indicate that they find there the tradition through which their community most nearly comes to knowing and being faithful to the truth."

40. See Plato, *Resp.* 382abc, 389b, 414b, 459; *Leg.* 663d. Christian texts endorsing the medicinal or noble lie include: Clement of Alexandria, *Stromateis* 7.9.53; Origen, *Contra*

Scripture but involves any number of possible cases where deciding what is right or wrong is next to impossible. He finally lists eight categories of lies, beginning with the worst sort and ending with those most easily forgiven. In the long run, however, he concludes that all lies are sins. In his treatise *Against Lying,* written in 420 to argue against pretending to agree with the Priscillian heretics in order to discover their hiding places, Augustine argues that the midwives of Egypt and Rahab are commended not because they lied but because of their humanity and mercy. While it is permissible to conceal the truth, it is wrong to do so by lying. The midwives and Rahab could have admitted their knowledge and have refused to reveal it, thereby becoming full witnesses and martyrs of the truth.[41] Being witnesses of the truth, then, is crucial for the community of character; and those who belong to that community must strive to be truthful in all things, since the quality of their lives is as much a witness to truth as is their confession of the Christian faith.[42]

Conclusion: The Peaceable Kingdom

Augustine, as I have noted, makes a sharp distinction between the Christian life in this world and the destiny of the saints in the age to come. Only after this world passes away will the citizens of the city of God have full vision of the Truth and find their virtues in a settled character rather than in a constant struggle against vice. Only then will their truthfulness finally overcome tragedy, no longer engendering hatred in those who love a false truth (*Conf.* 10.23.34). And it is in that future beyond all futures that the city of God will be purged of the tares suffered by the community of the church before the time of harvest. Augustine has a great many ways of speaking of the destiny of the saints. In Book 19 of the *City of God* he describes it as "peace in life everlasting" or "life everlasting in peace" (*Civ.* 19.11). He follows Varro's account of Antiochus

---

Celsum 4.18–19, *Homilies on Jeremiah* 19–20; John Chrysostom, *De sacerdotio* 1.6–8; Paulinus of Nola, *Carmen* 16.52–74; John Cassian, *Conference* 17. See the entry "Mendacio, De/Contra Mendacium," in *Augustine through the Ages: An Encyclopedia,* ed. Allan D. Fitzgerald (Grand Rapids, Mich.: Eerdmans, 1999), 555–57.

41. *C. mend.* 33. Cf. *De mend.* 22–23, where Bishop Firmus responds to the imperial officers who demand he hand over a man who had taken sanctuary with him, by saying, "I will neither betray nor lie."

42. Cf. Stanley Hauerwas, *With the Grain of the Universe: The Church's Witness and Natural Theology* (Grand Rapids, Mich.: Brazos Press, 2001), 212: "Witnesses must exist if Christians are to be intelligible to themselves and hopefully to those who are not Christians. . . . Martyrs—who are but the most determinative display of what being a witness entails—go to their death convinced that the gospel is true."

of Ascalon's Platonism (which is partly Stoic and partly Aristotelian) by arguing that the chief good for humans involves the combination of virtue with the primary goods of nature, and that this chief good includes a social dimension. The individual must appropriate to the natural instinct of self-preservation a care for the family, the city, the state, and the entire universe. But this understanding of the chief good is one Augustine opposes to the chief evil, which alone is the final end of the earthly city. The chief good is firmly located in the next life and, consequently, radically distinguished from the views of the philosophers who "have wished with amazing folly to be happy here on earth and to achieve bliss by their own efforts" (*Civ.* 19.4).

This world, then, is far from being the peaceable kingdom. At the same time, once the saints embrace the vision of the peace to come, they are able to discern anticipations of that peace in this life. They claim "that though human life is compelled to be wretched by all the grievous evils of this world, it is happy in the expectation of the world to come" (*Civ.* 19.4). One possible implication of Augustine's view would be a quietist sectarianism. Should the saints repudiate the earthly city and simply endure the world by holding fast to their confident expectation? Perhaps paradoxically, Augustine does not draw that conclusion. No matter how flawed human societies are in this world, the resident aliens (*peregrini*) of the city of God must seek to make the best of this bad bargain. "Thus even the Heavenly City in her pilgrimage here on earth makes use of the earthly peace . . . so far as may be permitted without detriment to true religion and piety" (*Civ.* 19.17). Warfare is a mark of how far the earthly city is tied to original sin and is obliged to make peace by war. The *Pax Romana* has been won at great cost. "Consider the scale of those wars, with all that slaughter of human beings, all the human blood that was shed!" (*Civ.* 19.7). Nevertheless, "so long as the two cities are intermingled we also make use of the peace of Babylon" (*Civ.* 19.26). Augustine sows the seeds of the medieval theory of the just war; but while he is no pacifist, his ideas are based upon his horror of war and his conviction that it is always an evil.[43]

Augustine's discussion of the peaceable kingdom in *City of God* 19 makes no mention of truth. Yet he does equate peace with the perfect ordering of the created world under God, and one can argue that this

---

43. See the entry "War," in Fitzgerald, *Augustine through the Ages*, 875–76. Cf. Stanley Hauerwas, *Dispatches from the Front* (Durham, N.C.: Duke University Press, 1994), 139–40: "Christians created just war reflection because of their nonviolent convictions; they assumed that those who would use violence bore the burden of proof for doing so. Thus, the wide reach of pacifism becomes clear."

order is the final truth of creation.[44] It may not be going too far to suggest that in *On the Trinity* 4.24 he makes the point explicit. He cites Plato: "As eternity is to that which has originated, so truth is to faith" (*Timaeus* 29c). Augustine understands Plato to mean that time in this world contrasts with eternity in the world to come, just as faith now contrasts with truth hereafter. Thus, "when we come to sight and truth succeeds to faith, eternity might likewise succeed to mortality." As Christ says: "You will know the truth, and the truth will set you free" (John 8:32). This freedom is "from death, from perishability, from liability to change." The knowledge of truth, then, is the perfection of the soul's ordering under God and the completion of the image of God. That ordering, in turn, enables the perfect ordering of the body in the changeless and eternal life of the resurrection.

My Hauerwasian attempt to describe Augustine's understanding of truth is as complete as it can be. Needless to say, much more would need to be said; and my account is only one among other ways of approaching Augustine's thought. It does not pretend to be complete; indeed, it implies that we cannot isolate Augustine's treatment of truth from other themes in his writings. Truth overlaps with humility, love, and peace.[45] The focus on truth is one way of speaking of God, of the Trinity, and of God's revelation in creation, in Scripture, and above all in the incarnate life, death, and resurrection of God's Word. Truth finds expression in the virtuous life and in the simple honesty toward which the Christian must aspire. Much of what Augustine says correlates with Stanley's ways of speaking of truth and truthfulness. But Stanley and Augustine do not always agree, and I have a cheerful imagination of them in the city of God, talking and arguing with one another as they move endlessly toward ever deeper understandings of the Truth that is God himself.

44. Cf. Hauerwas, *The Peaceable Kingdom,* 114–15: "For true justice never comes through violence, nor can it be based on violence. It can only be based on truth, which has no need to resort to violence to secure its own existence."

45. Cf. Hauerwas, *Christian Existence Today,* 92: "Just as love without truth cannot help but be accursed, so peace without truthfulness cannot help but be deadly."

2

Can We Be Free without a Creator?

David B. Burrell, CSC

Certainly the best way to celebrate and to take the measure of forty years of engagement with Stanley Hauerwas is to propose an outrageous thesis: no creator, no freedom. Before I elaborate, however, let me say a few words about the beginning of the relationship that this thesis celebrates.

My friendship and collaboration with Stanley Hauerwas began in the wake of Vatican II, when James Tunstead Burtchaell, CSC, then chairing Theology at Notre Dame, had the temerity to engage a rancorous Protestant who, when his archetypal Texan identity demanded an ecclesial counterpart, would soon identify himself as a "Catholic Mennonite." Stan conspired with others to persuade me to chair Theology when Burtchaell was made provost in 1970, thereby awakening my passion for philosophical theology. It was my growing sense of the affinity between Wittgenstein and Aquinas—a sense nourished by Victor Preller's prescient inquiry, *Divine Science and the Science of God* (which I had reviewed in 1969), and explored in my *Aquinas: God and Action*

35

(to be published in 1979)—that brought us together.[1] We worked with other engaging colleagues—among them Joseph Blenkinsopp, Robert Wilken, John Howard Yoder—to create a catholic climate of theological inquiry (including a Judaica position) under the aegis of a Catholic university. Those were heady days, buoyant with visions of "faith seeking understanding," yet (in retrospect) far too sanguine about the faith dimension of that mandate. Not so Stanley. He kept reminding us how presumptive were traditional Catholic strategies of "natural law." Amid these reminders, and letting Julius Kovesi's *Moral Notions* provide a fruitful meeting ground,[2] I tried to delineate the significant intent of these Catholic strategies: that ordinary discourse was already replete with evaluative expressions. Yet as Stanley intuited and I came to see, employing those "moral notions" with pragmatic consistency would require nothing less than a vibrant faith community—the Mennonite counterpart of Catholic "grace." It took a few more years—and the preemption of "ordinary discourse" by the Pentagon and late capitalism—for us to express our convergence in a resounding approbation of Aquinas's "infused moral virtues." In fact, this apparently recondite notion will offer a handy way of introducing my thesis about the indispensability of faith for an authentic human freedom.

It was part of the ideology of the Thomistic revival, inaugurated by Pope Leo XIII at the end of the nineteenth century and extending until Vatican II, that Aquinas's perspicuous use of human reason could bring together "those of good will." Moreover, his treatment of morality under the rubric of virtue offered to buttress the renewed appreciation of Aristotle stimulated by Alasdair MacIntyre's *After Virtue.*[3] Yet whether one simply presumed a communal context for virtue (as Catholics tended to do) or trumpeted the need for it (as Hauerwas's early preachments contended), the presence of "infused moral virtues" seemed a useless redundancy. One had come to expect an explicitly theological step to the "gifts of the Holy Spirit" that underscored a shared ecumenical concern for *sanctification,* but why this hybrid of "infused virtues" straddling the natural/supernatural divide?

Events soon forced us to recognize (with Henri de Lubac) that there could be no such "divide" and that the natural/supernatural *distinction*

1. Victor Preller, *Divine Science and the Science of God* (Princeton: Princeton University Press, 1967), reviewed in *Review of Metaphysics* 22 (1969): 676–99; David Burrell, *Aquinas: God and Action* (London: Routledge; Notre Dame, Ind.: University of Notre Dame Press, 1979).

2. Julius Kovesi, *Moral Notions* (London: Routledge and Kegan Paul, 1967).

3. Alasdair MacIntyre, *After Virtue* (Notre Dame, Ind.: Notre Dame University Press, 1984).

pervaded all of life. As tenacious ideologies, with their mirror images (communism/anticommunism), impeded the implementation of the heady rhetoric of "human rights," we were "impelled by the facts" (as Aristotle liked to say) to recognize that the *humanum* needed something more than the human to be realized in our time. To effect Plato's intended goal for the *Republic*—to show one how to live justly in an unjust world—came to require what we once called "heroic virtue," yet heroes were few. So driven to a closer reading of Aquinas and allowing ourselves to be instructed by his detailed treatment of the relevant moral virtues, we came to see that their actual exercise would require even more than Aristotle's sustained formation—already a stiff demand. Indeed, the actual exercise of the traditional moral virtues would require participating in a faith community; to speak of such participation was a useful way of capturing Aquinas's demand for "infused moral virtues."[4] What I propose to show here are the ways such a faith community is grounded in an operative belief in a free creator, a belief shared by Jews, Christians, and Muslims alike.[5] And even more: that absent such an operative belief, sustained by a community of faith, we lack a coherent account of the freedom we prize and require to sustain our human community.

Beyond Standard Accounts of Freedom

Current philosophical treatments of freedom prove to be remarkably thin, content to demonstrate that there is such a thing in the face of the bugbear of "determinism."[6] Moreover, the thing in question is identified with "the ability to do otherwise," a formula that proves to be quite unstable in the face of actual practice, as Eleonore Stump's maternal counterexamples display.[7] What seems unaccountably missing is any sustained description of the dynamics of free action. Yet that

4. For a recent penetrating analysis, see Angela Smith, "The Infused and Acquired Virtues in Aquinas' Moral Philosophy" (PhD diss., University of Notre Dame, 2004). It is illustrative to note how this strategy not only responds to the criticism of Thomas O'Meara, OP, "Virtues in the Theology of Thomas Aquinas," *Theological Studies* 58 (1997): 254–68, but also serves to give body to his references to "grace."

5. See my shared work with Elena Malits, *Original Peace: Restoring God's Creation* (New York: Paulist Press, 1997).

6. For a clear and cogent account, see Peter Van Inwagen, *An Essay on Free Will* (Oxford: Oxford University Press, 1983).

7. See her critical exploration in "Intellect, Will, and the Principle of Alternate Possibilities," in *Perspectives on Moral Responsibility*, ed. John Martin Fischer (Ithaca, N.Y.: Cornell University Press, 1993), amplified in *Thomas Aquinas: Contemporary Philosophi-*

is precisely what Aquinas supplies, as Eleonore Stump has so clearly
shown in her recent *Aquinas*. Why such insouciance for the details in
standard philosophical accounts? Anxieties about "determinism" may go
a long way toward explaining a blindness to other features of freedom,
but once that bugbear has been set aside, why rest content with the thin
and contentious "ability to do otherwise"? Surely human freedom holds
more promise than that?

My admittedly speculative diagnosis may appear to carry us far afield,
but it could also prove useful in identifying some presumptions that may
well render us myopic to the issues involved in human freedom. My contention is that as neo-Thomistic philosophy was unwittingly truncated by
regarding the natural/supernatural distinction as a divide, modern and
contemporary philosophy felt compelled to account for humanity without reference to a transcendent goal—or to employ tendentious terms,
sought to speak of "creatures" without reference to a creator. Ironically
enough, we shall see how standard analyses of a "libertarian" cast foster
a dualistic picture, whereas Aquinas's account (replete with a creator)
offers a holistic account of human freedom. The difficulty does not rest
with what distinguishes "libertarian" analyses from their alternatives
("compatibilist" or even "hard determinist"), yet for strategic reasons
my critique will focus on philosophers who adopt "libertarian" analyses
while they aver creation. Indeed, I shall contend that their unwitting
adoption of categories constructed to avoid reference to a creator can
prevent them from seeing how crucial that omission can be. Allow me
to suggest a scheme in which to locate references to a creator.

The regular teaching of a course in ancient and medieval philosophy
has led me to identify the difference between the two quite clearly:
the presence of a free creator. Jewish, Christian, and Muslim thinkers
converged in their efforts to insert a free creator into the apparently
seamless Hellenic philosophy they inherited.[8] (Josef Pieper's observation
that "creation is the hidden element in the philosophy of St. Thomas"
alerted many of us to this operative difference from Aristotle, which many
Thomists had managed to overlook in their anxiety to mark a divide
between philosophy and theology.)[9] Yet if we can say schematically that

---

cal Perspectives, ed. Brian Davies (Oxford: Oxford University Press, 2002), 275–94; and
in her "Freedom: Action, Intellect, and Will," in *Aquinas* (New York: Routledge, 2002),
277–306.

8. This is the burden of my *Knowing the Unknowable God: Ibn-Sina, Maimonides,
Aquinas* (Notre Dame, Ind.: University of Notre Dame Press, 1986).

9. Josef Pieper, "The Negative Element in the Philosophy of St. Thomas," in *The Silence of St. Thomas: Three Essays* (New York: Pantheon, 1957; repr., South Bend, Ind.:
St. Augustine's, 2002), 47–67.

the presence of a free creator divides medieval from ancient philosophy, what marks the subsequent transition to modern philosophy?

Many things, of course, but to continue speaking schematically, modern philosophy wanted to distinguish itself by eliminating the theological overtones of the "scholastics," and so proceeded by avoiding reference to a creator. Yet the creator is a bit large to overlook, so the gradual tendency was to deny its relevance, as evidenced in Enlightenment fascination with "the Greeks" (for the Enlightenment, more a construct than a historical reference). Aristotle, after all, had managed quite well without a creator. Now if that be the case—again, speaking quite schematically—we can characterize modern philosophy as "postmedieval," where the "post-" prefix carries a note of denial—in this case, of a creator, either directly or implicitly. However, a cursory look at the strategies whereby modern philosophers compensated for the absence of a creator shows them to lead inescapably to foundational grounds, be they "self-evident" propositions or "sense-data" or whatever. When these foundations prove illusory, we cannot help but enter a "postmodern" world. And if our understanding of "philosophy" itself (à la Rorty) is inherently linked to such strategies, then we will inevitably regard a postmodern context as one in which "anything goes."

Here is where our scheme can help: if modern philosophy can be seen as "postmedieval," then "postmodern" philosophy will have to be read as "post-postmedieval." And although the "post-" prefixes may not connote the same sort of denials, we will be directed to a sense of "postmodern" that bears affinities with medieval inquiry. Put more positively and less schematically, both medieval and postmodern inquiry are more at ease with Gadamer's contention that any inquiry whatsoever rests on fiduciary premises. In practice, this means that faith may be regarded as a way of knowing, though like any other way of knowing, never uncritically, however startling such a contention would prove to Descartes!

This scheme can help us to see three things: (1) that Gadamer's contention about all inquiry resting on fiduciary premises, already anticipated by Newman's *Grammar of Assent*,[10] can lead us to a constructive reading of the inescapably "postmodern" world into which we have been thrust; (2) that such fiduciary premises will have to be tested themselves so the hermeneutics developed in theological arenas may prove useful to philosophical inquiry; and (3) that presuppositions extant in modern

---

10. Consult, preferably, Nicholas Lash's edition of Newman's *An Essay in Aid of a Grammar of Assent* (Notre Dame, Ind.: University of Notre Dame Press, 1979) for its illuminating introduction, yet also note the way in which Joseph Dunne utilizes Newman to initiate his recovery of Aristotle's *phronesis* in his *Back to the Rough Ground* (Notre Dame, Ind.: University of Notre Dame Press, 1993).

inquiries may prove misleading in a world that has "lost faith in reason"—a contention that would be oxymoronic to Descartes yet is perfectly understandable when the "reason" in question is presumed to be a "pure reason" absent all presuppositions. Armed with these strategies, we can proceed to my outrageous thesis: Currently standard accounts of freedom (with strategic focus on "libertarian freedom") prove radically inadequate to parsing the nuances and complexities of human freedom. Moreover, these accounts lead to antitheological conclusions precisely because the analytic categories such accounts presume have been developed in an intellectual atmosphere inattentive to the presence of a creator—or indeed to the presence of any significant finality to the *humanum*. (To find "theists" espousing such accounts, quite unaware of the negative contexts such categories presume, is especially bizarre.) Finally—as if this were not enough—such truncated accounts of freedom will prove unable to counter the corrosively postmodern contention that "all is power," since the way in which they identify freedom with choosing, so as to eschew any telos inherent in free actions, allows freedom to be rendered as "doing what I wanna do." As a result, gratification and domination quickly fill the void left by an account of freedom that had neglected the dynamics of desire from the outset.

I shall illustrate this complex thesis with salient examples from customary practices of dominating groups (like Israeli settlers) to show how such accounts of freedom license corruption by motives of power lightly masked with ideological "justification." Ironically enough, once freedom is simply identified with choosing (as in the slogan "pro-choice"), there will be little to keep it from being exercised coercively on others, for any telos inherent in free action has been explicitly eschewed, leaving open the unabashed use of one's freedom to promote one's own gratification. If that account describes the policies of the hefty actors on our world stage, then we may have traced a path to one of the intellectual supports for this pervasive evil.

Free Action as Initiative or Response?

Perhaps the most telling insight into the skewed dynamics of "libertarian freedom" occurs in a 1964 lecture by Roderick Chisholm where, citing Aristotle, he insists that the will must be a prime mover.[11] Chisholm presumes Aristotle's prime mover to be an initiator, a "pusher," if you will, but this presumption is mistaken. A coherent account of a prime mover

---

11. Published as "Human Freedom and the Self," in *Free Will*, ed. Gary Watson (New York: Oxford University Press, 1982), 24–35, citation at 26.

requires that it be unmoved and that it cause whatever moves to move by being the object of desire. In short, Aristotle's account of movement incorporates Plato's accent on "the good" by postulating a world of essences, each intent on a proper end and all drawn, in an orderly fashion, to the good itself. But in a world bereft of teleology, a prime mover would have to initiate; what else would make it primary in movement? Yet although the dynamic scheme from Plato through Aristotle to Aquinas offered a coherent account of action as a response to a proper good, simply postulating an initiating power offers no account at all. Whence this mysterious "power"? Here we see the temptation to a form of dualism: one must postulate a power of a special sort, operating within the world of nature, to account for the presence of such prime movers with their innate power to initiate. Moreover, the tendency of this account to eschew any further articulation of the dynamics of free action will also make one wonder why one path is chosen rather than another. In short, there seems a direct lineage from early forms of "voluntarism" to libertarian accounts of freedom, for any account of why one may choose one direction in preference to another will have to invoke teleology. And teleology shifts our focus to the end in view. Put simply, does one push oneself out of bed in the morning, or is one rather drawn by the prospect of something enticing? Anything else, like punishment for being late for work, would threaten the freedom of one's rising. Moreover, to acknowledge that there may always be a little of both retains the focus on the goal, whether it be more compelling or more enticing.

So if the classical scheme simply makes more sense, is phenomenologically more compelling, why is it so conspicuously absent from current accounts of freedom? And why are those who give such accounts not embarrassed by their inability to depict the dynamics of free action? My contention is that these accounts have been schooled to avoid any reference to an orderly universe so as to pretend to focus on the action of individuals. But individuals respond to situations and are already embedded in linguistic (as well as prelinguistic) patterns of response. Once we are reminded of this fact, as Alasdair MacIntyre has done so effectively, then his contention that "the individual" is an eighteenth-century abstraction begins to ring true.[12] Alternatively, as Eleonore Stump has developed so clearly (and Mary Clark had sketched before her), the subtle interactions of intellect and will delineated by Aquinas offer a promising path for displaying the dynamics of human freedom.[13] Moreover, a classical ac-

12. Alasdair MacIntyre, *Dependent Rational Animals* (London: Duckworth, 1999).

13. See note 5 for Stump references; also, Mary Clark, "Willing Freely according to Thomas Aquinas," in *A Straight Path*, ed. Ruth Link-Salinger et al. (Washington, D.C.: Catholic University of America Press, 1988), 49–56. This book is a Festschrift for Arthur Hyman.

count readily explains the indeterminacy of freedom that moderns seem to value as its very core, for an inherent orientation to "the good" can never settle the best way to attain it. The same architectonic scheme also allows for a moment in free action that even radicalizes the celebrated "ability to do otherwise," in that each of us retains the ability to reject the dynamic itself, and so perform actions that are evil.

Here, too, the classical scheme offers a more phenomenologically satisfying analysis, since "good" and "evil" do not appear as simple contraries, as though one could readily "choose" either option. Indeed, the very grammar of "evil" demands that we acknowledge first the primacy of "good"; otherwise there is no evil, but only an alternate way of acting. On this account, an evil act is less of an act, illustrated in its limit by a person caught in the downward spiral of addiction, who can hardly be said to be acting in a full-blooded sense. So although rejecting the dynamic itself may offer a manifest case of our being "able to do otherwise," it can hardly be considered paradigmatic for free action, since acts flowing from such a refusal are manifestly deficient as acts.[14]

Any account of freedom that would make human beings mere "choice-machines" must overlook the goal-directedness of human development. Yet this caricature is clearly just that; choosings are always embedded in a rich texture of desires, and it is, finally, the attention to desire that most recommends the classical account of freedom. Ironically enough, by eschewing reference to desire, a standard account of freedom—particularly a "thin" libertarian one—leaves our "choices" at the mercy of desire. Failing to advert to the dynamics of our desires simply invites self-deception regarding the "freedom" of our actions, since "what we wanna do" seldom originates from our very selves, and is usually elicited by multiple (and often powerfully presented) enticements to which we are ever vulnerable. Indeed, when we contrast Platonic (and later, Augustinian) depictions of the tyranny of desire with accounts that focus on "the ability to do otherwise," the latter accounts are manifestly limp, notably from failing to attend to desires. Moreover, desire roots our actions in the world of nature in which we partake, so paying attention to desire heads off dualist temptations.

But given the ubiquity of desire, where does our "freedom" lie? It does not lie in mere (and usually nugatory) "willpower." In fact, to what end would such "power" be directed were we able to muster it? Rather, our freedom lies in assenting or not to desires in a way that calls upon a hierarchy of desire. Here the classical scheme can be enriched with a

14. See my "The Surd of Sin," in *Freedom and Creation in Three Traditions* (Notre Dame, Ind.: University of Notre Dame Press, 1993), 157–59.

creator who names and personifies Plato's "good." And that creator, as Aquinas insists, will be present in all authentically free actions, and absent only from those that deny the orientation inherent in our intellect and will, and even then only from the orientation itself.[15] Every action qua action will be a created action, though what makes an action evil—its departure from the orientation to the good sketched above—will come from the creature alone, as it exercises its power to disconnect from its creator in acting. But more on this later; for now, let us trace the curious path whereby free action became detached from desire.

"Only the Will Can Be Good"

Kant's famous phrase can begin this brief etiology explaining how "will" became separated from "desire"—brief, because the story has been often recounted.[16] In Kant, of course, the separation was a strategic one: desire was part of nature, so will had to be part of the noumenal world. Yet the roots of the separation lie in Scotus's bifurcation of will from intellect, a strategy apparently executed in response to the famous condemnations of 1277.[17] (We shall see that although Aquinas spoke of "intellect" and of "will," the two are intimately interconnected for him.) The agent for Scotus is the will, counseled, if you will, by the intellect; yet what makes one move is the will's so-called *actus elicitus*.[18] The resulting primacy of the will served Scotus's Franciscan roots. Although Kant's concerns, notably his epistemological strategies, were quite different, "will" also became crucial for him; it allowed human beings access to realities that lie beyond the "scientific" knowledge appropriate to them. Yet the will in question was that already isolated by Scotus, with the inevitable result that its activity would be governed not by intellectual discernment but by commands, or (in Kant's language) imperatives. (A peculiar "divine command theory" of ethics originates in this strategy.)

15. See Hugh McCann, "Divine Sovereignty and the Freedom of the Will," *Faith and Philosophy* 12 (1995): 582–98, as well as his "Author of Sin," to appear in the same journal (2004); also my "On the Relation between the Two Actors," in *Freedom and Creation*, 95–140.

16. Among others, see Bonnie Kent, *Virtues of the Will: The Transformation of Ethics in the Late Thirteenth Century* (Washington, D.C.: Catholic University of America Press, 1995).

17. On the condemnations of 1277, see Roland Hissette, *Enquête sur les 219 articles condamnés à Paris le 7 mars 1277* (Louvain: Publications Universitaires, 1977), as well as the more general discussion by J. M. M. H. Thijssen, *Censure and Heresy at the University of Paris 1200–1400* (Philadelphia: University of Pennsylvania Press, 1998).

18. See my "Creation, Will, and Knowledge in Aquinas and Duns Scotus," in *Pragmatik I* (Hamburg: Felix Meiner, 1986), 246–57.

Moreover, for Kant desires (as part of nature) become irrelevant to moral decision, often clouding and hindering an authentically ethical stance. The resulting "puritan" picture is evident in the center of Milton's hell—a raging fire stoked by wayward desires during one's lifetime—and stands in stark contrast to Dante's classical picture of a block of ice, the utter absence of desire.

We shall develop, with Augustine's help, the role that desire plays in the classical dynamics of intellect and will, yet for now there is one more salient step. A Kantian sovereign will best exercises itself in controlling one's life, notably, of course, one's desires, but "control" becomes the key term. Control suggests willpower, which then allows us to ask: does the will control me, or do I control my will? The question is endemic to any "faculty" account of being human: is it my intellect that knows, or do I know in virtue of my intellect? The coherent answer has to be that it is the subject who knows or wills, of course, though the mode of discourse that Scotus introduced of a detached will tends to make the question quite intractable here. Yet however that difficulty be resolved, it is the preoccupation with control that attends our analysis; for with control comes independence, the distinguishing feature of free action on this model.

Here matters take a theological turn, as exhibited in standard forms of the "free will" defense attending the "problem of evil." If human freedom is to be the source of evil (as Augustine insisted), then the strategy demands that human free actions be utterly "free," that is, bereft of any divine influence. If those who have promoted this strategy had been alert to precedents in the history of philosophy, they would have recognized the lineaments of the early Islamic Mu'tazilites, who were similarly intent on preserving "divine justice" as well as the autonomy of human freedom.[19] The crucial step lies in removing free human actions from divine sovereignty, though the premise explicit for Muslims (yet normally implicit for our contemporaries) is that any authentic action must be explained as a "creating." So although the creator must be understood to create everything, this strategy neatly exempts human actions from that universal set: human beings alone create their actions, else they could hardly be said to be free. Although political influences soon began to undermine this teaching in early Islam, inherent factors also worked against the idea: exempting human actions from the creator's sovereignty removes a considerable chunk of the created universe from creation! In the face of this problem, orthodox Islam soon adopted a subtle strategy whereby God creates what we perform,

---

19. For the Mu'tazilite strategies, see my *Freedom and Creation*, 51–52, 77–79.

reserving responsibility to humans for their actions, good or evil, while respecting divine sovereignty.[20]

Not so for many of our contemporaries, however, largely because their discourse remains remarkably unsophisticated regarding both the founding activity of creation and the resultant unique relation of creatures to their creator.[21] Lacking a coherent picture of creation as the unique *causal* activity it must be, many contemporary accounts of freedom inevitably regard the creator as another operator in the scene, and so as a rival to created agency. In the face of this problem, such accounts then withdraw free human actions from the created realm, as oxymoronic as that sounds and is. Yet the effect is even worse, since the resultant "creator" can no longer be the God whom Jews, Christians, and Muslims worship, but can only be "the biggest thing around."[22] So failing to attempt a proper articulation of creating will effectively remove from proper consideration the unique relation that both distinguishes creator from creatures and unites them.[23] Although there is neither time nor space here to elaborate this point, it should suffice to note how others, notably Aquinas, had recourse to Neoplatonic strategies to articulate the creator as "cause of being."[24]

This articulation requires a robust understanding of "being" as "act," to which Aquinas was able to give philosophical voice by transforming Avicenna's celebrated distinction between "being" and "essence."[25] The result is a rich scenario of the universe "participating" in being as it emanates from a creator. Here a great deal of work has been done to clarify Plato's original notion of "participation," which Aristotle had criticized

20. On what is called the Ash'arite (or orthodox) teaching, see Daniel Gimaret, *La Doctrine d'al Ash'ari* (Paris: Cerf, 1990).

21. Brian Davies' summary description of this "school"—in "Letter from America," *New Blackfriars* 84 (2003): 377—makes this point in a telling way: "It is false, we are told, that God is incomprehensible. He is, in fact, something very familiar. He is a person. And he has properties in common with other persons. He changes, he learns, and is acted on. He also has beliefs, which alter with the changes in the objects of his beliefs. And he is by no means the source of all that is real in the universe. He is not, for example, the cause of my free actions. These come from me, not from God. He permits them, but they stand to him as an observed item stands to an observer. He is not their maker. He is only their enabler."

22. See my "Creation, Metaphysics, and Ethics," *Faith and Philosophy* 18 (2001): 204–21.

23. What Robert Sokolowski has denominated "the distinction" in his seminal *God of Faith and Reason* (Washington, D.C.: Catholic University of America Press, 1995).

24. See my "Aquinas' Appropriation of *Liber de causis* to Articulate the Creator as Cause-of-Being," in *Contemplating Aquinas*, ed. Fergus Kerr (London: SCM Press, 2003), 55–74.

25. See my "Essence and Existence: Avicenna and Greek Philosophy," *MIDEO* [*Mélanges Institut Dominicain d'Études Orientales* (Cairo)] 17 (1986): 53–66.

as a "mere metaphor."[26] Yet even these sophisticated accounts may still appear to be so much "metaphor" to those who fail to struggle with the way in which creating a universe must exceed any understanding of "causing" that we regularly employ—as Kant saw so well.

So once a creator emerges on the scene, it appears that we cannot have a proper grasp of human freedom without embedding it in that created order. Otherwise, the very presence of a creator—now regarded as the largest item in the universe—will threaten human freedom, leaving self-styled "theists" the sole exit strategy of removing human free action from the creator's ambit, thereby undermining the original avowal of the Abrahamic faiths of a free creator of the universe. To return to our orienting scheme relating classical to medieval to modern to postmodern presumptions for philosophical inquiry, it seems that the imposing presence of a creator impedes a simple return to the classical picture of human beings oriented to "the good." As Kierkegaard has suggested, that picture may now appear too naïve, or perhaps the very introduction of a creator suggests a previously unimagined model for human agents: creators in their own right, as it were.[27] Yet both Bible and Qur'an warn us that adopting that image for ourselves will lead to unimaginable evil: to be "like God" is tantamount to refusing the original covenant, whereby human beings vow their obedience to the Lord of all.[28] Of course, we have adopted this image for ourselves, and so live in a human world of our own making, a world that Aquinas neatly distinguished from the world of nature that God creates by noting how in the world that human beings have made "evil for the most part prevails."[29] Can we early twenty-first-century people gainsay that radical observation? Yet it may help, as I move ahead with my thesis, to trace the path from a metaphysics that views free action as an unexplained initiative to a rudderless view of freedom that can no longer ask "what freedoms are for," and so leads ineluctably to a general insouciance about domination of the rich and

---

26. For an astute analysis of the tradition of participation, see Rudi teVelde, *Participation and Substantiality in Thomas Aquinas* (Leiden: Brill, 1995).

27. Kierkegaard, as Anti-Climacus, enjoying parrying with "Socrates" over the presence and execution of evil actions, in his *Sickness unto Death*, trans. and ed. Howard and Edna Hong (Princeton: Princeton University Press, 1980).

28. Genesis 3 is more explicit about the temptation to "be like God" (Gen. 3), whereas the Qur'an is more clear about the original covenant: 3:80–83.

29. *Summa Theologiae* 1.49.3.5. The question addresses one of Aquinas's prevailing concerns: the Manichean contention that "there is one supreme evil which is the cause of all evil." In reply to the fifth objection, which presumes that evil has the upper hand (*ut in pluribus*) in the universe, Aquinas notes that defects in natural processes are minimal, whereas "in human affairs evil appears to prevail," offering as the reason that "most human beings follow sense rather than reason," that is, are intent on their gratification.

powerful. As I proceed, I shall try to relieve the bleakness of this analysis by presenting comparative views of contrasting alternatives.

From Freedom as Assertion to Raw Assertion of Power, with Some Powerful Antidotes

When freedom is celebrated as the sheer power to initiate action, or identified with choosing, it cannot help becoming in practice "doing what I wanna do." However, the original picture of freedom in these terms left no room to appreciate or to assess the power of our wants, and so the Promethean image of "control," with its cognate "willpower," dominates. Yet when agents lack such control, as we often do, some authority will be required to constrain them, the most interior of these constraints being the imperatives of practical reason, reinforced for believers in divine commands. In this view, individuals no longer need a creator to empower them; rather, God enters the picture as the one who constrains this unlimited freedom by divine legislation. Pace Paul as well as Luther, "law" becomes the centerpiece of Puritan Christianity. Yet as Nathaniel Hawthorne and others have poignantly reminded us, however internal such constraints were meant to be for believers, they remain external to the Promethean picture of freedom they were intended to constrain, so they will succeed in constraining freedom of action only in a social order as effective as Puritan society. But what happens when that society collapses? The minimal characterization of freedom as "the ability to do otherwise" deprives human freedom of any internal structure, stripping it of any inherent constraints. So when the constraining social order collapses—as social orders tend to do, especially when undermined by a notion of freedom as "doing what I wanna do"—individuals emerge, constrained only by Kant's formal imperatives or those of revelation or, in practice, a combination of both. Yet as we shall see, since even these (purportedly interior) constraints remain external to the dynamic of free action, they can easily be manipulated to serve one's progress to gratification.

Doubtless many cultural and economic factors conspired to create the resulting "individual," but the view of freedom that has prevailed will help to assure that the "life and liberty" such persons stoutly defend will be a function of the "happiness" they are intent on pursuing, which can only be individual gratification. This picture of freedom offers no further resources; lacking an inherent telos, we have no way of asking what freedoms are for.[30] This description of freedom conveniently

30. See John Garvey's constructive essay in legal philosophy, *What Are Freedoms For?* (Cambridge, Mass.: Harvard University Press, 2001).

serves that picture of society called "political liberalism," of course, yet the inescapable logic of gratification assures that such "liberals" will before long become political "libertarians," as democratic ideals give way to economic power, reducing any touted republic to an oligarchy and mocking the "soft" constraints of "civil rights" and "international law" in the name of "interests," usually financially defined. Can we any longer doubt this disaster to be the outcome, or at least the inevitable concomitant, of a libertarian analysis of freedom? But we are asked, "What is the alternative?" as our interlocutors fear a return to the repressions of Puritan society. The alternative I shall try to elaborate takes its bearings from Augustine's analysis of wants and desires, especially as they conspire to form communities of discourse and of action. Such communities could offer striking witness to a society inspired by the vision of freedom outlined here.

Commenting on the promise in the First Letter of John that "we shall be like him, for we shall see him as he is" (3:2 NAB), Augustine presents "the entire life of a good Christian [as] an exercise of holy desire. You do not see what you long for, but the very act of desiring prepares you, so that when he comes you may see and be utterly satisfied." Sometimes, he says, we find that we need to stretch a sack or wineskin to receive an extraordinary amount: "This is how God deals with us. Simply by making us wait he increases our desire, which in turn enlarges the capacity of our soul, making it able to receive what is to be given to us. So, my brethren, continue to desire, for we shall be filled. [Yet] this exercise will be effective only to the extent that we free ourselves from desires leading to infatuation with this world."[31] We find ourselves to be a battleground of desires, yet it is desire itself that will lead us to victory, which is always a gift. Augustine presumes that our orientation to "the good" represents an endowment from the creator, itself an original gift, which when followed will be crowned with the supreme gift to be like that very creator. So all is gift, which we will be enlarged to receive once we free ourselves from infatuations leading (as Paul said) to death. The gift of the promise together with the gift promised entail a task. That task defines the context and the point of our freedom: to return everything to the One from whom we have received everything. A task of that sort will take nothing short of a lifetime to accomplish, but it can be accomplished little by little through discrete actions embodying an orientation to the good. The image is progressive: as infatuations are sloughed off, noble desires are consummated, and the true self emerges. Indeed, on

31. *Tractates on the Gospel of John 112–124; Tractates on the First Epistle of John,* Fathers of the Church 92, trans. John Rettig (Washington, D.C.: Catholic University of America Press, 1995), 4.6, p. 179.

this account there can be no definition of "true self" other than one completely open to receiving the gift of this promise: to be assimilated to the One whose gift of being constitutes our very existence. This is of course very heady stuff, nor does Augustine expect us to understand the words; it is rather our desires that will show us the proper way, as we learn to discriminate among them, following those that lead to life and renouncing those leading to death.[32]

So "will" for Augustine (as well as Aquinas) is suffused with desire and discernment, which together will lead us to our true self as we follow the orientation with which we are endowed at creation, and which is bolstered by "an anointing by the Holy One which teaches us inwardly more than our tongue can speak."[33] In his *Confessions*, Augustine details the dialectic of desire in his own case, tracing his journey through multiple infatuations to the point where he will allow the guiding desire to fill his soul and take over the direction of his life: "The light of confidence flooded into my heart" (8.29). This account of freedom differs from the standard analysis in that a free act becomes a response rather than an initiative, as one accepts the invitation to fulfill the original orientation. Moreover, this account offers a progressive view of freedom: an action becomes more authentically one's own, and hence more integrally free, to the extent that one is freed from the hold of infatuations and thus able to follow those desires that contribute to fulfilling the orienting desire. So all is gift, and all is desire, while desires properly discerned lead to a freedom liberated from infatuations—*non est liber nisi liberatus;* no one is free until freed.

We are as far from an off/on exercise of freedom as we are from an off/on picture of existence.[34] It is rather our inbuilt orientation to the creator that empowers this activity of responding, so that a proper appreciation of the creator/creature relationship, far from being a hindrance, actually makes possible a created freedom that can be positively characterized as a return to one's source rather than as a pointless assertion of a posited power. This exercise of freedom offers a path to the true self, however sinuous and twisting its route may be. Alternatively, allowing

32. For a fascinating parallel with Ghazali, see the introduction to my translation of his *Book of Faith in Divine Unity and Trust in Divine Providence* (Louisville, Ky.: Fons Vitae, 2001).

33. I have been aided in these matters by the astute investigation by D. C. Schindler, "Freedom beyond Our Choosing: Augustine on the Will and Its Objects," *Communio* 29 (2002): 618–53; citation from 640.

34. See Barry Miller's treatment of this issue in *The Fullness of Being: A New Paradigm for Existence* (Notre Dame, Ind.: University of Notre Dame Press, 2002), by contrast with Christopher Hughes, *On a Complex Theory of a Simple God: An Investigation in Aquinas' Philosophical Theology* (Ithaca and London: Cornell University Press, 1989), 27.

oneself to be caught in the tangle of infatuations will divert one from one's true self, so that the exercise of freedom will be deficient in that it stems from refusing rather than accepting the gift. Although we are uncannily skilled in keeping this deficiency from becoming manifest, this account presumes that it will tend to become so, since staving off the demands of the orienting desire will come to prove awkward. That is indeed the hope, and the grounds for hope, even though the radical reach of this freedom can extend to the very loss of self. What this account avoids, however, is elevating the refusal of the gift into the paradigm of freedom itself, though a rich contemporary literary vein suggests that an account that rejects a creator with its grounding orientation may be led to do just that.

A libertarian account of freedom does not lead of itself to such a self-defeating end, but the way it eschews offering a point to the exercise of freedom can introduce a pointlessness that opens the gates to gratification masked as freedom. (Recall how Augustine's "pear tree incident" introduces pointlessness as the core of evil.) The dynamics are quite simple. If freedom amounts to choosing, and my choices are directed by and to what I want, then beginning with my wants invites harnessing my intellectual powers to justify what I want to do, rather than to discern what I ought to do. Moreover, if "oughts" are Kantian-wise opposed to "wants," then personal and collective experience show which one wins. Our resourcefulness at finding justifications is matched only by our virtuosity for making excuses, so "will" as "want" will prevail. Levinas had hoped that the very presence of the "other," notably of another person, would confront our endemic inertial tendency to gratification, thereby lifting us to an ethical plane not unlike that envisaged by Kant. But collective mind-sets seem able to obscure even this dynamic by the handy ruse of demonization. West Bank settlers no longer see Palestinians as fellow human beings but as obstacles to completing the settlement of a land that is exclusively theirs by divine right. So however inhuman their gratuitous actions of expropriation and humiliations may appear to onlookers, any move to regard their Palestinian neighbors as neighbors would require rejecting an entire justificatory scheme. Yet the ease with which that scheme can obscure what we (and Levinas) take to be simple human decency is certainly facilitated by an account of freedom that leaves all constraints external to itself, since it is itself bereft of any inherent goals. Yet if that be the case, it suggests that "simple human decency" will require a richer view of human freedom to make its demands felt. So it may well be that something like the normative account that I have offered, replete with a creator to empower its direction and execution, may come far closer to the kind of freedom we need to be human and decent. Indeed, attempts to avoid so potent a metaphysics by simply equating freedom with choosing lead rather to an illusory freedom whereby we effectively become prey to wayward desires.

Some Startling Conclusions

At this point I come full circle to my original contention about "infused moral virtues," for the view of freedom that I am promoting cannot be articulated without its internal relation to a transcendent source in creation. Indeed, this grounding relation constitutes its power as well as its scandal. In his *Thick and Thin*, political philosopher Michael Walzer celebrates the way medieval Christians elaborated "the social meaning of the good that was being distributed: eternal life."[35] Freely acknowledging that "the everyday role of eternity is no doubt a difficult matter, especially for those of us who have lost or given up its comforts," Walzer goes on to show how as "ordinary men and women came increasingly to question the reality or the central importance or the public availability of eternal life, . . . they substituted longevity for eternity" (30). So, in his words, care of souls transmuted into care of bodies. I am proposing a return to the soul, the inbuilt orientation of human persons to "the good," and with it an understanding of *eternity*, not as a "comfort" but as a demanding presence in everyday life, not as an extrinsic reward of a life well lived but as the structure directing our freedom to its proper exercise. Let me offer a Muslim and a Christian example.

When Anwar Sadat was asked by the BBC why he risked his life to go to Jerusalem (in 1979), his response was telling. This sophisticated head of state reverted to a *hadith* (one of the stories of the Prophet's life and works that shape Muslim practice): "When I die and meet Allah, I want to be able to say that I have done everything possible for peace." Imagine a set of questions that, Muslims learn, will be asked of each person, articulated according to their role in life. The questions serve to specify the way each person will go about attaining the inbuilt goal of "returning everything to the One from whom they received everything." So the "last judgment" is effectively present in every action for those who keep their wits about them. Or, put differently, eternity, in Walzer's terms, will be present in the temporal execution of our God-given freedom as its inherent structure or inbuilt telos.

We could no doubt think of examples of Christian men or women paralleling that of Sadat, but let me shift to Jesus's admonition to his disciples as they "argued with one another who was the greatest. Jesus

---

35. Michael Walzer, *Thick and Thin: Moral Argument at Home and Abroad* (Notre Dame, Ind.: University of Notre Dame Press, 1994), 29.

sat down, called the twelve, and said to them: 'Whoever wants to be first must be last of all and servant of all'" (Mark 9:33–35). Jesus's own actions will fulfill this injunction, as he reminds his disciples at their last supper together: "You call me Teacher and Lord, and rightly so, for that is what I am. Then if I, your Lord and Teacher, have washed your feet, you also ought to wash one another's feet. I have set you an example: you are to do as I have done for you" (John 13:13–15). Just as he knows who he is, so he realizes that everyone must "want to be first"; the issue is how to proceed to fulfill that egotistical aim. He does not challenge the aim itself, but directs us to a way, which when followed will wean us from egotistical "infatuations" to activate the inbuilt goal directing us to our true self. This ethical jujitsu, if you will, gains credibility from his own witness: we can come to discern how authentic is this way, for he shows himself to be "the way, the truth and the life" (John 14:6).

Neither of these examples can gain any purchase on us, of course, without its being rooted in the gift of free creation, so that our inbuilt goal becomes articulated in our attempts to return everything to the One from whom we have received everything. Yet it is not as though we must first "believe in one God, creator of heaven and earth" (Nicene Creed). It may be far more natural to reflect on the antinomies inherent in standard "libertarian" views of freedom, crafted in the absence of this One, to realize that something like this astounding picture may in fact be more true than the one that offers us no direction and simply urges us to be "pro-choice." Moreover, the truth of this way will turn out to be more accessible to practice than to speculation, for this One necessarily exceeds our understanding, though with the help of an "anointing," together with a community sustaining that anointing, we can follow the way to this truth, as we attempt to orient our lives to return everything to the One from whom we have received everything.[36]

36. I want to express my gratitude to Robert Kane for some critical observations that saved me from a few egregious errors; those that remain are my own.

3

The Virtue of Writing Appropriately

Or:

*Is Stanley Hauerwas Right in Thinking He Should Not
Write Anymore on the Mentally Handicapped?*

Hans S. Reinders

My Friend Ronald

I have a friend named Ronald. Usually when I tell people about Ronald, they are amused by my stories. Most of the stories are funny, not because Ronald is a particularly funny guy, but because he does things differently. He might stop a lady in the street to tell her she has beautiful hair and that he would not mind marrying her. Or he might walk into a department store with seventy or eighty cents in his pocket to buy a new watch. Ronald does not worry about what other people may think of him. He knows what they think, has known it all his life. People respond differently when you are disabled. Ronald knows people think he is a little crazy, but that does not much matter. To him it is just a fact of life. It does not stop him from being the outgoing guy that he is. I once had lunch with him in a crowded fast-food place when all of a sudden he started to identify the people sitting around us as look-alikes of the actors and actresses in his favorite soap. "Hey, you look just like Ethel," he would say. "And you look just like Sam." And so on. Within five minutes he had the entire crowd examining one another as to who resembled which actor or actress. That's what I mean by "funny."

When I tell people I consider Ronald a friend, however, they are often surprised—even skeptical. "Oh, really?" they say. Their apparently Aristotelian intuition suggests to them that you cannot really be friends with someone so unlike yourself. I am after all an academic. I am presumed to embody intellect, which is about the opposite of what Ronald is presumed to embody. With regard to friendship, the old metaphysical truth still seems to be alive: sameness attracts sameness, not otherness. This in spite of postmodern celebrations of "otherness." Friends are people who make you feel at ease with yourself—as Aristotle would say—and that is what "otherness" usually does not do.

Once you start to pay attention to these things—as I have been doing for quite a while—you find out that friendship is a rare thing in the world of those we call "intellectually disabled." In talking with professional caregivers and support workers I have noticed that these people hardly ever think of their "clients" as friends. They may be very fond of them, they may even say they love them, but only reluctantly is such affection interpreted as friendship.

One might think that the explanation for this reluctance has something to do with "choice," the assumption being that professionals do not choose their clients in the same way they choose their friends. I do not think, however, that this explanation works. Apart from the fact that friends are "found" and "claimed" rather than chosen, it is simply not true that professionals do not become friends with their clients. It surely makes professional relationships more complicated, but it happens quite frequently. It does not happen frequently only in the lives of "clients" like Ronald.

If friends are found, how did I find Ronald? Well, I didn't. My wife did. Or, better, he found us. We were visiting a place where people with intellectual disability live when she was approached by a bold-looking young fellow. "I know you!" this fellow exclaimed. It turned out to be Ronald. He was not just being bold, however, because what he said was true. Years ago they had lived in the same town and had occasionally met. My wife recognized him, too. So they had a little chat, during which Ronald and I were introduced to one another. And when we said good-bye, he made us promise to come back and visit him. That is how Ronald found us.

I remember very well our first visit to his group home a few weeks later. It was late summer. Ronald took us out for a walk on the grounds of the institution. Since it was a nice, sunny day, there were many people out, most of whom Ronald knew. And not a single one passed that he did not stop to tell that "these two people here" were his friends. So I was claimed as a friend.

My Friend Stanley

The lives of people like Ronald have for a long time been a recurring theme in the writings of Stanley Hauerwas. In his many collections there are a number of essays on caring for the "mentally handicapped," as he calls them.[1] But Hauerwas has never written about these people to discuss an "ethical issue." Those people who think there are "ethical issues" to be discussed in this connection are the same people who believe that the existence of persons with disabilities confronts us as a "problem." Hauerwas has written on intellectual disability to support those who dedicate their lives to the task of resisting this view.[2] Apart from this, Hauerwas does not believe in being an "ethicist." Nor has he ever believed in ethical expertise. Ethical experts are those who consider it their job to address "ethical issues" on our social and political agenda in ways that help establish a moral consensus. Hauerwas has never taken much interest in that agenda, because he thinks the way our society construes its "ethical issues" is but another way of how political liberalism manipulates our political allegiance.

His rejection of being an "ethicist" notwithstanding, Hauerwas's name was attached to intellectual disability long before it became a "subject" of ethical interest.[3] All the more remarkable, therefore, was his confes-

1. Hauerwas has never had much patience for political correctness, so he does not bother about the changing terminology in the field. The term commonly accepted nowadays is, of course, "persons with intellectual disabilities," which is also the term that I will use.

2. Stanley Hauerwas, "The Church and the Mentally Handicapped," in *Dispatches from the Front: Theological Engagements with the Secular* (Durham, N.C.: Duke University Press, 1994), 177: "The challenge of being as well as caring for those called 'mentally handicapped' is to prevent those who wish they never existed or would 'just go away' from defining them as 'the problem' of the mentally handicapped. It is almost impossible to resist descriptions that make being mentally handicapped a 'problem,' since those descriptions are set by the power of the 'normal.'"

3. One of his earliest publications on the subject is the essay "Community and Diversity: The Tyranny of Normality," in Stanley Hauerwas, *Suffering Presence: Theological Reflections on Medicine, the Mentally Handicapped, and the Church* (Notre Dame, Ind.: University of Notre Dame Press, 1986), 211–17; originally published in *National Apostolate with Mentally Retarded Persons Quarterly* (Spring/Summer 1977).

sion a few years ago that he had been promising himself not to write on the subject anymore.[4] I have been in close conversation with him for a number of years, so this confession did not escape my attention, and the occasion of the present Festschrift—to which it is a great honor to contribute—provides me with an opportunity to reflect on it. It also provides me with an opportunity to reflect upon what I take to be an absolutely crucial question in the ethics of caring for persons with intellectual disabilities, the question of how to be their friends.

In addressing this question it will become apparent—I hope—how much I am indebted to Hauerwas's work. When some fifteen years ago I became involved in the field of intellectual disability, I did not much know what to think about the people I met there. Reading Hauerwas (and MacIntyre) taught me that knowing *how* to think might be the more important ethical question than knowing *what* to think. Ethics is no doubt an intellectual discourse, but the ways in which this discourse is construed reflect different practices, as is true for all other discourses as well. Coming to the field of intellectual disability, I sensed that the question of what kind of practice I wanted to be engaged in would be decisive. The dominant practice of the day was—and still is—that of "applied ethics." Accordingly, the demand for "ethical expertise" was—and still is—quite strong. Hauerwas and MacIntyre recognized that demand as a reflection of modernity's approach to all of human activity as a form of technology. Within that approach, questions about "the right thing to do" can be answered independently of questions about the character of the agent. The only thing needed is a procedure for right reasoning, which is what "ethical expertise" supplies.

But although their relentless criticisms were sound and convincing, at least in my view, the alternative was less easy to define. I noticed that many colleagues in the field who were dissatisfied with the formal and procedural approaches to applied ethics were very much inspired by the turn to Aristotelian virtue ethics, but they mistakenly regarded it as an alternative that would allow them to do what they did in a more "substantial" way. Many failed to see that the critical arguments did not support a "better" version but implied the rejection of the project of applied ethics in its entirety. Therefore, the question of what practice I wanted to be engaged in was not merely a question of an alternative. It was a question of an alternative for what. Given the direction in which my thinking was developing, my own way of putting it at the time was as the question of how to "do" virtue ethics.

4. Stanley Hauerwas, "Timeful Friends: Living with the Handicapped," in *Sanctify Them in the Truth: Holiness Exemplified* (Nashville: Abingdon, 1998), 143–56; 144.

In what follows I will concentrate on Hauerwas's writing on persons with intellectual disabilities. I will ask why he came to believe that he should not write about these people anymore. In doing so I will consider how to practice an Aristotelian type of Christian ethics if one does not believe in theorizing about it. Hauerwas thinks theorizing about ethics is a bad idea. I agree. But then what to do? What is the purpose of writing about ethics? What is its appropriate style? These are the questions I will address, but I will do so only indirectly. That is to say, I will not approach them in a formal way. Nor will I proceed by offering a systematic account of Hauerwas's thoughts (which in any case would signify a profound misreading of his work). Instead, I will reflect on friendship and truthfulness, on what it means to be claimed as a friend by someone like Ronald, on what it takes to be such a friend as well as what that means for our conception of what it is to be a true friend, and finally, on what it means to be claimed as a friend by Stanley M. Hauerwas.

Theological Realism

In his essay "Timeful Friends" Hauerwas explains that his writings on persons with intellectual disabilities have been crucial for his critique of modernity, for the disabled live lives of which the moral beliefs of modernity cannot make sense. According to these beliefs, our lives are meaningful to the extent that they are meaningful to ourselves. We are supposed to be "authors" of our own lives. That is what modern people believe. Christians, however, do not believe the same. "As Christians," Hauerwas says, "we know we have not been created to be 'our own authors,' to be autonomous. We are creatures. Dependency, not autonomy, is one of the *ontological characteristics* of our lives."[5] Hauerwas realizes, however, that the very assertion will be mistaken by his secular critics as a performative contradiction. "If being dependent is what you choose," these critics will say, "that's fine, but don't tell me I should choose the same." The critics reject "dependency" as if it were a matter of choice. Thus they mistake Hauerwas's claim about dependency as a claim to a moral value that Christians may embrace to counteract the modern value of autonomy.

We see then why and at what point the existence of persons with intellectual disabilities is pertinent to Hauerwas's argument. Their existence shows him why the critics' rejection of dependency is mistaken; their lives testify to what it means to be a creature. The fact that these lives are

---

5. Hauerwas, "Timeful Friends," 147 (italics added).

not chosen, that these people are not the authors of their own narrative, this fact "reveals the character of *our* lives," he says.[6] He thus takes the existence of persons with intellectual disabilities as paradigmatic—rather than exceptional—for what human existence is like. Acknowledging the fact that we are constituted as creatures is no less than a claim to theological realism, for which the existence of these persons provides Hauerwas with a warrant: "I have used the mentally handicapped as *material markers* to show that Christian speech can and in fact does make claims about the way things are."[7]

Theological realism for Hauerwas is, of course, couched in the narrative of the cross and the resurrection of Jesus Christ.[8] Only the Christian narrative can make us free to face our own incompleteness without despair and share our lives with one another as gifts. The presence of the intellectually disabled therefore does not present Christians with a particular challenge. Their lives do not need a justification. Quite the contrary. In the Christian community persons with disabilities are welcomed, not questioned.[9] Accordingly, the Christian narrative is capable of nourishing practices of sharing our lives with them. Without this narrative such practices are difficult to sustain.

Hauerwas's view is correctly summarized, I think, by saying that without the Christian narrative the experience of sharing one's life with an intellectually disabled person does not make much sense unless it is undergirded by a moral justification. But the very need for a moral justification is problematic, according to Hauerwas, because it suggests that the existence of that person per se is "unintelligible."[10] The need to produce "justifying reasons" for the care and support of people with disabilities indicates the force of the moral beliefs of modernity. If autonomy and self-representation are what make our lives worthwhile, then the lives of these people stand in need of a justification. That much is obvious. But Hauerwas believes this need to be dangerous. If rationality and self-consciousness are taken to be the very essence of what makes us human, then it is not at all clear that we ought to treat human beings lacking in these characteristics as our equals.

Hauerwas is not making an apologetic claim at this point, however. He is not telling secular humanists that their moral beliefs cannot make sense of the existence of intellectually disabled people and that only

6. Ibid. (italics added).

7. Ibid., 147–48 (italics added).

8. See Hauerwas's *With the Grain of the Universe: The Church's Witness and Natural Theology* (Grand Rapids, Mich: Brazos Press, 2001).

9. Hauerwas, "Timeful Friends," 147.

10. Ibid., 144.

Christian beliefs can. Instead, his attempt is to sustain Christians willing to share their lives with such people by showing how their intentions are nourished by the practices of the church. In that sense there is a connection between his claim to theological realism and his understanding of the Christian moral life: "Theologically thinking about the mentally handicapped helps us see . . . that claims about the way things are cannot be separated from the way we should live."[11]

Writing as Witness

Despite the crucial importance of persons with intellectual disabilities to his project, however, Hauerwas confesses to being uneasy about his writing in this regard.[12] Writing "about" these people is not what you do when you really care for them. If you care, you write "with" and "for" them. But then you have to know such people.

> By "know" I mean you must be *with* the handicapped in a way they may be able to claim you as a friend. I was once so claimed, but over the last few years I have not enjoyed such a friendship. So when I now write about the ethics of caring for the mentally handicapped, I fear I am not talking about actual people but more of my memories of the mentally handicapped.[13]

Intellectually disabled persons once claimed Hauerwas as a friend, but that is now only a memory. The real cause of his uneasiness, however, is not this loss. The uneasiness has been there from the beginning of his writings. It was caused by the particular purpose of these writings. He did not write "with" and "for" the intellectually disabled but—as he puts it—for his own theoretical purposes.[14]

Now, the interesting question is why Hauerwas thought he could break the promise he had made to himself. If he believed he was using other people for his own theoretical purposes, what excuse allowed him to do so again? The answer he gives is somewhat surprising. He traces his own uneasiness to the moral pangs about using other people in our culture, attributable to the dominance of "the Kantian narrative." Apparently we are to understand that for this once he has fallen prey to Kantian presuppositions. Apart from the fact that Hauerwas usually smells the

11. Ibid., 148.
12. Ibid., 144.
13. Ibid.
14. Ibid.

odors of Kantianism long before other people start to have their noses cleaned, this is a curious move for an Aristotelian.

The argument suggests that if we dispel the Kantian narrative, the moral objection against using other people loses its force. That may be. But even then an important question remains to be addressed, and it is the question that an Aristotelian Christian should ask. Indeed, the question is not whether we may use persons with intellectual disabilities as part of our theological agenda. The question is what good we are depriving ourselves of by giving up their friendship. Kantian ethics supposes the nature of ethical questions about "using" people to be other-regarding. Once Kantian ethics is removed, however, the concern remains how our relationships with those others are part of our own good. Therefore Hauerwas's argument about appropriate writing in this connection is not very convincing. Now that the Kantian worry has been dispelled, have we solved the problem of writing "about"? I don't think we have, and neither does Hauerwas. If appropriate writing is not at odds with writing "about" other people, it certainly poses the issue of our relationships with those people, as Hauerwas will be the first to concede.

The point is even more compelling once we think not only as Aristotelians but also as Christians. Hauerwas has been the theologian who for decades has reminded us more than anyone else that Christian speech cannot be separated from Christian witness. There is no way to establish the truth of theological claims independently of being engaged in the practices from which they spring. From the many, many passages that could be quoted from Hauerwas's work to support this claim, let me highlight one from his book with Charles Pinches—in many ways a book about friendship and truthfulness. In arguing for a Christian account of the virtues, the authors claim that

> any adequate account of the virtues Christianly considered will, we believe, render the distinction between theology and ethics problematic. The way we are taught to speak as Christians, what it means for us to be in the Christian faith, is not separable from how we are to live. Because the virtues presume what we say and what we do are inseparable they are an indispensable resource for the display of the Christian life.[15]

For Christian theology truth is necessarily related to witness. Consequently, Christian theologians cannot speak truthfully without examining how their writing supports, or contributes to, witnessing the narrative of

15. Stanley Hauerwas and Charles Pinches, *Christians among the Virtues: Theological Conversations with Ancient and Modern Ethics* (Notre Dame, Ind.: University of Notre Dame Press, 1997), x.

Christ. This is the central claim Hauerwas has been hammering home to the theological world since well before the end of the last century. There is no doubt in my mind that he deserves our gratitude for reminding us of the importance of witness, whatever else we may think of his work. It is only once we begin to take the responsibility of witnessing to Christ seriously that we begin to see the poverty of academic theology as it is practiced in most of our institutions of higher education. But it is also only then that we begin to fathom what the culture of modernity, from which these institutions originate, means for the possibility of living the Christian life.

"We Are Friends, Aren't We?"

The analysis in the previous section is not an ingenious way to tell Hauerwas that he should practice what he preaches. Even though Hauerwas needs to be told that, it is certainly not for me to do. So in the last part of "Timeful Friends" Hauerwas sings the praises of the people of L'Arche who share their lives with persons with intellectual disabilities as a way of witnessing to Christ. If excusing ourselves by way of praising others is a theological mistake, I plead guilty: long after Hauerwas did so with regard to the people of L'Arche, I did exactly the same.[16]

Not only is my analysis not meant to lecture Hauerwas; neither is my way of framing it in a story about my friendship with Ronald meant to suggest that I am improving my life. The pitfalls of writing appropriately on ethics are many. One of them is the temptation to engage in certain practices as a way to obtain legitimacy. After all, we can also use people by becoming their friends, as Aristotle tells us. Doing so not only produces no true friendship; it also offers very little chance of success. This is particularly true in the case of people like Ronald. More often than not such people do not make easy friends. Attempting to be friends with them is a quite hopeless undertaking if we lack the virtues of patience, sincerity, and constancy.

My friendship with Ronald taught me this lesson. Let me tell you a bit more about it. Where Ronald lives, social life is bleak. As soon as you enter the residence you sense that there is not much of a shared communal life. Rather, the atmosphere is one of what I would call a *modus vivendi*. Ronald's life is regulated by a set of explicit and implicit rules to live and let live. Sharing one another's time in the living room is an

---

16. Hans S. Reinders, "Being Thankful: Parenting the Mentally Disabled," in *The Blackwell Companion to Christian Ethics,* ed. Stanley Hauerwas and Samuel Wells (London: Blackwell, 2003), 427–40.

obligation for Ronald, whereas being allowed to go to his room is his escape. Living in such a place makes fellowship a scarce good. Competition for positive attention is a necessity. Ronald would call neither the people he lives with nor the people who work with him his friends. He is stuck with them, which he takes as another fact of life. Within this kind of social environment having a friend is an asset. Having a friend from "outside" is a cause for envy. It enhances your status; it is something you can show off with.

So Ronald is thrilled when I visit him. In fact, he phones two or three times a week to ask when I will visit him, even though he already has our next appointment on his calendar. As soon as I arrive on the grounds of the institution, Ronald hops in my car and wants to leave. His preferred destination is a small village nearby, where he likes to go shopping. Buying things is an obsession for him. CDs, videos, watches, and pens are his favorites. He usually does not have enough money to buy what he wants, but he has no problem with relying on the fact that I do.

When we started these trips, it frequently happened that he would run into the local music store, throw a fistful of nickels and dimes on the counter, and ask for the latest production of his favorite band. When the owner would tell him that he could not buy a CD for that kind of money, Ronald would look imploringly at me. Then the owner would start to grow impatient with the situation. Was I going to pass on the amount needed, or what? I didn't like that, of course. I felt used.

I have since learned, however, to anticipate these moments and lay out the rules in advance. I announce that I want to visit him but I don't want to go buy something. I convince myself that in setting this rule I am seeking his good because "buying" is a compulsive obsession for him. Ronald is "buysick," as he himself prefers to call it. So we are not going shopping. You don't give sweets to someone who suffers from diabetes, do you?

Ronald accepts this. Of course he does; what else can he do? I realize that in refusing to go shopping with him I am depriving him of one of the very few opportunities he has to exercise some form of power over his life, the power of spending money. But I can't stand the way he does it. It drives me crazy. The other day he wanted to buy a new CD box. It had to be a box that would hold five disks. He needed it to replace one that was broken. The old box had acquired two holes on the side—at least that was what Ronald believed. But when I looked at it, I saw that it was not broken at all. The holes had been there all along. They were there for opening the box. Ronald remained unconvinced. The box was broken. In order not to be the "bad guy," I gave in, and we went to the music store. The owner told him what I had told him, but Ronald continued to explain that we had it wrong. Because he was completely obsessed with the idea of buying a new box, he would not let go. Finally, the owner lost patience. I had to take Ronald out of the shop. He was disappointed, and I was angry, more with myself than with him. Like most people, I am not a very communicative character when I am angry, so I drove back to Ronald's home in silence. He became very anxious. "Please Hans, we are friends, aren't we?"[17]

Aristotle's Friends

When people respond skeptically to the notion of being friends with someone who is intellectually disabled, do they have a point? Can such a relationship in truth be called a relation between friends? As the account of my friendship with Ronald suggests, the question is a serious one. In the history of ethics no one has paid more attention to the practice of friendship than Aristotle, as is well known. But it is equally well known that his account of true friendship has its limitations. For the present context, the notion of true friendship as friendship between "equals" is particularly troublesome.

Whatever there is to be learned from Aristotle's account of true friendship, I don't think this account is capable of including friendship with persons with intellectual disabilities. The reason is, briefly, that true friendship involves persons of good character or virtue, and persons of good character or virtue are distinguished by a particular kind of life, namely, a life of "activity or actions of the soul implying a rational principle."[18] Even on the most favorable interpretation, it is impossible to include in this view people whose actions and activities do not seem to display a rational principle.[19] Since true friendship is possible only

17. To be clear: being friends with Ronald is not just a pain in the neck. Such a limited characterization would do great injustice both to him and to our friendship. We laugh and make jokes; we have dinner, walk on the beach, go camping, and so on. But in all this I do want to stay focused on how I might make a true difference in his life, which my account here shows is not an easy thing to do given who I am, who Ronald is, and what his life is like.

18. Aristotle, *Nicomachean Ethics*, trans. W. D. Ross (Oxford: Oxford University Press, 1925), 1098a14; hereafter *NE*. Even though Aristotle's account can be saved from his bad reputation with regard to women and slaves, the disabled are in a different category. The discriminating ground is not social status but intellectual function.

19. Recent discussions on the definition of intellectual disabilities have been fueled by concerns that the focus on individual characteristics tends to disregard the social environment from which such characteristics draw their practical and political significance. These discussions notwithstanding, "subaverage intellectual functioning" is still regarded as a dominant characteristic. The classical source is R. Luckasson et al., *Mental Retardation: Definition, Classification, and Systems of Support* (Washington, D.C.: American Association for Mental Retardation, 1992).

between persons of good character whose lives imply a rational principle, it must follow that persons with intellectual disabilities cannot
be part of such friendships. That much is obvious. Less well known is
the fact that Aristotle's account of friendship does not exclude these
persons from friendship altogether, inasmuch as he allows for friendship between people who are "unequal" or "dissimilar."

Aristotle's account of friendship is fairly "liberal," to be sure, with
regard to who can count as a friend. It leaves room for such widely
different kinds of mutual relationships as mother and child, political
rulers and their subjects, and children and their peers. Friendship in
this broad sense is concomitant with justice in that it is concerned
with the same relation of mutuality. "Friendship and justice exist between the same persons and have an equal extension."[20] The difference between justice and friendship is that the demands of justice
are independent of the actual presence of fellow feeling, which in the
case of friendship is impossible. Friendship, according to Aristotle, is
defined by the fact of both wishing *and* doing good for the other *for the
other's sake* and by the fact that these good wishes and good deeds are
mutually recognized.[21] As John Cooper has pointed out, this condition
applies to all kinds of communal relationships.[22] Just as there can be
a relationship of justice with everyone who is capable of participating
in law and contract, so there can be friendship with everyone "in so
far as he is a man."[23]

Within the wide variety of possible friendships, there is a subset that
involves personal relationships between people who appreciate particular qualities in each other. The qualities operative in a given friendship

20. *NE* 1160a8.
21. *NE* 1156a3. See John M. Cooper, "Aristotle on the Forms of Friendship," in *Reason
and Emotion: Essays on Ancient Moral Psychology and Moral Theory* (Princeton: Princeton
University Press, 1999), 312–35; 313, 314.
22. See John M. Cooper, "Political Animals and Civic Friendship," in *Reason and
Emotion*, 356–77; 371 n. 18.
23. *NE* 1161b8. It is interesting to note the *conditio sine qua non* that Aristotle defines
here. One cannot be friends with a slave insofar as he is a slave. The slave resembles the
citizen under the rule of a tyrant: he is used as a mere extension ("a tool") of his master.
One cannot be friends with what is only an extension of oneself. "*Qua* slave then, one
cannot be friends with him. But *qua* man one can" (*NE* 1161b8). In this connection Julia
Annas points out that the very broad scope of friendship may raise the question whether
Aristotle's conception is at all coherent when friendship can take so many different forms;
see Julia Annas, *The Morality of Happiness* (New York: Oxford University Press, 1993), 250.
The answer is found in Aristotle's method of examining ethical questions. He asks how
his fellow Athenians use words (*NE* 1155a33, 1157a25, 1157b5, 1159b27), or what can
be learned from proverbs and popular sayings (*NE* 1155a35, 1156b26, 1157b12, 1158a1,
1159b31). It is from the many opinions that educated people may have on a given subject
that Aristotle seeks to find the truth in some of them (*NE* 1145b2).

determine its nature. Aristotle distinguishes the qualities of utility, pleasure, and virtue.[24] Only virtue—a function of character, which endures
over time—enables true or "perfect" friendship, as he calls it.[25] Perfect
friendship is that between people of good character where the parties
seek one another for the love of virtue. Such friendship will also be
perfect in equality and similarity. As noted, however, for Aristotle not all
friendships are "perfect," since he allows for friendships between people
who are unequal and dissimilar.[26] Friendships of equality are those in
which both parties extend the same benevolence to one another. Both
receive the same benefits from their friendship. In contrast, unequal
friendships involve superiority of one party over the other. These friendships are viable only to the extent that the benefits rendered to each
of the parties are proportionally compensated. "The better [of the two
parties] should be more loved than he loves, and so should the more
useful, and similarly in each of the other cases; for when the love is in
proportion to the merit of the parties, then in a sense arises equality,
which is certainly held to be characteristic of friendship."[27]

More or less the same rules hold for friendships marked by dissimilarity. These are friendships in which the parties do not necessarily
get a proportionally unequal share of the same benefits; rather, they
receive benefits of different kinds. For example, a wealthy person may
be friends with an intelligent person. In these cases, Aristotle explains,
all sorts of difficulties may arise in determining what return the parties
are due, because there is no fixed standard.[28] None of these difficulties
will arise in a friendship based on good character, however, because
there the mutual benefits are in proportion to intention.[29] True friendship, in other words, does not give rise to problems that derive from
inequality or dissimilarity, because friends of good character will seek
one another's good for the sake of the other and not for some transient
quality such as utility or pleasure.

---

24. *NE* 1156a4–1156b12.
25. *NE* 1156b6.
26. Cooper, "Aristotle on the Forms of Friendship," 320.
27. *NE* 1158b25–28.
28. Hauerwas explains Aristotle's tolerance with regard to the lesser forms of friendship
by arguing that friendship does not presuppose virtue but is itself "a process that makes
possible our becoming virtuous." Thus the lesser forms of friendship have "the potential
of putting us on the road to virtue." See Stanley Hauerwas, "Companions on the Way: The
Necessity of Friendship," *Asbury Theological Journal* 45 (1990): 35–48; 39. This appears
to me a quite favorable interpretation, given Aristotle's insistence that inequality and
dissimilarity between friends must be compensated proportionally. Between unequal or
dissimilar friends the "better" of the two deserves to get more out of the friendship.
29. *NE* 1164b1.

But true friendship not only does not give rise to these problems; it also fosters a growing equality and similarity. Friends not only seek to promote one another's good for the sake of the other; they also desire to be in one another's company and share one another's delights and sorrows. And each of these things, Aristotle observes, "is true of the good man's relation to himself."[30] Indeed, a man of good character desires for his friend what he also desires for himself. True friends thus grow together in virtue, becoming more and more similar over time. For the good man, Aristotle concludes, "his friend is another self."[31]

Let me return at this point to my observation of the typically skeptical response to the notion of friendship with an intellectually disabled person. Through the lens of such doubt, Aristotle's claim to equality as the mark of true friendship appears right on target. Whatever the fruits of my friendship with Ronald for each of us, it seems unlikely that what I get from it equals what he gets from it. This inequality may well be what people have in mind when they question whether I can "really" be friends with a disabled person. When I confirm Ronald's claim that we are friends, the responding look is usually one of incredulity. One of us must be joking.

This incredulity is readily displayed by the professionals in Ronald's home, who regard me as a "volunteer." Usually, being a volunteer means doing things that do not pay off, which is why most people don't do them when they are under no obligation. This makes "reward" the critical aspect of being a volunteer. So to the people who work in Ronald's home, it is clear what he gets out of our friendship—trips to the village, free meals, visits to my apartment—but it is unclear to them what I get out of it. Since in their view it is surely very little, they frequently tell Ronald not to be too demanding. It is as if they are saying to him: "Don't push your luck." Presumably their reaction is based on how they know volunteers to respond when disabled people become too demanding. They quit.

In sum, Aristotle's account of true friendship suggests that the skepticism with which people view my friendship with Ronald is warranted. Moreover, Aristotle's theory explains not only these intuitive responses of others, but also—whether I like it or not—my own negative reactions to some of Ronald's habits.[32] These are the kinds of experiences we would expect to occur in friendships that are unequal and dissimilar. It appears, then, that we can argue the question of true friendship with

30. *NE* 1166a10.
31. *NE* 1166a31.
32. No doubt many persons with intellectual disabilities are blessed with better friends than myself, but I am confident that quite a few of these friends face similar challenges.

an intellectually disabled person in one of two opposing ways. We can reject Aristotle's account because it excludes people like Ronald from being part of such friendships. But we can also invoke Aristotle's account to explain the tensions in such friendships, as is evident in my relationship with Ronald. Apparently that tension attests the lack of virtue that prevents friendship from flourishing, at least for the time being. At this point it seems that the argument can go either way.

Christian Friends

Can a Christian account of friendship accommodate the difference between these two views of Aristotle? Let me offer a hint about which direction a positive answer to this question might go. In doing so, I will address once again Hauerwas's work, this time his discussion—co-authored with Charles Pinches—on the difference between Aristotelian and Christian friendship.

The problem with Aristotle's account of true friendship, from a Christian point of view, is that it is unclear how one could ever be certain of being involved in true friendship. For the virtuous person there is no distinction between love for self and love for the friend, because both are similar with respect to the good. But this implies that perceiving oneself and perceiving one's friend as a person of good character are one and the same. In their comments on Aristotelian friendship, Hauerwas and Pinches make a similar point by saying that Aristotle's account leaves no space to appreciate the friend as another. The authors notice that even though Aristotle denies true friendship to be instrumental—the friend is not just an extension of the self—his description "fails to reflect otherness in friendship."[33] It is their experience that "when we love the friend, we love not just what we share with her, but also, and often more importantly, that in her which differs from ourselves."[34]

Regarding this objection from otherness, I would argue that on its own account it does not capture the real problem in Aristotle's views. For Aristotle, true friendship distinguishes itself in that it excels in constancy. True friendship can stand the test of time because friends participate in virtue, and virtue remains constant. The problem here is not so much that "Aristotle comes close to requiring that the constancy we share protect us from one another's difference."[35] The problem is the

33. Hauerwas and Pinches, *Christians among the Virtues*, 40.
34. Ibid.
35. Ibid., 41. Insofar as Hauerwas and Pinches—at this stage of their argument—are offering an internal objection to Aristotle, I don't think this objection is very strong. As

necessary act of self-affirmation that his conception of true friendship implies. I can consider myself to be involved in true friendship only to the extent that I know myself to be a virtuous person. It is not easy to see how Christians could perform such an act of self-affirmation. Not even saints could perform such an act, because it would mean that they regarded themselves as no longer in need of the Lord's Prayer not to lead them into temptation. Conspicuously lacking in Hauerwas and Pinches's text on Aristotelian friendship is the notion of sin.[36]

A Christian conception of true friendship, I suggest, must include the notion of confessing our failure to be true friends.[37] The reason is not hard to grasp. As Hauerwas and Pinches themselves point out, Christians believe that "the God of the universe, who has extended Himself to us in the Jewish people and in Jesus, invites us to become His friends by sharing in His suffering."[38] That is, of course, precisely what we want to avoid. We surely want to be friends with God, but not in order to share in His suffering. Most of us do not want to be affiliated with suffering, nor with poverty, nor with abnormality. From a Christian point of view, the notion of betrayal because of our sinfulness is crucial in our account of friendship. Without it, that account may incorporate terrible mistakes. For example, I might be tempted to regard my friendship with Ronald as a way to respond to God's invitation. This would render our friendship as an act of compassion on my part, in which I offer friendship to the one who is suffering from otherness. The mistake here would be my misconstruing my act of friendship toward the other as analogous to God's act of friendship toward me. Within this false analogy, I would place myself at the wrong end of the invitation. The important thing about our friendship *for me* is not what I offer the other person. A history of hypocrisy in Christian charity testifies to the sinfulness of this mistake. The important thing for me is what the other person does—in Hauerwas's salutary way of putting it—by *claiming me as a friend*. It is a

---

I remarked in my introduction, Aristotelian friendship is what makes us feel at home with the other, which is usually not what "otherness" does. If disregard for otherness is a failure, a quite different view of friendship must already be in place.

36. See Hauerwas's "Companions on the Way," where he is more explicit on this point when he argues that in our friendships we like to mirror "a God who bears a closer resemblance to Aristotle's 'high-minded man'" (44). That is to say, in our friendships we like to affirm ourselves in our self-sufficiency rather than in our capacity to receive.

37. Hauerwas does make this claim; see Stanley Hauerwas (with Laura Yordy), "Captured in Time," in *A Better Hope: Resources for a Church Confronting Capitalism, Democracy, and Postmodernity* (Grand Rapids, Mich.: Brazos Press, 2000), 181: "Friendship for Christians is both a necessary activity for the discovery that we are less than we were meant to be and the resource to start us on the journey through which we become what we were created to be."

38. Hauerwas and Pinches, *Christians among the Virtues*, 44.

calling, a task that I am invited to perform.[39] Friendship, in other words, is in an important sense something I receive before I can give:

> Christians must not only see friends as gifts to one another, they must see their friendship itself as a gift. They can do this precisely because they understand themselves to be actors within a story authored not by them but by God. As Christians, our friendship is not made constant by an act of our own will, individual or corporate, or even by our own virtue, but rather because we and others find ourselves through participation in a common activity that makes us faithful both to ourselves and the other. That activity is not, as it seems to be in Aristotle, mutual enjoyment as an end in itself, but rather it is the activity of a task we have been given. That task is nothing less than to participate in a new way of life made possible by the life of the man Jesus.[40]

That task, I might add, is not so much an assignment as an invitation. It is an invitation to be truthful to the story of the triune God whom Christians confess as the One who rules the world. Put differently, it is an invitation to remain faithful to the gifts we have received through his action.

Being Claimed by Hauerwas

There are different ways in which such gifts are delivered. Let me conclude by telling the story of one of my encounters with Hauerwas, an encounter I will not soon forget. In 1994 I visited the annual meeting of the American Academy of Religion in Chicago. I had contacted Stanley Hauerwas about my coming, upon which he had told me to come and see him at the booth of Duke University Press, where they were to have a reception. I believe the occasion was the publication of *Dispatches from the Front*. Feeling lost in the sheer magnitude of that meeting, I was happy to be expected by someone somewhere. So I went down

---

39. In this connection let me point to a text in the Gospel of Luke that appears right after the Lord's Prayer, which underlines this characterization. Suppose, Jesus suggests to his disciples, that someone approaches a friend at an untimely hour for some bread because he has an unexpected guest. Suppose further that this friend makes excuses for not being able to help him because the door is locked and the family is already asleep. "I tell you," Jesus then claims, "even though he will not get up and give him anything because he is his friend, at least because of his persistence he will get up and give him whatever he needs" (Luke 11:5–8; 8 NRSV). Accordingly, it is not necessarily my conception of what it is to be a friend that provides me with sufficient motive to respond positively but rather my friend's persistence in calling upon me.

40. Hauerwas and Pinches, *Christians among the Virtues*, 49.

to the basement where the publishers and booksellers were located in order to meet the famous author. Having no map, I did not know where to go. Then my ears caught this very peculiar noise, unmistakably Stan Hauerwas laughing at one of his own jokes at the top of his high-pitched Texan voice. There he was, surrounded by a bunch of people, among whom I recognized some of his American colleagues. Not sure how to approach him, I hesitated, when suddenly he turned around, saw me, grabbed and hugged me, and then welcomed me and introduced me to his colleagues, saying: "Hey guys, let me introduce you to Hans Reinders—a friend from the Netherlands who's a Calvinist but doesn't know it." What a great way to be claimed as a friend and invited to be true to oneself at the same time!

Part 2

Being a Christian . . . and Facing (Post-)Christendom

4

A Constantinian Bishop: St. Ambrose of Milan

Robert Louis Wilken

Stanley Hauerwas likes the idea of bishops, and in his Gifford Lectures, *With the Grain of the Universe,* he has warm words of appreciation for a particular bishop, the current bishop of Rome, John Paul II. Of course as a Methodist he belongs to a Christian communion that recognizes the role of bishops in the church's life. Whether Hauerwas would be as enthusiastic about a bishop to whose authority he was genuinely subject is, however, a topic for another time and occasion.

I got to thinking about bishops when I was asked to contribute an essay to a Festschrift in honor of Stanley. For long periods in the church's history, bishops, along with emperors and kings, were an integral part of the establishment between the church and political authority. In his *Constantine and the Bishops,* Harold Drake observes that during Constantine's rule "bishops became players in the game of empire."[1]

---

1. Harold Drake, *Constantine and the Bishops* (Baltimore: Johns Hopkins University Press, 2000), 73.

73

For two decades Stanley and I have debated the merits and demerits of Constantinianism, so it seemed fitting on this happy occasion, while I have Hauerwas's ear, to draw attention to one bishop, St. Ambrose of Milan, *doctor ecclesiae*, who came to office a generation after the death of Constantine in AD 337. Here, then, my dear friend, are some thoughts not on the idea of Constantinianism, but on Constantinianism as it sprang from the ground, so to speak, at the point when the new Christian rule was beginning to settle in for the long haul.

Becoming a Bishop

Ambrose was born in AD 339 in Trier, where his father was praetorian prefect of Gaul at the court of Emperor Constantius II, the son of Constantine the Great. His father, Aurelius Ambrosius, died while Ambrose was an infant; with his mother, older brother, Satyrus, and sister, Marcellina, Ambrose moved to Rome, where he had his schooling. The family was well placed in ecclesiastical circles, and Ambrose's sister received the veil from Pope Liberius at an elaborate ceremony in the recently constructed Basilica of St. Peter in Rome. Like other youths from well-to-do families Ambrose received a traditional education in Latin grammar and rhetoric, but he also learned Greek, making him part of a small company among the Latin Fathers (Jerome was another) who could read Origen and other Greek Christian writers, as well as the Alexandrian Jew Philo. When he completed his education, Ambrose began to practice law but was soon pressed into service on the staff of the praetorian prefect of Italy. From there he was appointed governor of the provinces of Liguria and Emelia in north central Italy, with his seat at Milan.

When the bishop of Milan, Auxentius, died in 373 partisan crowds began to gather in the cathedral. The city was deeply divided between the Nicenes, supporters of the decisions of the Council of Nicaea in 325, and the Arians (or more accurately the Homoeans), who confessed Christ as "like," not "of one substance with," the Father. Auxentius was an Homoean, and Ambrose, though only a layman, was known, because of the Nicene lineage of his family and his tutoring in Rome as an adolescent, to favor the Nicenes or Catholics. As soon as he heard that crowds were milling about the cathedral quarreling over Auxentius's successor, Ambrose came to the church to quell the unrest. According to his ancient biographer, when Ambrose entered the great basilica, he proceeded at once to the front of the church to address the crowd. Suddenly the voice of a small child far back in the church cried out: "Ambrose for bishop!" At once the mood of the crowd changed, and the people took up the cry: "Ambrose for bishop." Whatever Ambrose himself thought of the proposal, he did not respond to the acclamation but left at once to attend to his duties as judge. Later he would write that he had been "snatched from the magistrate's tribunal and my robes of office into the priesthood," and then add: "I began to teach what I had myself not yet learned."[2]

Ambrose seems to have made a half-hearted attempt to flee the city, but the next morning, in the revealing phrase of his ancient biographer, he "found himself" at the chief ceremonial entrance to the city, the so-called Roman gate.[3] Soon a petition was addressed to Emperor Valentinian requesting that he rule on the circumstances of the "election." In the meantime, Ambrose went into hiding in the home of a friend.

No doubt the emperor saw in Ambrose a proven civil servant, a man sound in judgment, and word soon came of the emperor's satisfaction and pleasure at the election. At once Ambrose's friends handed him over to the bishops in charge of the consecration. In rapid succession, he was baptized, marched through the several ecclesiastical offices (e.g., deacon and presbyter), and consecrated bishop. His baptism took place on one Sunday, his ordination during the week, and his consecration as bishop the following Sunday. Everything, according to his ancient biographer, was carried out with "the utmost grace and rejoicing" among the faithful, though his opponents (of which there were many) later said the whole affair was irregular and ill-considered, a scheme worked by his influential friends.[4] The date was December 7, 374.

It was an auspicious time and place to become bishop.

Bishop in Milan

Sitting astride the great east–west highway from the Balkans to Gaul and the north–south highway from North Africa to the alpine passes leading to the Rhineland, Milan was centrally located with good communications to all parts of the empire. Up until the end of the third century it was a respectable provincial capital, the commercial and administrative hub of the region. Then in 300, the emperor Maximian moved his residence to Milan, and with him came the imperial court. The city quickly became the empire's political center, its power and influence eclipsing even the ancient capital of Rome. By Ambrose's day

2. *De Officiis* 1.4.
3. Paulinus, *Life of St. Ambrose*, 8.
4. Palladius, *Apology*, 120. On this text, see R. Gryson, *Scolies Ariennes sur le concile d' Aquilee* (Paris: Sources Chrétiennes 247, 1980), 264–325.

the city was largely Christian, and as head of the Christian community Ambrose was, next to the emperor, the most important public figure in the city. This was a new role for a Christian bishop.

Take, by comparison, the case of Cyprian (d. 258), who was bishop of Carthage, the chief city in North Africa, a century earlier. Like Ambrose, Cyprian had come from an upper-class family of considerable means (he sold much of his property on election), he received a thorough education, he was a gifted speaker and skilled Latin stylist, and seems also to have studied law. Unlike Ambrose, he was a convert to Christianity. In his day, the church in Carthage was a small, closely knit community—we might call it an intentional fellowship, a city within the city—whose life moved by its own rhythms independent of the society at large: regular worship; caring for the poor, widows, orphans, the sick; burying the dead; visiting prisoners; welcoming Christian visitors; the inevitable petty squabbles of a small community. Christians may have owned some buildings, but there were no "churches," that is, Christian structures that were conspicuous. It is estimated that out of a population of sixty million people in the Roman Empire in the year 200 there were only about two hundred thousand Christians, less than 1 percent of the population, 0.36 percent by one measure. By the middle of the century, when Cyprian was bishop, this number had increased to a little more than a million, perhaps 2 percent of the citizenry. Carthage was a large city of some three hundred fifty to four hundred thousand inhabitants, which meant that Cyprian was head of a community that numbered well under ten thousand, perhaps closer to five thousand in a good-sized city.

Origen, Cyprian's contemporary in Alexandria, believed that Christians belonged to "another society created by the Logos." This was a theological judgment as well as a social fact. The critic Celsus had urged Christians to "accept public office," but Origen replied that those who are competent to hold office are asked "to rule over the churches," not accept positions in civil or imperial administration. Christians serve the good of the civic community by their prayers and their virtuous lives, he said, a view that was shared by Cyprian.[5]

As bishop, Cyprian was certainly known outside the church, but he was not a public figure. The emperor was an august and distant personage across the sea in Rome; as bishop, Cyprian's charge lay with his clergy (numbering less than ten) and the affairs of Christians under his care. For example, his correspondence was chiefly with presbyters, deacons, confessors, and other Christians. Political authority, whether in Rome or in Carthage, was "other"—in some cases a benign other, in others

5. *Against Celsus* 8.73–74.

a menacing and harshly repressive other. Persecution was not only a possibility but became a bitter fact of life. The great crisis of Cyprian's episcopacy was an aggressive and systematic effort, led by the emperor, to weaken if not destroy Christianity, beginning with the bishops. In the decree prescribing the death penalty for Christians who refused to sacrifice to the gods, bishops were the first to be named.[6]

Ambrose came to the office of bishop several generations after the last great persecution of Christians in the first decade of the fourth century. After the accession of Constantine to the imperial throne in 306, all the emperors were Christian (with the exception of Julian [361–363], known in Christian memory as the Apostate), though not all were Nicene. By Ambrose's day, in sharp contrast to that of Cyprian, the civic life of the cities of the Roman Empire had begun to move to the rhythms of Christian time and the urban landscape had started to take on the contours of a new Christian space. In Milan there were five church buildings in the city and suburbs. The cathedral, over which the present cathedral of Milan is built, was particularly grand, measuring some eighty by forty-five meters. It was nearly as large as St. John Lateran, the huge church in Rome built by Constantine. Its imposing size and solidity of construction not only changed the look of the city; it also conferred authority and dignity on the bishop who spoke from its cathedra. A community that was previously scorned now had a very public podium on a majestic stage, especially when the bishop was a gifted public speaker.

The mores of the society were also changing. Sunday was a religious holiday, and Christian festivals (e.g., Easter, Christmas, Pentecost) had begun to displace the traditional calendar. These celebrations, as well as days set aside to venerate the martyrs and saints, were supplanting civic rituals keyed to the worship of the Roman gods and the glorification of the emperors. The relics of the martyrs were a potent new force that drew the affections of the people to new objects (and forms) of devotion while creating a new Christian past. A dramatic demonstration of the potency of relics during Ambrose's episcopacy was the discovery of the remains of the martyrs Gervasius and Protasius.

Christians have always liked bones, particularly the bones of martyrs. From the earliest period of the church's history, the faithful built shrines for the martyrs and gathered at their tombs to offer the Eucharist and celebrate their faithfulness. By the fourth century, church buildings had begun to be sanctified with relics of the martyrs. In the summer of 386, Ambrose planned to dedicate a new church with a celebration of the Eucharist, a sermon, and special prayers for the occasion, but the people demanded more. They wanted relics and implored him: "Consecrate this

6. Cyprian, *Letter* 80.

building in the same way you consecrated the Roman Basilica." In that church relics of Saints Peter and Paul were deposited. Ambrose replied that he would meet this request "if he could find relics of martyrs."[7]

A search was undertaken, and Ambrose instructed the diggers to probe beneath the floor of another church built over an ancient Christian cemetery. Ambrose's premonition turned out to be sound, and soon bodies were uncovered with bones intact, except for the heads—a sign that they might indeed have been martyrs. On the testimony of several elderly men, it was determined that the remains belonged to the martyrs Gervasius and Protasius, who were thought to have suffered martyrdom during the reign of Emperor Nero, though more likely at the end of the second century. Two days later the relics were carried in procession to the new church; a blind man, formerly a butcher, touched the fringe of one of the biers with a handkerchief, applied it to his eyes, and his sight was restored—certain proof that the relics were genuine.

When the procession reached the church, Ambrose was so overcome with emotion that he was at first unable to speak (according to his account). But during the reading of the lessons he gained his composure. Taking his place between the biers, "holy relics on my right hand and on my left hand," he gave thanks to God for the discovery of the tombs of the martyrs. This was a gift beyond telling, he said, for the church of Milan was "barren of martyrs" for too long. Now she had become a "joyful mother of children." In the words of a hymn composed for the occasion: "We were not able to be martyrs, but we have found martyrs."[8]

This whole affair seems staged, and what we know about the "invention" (i.e., finding) of the relics comes primarily from a letter Ambrose wrote to his sister, Marcellina. Augustine, however, was in Milan at the time and in his *Confessions* describes the event in terms similar to those of Ambrose.[9] What is significant is not so much what Ambrose did, but what the people of the city demanded of him. As a modern biographer has observed, the fourth century cult of the martyrs "was not a pantomime staged for the vulgar but a channeling of powerful energies too intractable for the bishop to have controlled at will, and too pervasive for him to have thought to try."[10] There is no more telling mark of the new society being constructed in the wake of Constantine than this

7. *Letter* 77 [22].1.
8. *Hymn* 11.
9. *Confessions* 9.7.16.
10. Neil B. McLynn, *Ambrose of Milan* (Berkeley: University of California Press, 1994), 215.

liaison between city, people, and religious devotion as embodied in the veneration of martyrs and saints. Constantinianism sprang from the ground; it was not imposed from above.

The city had now begun to be identified with Christianity: its institutions and practices, its way of life and beliefs, its martyrs and saints, its history, and its hopes. By Ambrose's day the social fact of Christian success (no matter how tenuous the hold of the faith on many new Christians) had undermined comfortable assumptions about the relation between the church and society that had governed Christian thinking for three hundred years. Yet Origen's vision of "another society created by the Logos" still formed Ambrose's outlook. The challenge facing him was how to keep this vision alive as the church became coextensive with the society. As bishop of Milan, Ambrose was in a position to have a say about what the new society would look like; not, however, the only say, because in the Roman Empire the emperor traditionally had the final say in religious matters.

Bishop versus Emperor

When Constantine came to office he assumed that the new religion could be dealt with in much the same way earlier emperors had dealt with traditional Roman religion. He retained the title *pontifex maximus*, chief priest, for example, and inserted himself at once into the affairs of the church, calling a council at Arles in 314 to deal with the dispute over the Donatists. Whatever else his conversion to Christianity may have been, it had to do with state policy. Constantine hoped that the new religion could unify the empire and give him a secure and successful reign. Religion had long been a matter of civic peace and unity, and Constantine believed that Christianity could provide the emotional glue to hold together the disparate forces loose across the vast empire. In ancient Rome there was neither politics nor statesmanship without the buttress of religion, and Christianity was the religion of the future. The old policy of defining citizenship by the ritual worship of the traditional gods had failed. Even Constantine's immediate predecessors, who had persecuted Christians, beseeched them to join their prayers with those of others on behalf of the empire.

Rome was not a secular state, and priests were a familiar feature of public life. The priesthood was not a separate office or profession. With few exceptions the major religious offices were held by prominent political figures. Cicero had written that "the most distinguished citizens safeguard religion by the good administration of the state and safeguard the state by the wise conduct of religion."[11] During the empire, the priest-hoods became even more closely linked to political power, and one of the most familiar ways of depicting the emperor was in priestly garb.

Bishops, the Christian priests, were stamped from a different mold, and the strength and independence of the office created a new religious fact. Bishops were not functionaries of the state, and political authorities had no say in their selection. They held office for life. Unlike the Roman priests, whose role was primarily cultic, the office of the bishop included oversight (the meaning of *episcopos*), which involved governing a distinct and well-defined community, teaching (exercised chiefly, but not wholly, in expounding the Bible), and leading the church's worship. Bishops thought of themselves as leaders of an alternate society. They were well organized with a powerful network of communications (many of the major bishops in the early church left a significant corpus of letters) and met together regularly (often in contentious circumstances) to discuss matters of mutual concern. And they had a large and growing constituency. As a consequence, the emperor had to develop a relationship with the leaders of a new kind of community over which he had no formal control.

But the emperors did exercise control, and one of the central story lines of the fourth century is how Christian emperors—beginning with Constantine, followed by his sons who succeeded him in office—were able, often with great success, to dominate the affairs of the church. It should not be forgotten that it was the emperor who called together the bishops for the first ecumenical council, the Council of Nicaea in 325 (and the councils that followed). And it was the same emperor, Constantine, under the influence of the powerful Arianizing bishops, who banished Athanasius, the vigorous defender of Nicaea, and sent him into exile. Athanasius was also banished by Constantius II (Constantine's son) in 339 and 356, by Julian in 362, and by Valens in 365. Though Arius had been anathematized by the bishops at Nicaea, modified forms of teachings similar to his had survived and even flourished in some regions through the support of certain emperors. The emperor assumed for himself the authority to order bishops to attend councils; he set the agenda; and he appointed imperial officials to preside over the deliberations.

Although the Council of Nicaea had ended fifty years before Ambrose's consecration, its creed still provoked dissension and partisan maneuvering (just as debate after Vatican II is no less fervent forty years after its close than it was during the council itself). During his first years as bishop, however, Ambrose gave himself to pastoral and catechetical

11. *On His House* 1.

matters. He wrote a treatise on virginity to his sister, Marcellina, and other essays promoting the religious life. He led the faithful in common prayer, preached regularly, and encouraged the veneration of the relics of the saints. But these halcyon months were not to last. In November 375, the Western emperor, Valentinian, died. He was replaced by his teenage son Gratian; meanwhile, Valentinian II—also Valentinian's son and half brother to Gratian—was acclaimed by the army in Trier. He was only five years old, and his ascension effectively gave power to his mother Justina, an aggressive Homoean.

Valentinian II's realm included the Balkan provinces where Arianism had become an accommodating form of state religion. When the bishop of Sirmium (a city on the Sava River in Pannonia in the Balkans) died, Ambrose saw an opportunity to advance the cause of Catholic Christianity, though the city was five hundred miles to the east of Milan and not in his jurisdiction. He made the arduous trip and was able to secure the ordination of a Catholic bishop. But the Arians were not so readily defeated. They pressed Gratian to convene a council of Western and Eastern bishops, confident that with the support of the East they could carry the day. Realizing it was folly to agree to such a council, Ambrose persuaded the youthful Gratian to convoke a council in Aquileia in Italy that would be attended chiefly by Western bishops supportive of Nicaea. By skillful maneuvering, Ambrose was able to secure the deposition of two of the most notorious Arian bishops from the Balkans.

The same sagacious stubbornness, this time with much higher stakes, allowed Ambrose to rebuff renewed efforts of Valentinian II's mother, Justina, to win privileges for the Arians in Milan. Upon Gratian's death in 383, Valentinian II (who was now twelve years old) had succeeded him as emperor of the West. Though most of the townspeople in Milan were Nicene Christians, a company of Gothic troops quartered in the city were Arians with no church of their own. According to old Roman law, religious buildings were under the authority of the emperor. In an earlier dispute between Catholics and Arians, Emperor Gratian had sequestrated (i.e., taken into his own custody) a church building without any protest from the Catholics (i.e., the Nicenes). Emperor Theodosius, who became emperor of the East in 379, had handed over churches to Catholics, and Justina thought if it could be done for the Catholics, why not for the Arians.

At the beginning of Lent in 385, Ambrose was summoned to the imperial palace and told that he had to give up the Basilica of Portius, a church in the possession of Catholics outside the walls of the city. He refused. A few weeks later, Justina, acting in the name of her son Valentinian II, tried another ploy. There were two principal churches in the city, the Old Basilica and the New Basilica, and she requested that one of these churches be given to the Homoeans. On Friday before Palm Sunday the order came down to relinquish the building. Ambrose replied: "A bishop cannot give up the temple of God."[12]

On Saturday the praetorian prefect of Italy showed up in the church where Ambrose was presiding to request once again that he give up the Portian Basilica (outside the walls of the city, hence a less important church). Ambrose stood firm. On Tuesday, a delegation from the emperor again met with him, reminding him that disposal of religious buildings was within the rights of the emperor. Ambrose responded: If the emperor asked of me anything of my own, "my estates, my money, everything that is mine," I would not refuse him, but "the things of God are not subject to the authority of the emperor."[13]

The next morning, before daybreak, Ambrose went to the Portian Basilica to celebrate the liturgy and found the church surrounded by soldiers. When he finished his sermon an imperial secretary approached him and in the name of the emperor said: "What is your aim in acting contrary to my wishes?" Ambrose responded: "I cannot surrender the basilica, but I must not fight." Ambrose spent the night in the Portian Basilica reciting psalms with his clergy. The next morning, Holy Thursday, as Ambrose was preaching on repentance (the text was from the prophet Jonah), word arrived that the emperor had relented and given orders that the soldiers leave the church. The emperor had not only misread the mood of the populace; he had misjudged Ambrose's strength and resolve.

Ambrose could not afford to be moderate. Beneath his studied poise was an indomitable will driven by the resolute conviction that the emperor could not be the arbiter in religious matters. In his language: "In a matter of faith it is the practice for bishops to judge Christian emperors, not emperors bishops."[14] Christianity is a religion of creeds, not only rituals and attitudes; hence there could be no compromise with the Arians. The initial Christian portrayal of Constantine as reflected in the writings of Eusebius of Caesarea depicted him as a hieratic figure, but Ambrose effectively desacralized the office by insisting that the emperor was a layman who had to reckon with an alternate authority. The establishment of Christianity took place as much against political power as in collusion with it. This is evident in a more famous and quite different confrontation that had taken place a year earlier.

Since the days of Emperor Augustus a statue to the goddess Victoria had stood in the senate house in Rome, and as senators entered the

12. *Letter* 76 [20].2.
13. *Letter* 76 [20].8.
14. *Letter* 75 [21].4.

chamber they made an offering of incense at her altar. As the number of Christian senators mounted, the altar became an embarrassment if not an offense to Christian sensibilities. In 357, Emperor Constantius had removed the altar, but a few years later it was restored. In 382, however, against the protests of conservative pagans in the senate, Emperor Gratian again ordered its removal and cut off subsidies of the state cult, effectively severing one of the last ligaments that bound the Roman state to traditional religion.

Gratian, however, died a year later (383), and with the accession of the youthful Valentinian II as emperor of the West a group of pagan senators seized the opportunity to stage a public procession on the occasion of a traditional festival. In the summer of 384, Symmachus, a distinguished senator and prefect of the city of Rome, at the request of members of the senate (some may have been Christian), penned a memorable plea to the emperor. In his famous "Memorial" (*Relatio* in Latin), Symmachus called for a return to "the religious condition that for so long has benefited the commonweal."[15] What gave the "Memorial" enduring significance is that Symmachus did not simply plead for a return to ancient ways; he shrewdly couched his plea in the language of tolerance.

The "Memorial" is beautifully written, and even Ambrose acknowledged Symmachus's "glittering eloquence" and "golden tongue."[16] The "Memorial" appealed not only to a sense of fairness and justice but also to the affections of citizens of the empire: "Grant us, we beseech you," he wrote, "that what we received as boys we may as old men leave to those who come after us."[17] The driving idea behind the "Memorial," however, is what seems a modern notion of religious pluralism resting on belief in a universal providential deity. "We gaze upon the same stars, the sky is common to all, the same world envelops us. What difference does it make by what wisdom a person seeks the truth? We cannot attain to so great a mystery by one path."[18] Unlike many modern Christians who would find the "Memorial" a model of sweet reasonableness, few in Ambrose's day were beguiled by Symmachus's argument. Prudentius, the Christian Latin poet, praised the "unfading golden sheen" of Symmachus's speech, but wickedly added that when one considers the content it is as though a man had set about to till "muddy ground with a golden fork."[19]

15. "Memorial" 3.3.
16. *Letter* 73 [18].2.
17. "Memorial" 3.4.
18. "Memorial" 3.10.
19. *Against Symmachus* 1, 635–38.

Ambrose's response was forceful, pointed, and uncompromising. Again his argument turned on his authority as bishop. In addressing the emperor, Ambrose said that if it were a "civil matter" it would be one thing, but since it is a "matter of religion I appeal to you as bishop."[20] Ambrose addressed Valentinian II as a fellow Christian and member of the church. The issue, as he saw it, did not turn on toleration but idolatry, specifically whether a Christian emperor could lend his support to the worship of false gods. Ambrose rejected the notion that there was a neutral place to stand. Even in the public sphere one must choose between paganism or the worship of the one God. As Augustine would say a generation later, it is this one God to whom the Romans owe obedience.[21]

Ambrose's next move was as audacious as it was unexpected. If Symmachus's request is granted and the altar restored, Ambrose wrote the emperor, don't for a moment think that the bishops will turn the other way and allow the matter to pass unnoticed. And then he added: "You may come to the church if you wish, but you will not find a bishop there, or if so, it will be one who will resist you."[22] It is a characteristically flamboyant gesture. No one had ever challenged the emperor so directly and on a matter that traditionally fell within his authority. But the grounds for his challenge were pastoral and personal; Ambrose urged Valentinian II to be faithful to his calling as a Christian. Though the church may be complicit with power, that complicity does not give a Christian the right to promote idolatry.

Given the political and ecclesiastical setting in which Ambrose became bishop, the struggle with the Arians and the resistance of pagan senators to the impending triumph of the church could be expected. But in the summer of 388, Ambrose was caught off-guard by an unexpected challenge from a quite different quarter. In a border military town on the Euphrates, Callinicum, a group of Christians set fire to a Jewish synagogue. The count of the East referred the matter to the emperor of the East, Theodosius, who ordered that the bishop rebuild the synagogue out of his own funds. When Ambrose heard of the incident and the emperor's response, he wrote Theodosius at once to protest. His argument was that the emperor had no business ordering a bishop to rebuild a synagogue with Christian funds.

Understandably Ambrose's action has provoked much negative commentary among modern scholars. He is said to be "plainly wrong," a "bully" and "bigot," a religious zealot acting out of "unbalanced zeal" and "fanaticism." To be sure, his actions were morally dubious and legally

20. *Letter* 72 [17].13.
21. *City of God* 19.22.
22. *Letter* 72 [17].13.

tenuous, yet his reasoning had a certain logic in the late-fourth century, particularly in the Eastern provinces where Jews were numerous and their practices attractive to some Christians. In Antioch during the same decade, John Chrysostom complained that during the Jewish festivals in the fall Christians were attracted to Jewish rites. The issue of the synagogue at Callinicum, as Ambrose depicted it, was not whether the Jews had a right to their own building and freedom to worship according to their traditions, but whether a Christian bishop could in good conscience contribute to the reconstruction of a house of worship of a rival religion. In Ambrose's melodramatic language, the emperor's order would force the bishop to become either an "apostate" if he acceded to the order or a "martyr" if he refused to.[23] Reluctantly, and no doubt with a troubled conscience, Theodosius accommodated Ambrose's demands.

The most memorable event during Ambrose's tenure was his confrontation with the Emperor Theodosius over a bloody incident in the city of Thessalonica. One evening in a tavern a popular charioteer had made sexual advances to an attendant of Butheric, the commander of troops quartered in the city. The charioteer was arrested. When the people clamored for his release, Butheric refused. The mob then savagely murdered him and dragged his body through the streets. Theodosius was outraged, and he ordered that the people of Thessalonica be invited to a spectacle in the circus. In the midst of the show, soldiers rushed in and for three hours massacred several thousand citizens, mowing them down "like wheat at harvest time," according to an ancient historian.[24] Ambrose received news of the massacre while attending a council of bishops and realized that the eyes of the other bishops were on him. Whatever political miscalculations may have been made by the emperor (he apparently tried to rescind the order, but Thessalonica was five hundred miles from Rome, and the message arrived too late), mass murder was a grave sin in the eyes of the church.

In the historical memory of the West there seems a direct line between Ambrose's confrontation with Theodosius and the encounter between Gregory VII and Henry IV at Canosa in the eleventh century. In the famous painting by Peter Paul Rubens, *Emperor Theodosius Refused Entry into Milan Cathedral,* two figures stand at the door of a church—Theodosius in the garb of a Roman soldier, Ambrose in brocaded cope and miter, his outstretched left hand blocking Theodosius's entry. But the standoff never reached that point; nor was it a showdown between ecclesiastical authority and political might. The issue, as Ambrose presented it, was how as bishop he could persuade the emperor, a faithful member of

23. *Letter* 74 [40].7.
24. Theodoret, *Ecclesiastical History* 5.17.3.

the church, to submit to penance. My aim, he wrote, is "not to put you to shame . . . but to put this sin away from your kingdom."[25] The letter to the emperor was written in his own hand for the emperor alone to read.[26] Significantly, Ambrose did not include this letter in his official correspondence to be published after his death. He wished neither to humiliate Theodosius nor to diminish his authority. Insofar as he was thinking about how things would play, he may have hoped humility would be seen as a necessary virtue for a Christian ruler.[27]

It must be remembered that in the early church it was not possible for the emperor to present himself privately before the bishop, confess his sin, and receive absolution. The penitential discipline of the early church was unremittingly harsh and very public. The penitents were segregated from the rest of the community, assigned a special section in the church, and forbidden to receive the Eucharist. As Ambrose reminds Theodosius: "I dare not offer the Sacrifice if you intend to be present."[28]

Theodosius was not an adolescent under the thumb of an ambitious and manipulative mother but a mature and self-assured leader. Yet Ambrose insisted that he submit to the discipline of the church and join the company of penitents. The emperor was "within not above the church."[29] Ambrose was not laying down a principle about the relation of church and state; he was invoking the ancient discipline that had long governed the way the church dealt with grave sin. What is new in the confrontation with Theodosius is not what Ambrose says, but that he says it to an emperor, the august and lordly potentate. It is not the priest who is at center stage but the penitent ruler.

Though Ambrose followed well-established practice in dealing with Theodosius, he had, as bishop in fourth-century Milan, embarked on a voyage into unknown waters. But he never forgot where he would make port. His confident assertion of the freedom of the church even when identified with the power structures of society shows that he had a vision of what a Christian society should look like. At a time when the Christian cult could have become a department of the imperial administration, Ambrose drew clear boundaries around the church. This delineation is all the more impressive because the growth of the Christian community blurred, if not erased, the lines separating the church and the "world." When the social fabric seemed to have no seam, Ambrose stitched in a

25. *Letter* 11 extra collectionem [51].11.
26. *Letter* 11 extra collectionem [51].14.
27. *On the Death of Theodosius* 27.
28. *Letter* 11 extra collectionem [51].14.
29. *Against Auxentius* 36.

well-defined border. He did not use the language of two cities, but he left no doubt that his community was the church, not Rome. The Latin poet Prudentius imagined that Christianity had inaugurated a new era in the history of Rome. "Can we doubt that Rome is dedicated to you, O Christ, and has placed herself under your rule." Ambrose was not enamored with Christian Rome boosterism.

Even as he made his way in the halls of power of the earthly city, his feet were firmly planted in another city whose visible and public magistrate was the bishop. In the long history of the church, the failings of the bishops have been many, but the office has proven remarkably resilient. When the church was young and innocent, Ignatius, a bishop in Antioch, said that the bishop is the sign of the church.[30] This was no less true in Ambrose's day when the church was making the gradual adjustment to the new age ushered in by Constantine. Only as bishop could Ambrose have urged a Roman emperor to make the words of David the king of Israel his own: "I have sinned greatly in that I have done this deed; and now, O Lord, take away the iniquity of your servant, for I have failed miserably."[31]

30. *Trallians* 3 and *Smyrneans* 8.
31. *Letter* 11 extra collectionem [51].8, citing 2 Sam. 14:10. Theodosius heeded Ambrose's admonition and—in the fashion befitting an emperor, of course—humbly acknowledged his sin and publicly submitted to the church's discipline of penance.

5

The Politics of Diaspora

The Post-Christendom Theologies of Karl Barth and John Howard Yoder

Arne Rasmusson

The Church did not prevent the two world wars, and could not prevent them. They simply broke over it. But what is disturbing today is something beyond the mere fact of the two wars: the Church is the body of Christ, beyond all boundaries, the people of God among the nations. That in 1914 Christians went enthusiastically to war against Christians, baptized against baptized, was not seen in any way as a destruction of what the Church is in and of its very nature, a destruction that cried out to heaven. That was the real catastrophe.

—Gerhard Lohfink[1]

1. Gerhard Lohfink, *Does God Need the Church? Toward a Theology of the People of God* (Collegeville, Minn.: Liturgical Press, 1999), 315.

Christians are a people whose imagination has been challenged by a God who has invited us into an otherwise unimaginable kingdom. For only God could have created a world in which forgiveness rather than force could be both a possibility and a duty. Our own limited imagination often occasions our sin, as we imprison ourselves in attachments for which we are normally willing to kill. Only as we fulfill our obligations to let our vision be governed by the kingdom inaugurated in Jesus can we become free to face death as faithful servants. . . . Because we have been called to discipleship in a community of the new age proclaimed by Jesus of Nazareth, we have become capable of the unimaginable: forgiveness of enemies even unto death, loving service knowing no boundaries or limits, trust in the surprising power of God's peace.

—Stanley Hauerwas[2]

In his Gifford Lectures,[3] Hauerwas argues that Karl Barth is the great natural theologian of the twentieth century. These lectures display how important Barth is for Hauerwas. The book, however, does not end with Barth but with John Paul II, John Howard Yoder, and Yoder's concept of witness. Moreover, the title of the book, *With the Grain of the Universe*, is taken from Yoder. In this essay, I will discuss the connection between Barth's and Yoder's theologies with a focus on the relationship between church and nation-state. I will discuss the nation-state instead of (as theology has often done) "society," "culture," or "state," because the nation-state (although a contested and confused concept) has been the most determinative political reality during the last century or two. Yoder claimed in some of his quite extensive writings on Barth that there is a trajectory in Barth's theology in which he moves from a Christendom mode to a more "free church" mode.[4] In this essay, I will describe and analyze this trajectory. I will also point to certain problematic aspects of Barth's discussions of church and state and show how Yoder's articulation of a type of diaspora theology is a fruitful way to go forward.[5]

2. Stanley Hauerwas, *Against the Nations: War and Survival in a Liberal Society* (Minneapolis: Winston, 1985), 57–58.

3. Stanley Hauerwas, *With the Grain of the Universe: The Church's Witness and Natural Theology* (Grand Rapids, Mich.: Brazos Press, 2001).

4. Yoder's main work on Barth is his critical analysis of Barth's views of war. However, for our purposes it is some of his other writings on Barth that are of greatest interest. Most of Yoder's writings on Barth are now gathered in John Howard Yoder, *Karl Barth and the Problem of War and Other Essays on Barth* (Eugene, Ore.: Cascade, 2003).

5. The only major discussion of Yoder's thesis on Barth's free church trajectory that I am aware of is a 1980 article by George Hunsinger, now republished in George Hunsinger, *Disruptive Grace: Studies in the Theology of Karl Barth* (Grand Rapids, Mich.: Eerdmans, 2000), 114–28. While Hunsinger is generally sympathetic to Yoder's argument, he offers

Theological Imagination and "1914"

Christian practice is a question of imagination. So is all politics.[6] Politics has to do with the material reality of economic and political institutions, borders, armies, and so on. But how these realities are envisioned and practiced are questions of imagination. Material reality is shaped by political imagination, just as imagination is limited and shaped by material reality. The events of 1914, which decisively shaped the twentieth century, are a formative and tragic example of this relationship between material reality and imagination. How was it that German workers, allied with the aristocrats against whom they otherwise fought, enthusiastically (at first) wanted to kill French workers because they lived on the other side of a border, and vice versa? And how could German Christians, even German Catholics, want to do the same to French Christians/Catholics, and vice versa? Why did almost no church leader or theologian see this killing as a scandal? As William Cavanaugh writes: They "must be convinced of the reality of borders, and imagine [themselves] deeply, mystically, united to a wider national community that stops abruptly at those borders."[7]

Of course, not everyone failed to see the scandal; there were some protests, and the events of 1914 became the occasion for a new start in theology. Indeed, it was the double failure of Protestantism—and Protestant public theology—and socialism in the face of nationalism and war that prompted Karl Barth to develop an alternative to the liberal Protestant theology that dominated at the time (and that in various forms dominates still).

Barth had been trained in the tradition of German culture–Protestantism represented by people like Wilhelm Herrmann, Ernst Troeltsch, Adolf Harnack, and Martin Rade. Back in Switzerland, working as a pastor, he was radicalized and became part of the religious socialist movement. Still, his theology retained the basic structure that he had learned from his German teachers. Barth saw social democracy as God's word to the present and the "continuation of the spiritual power which . . . entered into history and life with Jesus."[8] In the summer of 1914,

---

some sharp criticism. I partly disagree with Hunsinger, but I will not explicitly discuss that here. See also ibid., 34–40 and 102–8, where Hunsinger seems almost to identify Barth's and his own views with Yoder's.

6. In the following I have adapted and developed William T. Cavanaugh, *Theopolitical Imagination* (Edinburgh: T. & T. Clark, 2003), 1.

7. Ibid.

8. Karl Barth, "Jesus Christ and the Movement for Social Justice (1911)," in *Karl Barth and Radical Politics*, ed. George Hunsinger (Philadelphia: Westminster, 1976), 20.

he was confident that the international labor movement would not compromise with nationalism and militarism.[9]

In August 1914, however, both the church and the labor movement failed. What seemed to shock Barth most was the enthusiasm for the war among German theologians and their absolute faith in Germany.[10] One might think that he hardly should have been surprised.[11] German theologians were part of, and even co-creators of, a political and cultural imagination that made the war more or less unavoidable. This was as true of Herrmann as of Troeltsch, "leaders" of opposing theological schools. It was also true of more conservative theology.

Herrmann was the theologian who had influenced Barth the most. Herrmann was a strong defender of the idea of a culture-state, which, he asserted, it was the task of the church and Christians to support. A legitimate national state, formed by nature and history, presupposes the full and sustained development of a distinctive culture, such as had existed long before the modern German state was created.[12] According to Herrmann, the task of the German state was to defend and promote the German people and the German culture. However, because the state is a necessary product of human nature, it is not an expression of morality. One cannot therefore ask it to deny itself if it comes into conflict with other states. The state can be used for moral purposes, but it is not in itself moral. When the interests of a state clash with the interests of another state, the inevitable result will be open or latent war. Hermann stressed that warfare in itself is neither moral nor immoral, neither Christian nor non-Christian; in specific historical circumstances it is simply necessary as an expression of a national culture's life. When war is seen as politically correct, as an expression of cultural self-assertion, it is also morally justified. To desire a state but eschew war is thus simply hypocrisy.

According to Herrmann, if Christians properly understand the moral significance of the state, they will recognize that their primary duty is obedience and that the perspective from above, from the political center,

9. Karl Barth, "'Die Hilfe' 1913," *Die Christliche Welt 28,* no. 33 (1914), col. 774–78.

10. The best place to follow his reactions is his letter exchange with his former teacher Martin Rade. See Christoph Schwöbel, ed., *Karl Barth–Martin Rade: Ein Briefwechsel* (Gütersloh: Gütersloher Verlagshaus, 1981). For a much more detailed description and discussion of Barth's reaction in 1914 and the first beginnings of his theological reconstruction, see my forthcoming article "Church and Nation-State: Early 20th Century German Developments and Public Theology Today."

11. Cf. his critical analysis, in Barth, "'Die Hilfe' 1913," of the influential pastor turned politician Friedrich Naumann, whose perspective was similar to Troeltsch's.

12. He did not think that Poles or Czechs had the type of characteristic culture that should legitimate their own states.

is superior to any perspective from below, however well informed. They will also promote a right use of the state's power, but with an awareness that what is right cannot be understood solely from the perspective of Christian morality. To be able to talk about what is right one has to attend to the political reality and nature of the state. Finally, if Christians properly understand the significance of the state, they will foster patriotism. So the Christian duty in 1914 was never in doubt for Herrmann. In the autumn of 1914, he sent Barth a whole shipment of war writings.[13]

Troeltsch in 1914 was as enthusiastic about the war as Herrmann. Troeltsch's enthusiasm was not a momentary passion aroused by the war itself; it was a logical implication of his basic views of the reality of the nation-state.[14] Troeltsch developed his case in more direct sociological categories than Herrmann. He saw the modern state, and the nation-state, as a quite recent construction but also as modernity's main social force, together with capitalism and science. For Troeltsch, the state is built on power and violence:

> The state must be power and cannot be anything else. In the struggle for existence, only that intensified and ruthless power survives which increases by the absorption of all that it has vanquished. [This power] can entertain sentimentalities and general principles only at the price of its own perdition.[15]

From this view it follows that war is an unavoidable element of history. Moreover, nationalism is the primary ethical principle of the modern nation-state. Although Troeltsch recognized that nationalist discourse is largely fictitious—and that it is totally alien to Christian ethics—he argued that it has to be accepted and affirmed by the church because it creates its own forceful reality. He could therefore say in 1914 that although God's ultimate word about God and the soul transcends nationalism, God's first and immediate word in the current situation was about "the love for state and fatherland as the embodiment of the divine thought in the German spirit."[16]

---

13. See Schwöbel, *Karl Barth–Martin Rade*, 113–19.

14. I have dealt extensively with Troeltsch's views in Arne Rasmusson, "Historicizing the Historicist: Ernst Troeltsch and Recent Mennonite Theology," in *The Wisdom of the Cross: Essays in Honor of John Howard Yoder*, ed. Stanley Hauerwas et al. (Grand Rapids, Mich.: Eerdmans, 1999), 213–48.

15. Ernst Troeltsch, *Religion in History* (Minneapolis: Fortress Press, 1991), 175.

16. Ernst Troeltsch, *Deutscher Glaube und Deutsche Sitte in unserem Grossen Kriege* (Berlin: 1914), 28.

Herrmann and Troeltsch participated in and contributed to the political and cultural imagination that shaped this nationalism and that made the First World War "normal" and understandable, even something that could be celebrated. Most other theologians, and Protestantism in general, were similarly involved in this shaping of nationalism. One may even argue, as the leading war historian John Keegan has done, that the First World War was actually created or made more or less unavoidable by the nationalist culture.[17] Indeed, it was extremely difficult to think outside this hegemonic discourse. As Liah Greenfeld has written about nationalism: "It acquired its own momentum; it existed in its own right; it was the only way in which people now could see reality and thus became reality itself. For nationalism was the basis of people's identity, and it was no more possible at this point to stop thinking in national terms than to cease being oneself."[18] One should note that theologians at this time played an important role in the public discussion. They were doing the sort of influential public theology that theologians today often dream of. According to Mark Chapman, 12 percent of all German university professors in 1903 were theologians.[19] Still, for theology, it was simply taken for granted that the church is integrated within and serves the nation-state. This assumption was as true for liberals as for conservatives. The theological imagination, then, was essentially informed by the political.

The Beginnings of a Post-National Theology

Barth had taken a step away from this nationalistic thought—which also existed in Switzerland, though naturally without Germany's imperial ambitions—through his participation in religious socialism. But when in the summer of 1914 both liberal theology and social democracy failed, this double disappointment forced Barth to rethink the bases for theology. The first result is found in his commentary on Romans, published, in its first edition, in 1919. It can be read as a sustained attack on theology's ideological support of the culture that created capitalism and the war. But Barth is also criticizing religious socialism, and that is the emphasis of the second edition, published in 1922. Christians should not believe in and religiously legitimate the nation-state or the

17. John Keegan, *A History of Warfare* (New York: Knopf, 1993), 20–24, 340–66.

18. Liah Greenfeld, *Nationalism: Five Roads to Modernity* (Cambridge, Mass.: Harvard University Press, 1992), 87.

19. Mark D. Chapman, *Ernst Troeltsch and Liberal Theology: Religion and Cultural Synthesis in Wilhelmine Germany* (Oxford: Oxford University Press, 2001), 3.

revolution. Barth is not calling for withdrawal. Rather, he is calling for political life to be dissociated from the absolute, from the warfare between good and evil, and to become instead "a prudent reckoning with reality." This does not eliminate politics; it makes politics possible. Christians should put their faith in the reality of the living God, who is independent of our knowledge of God and who judges all that is called "reality."[20]

The way Barth develops his theology in the Romans commentaries creates new problems. In a certain respect, he accepts too much of Herrmann's and Troeltsch's descriptions of reality, simply turning them on their heads. Barth wants to free the Christian imagination from its imprisonment in dominant cultural imaginations. His first attempts emphasize the negative, the necessity of not legitimating either the current hegemonic discourse and practice or its revolutionary alternatives. In the process, Barth tends to describe the state and politics as completely and necessarily embedded in the realm of sin. He thereby seems to confirm Troeltsch's and Herrmann's accounts not only empirically but also theologically and metaphysically.

Later on Barth tried to develop more constructive alternatives, which rested on two essential developments in his thought during the 1920s: (1) a specifically Trinitarian theology based on his rediscovery of classical Christology, and (2) a more positive ecclesiology. Bruce McCormack thinks the latter development was the most significant change in Barth's thinking during the first couple of years after he came to Germany in 1921: it meant that the primary context for doing theology became the church. In Barth's new ecclesial hermeneutics, the reading of Scripture is to be carried on within and guided by the church. Only so can the person of Jesus Christ be given the role he has in Barth's theology.[21]

Barth continued to vacillate, however, over how to conceive the church in relation to the state. He continued to talk about the state (and the church) in generally timeless terms. In his writings from the 1920s, he develops a much more positive view of the state than in the Romans commentaries, perhaps because he wants to support the Weimar democracy, but his criticism of national theology in those writings is as sharp

20. See especially Karl Barth, *Der Römerbrief (Erste Fassung), 1919* (Zürich: Theologischer Verlag, 1985), 495–524, and Karl Barth, *The Epistle to the Romans* (Oxford: Oxford University Press, 1968), 475–97. The citation is from *Romans*, 489.

21. Bruce Lindley McCormack, *Karl Barth's Critically Realistic Dialectical Theology: Its Genesis and Development 1909–1936* (Oxford: Oxford University Press, 1995), 302–3, 318, 322–23, 335, and 347. For a particularly powerful account of how theology should be done in the service of the church, see Karl Barth, "Church and Theology" (1925), in Karl Barth, *Theology and Church: Shorter Writings, 1920–1928* (New York: Harper & Row, 1962), 286–306.

as ever: he describes it as idolatry. In his ethics lectures from 1928–1929 and 1930–1931, Barth works inside a Christendom model, seeing church and state as two divine institutions with the same aim. He depicts them as two circles, with the church as a broader, encompassing circle within which the state, as a narrower circle, exists. He thus thinks, contra the Weimar constitution, that a state church system is to be preferred.[22]

More interesting is Barth's discussion of the idea of the nation.[23] After having relativized the reality of peoplehood and nationhood, he argues that the fact that we live in such relationships and are part of such nations is ethically relevant because it describes the situation or framework in which we hear God's command. I am loyal to my people because they are my people, and in that sense loyalty provides a criterion for action. However, "the bonds are not unequivocal and ultimate and therefore the criteria are not absolute."[24] In addition to the fact that there is no unambiguous way to define one's "people," one's loyalty to that people is qualified by other loyalties, such as marriage, family, state, church, and humanity. In German theology of the time, the concept of humanity was often sharply criticized as "an empty rationalistic phrase as compared with that of kin or people."[25] For Barth, in contrast, humanity is foundational, the first and most basic of the "circles" of human existence he names.[26] Barth's concept of humanity does not abolish the fact that we are also part of a people and that this is ethically relevant. It does, however, call into question anti-Semitism and modern nationalism.

Yet the *völkisch* and nationalist movements won in the form of Hitler and National Socialism. The Nazi revolution in 1933 was greeted with much enthusiasm in German Protestantism, although the German Christians' attempt to take over the church also met with much resistance. For Barth this revolution again showed the importance of the independence of church and theology. Barth was clear that he saw the German Christians "as the last, most complete and worst product of the being of neo-Protestantism."[27] It was only too easy to go from neo-Protestantism to support of or at least understanding for the Nazi revolution. "The whole proud heritage of the eighteenth and nineteenth

22. Karl Barth, *Ethics* (New York: Seabury Press, 1981), 440–51.

23. Ibid., 191–96. He develops the same theme at much greater length in *Church Dogmatics* (Edinburgh: T. & T. Clark, 1956–1975), 3/4:285–323; hereafter *CD*.

24. Barth, *Ethics*, 193.

25. Ibid., 194. Cf. 179.

26. Ibid., 178–81.

27. Karl Barth, *The German Church Conflict* (Richmond: John Knox Press, 1965), 41. He included both liberal and conservative theology in this description (ibid., 25).

century proved incapable of resistance, obviously because it contained nothing that *had* to resist and *could* not give way."[28]

The 1934 Barmen Declaration, which Barth drafted, stressed the fundamental independence of church and theology. However, it talked about the state in the same general and timeless way that theologians, including Barth, were accustomed to—arguably a weakness. It said nothing about the nation-state, nationalism, or war. In a text from 1925, in which he discusses the possibility of making a new Reformed confession, Barth had argued that if one were to make such a confession it should be so concrete as to condemn concrete things like fascist-*völkisch* nationalism, anti-Semitism, and war.[29] Of course, if he had followed this line in 1934, there would have been no Barmen Declaration. Most people at Barmen and in the Confessing Church were strong nationalists or patriots. The sort of church practice that could have made meaningful a confession of the kind for which Barth argued in 1925 hardly existed. What was stressed in the declaration—and by Barth in the early years—was faithful preaching. But the preaching lacked the context of a communal discipleship and an ecclesial imagination that could have functioned as an alternative to the nationalism of German Protestantism.

Post-Christendom Theology and a Post-Secular Reading of Reality

After the war, in 1946, Barth published a famous text on the relationship between church and state: "The Christian Community and the Civil Community."[30] Yoder thinks that here Barth makes some important moves that clearly distance him from the dominant Christendom model. These moves are not radical but are implied, so to speak, in the theology he had long since begun to develop. Here, however, they are stated clearly. For Yoder the most important feature of this text is the way that Barth assumes a distinction between the church, which thinks and lives in terms of the reality of Jesus Christ, and the civil community, which uses another language based on another description of reality. Barth defines both communities—Christian and civil—in political terms: "The Christian community exists at all times and places as a *politeia*

28. Ibid., 41.

29. Karl Barth, *Vorträge und kleinere Arbeiten 1922–1925* (Zürich: Theologischer Verlag, 1990), 604–43; here 640–41.

30. Karl Barth, "The Christian Community and the Civil Community," in *Against the Stream: Shorter Post-War Writings, 1946–52* (New York: Philosophical Library, 1954), 15–50.

with definite authorities and offices, with patterns of community life and divisions of labour. . . . In this sense, therefore, the existence of the Christian community is political."[31] But the Christian community as a community of discipleship sees reality in the light of Christian faith. The civil community does not. Thus the church cannot address the civil community directly in terms of the Christian faith. It is in this context that Barth claims Christians can use analogies from the church and Christian faith for the political community, as well as the other way around. Barth's exemplification of such analogical reasoning is probably the most well-known part of the text, not because of its strengths, but because of its seeming arbitrariness and its far-fetched examples. Yoder is sharply critical on this point.[32] But Yoder thinks the basic idea behind Barth's analogical reasoning—the type of distinction he makes between the church and civil community—is correct. Barth, says Yoder, is the first mainstream Protestant theologian who works out the full implications of this distinction, and in doing so makes his theology a free church theology.[33]

> What Barth is distinguishing is not levels or realms in either of those ways but rather two different kinds of political and social identification. Both are social. Both are outward, institutional, "worldly." But the difference is that in one of them the commonality of all the people who form together a *"Gemeinde"* is that they are Christian: they all confess Jesus as Christ and as Lord, and the members of the other group do not.[34]

In the modern context, this post-Christendom theology is also post-national. The nation-state is not the primary social and political context for doing theology.

The type of theology Barth reacted against made "secular" readings of the social and political reality basic for the sort of ethics and politics such theology supported (one could, of course, give theological reasons for why this was necessary). These readings were not free-floating, "scientific" proposals but closely related to specific cultural, social, and political forms of life, in this case the nation-state. In Herrmann's and Troeltsch's case we see a sort of ontological generalization of a specific historical experience in Wilhelmine Germany, in which the struggle for existence understood in nationalistic terms was made into a necessary historical "law." It is easy to find parallels in more recent theology.

---

31. Ibid., 18–19.
32. Yoder, *Karl Barth and the Problem of War,* 150.
33. Ibid., 142.
34. John Howard Yoder, *The Royal Priesthood: Essays Ecclesiological and Ecumenical* (Grand Rapids, Mich.: Eerdmans, 1994), 108.

Against this type of secular reading, Barth offered a specifically Trinitarian reading of the world we live in, a reading that makes Christology central. In this limited sense, his post-national theology is also a post-secular theology, the beginnings of which we find in his Romans commentaries. He then continued to develop this theology—most extensively, of course, in his *Church Dogmatics*. According to Yoder, there is a strong tendency in *Church Dogmatics* 1–3 for "Jesus Christ" to become a cipher for revelation or (in volume 3) for creation to be claimed as part of the covenant. However, when Barth, in volume 4, again takes up Christology, this time in the context of sanctification, his approach is different, because he now needs to give content to the life of holiness in terms of following Jesus Christ.[35] Here it becomes necessary to describe the human life and preaching of Jesus and the call of the kingdom in terms of a call to follow him.[36] Discussing the concrete form of Jesus's demand, Barth says:

> It is common to every instance that the obedience concretely demanded of, and to be achieved by, the disciple, always means that he must move out of conformity with what he hitherto regarded as the self-evident action and abstention of Lord Everyman and into the place allotted to him, so that he is inevitably isolated in relation to those around him, not being able or willing to do in this place that which is generally demanded by the gods who are still fully respected in the world around. At this particular place he is freed from the bonds of that which is generally done or not done, because and as he is bound now to Jesus.[37]

The disciple is freed from what is generally done, bound now to the concreteness of the particular commands addressed to him or her in this or that situation, not to an alternative general system of ethics, a new general law. But the Gospels do point to certain general lines of concrete obedience to Jesus. Discussing this topic, Barth takes up the issue of force, saying that the command of Jesus "takes the concrete form of an attestation of the kingdom of God as the end of the fixed idea of the necessity and beneficial value of force."[38] Pointing to several sayings in the Gospels that declare or imply that the disciples should not use force, Barth says that this prohibition, which is grounded in the new reality of the kingdom come in Jesus Christ, "invalidates the whole friend-foe relationship." Barth concludes that although the prohibition of force should not be made into a general rule, the direction is clear and must be carried out. "According to the sense of the New

35. Yoder, *Karl Barth and the Problem of War,* 140–41.
36. On the call to discipleship, see *CD* 4/2:533–53.
37. *CD* 4/2:546.
38. *CD* 4/2:549.

Testament we cannot be pacifists in principle, only in practice. But we have to consider very closely whether, if we are called to discipleship, we can avoid being practical pacifists, or fail to be so."[39] This pacifism is not an abstract command or an ethical principle. It is based on the nature of reality, the nature of God.

As Barth says, this ethics is "only the reflection of God's own being." God is not a transcendent lawgiver; rather, it is God's "divine nature to exist in the sense of this ethics."[40] This is the God we meet in Jesus Christ and in Jesus Christ crucified. George Hunsinger can therefore claim that "enemy-love in Karl Barth's theology is the heart of the gospel."[41] It shapes our understanding of both God and Christian discipleship. "The enemy-love enacted in the cross is what gives New Testament ethics its direction, its freedom, its dynamic."[42]

Barth's reading thus differs from the "secular" readings of social and political reality of Herrmann, Troeltsch, and others because Barth understands reality differently. It is not a question of different abstract ethical principles. The issue is the nature of reality. John Webster notes that "for Barth, ethics is rooted in nature":[43]

By "nature" is meant, not a reality prior to or existing as a condition of possibility for "grace," nor some general *humanum* which grace perfects or completes. . . . What is meant, rather, is simply nature as *that which is*. Barth believes that good human action is generated, shaped, and judged by "that which is," and that "that which is" is a Christological, not a pre-Christological, category.[44]

The task of Christian ethics is thus to describe "that which is." *Church Dogmatics* is ethical because it attempts to Christianly describe the world in which we live. "Christian moral theology is essentially an assertion that good human action is action which is most in accord with the way the world is constituted in Jesus Christ."[45] Elsewhere I have described Yoder's theology as a development of this thesis.[46]

---

39. *CD* 4/2:550.
40. Both citations are from *CD* 4/1:191.
41. Hunsinger, *Disruptive Grace*, 35. For Hunsinger's extended discussion of this theme, a forceful confirmation of the reading of Barth I propose here (and also, indirectly, of the closeness between Barth's and Yoder's theologies), see 34–40.
42. Ibid., 37.
43. John Webster, *Barth's Ethics of Reconciliation* (Cambridge: Cambridge University Press, 1995), 214. For the following, see further 214–30.
44. Ibid., 214.
45. Ibid., 219.
46. See Rasmusson, "Historicizing the Historicist," further developed in Arne Rasmusson, "Revolutionary Subordination: A Biblical Concept of Resistance in the Theology of

However, neither for Barth nor for Yoder is describing "that which is" a question of developing a free-floating theological theory. A crucial part of this Christian metaphysics is the role of the church. Yoder especially notes Barth's ecclesiological account in *Church Dogmatics* 4/2. Here Barth talks about the upholding of the church against the world, against outer pressure and indifference, and against inner secularization and sacralization. By secularization he means letting the church be determined by "secular" philosophies, claims of historical *kairos,* or political and economic forces. Such concessions are usually defended in terms of "mediation," "translation," or "baptizing."[47] Sacralization, on the other hand, refers to the temptation of the church to make itself the end, to assert itself instead of serving.[48]

This very way of describing the situation, Yoder again claims, presupposes a post-Christendom theology, which becomes even clearer in the section of *Church Dogmatics* entitled "The Order of the Community."[49] The community order, which is christologically derived, should be an order of service; it is liturgical, living (evolving), and exemplary. As Barth writes: "The decisive contribution which the Christian community can make to the upbuilding and work and maintenance of the civil consists in the witness which it has to give to it and to all human societies in the form of the order of its own upbuilding and constitution."[50] The church should not give witness to itself but "to the kingdom of God already set up on earth in Jesus Christ, and a promise of its future manifestation."[51] Here ecclesiology and ontology are combined. The church witnesses to other possibilities. Part of Yoder's work has been to show the fruitfulness of this approach.

Barth's Abstract Theological Doctrine of the "State"

Barth was active during a time when the nation-state was the object of much discussion and political upheaval. In his writings, however, he seldom discusses the nation-state concretely. He treats in an illuminating way the issues of peoplehood and nationhood, and he often discusses the tasks of the state, but he seldom puts nation and state together. When

John Howard Yoder" in *Peace in Europe, Peace in the World: Conflict Resolution and the Use of Violence,* Iustita et Pax Dokumentation 3, (Wien: Südwind-Verlag, 2002), 35–67.
47. *CD* 4/2:667–68.
48. *CD* 4/2:668–70.
49. *CD* 4/2:676–726.
50. *CD* 4/2:721.
51. *CD* 4/2:721.

he does, it is clear that he does not see the nation-state, understood as "limited to a specific land and people and serving only national interests,"[52] as more than one specific form of the state, a form that became dominant in the nineteenth century and that may be short-lived. For Barth, insofar as the nation-state is the present reality, the church must strive to live loyally and obediently within it. Even a state that is national is instituted by God, and there is no intrinsic contradiction between the universal church and the nation-state "in so far as the latter, *in its sphere* is in itself that essentially international, God-instituted *true* State."[53] The true and just state can never serve only national interests but has to see itself as part of a supranational universal order of rights and responsibilities. Barth thus says about the Christian: "He will of course always be found among those who champion the effort to place international relations more and more completely on a basis on which national states can stand together as true states."[54]

For the most part, Barth discusses the "state" in general and ahistorical terms, as any supreme political authority in a specific geographical area. This timelessness has some unhappy consequences, which become evident if we consider, by contrast, Barth's discussion of the "nation" (the near and the distant). This discussion is, to a larger extent, built on empirical and historical observation. The perspective is theological and biblical, but what is interpreted theologically is an empirical and historical phenomenon and is dealt with as such. Barth's discussion of the "nation" is part of the doctrine of creation and describes the situation into which the command of God is spoken and in which it is lived. Tribe, ethnicity, nation, and so on are important realities that we cannot ignore, but they are always relativized by each other and by the universality of the neighbor and humanity.

Barth's discussion of the state is quite different. He sees the state, together with the church, as part of God's reconciling work and therefore treats it as part of the doctrine of salvation. It is perhaps, in part, because of its place in the doctrine of salvation that Barth combines, in a quite unmediated way, an ahistorical description of state (grounded primarily in the Bible: e.g., the confrontation between Jesus and Pilate; Romans 13; Revelation 13; the texts about Christ conquering the powers; and so on) with both detailed descriptions of the ideal of a social–democratic or social–liberal constitutional state and specific political judgments on this or that type of situation. It is unclear how his theological account leads to such concrete judgments, or, put dif-

52. Karl Barth, *The Church and the War* (New York: Macmillan, 1944), 22.
53. Ibid., 23.
54. Ibid., 24.

ferently, how his theological account actually disciplines these concrete judgments. The way he talks about the state in concrete, "timeless" situations tends to be strongly—but tacitly—colored by the historical situation he is in, although it seems, on the textual surface, to be shaped "only" by the Bible. Barth is sometimes aware of the influence of his own situation.[55] But the problem is not the contextual influence as such; it is the lack of thick historical and political description, which makes his positions seem quite dogmatic, arbitrary, and undiscussable. Although Barth himself usually relativizes the political reality, his approach invites a dogmatic politics where people strongly claim exclusive theological warrant for their specific political views, something we have seen in the sometimes bitter struggles for the "correct" political legacy of Barth.

Nicholas Healy has argued that there is a similar abstractness concerning Barth's ecclesiology, and perhaps, to some extent, for the same reason.[56] Both church and state are, as we have seen, described by Barth as part of God's reconciling work. According to Healy, Barth (implicitly) works with three rules as he develops his ecclesiology. The first rule says that the church as an event of the Holy Spirit is an object of faith and thus an object for theological description. The second rule says that the church is made "visible in the form of human activity."[57] The third and most fundamental rule says that ecclesiology has to be understood as a function of christology. Like Yoder, Healy contends that Barth uses Scripture in two different ways when explicating christology, one more conceptual and the other characterized more by narrative. It is the former mode that dominates his account of christology in the context of ecclesiology, and he tends to apply these theological concepts directly to the church. The concrete church for Barth is thus the church as the body of Christ, visible to faith, while the church as sinful human phenomenon, visible to anyone, is only the *Scheinkirche*, though it can become the true church through God's action.

Healy asserts that Barth's thought in this area is determined primarily by the first and third rules, while the second rule, concerning human agency, is generally placed in the background. The result is that the exclusive use of christological concepts "makes it difficult to describe our ecclesial response to Jesus Christ as a concretely *human* response."[58] In a sense, the sufficient human response to God's saving

---

55. See, e.g., Karl Barth, *Fragments Grave and Gay* (London: Collins, 1971), 81.
56. Nicholas M. Healy, "The Logic of Karl Barth's Ecclesiology," *Modern Theology* 10, no. 3 (1994): 253–70.
57. Ibid., 255.
58. Ibid., 264.

action has already happened in Jesus Christ, and the church's task is simply to acknowledge it. Healy tends to stress only this side of Barth's dialectic. On the other side, although everything is fulfilled in Christ, the importance of human action is not diminished. However, Barth is hesitant to explicate this other side in concrete human, social, and historical terms lest he fall into the neo-Protestant attempt to identify God's saving action with a historical phenomenon.

One may say that the same thing happens with Barth's way of talking about the state. He thus describes the state in purely christological language—and then not even in terms of a narrative christology but in timeless, ahistorical categories. The state becomes, in the theological account, a saving institution. The contingent, historical nature of political authority is placed in the background. One result is that it is difficult to see how his analysis is theologically disciplined; another is that some habits of thought inherited from Christendom tend to linger here longer than in other parts of his theology.

The Politics of Diaspora

One can read Yoder's work as an attempt to develop an ecclesiology with much more sociohistorical thickness, while still keeping much of Barth's theological basis. Barth's account of Christology, ecclesiology, discipleship, and politics read in the light of or inserted into Yoder's account looks quite different. This difference has consequences for how to talk about the relationship between church and the political entities with which the church coexists.

Yoder does not develop his account of ecclesiology on the basis of an isolated Christology. Neither Jesus nor the church, for Yoder, represented something entirely new. Central for any understanding of Yoder's thought is his account of the Jewishness of Christianity. Yoder claims that the emergence of Christendom correlated with a de-Judaization of Christian faith, as the original eschatological perspective was overwhelmed by a vertical approach to Christian faith. A distinct sacramental economy then developed that was partly separated from ordinary life. The church became more an institution that managed sacramental grace than a concrete people. Peoplehood was transferred to the Roman Empire and other cultural and political entities. All of this had immense consequences for "ethics" and "politics."[59]

59. See, e.g., John Howard Yoder, *The Jewish–Christian Schism Revisited*, ed., Michael G. Cartwright and Peter Ochs (Grand Rapids, Mich.: Eerdmans, 2003), 72–75, and John

Of course, Christianity's Jewish heritage (as well as present-day Judaism) can be understood in different ways. Defenders of Christendom might have argued that their understanding affirmed God's election of and dealing with the Jewish people, but now transferred to Christian peoples. Later on, this way of reading the Old Testament was important for emergent national consciousness.[60] Yoder, however, follows another trajectory of the Jewish experience: life in the Diaspora and the antiroyal strand in Israel's tradition.[61] The Diaspora has been the normal existence for most Jews in most times. Yoder sometimes talks about a "Jeremian shift," but he thinks that the exilic abandonment of ordinary "statehood" built on an earlier antiroyal tradition.[62] In any case, the Jewish experience of living within other cultural groups and political powers and of not being in charge created, Yoder thinks, "the culturally unique traits which define 'Judaism,'" a set of social innovations that shaped Jewish identity and thereby also Christianity:

- the phenomenon of the synagogue; a decentralized, self-sustaining, non-sacerdotal community life form capable of operating on its own wherever there are ten households.
- the phenomenon of Torah; a text around the reading and exposition of which the community is defined. This text is at once narrative and legal.

Howard Yoder, *The Priestly Kingdom: Social Ethics as Gospel* (Notre Dame, Ind.: University of Notre Dame Press, 1984), 135–47.

60. Cf. Adrian Hastings, *The Construction of Nationhood: Ethnicity, Religion, and Nationalism* (Cambridge: Cambridge University Press, 1997), 186, 195–97.

61. Many of the essays that develop this theme are now gathered in Yoder, *The Jewish–Christian Schism Revisited*, with a fascinating commentary by the Jewish scholar Peter Ochs and a long discussion by Michael Cartwright. For a Jewish account that has remarkable similarities to Yoder's and that makes the Diaspora normative, see Daniel Boyarin, *A Radical Jew: Paul and the Politics of Identity* (Berkeley: University of California Press, 1994). He has, together with Jonathan Boyarin, developed this theme in Jonathan Boyarin and Daniel Boyarin, *Powers of Diaspora: Two Essays on the Relevance of Jewish Culture* (Minneapolis: University of Minnesota Press, 2002). Daniel Boyarin's interpretation of Paul, however, is different from Yoder's. For support of Yoder's reading of Paul, see Douglas K. Harink, *Paul among the Postliberals: Pauline Theology beyond Christendom and Modernity* (Grand Rapids, Mich.: Brazos Press, 2003).

62. See Yoder, *The Jewish–Christian Schism Revisited*, 70–71. Boyarin sees "the 'invention' of Diaspora" as a further advancement in a new situation of the "radical experiment of Moses." See Boyarin, *A Radical Jew*, 253–55; 254.

- the phenomenon of the rabbinate; a non-sacerdotal, non-hierar-
  chical, non-violent leadership elite whose power is not civil but
  intellectual, validated by their identification with the Torah.[63]

This social life was and is possible without conventional political structures, a military, or cultural homogeneity. It gives space for different
ways of living and different philosophical systems because "the ground
floor of identity is the common life itself, the walk, halakah, and the
shared remembering of the story behind it." The people's international
unity "is sustained by intervisitation, by intermarriage, by commerce,
and by rabbinic consultation."[64]

Part of this is also God's command in the book of Jeremiah (29:7)—the
Jews are to seek the welfare of and pray for the people in whose midst they
live, while at the same time living faithfully to God. Yoder can thus describe
the Jewish vision as more universal than the imperial vision of Rome or of
any other empire. "The Jewish world vision was *in lived experience* wider
than was the Roman Empire."[65] Many Jews lived outside the Roman Empire,
and Jews inside the empire had intense contacts with them. This correlates
with Jewish monotheism, in which God is Creator and Lord of the entire
world. Justice is not the word of the king or the emperor but transcends
kingdoms and empires and is known through the Torah.

This nonsovereign, nonterritorial, and "not-in-charge" existence created, Yoder says, a sort of inherent Jewish pacifism out of which the
pacifism of the early church grew. Jewish nonviolence was not simply a
result of the social situation; it was also articulated in theological terms:
God is sovereign over history; the establishing of a final righteous order
is a task for the Messiah; the failed military experiments were for lack
of God's blessing; God's people should not defend themselves against
God's chastisements; the death of the righteous "makes a doxologi-
cal contribution on the moral scales of history."[66] Yoder can thus say
that "for over a millennium the Jews of the diaspora were the closest
thing to the ethic of Jesus existing on any significant scale anywhere
in Christendom."[67]

63. Yoder, *The Jewish–Christian Schism Revisited*, 171.
64. John Howard Yoder, *For the Nations: Essays Evangelical and Public* (Grand Rapids, Mich.: Eerdmans, 1997), 59. "This cultural *novum* was capable of enormous flex-
ibility. . . . Wherever they went they created new trades, new arts, new literatures, even
new languages, without losing their connections to Moses or one another, or their hope
of return" (ibid., 59–60).
65. Yoder, *The Jewish–Christian Schism Revisited*, 73.
66. Yoder, *For the Nations*, 67–68. See also the somewhat different account in Yoder,
The Jewish–Christian Schism Revisited, 82–87.
67. Yoder, *The Jewish–Christian Schism Revisited*, 81–82.

Jesus and the early church reinforced and developed this Jewish tradition, which Yoder describes as "the already well established ethos of not being in charge and not considering any local state structure to be the primary bearer of the movement of history." When the earliest church added further reasons for this understanding, "having to do with the messiahship of Jesus, his lordship, and the presence of the Spirit,"[68] they were still working inside a Jewish framework.

Yoder is critical of the common depiction of Judaism as particularistic, nationalistic, and earthly in contrast to Christianity's universal, individualistic, and spiritualistic vision.[69] From his perspective, the de-Judaizing of the Christian faith in emergent Christendom meant in practice the loss of the Jewish and Christian universalism where God was transcendent above kings and empires and where faithfulness to God's Torah or God's Word stood above a morality of political "necessity" and "responsibility"—the morality of "Lord Everyman," to use Barth's term. The self-evident object of such "necessity" and "responsibility" was the Roman Empire, and the evolving church saw its own responsibility as directed toward that empire. This shift led in turn to a "normalization" of violence, as the church increasingly identified itself with the ruling elite.[70] Yoder reads this history—recurring in different ways in Byzantium, Aachen, Moscow, Berlin, and so on—as a repetition of the mistake of 1 Samuel 8. It thus follows, he thinks, that "authentic reverence before divine sovereignty must accordingly mean a critical judgment upon nationhood/statehood in its modern as well as its medieval forms."[71]

In this sense, Yoder supports Troeltsch's claim about the mutual and dialectic connections between theology and social location.[72] Does he not then confirm Barth's suspicions about the neo-Protestant derivation of theology from history, a form of "natural theology"? The answer is that Yoder reads this history in a theological framework. Moreover, this historical practice, in both its Jewish and its Christian forms, has always been theological through and through. However, theology and social location cannot, for Yoder, be separated. Yoder differs from Barth in stressing the (ambiguous) social reality of Israel and the church and how theology is directly related to its lived reality. To put it another way, one might say that Yoder places more emphasis on Healy's second rule

68. Yoder, *For the Nations*, 69.
69. Yoder, *The Jewish–Christian Schism Revisited*, 69–70.
70. Cf. Arne Rasmusson, "Not All Justifications of Christendom Are Created Equal: A Response to Oliver O'Donovan," *Studies in Christian Ethics* 11, no. 2 (1998):1 69–76.
71. Yoder, *The Jewish–Christian Schism Revisited*, 163.
72. Yoder, *The Priestly Kingdom*, 80.

than does Barth, that is, on human agency and the historical human response to God's action.[73]

The Ethics of Diaspora

From the perspective of a diaspora theology and ecclesiology, Yoder can affirm Barth's understanding of the church's witness to the world.[74] From such an ecclesiology it clearly follows that there is no general theory or systematic theology of the relationship between the church and the civil community or the state. Yoder could never have written the sort of ethical summa that has been standard in European, especially German, theological ethics. This genre is so common, and still in practice, that it is difficult to recognize what it presupposes and in fact how odd it is. One develops a general system of ethics, often on the basis of some systematic principle or set of principles, and then deals with "most" areas of individual and social life in terms of that system. One can thus proceed to develop a general theory about the state, culture, technology, economy, and so on. This approach casts the ethicist as a sort of legislator in service of the managers of society. Society is assumed to be a potentially harmonious, well-ordered system, and the ethicist is assumed to be able to find or create this order. The approach presupposes an established position, such as German theology professors may once have held, from which this practice may seem meaningful. It also tends to assume that the church should work with the descriptions of reality and with the language dominant in a given society. Furthermore, it assumes that ethics should be done in a generalizable logic so that it can effectively fill all the slots in society and be seen in terms of what the sovereign should do. To glimpse the oddity of this idea, imagine that a nonassimilated German rabbi should do something similar, including systematically placing Judaism and the synagogue in this system.[75]

73. One might still say, as has Douglas Harink, that Yoder would have strengthened his case if he had explicated more strongly, in a Barthian way, the primacy of God's act of electing "Israel and through Jesus Christ the *ekklesia* as Israel's extension into the nations." Harink, *Paul among the Postliberals*, 207; see further 205–7.

74. Yoder, *For the Nations*, 23–33.

75. Similar perspectives have permeated the imaginations of other modern "experts" in such areas as economics, sociology, political science, and international relations. For a brilliant analysis and critique of such views, see James C. Scott, *Seeing Like a State: How Certain Schemes to Improve the Human Condition Have Failed* (New Haven, Conn.: Yale University Press, 1998).

A large part of Yoder's writing has attempted to undermine the imagination that makes this ethics for "Lord Everyman" reasonable. What Yoder (and Barth) is saying is that one should think instead in terms of a Christian description of reality, though one may well use dominant languages for tactical reasons—using, for example, the language of the sovereign against the sovereign. Instead of thinking in terms of filling all the slots, of a generalizable ethic, one should consider where a specific Christian presence might make the most difference. There is no general answer to the question of how the "church" should relate to "society" and "culture." Instead of seeing reality from the perspective of the sovereign, one can identify with and think from the perspective of the victim or the opponent. Instead of assuming some form of value homogeneity, one can assume the existence of various communities, and acknowledge the fact that the church is giving witness to a reality that is not universally recognized.[76]

It is important to note the close mutual relationship Yoder sees between Christian speech and Christian practice. This is the strength he sees in Barth's articulation in *Church Dogmatics* 4/2 of the church's order as witness:

> The faith community and the human community are connatural; each is human, historical, social. No apologetic bridge needs to be built from one to the other. No deductive derivation of concrete specifications from general theories or metaphors is needed. If and when and to the extent to which women and men order their common life in the light of Christ's lordship, they are already actualizing in, with, and under ordinary human forms the sanctification of creaturely life. That action is public by nature, with no need for it to be translated or buffered or diluted. The *reason* for that action may not be transparent to those uninformed or misinformed about the witness of resurrection, ascension, and Pentecost, but that does not diminish its public accessibility or pertinence.[77]

Yoder lists five dimensions of this witness: baptism, forgiveness, the Eucharist, the open meeting, and the universality of giftedness.[78] Let me summarize each in turn.

Yoder describes baptism as the breaking down of social barriers such as gender and ethnicity through individuals' dying and rising with Christ

---

76. Yoder, *The Priestly Kingdom*, 160–66.

77. Yoder, *For the Nations*, 27.

78. For the following, see ibid., 29–33. For fuller discussions, see John Howard Yoder, *Body Politics: Five Practices of the Christian Community before the Watching World* (Nashville: Discipleship Resources, 1992), and Yoder, *The Royal Priesthood*, 359–73.

to new communal life. If the body of Christ had been experienced in as "real" a way as people experienced the national body, the events of 1914 would at least have been a trauma for Christians. They were not. Christian baptism, Yoder says, should be more powerful than Enlightenment humanism, which only postulates universal equality as self-evident—even when it is not.

Forgiveness is central for Christian faith and practice. Yoder describes the function of forgiveness in the Christian church and how it is and can be used in other communities, referring to Hannah Arendt's discussion of its crucial political importance.

For Yoder the Eucharist, the eating together, "is the paradigm for every other mode of inviting the outsider and the underdog to the table, whether we call that the epistemological privilege of the oppressed or cooperation or equal opportunity or socialism."[79]

In early Christian worship and church meetings everyone was allowed and encouraged to speak. "From this original Christian vision have come the stronger strands of what we call 'democracy,' a vision which does not say that 'the people' are always right, or that a majority is, but only that decisions will be better and community more whole if all can speak."[80]

Finally, the gifts of the Spirit give each individual a role in the community. This vision, Yoder thinks, can help us "rediscover the ways in which the individual, the local, the ordinary can be validated."[81]

Conclusion

Yoder claims that the early church—its theology and ecclesial practice—was shaped by and extended the Jewish Diaspora existence. In the center of the Christian extension of this existence is the claim that the Creator and Lord of the cosmos acts as the slain Lamb (Revelation 5), that Jesus as crucified and resurrected is the key to understanding the ultimate reality and the meaning of history. The church is called to witness this good news in life and speech—or, to use Webster's description of Barth's moral theology, to live in accordance with how the cosmos is constituted in Jesus Christ. It is Yoder's claim that there is a homology between the "diaspora politics" of the church and this christological understanding of the world. Travis Kroeker summarizes Yoder's view:

79. Yoder, *For the Nations*, 32.
80. Ibid.
81. Ibid., 33.

The mission of the church . . . is precisely to witness to the flaws in Babel-like unity, rooted in coercive, centralized, sacral authority, the idolatrous politics of empire that substitutes human for divine kingship and that tries to take charge of human history via external conquest. The rule of divine love and harmony represents a very different pattern of ecumenicity: a pattern of creative diversity, dialogue, a community that welcomes outsiders and understands leadership as servanthood. In the Jeremian shift this is represented by cultural linguistic plurality (diaspora culture is polyglot and on the move, not univocal and sovereign); the creation of a synagogue rather than a temple culture (the focus is now on the interpretation of the story in ever new cultural situations, not an altar that stands in cultic support of a sacral regime); and the building of God's city and God's rule "from below."[82]

Diaspora ecclesial practice presumes and lives a radical universality built on the assumption that the God of Jesus Christ is Creator and Lord of the whole universe and of all peoples. However, when the church becomes the established religion—as in the Roman Empire, medieval Christendom, and modern nation-states—the meaning of these ecclesial claims and practices is transformed. Beliefs and practices that have one meaning for the church as "resident aliens" take on another meaning for the church as "established power." Universal claims made by a diaspora community and by a hegemonic church that can use coercion function very differently. And it is worth noting that much modern, formally disestablished Christianity and theology still assume an "established perspective" on the world, still "see like a state," as James Scott says.[83]

Established Protestantism has generally given more or less unlimited support to modern nationalism. Although in theory the Roman Catholic Church can hardly give such strong support to nationalism and the nation-state, it often has. It is mainly in some of the so-called free churches—especially Mennonites and Quakers, but also others—that a diaspora-like theology and practice has existed in modern times.[84] Yoder stands in this tradition. He sought to insert much of Barth's theology into a diaspora theology and thereby develop it in a fruitful way. He could do so not least because Barth's theology itself increasingly moved in this direction. For Yoder, as for Barth, the resulting theology is not

82. P. Travis Kroeker, "The War of the Lamb: Postmoderntiy and John Howard Yoder's Eschatological Genealogy of Morals," *Mennonite Quarterly Review* 74, no. 2 (2000): 295–310; 302.

83. Scott, *Seeing Like a State*.

84. "But it is undoubtedly within this constituency that the most creative efforts have been made to free Protestantism and Christianity with it from nationalist bondage. It is groups like the Mennonites and the Quakers which have produced a Christian spirit most impervious to nationalism" (Hastings, *The Construction of Nationhood*, 205).

specifically free church theology. It is catholic. Indeed, leading Roman Catholic theologians have started to think in this direction. Karl Rahner could talk about the future of the church in terms of diaspora,[85] and Hans Urs von Balthasar has said that diaspora, not Christendom, is the normal condition for the church.[86]

Something like the diaspora ecclesiology of Yoder, though it may take many different forms, seems necessary for a church that wants a measure of freedom from its bondage to the nation-state or Christendom, which Christians today may see realized in the globalized "Western civilization." Such an ecclesiology will share space with others, use various cultural and social resources, and show a relative and critical loyalty to other local entities (such as regions, nations, international unions) in which it exists. It will not think of the church as forming a particular (or even private) identity and the nation-state or international communities as shaping more universal (and public) identities. For churches that call themselves catholic, the diaspora identity is, in the time between, a concrete way of living the Christian catholicity in a world of nations. Only in this way can Christians be shaped by an alternative imagination that trusts that things do not need to be as they are. "For there is perhaps no more serious Christian offense than to fail in imagination, that is, to abandon or forget the resources God has given as the means of calling us to his kingdom."[87]

85. Gerald A. McCool, ed., *A Rahner Reader* (London: Darton, Longman & Todd, 1975, 1975), 305–9.

86. See Hans Urs von Balthasar, *Explorations in Theology*, vol. 4, *Spirit and Institution* (San Francisco: Ignatius Press, 1995), 67.

87. Hauerwas, *Against the Nations*, 59.

6

God and King

Robert N. Bellah

I count myself honored to be a long-standing friend of Stanley Hauerwas. I am probably one of several of Stanley's friends whose friendship with him is in good part constituted by an ongoing argument. In my case the argument has been over the meaning of America and of the relationship between the American nation and the Christian church. In his contribution to my Festschrift, "On Being a Christian and an American,"[1] he furthered that argument. In this essay I am doing likewise.

Before beginning my substantive argument I need to remind the reader that my views have changed over time, as I am sure Stanley's have. I entered the discussion with my 1967 article "Civil Religion in America" because of my anguish over the Vietnam War, though quite unwillingly, as at that time I was primarily preoccupied with Japan.[2] My concern was to discover the resources in America's religious self-understanding that could provide critical leverage for opposing the war. By using Rousseau's

---

1. Stanley Hauerwas, "On Being a Christian and an American," in *Meaning and Modernity: Religion, Polity, and Self,* ed. Richard Madsen et al. (Berkeley: University of California Press, 2002), 224–35.

2. Robert N. Bellah, "Civil Religion in America," *Daedalus* 96, no. 1 (Winter 1967): 1–21.

term "civil religion" to describe those resources, I unwittingly set off a barrage of publications and a major debate over whether there was such a thing, and if there was, whether it was a good or a bad idea. I have long since ceased to use the term, nor am I at all interested in the controversy it sparked, though I have learned that for many people I am forever identified with that article and that term. When I published that article, though I considered myself a Christian, I was not a member of any church, and I was concerned almost exclusively with the nation and not the church. Without going into the story of my changing views over nearly forty years, let me just say that I am now much closer to Stanley's position than I was initially, in that I see my first loyalty as to the church, not to the nation. That does not mean that Stanley and I feel no responsibility to the nation, but that for both of us the relationship between church and nation is problematic, to say the least. Finally, and here too I think Stanley would agree with me, I do not see the church as exclusively "religious" and the nation as exclusively "political." Both nation and church are religious and political. That is the theme of this essay.

More specifically, I want to examine the relation between the Christian church and liberalism, a central theme of Stanley's work. Like Stanley, I am critical of the philosophical liberalism that is a product of the Enlightenment, though my criticism may be somewhat more tempered than Stanley's.[3] But whereas Stanley traces the baleful influence of liberalism on American Christianity primarily to liberal Protestant theologians from Rauschenbusch to the Niebuhrs to the present, I would argue that the link between Protestantism and liberalism long precedes the twentieth century and is, in fact, constitutive of them both. I want to start, however, by putting the whole question of the relation of religion and politics in a deep historical framework.

Origins of State Religion

I have taken as my title "God and King" because I believe historically these two terms were born together and have not ceased to be mutu-

---

3. My position is close to that of Charles Taylor, particularly as expressed in his "A Catholic Modernity?" in *A Catholic Modernity?* ed. James L. Heft (New York: Oxford University Press, 1999), 13–37. Assuming that Taylor means by "modernity" the same thing in a broad sense as "liberalism," I would agree with him when he suggests that he and his fellow Catholics "gradually find our voice from within the achievements of modernity, measure the humbling degree to which some of the most impressive extensions of the gospel ethic depended on a breakaway from Christendom, and from within these gains try to make clear to ourselves and others the tremendous dangers that arise within them" (36–37).

ally entangled ever since. Drawing on my lifelong work on religious evolution, I would argue that in pre-state societies neither God nor king exists. In such societies there are powerful beings, ancestors, spirits of the mountains and rivers, and so on in great number, but there is no creator god who rules the cosmos as a whole. And in such societies there are elders, chiefs, war leaders, and such, but no kings whose claim to rule is absolute. It is worth remembering that pre-state societies were small-scale affairs; a few hundred or a few thousand people were organized loosely in bands, villages, or chieftainships. The early state saw an enormous increase in scale, from hundreds to hundreds of thousands, or millions in some cases. Aggregations of such size, overriding ancient small-scale local solidarities, demanded new forms of self-understanding and social cohesion.

It is with the early state—in ancient Egypt and Mesopotamia, in North China, in Mesoamerica and Peru, as late as the eighteenth century in Hawaii—that we see high gods and kings emerge together, often suddenly and terrifyingly. Human sacrifice is almost missing in pre-state societies but appears on a remarkable scale in all the early states, particularly China, the New World, and Hawaii, and on a lesser scale in Egypt and Mesopotamia. In almost every case, ritual human sacrifice declined rapidly after the state was established, though we can ask whether every state is not based in some way or other on human sacrifice. The relation between high god and high king was everywhere close in archaic states, sometimes amounting to identity. Early dynasty (ca. 3100–2700 BC) kings in Egypt were identified with the sky god Horus; kings in Mesopotamia were identified as gods sporadically in the third millennium BC; the king in Shang China had a special relation to Di or Shang Di, the "god above" in the late second millennium BC; and from the beginning of the first millennium BC the Chinese king was styled Son of Heaven, just as the Egyptian pharaoh from the mid-third millennium BC was styled Son of Re, the sun god. The Japanese emperor, in some circles to this day, is believed to be descended from the sun goddess Amaterasu.

In all these archaic societies the king was high priest, the chief, and indispensable mediator and intercessor between humans and the gods. There were no church and no state as separate entities; there was only a single religio-political community. I want to argue that this archaic substratum has never completely disappeared, not in Japan and not in America—even the American president is at some level the lineal descendent of these archaic divine kings.[4] Although it is tempting to see the transition from tribal society to the early state as a "fall," that is not

4. For my views on the comparison between Japan and the United States in this regard, see Robert N. Bellah, epilogue to *Meaning and Modernity*, 259–64, and the introduction

my intention. It is true that early states are associated with an enormous increase in organized violence, so there is no reason to idealize them. It is also true that many early states inaugurated periods of sustained peace, making possible the rise of cities and of civilization, as indicated by the emergence of literature, monumental architecture, and the arts, so they need not be demonized either.

If, as Thorkild Jacobsen argued for ancient Mesopotamia (though the same was more or less true in all the archaic cases), the cosmos was seen as a state and the state as embedded in the cosmos, then it was the king who was the focus of order in society and nature.[5] Though kings claimed to embody eternal order, and it was in those early states that eternal order in the cosmos was first imagined, the order they embodied inevitably broke down. Empires disintegrated; civil war ravaged the land; and intermediate periods, to use the Egyptian term, occurred, during which the lack of centralized rule and the onset of large-scale social chaos created major "problems of meaning," as Max Weber put it. It was often in these periods that new understandings, new revelations we could even say, appeared. In small-scale pre-state societies shamans and priests often received messages from the spirits, but they were usually concerned with domestic and local issues: why so and so was sick, why the harvest in such and such a village was so bad this year. But in the intermediate periods of early civilizations, new conceptions of cosmic order, new ideas about ultimate reality, appeared, and we can discern the early intimations of what used to be called "higher religions."

Apparently a notion of the divine as having a concern for the welfare of humans was widespread enough to arouse reproaches in Egypt during the First Intermediate Period (ca. 2150–2040 BC), or at least in the memory of this period in the Middle Kingdom (ca. 2040–1650 BC). The "Admonitions of Ipuwer" complains that not only the king but also "the god" has been derelict in his duty of taking care of the people. Ipuwer reproaches the god who brought human beings into existence: "Where is he today? Is he asleep? His power is not seen."[6]

A remarkable defense of the "all-lord" is mounted in Coffin Text 1130 from the Middle Kingdom, a text that Jan Assmann believes belongs

to Robert N. Bellah, *Imagining Japan* (Berkeley: University of California Press, 2003), 1–62.

5. Thorkild Jacobsen, "The Cosmos as a State," in *Before Philosophy: The Intellectual Adventure of Ancient Man*, ed. Henri Frankfort et al. (1946; repr., Harmondsworth, U.K.: Penguin, 1949), 137–99.

6. Jan Assmann, *The Search for God in Ancient Egypt* (1984; repr., Ithaca, N.Y.: Cornell University Press, 2001), 171. For a complete translation, see Miriam Lichtheim, *Ancient Egyptian Literature*, vol. 1, *The Old and Middle Kingdoms* (Berkeley: University of California Press, 1973), 149–63.

in the developing tradition of wisdom literature. The text is an apology for the god against such accusations as Ipuwer's. In order to "still the anger" the god recounts his "four good deeds":

> (1) I performed four good deeds in the threshold of Light-land:
> I made the four winds,
> so that everyone could breathe in his time.
> That is one of my deeds.
> (2) I made the great flood,
> so that the poor man would have use of it like the rich man.
> That is one of the deeds.
> (3) I made each one like his fellow
> and forbade that they do evil.
> But their hearts resisted what I had said.
> That is one of the deeds.
> (4) I caused that their hearts cease forgetting the West,
> so that offerings would be made to the deities of the nomes.
> That is one of the deeds.[7]

What is striking about this text is the emphasis on equality. The god has given the wind (the prevailing north wind brings blessed cool to Egypt's otherwise desert heat) and the inundation of the Nile to all, rich and poor alike. And he made all humans alike, forbidding them to do evil. It is humans, not the god, who have created oppression and caused the difference between rich and poor, strong and weak. The king is not missing—the god has created rulers to protect the weak—but the focus is not on glorifying the king but on justifying the god.

In the late Shang dynasty (ca. 1200–1045 BC—it is only from the late Shang that we have texts) the king was the only mediator between the people and the high god Di; just as Di orders (*ling*) the natural elements, so the king orders (*ling*) his subordinates. But it should be noted that Di was not always favorable to the king; he could be responsible for enemy attacks on the Shang. From the surviving Shang documents, we have no idea why Di turned against the king, no indication that the king was being punished for a moral fault, but this idea becomes explicit in the ideology of the succeeding Zhou dynasty (Early Zhou, 1045–771 BC). For the Zhou, Tian (Heaven) usually replaced Di as the term for the high god, and Tian was very concerned with the moral behavior of rulers. In Zhou thought, it was the evil deeds of the late Shang kings, particularly the last one, that caused Heaven to transfer its mandate (*Tian ming*) to the new dynasty. Implicit in this idea was that kingship is

---

7. Assmann, *Search*, 174–75, and commentary, 174–77. For a complete translation of the text, see Lichtheim, *Old and Middle Kingdoms*, 131–33.

conditional. Should wicked kings arise, the mandate could once again be transferred. This idea persisted throughout the history of imperial China, being used to justify existing rulers, as well as, in the name of a changed mandate, their challengers.

What I want to demonstrate by these examples is that even in several of the mature archaic societies, though cosmos and state were still tightly fused, at least a crack was opened between god and king; some idea of a judgment transcending the existing society had appeared. With the Axial Age (roughly the first millennium BC, but dates vary in different societies and the idea of the Axial Age is not based on absolute chronology) that crack widens into a chasm. Kings do not disappear—they never do—but they are no longer the primary channel for relating the human and the divine; all existing institutions, including political ones, stand under divine judgment. Let me consider only a few moments in our own tradition.

From Moses to Monarchy

Surely the archetypal moment is the Exodus narrative, with its confrontation between Moses, the man of God, and pharaoh, worshipper of idols but also claimant of divinity itself. In the Hebrew Scripture, Egypt is rivaled only by Babylon as the very epitome of evil, and for the same reason: pride in self and rejection of God. Ezekiel puts it clearly when he writes that pharaoh is a "great dragon" who says: "My Nile is my own; I made it for myself" (Ezek. 29:3).[8] As we have seen above, this is not a fair depiction: the Egyptians believed the god created the Nile, not the pharaoh. But the Israelite indictment of Egypt—as evidenced in Jeremiah, and which Walter Brueggemann calls "staggering, both in its sheer quantity and in its hyperbolic fierceness"—was not intended to be fair. Egypt was charged, above all, not so much with its oppression of Israel as with its defiance of Yahweh.[9] Behind the demonization of both Egypt and Babylon was Israel's deep suspicion of the claim to divine kingship that was never absent in the great archaic monarchies, however tempered over time.

The great institutional achievement of Israel was to found a society not on the rule of one man who claimed to unite heaven and earth, but on a covenant between God and a people. That is the significance of the events at Sinai after the exodus from Egypt. But such a new community,

8. All biblical quotations are from the New Revised Standard Version.
9. Walter Brueggemann, *Theology of the Old Testament* (Minneapolis: Fortress Press, 1997), 505.

like the old one, had to be simultaneously political and religious—there was as yet no clear distinction between these realms—and therefore had to have a leader. The Egyptian king, however much he became the servant of the god rather than a god himself, never gave up the titles of Horus and Son of Re. Moses could make no such claim. He was God's prophet, nothing else. Yet his sheer responsibility as leader in so desperate an enterprise made him at times look like a king and even act like a king. Michael Walzer, in *Exodus and Revolution,* points out that there were two sides to Moses as leader: a Leninist side and a social–democratic side.[10]

The Leninist side is most clearly evident in the incident following Moses's discovery that while he was on the mountain receiving the commandments of the Lord, the people had made for themselves a golden calf, which they proceeded to worship. This is an incident that my students, even those who knew the Bible well, usually did not remember until it was pointed out to them. Moses called to those "on the Lord's side," and the sons of Levi gathered around him. Then Moses said to them:

> "Thus says the LORD, the God of Israel, 'Put your sword on your side, each of you! Go back and forth from gate to gate throughout the camp, and each of you kill your brother, your friend, and your neighbor.'" The sons of Levi did as Moses commanded, and about three thousand of the people fell on that day. Moses said, "Today you have ordained yourselves for the service of the LORD, each one at the cost of a son or a brother, and so have brought a blessing on yourselves this day." (Exod. 32:27–29)

Walzer calls this the first revolutionary purge. It must surely also be called the first revolutionary terror. The Exodus narrative insists that Moses was not a king, an important point to which we shall return, but in Exodus 32 he acts like a king. As David Malo, himself a member of the old Hawaiian aristocracy, put it with respect to the Hawaiian king: "The edicts of the king had power over life and death. If the king had a mind to put someone to death, it might be a chief or a commoner, he uttered the word and death it was. But if the king chose to utter the word of life, the man's life was spared."[11] Moses claimed that the word was the Lord's but its human voice was Moses's, and on this earth it is the state that authorizes the word of life and death; the spokesperson of the state is always, somehow or other, a king, even when, especially when, he claims the word comes from the Lord.

---

10. Michael Walzer, *Exodus and Revolution* (New York: Basic Books, 1985), 66.
11. David Malo, *Hawaiian Antiquities* (1898; repr., Honolulu: Bernice P. Bishop Museum, 1951), 57.

Exodus 32 is not the only place in the Exodus narrative where terrible things happen to those who oppose Moses, but Walzer insists the Leninist side is not the whole story. There is another Moses, a social–democratic Moses, who leads by teaching, exhortation, and example, not by violence; who defends the people from the wrath of God, asking the Lord not to make a catastrophic end to the project that God had initiated.[12] The important point here is that however "necessary" revolutionary violence may have been, and there have always been those down through the ages who have argued for that necessity, what emerged was a new political form, a people in covenant with God, with no king as ruler. Moses is a teacher and a prophet, not a king, and the Torah underscores this point not only by God's prohibition of Moses reaching the Promised Land, but also by the account of his death. Moses died in the land of Moab and "no one knows his burial place to this day" (Deut. 34:6). Walzer points out that there could be no greater contrast to the Egyptian pharaoh, whose tomb was so central to his identity. Moreover, Moses was not the father of kings—the Bible tells us almost nothing about his descendants.[13] But it remains an open question, as far as I am concerned, whether former slaves could have been transformed into a covenant people without Moses's Leninist side.[14]

Moses, in spite of his Leninist moments, was not a king, but there would be kings in Israel. This is not the place to tell the whole complex and, in the end, sad story, or to try to disentangle the monarchist and

12. Walzer, *Exodus*, 66–68.

13. Ibid., 126.

14. Machiavelli famously called Moses a "prophet armed," and went on to say that "all armed prophets win, and unarmed ones fall" because people are variable and the prophet must be ready "to make them believe by force." See chapter 6 of Niccolò Machiavelli, *The Prince*, in *The Chief Works and Others*, trans. Allan Gilbert (Durham, N.C.: Duke University Press, 1965), vol. 1, 26. (Machiavelli is silent about the ways in which unarmed prophets may also "win.") In the *Discourses*, Machiavelli discusses the passage from Exodus 32 cited above and writes, "He who reads the Bible with discernment will see that, before Moses set about making laws and institutions, he had to kill a very great number of men who, out of envy and nothing else, were opposed to his plans" (III.30.4); see *The Discourses of Niccolò Machiavelli*, trans. Leslie J. Walker (London: Routledge and Kegan Paul, 1975), vol. 1, 547. It is also of interest that Machiavelli insists that if a new commonwealth is to be formed or an old one thoroughly reformed, there must be one sole authority. He writes in the *Discourses*, in a context where Moses is mentioned as an example, "One should take it as a general rule that rarely, if ever, does it happen that a state, whether a republic or a kingdom, is either well-ordered at the outset or radically transformed *vis-à-vis* its old institutions unless this be done by one person. It is likewise essential that there should be but one person upon whose mind and method depends any similar process of organization" (I.9.2); see Walker, *The Discourses of Niccolò Machiavelli*, vol. 1, 234. This observation might be helpful in understanding the overwhelming emphasis on the single ruler in all the early states.

antimonarchist strands in Hebrew Scripture. But it is worth remembering that in Israel—unlike archaic societies such as ancient Mesopotamia, where the gods "sent down" kingship from heaven—the king was not God's idea but the people's. In 1 Samuel 8 we hear the people asking the aged Samuel for "a king to govern us, like other nations." When Samuel, though displeased, conveys their wishes to the Lord he receives this reply: "Listen to the voice of the people in all that they say to you; for they have not rejected you, but they have rejected me from being king over them. . . . Now then, listen to their voice; only—you shall solemnly warn them, and show them the ways of the king who shall reign over them" (1 Sam. 8:7, 9). God's warning, as recounted by Samuel, tells the people that the king will take their sons for his army and their daughters for his servants; he will take the best of their fields and vineyards and olive orchards for his courtiers; he will subject the people to corvée labor and heavy taxes. The warning concludes: "He will take one-tenth of your flocks, and you shall be his slaves. And in that day you will cry out because of your king, whom you have chosen for yourselves; but the Lord will not answer you in that day" (1 Sam. 8:17–18).

And so Israel, which had, after all, never been able to escape the violent conflicts of the Iron Age, entered the concert of nations in the ancient Middle East as a monarchy, with varying fortunes. And problematic though the Israelite monarchy was, it is again an open question whether Israel would have survived without it. Perhaps without a state, largely modeled on the states surrounding it, a tribal Israel would have been crushed and absorbed by neighboring empires so that we would not know that it ever existed.

From the Prophets to Jesus

The great prophets who, beginning in the eighth century BC, had so much to do with shaping the biblical tradition were, as Max Weber reminded us, very much prophets of foreign policy, and the foreign policy they advocated was often at odds with that of the kings.[15] In fact it was the very vulnerability of the Israelite states in the face of resurgent power from Egypt and Mesopotamia that gave rise to the great preexilic prophets in the first place. In the face of extreme danger, they were vehement in their criticism of their own kings and people. They counseled submission more often than resistance, not because they liked the great

---

15. Max Weber, *Ancient Judaism* (1921; repr., Glencoe, Ill.: Free Press, 1952), 267–69.

powers—they denounced Egypt, Assyria, and Babylon as strongly as they denounced Israel and Judah—but because they placed their trust in Yahweh, not in the nation. They called for repentance for sin and trust in God, not reliance on national power. They predicted doom for all the nations, including their own, and, as it turned out, their predictions were right on all points. If they were around today they would probably be called anti-American, utopian, pacifist, even, can we say, "sectarian"? Were the prophets religious or were they political? Clearly for them the distinction makes no sense. They were intensely concerned with the nations—in that sense they were intensely political—but their politics was the politics of God.

In this sense as in so many others, the Hebrew prophets were forerunners of Jesus of Nazareth. Jesus was not "spiritual" as opposed to "political" any more than was Jeremiah. In *The Politics of Jesus,* a book that I taught to undergraduates for many years, John Howard Yoder argues that Jesus was far from apolitical, but that his politics was the politics of God, not of the nations.[16] Nonetheless, Jesus was mindful of the nation of Israel, viewing his mission as primarily to Israel, though, through Israel, to all the nations.[17] The kingdom of God may be "within you," but it was to be realized in a community, first of all in a reformed Israel. As Yoder argues, it was the intensely political message of Jesus that drove the Romans to execute him, but the politics of Jesus was neither the politics of insurrection nor of collaboration, but of nonviolent witness. Yoder's view that Matthew 5:39, "Do not resist one who wrongs you," remains the fundamental text for Christian politics is a position hard to refute. Any Christian who would act on other grounds must do so in fear and trembling. Moreover, Yoder's careful reading of Romans 13 makes it clear that Paul, while accepting the legitimacy of existing political authority, does not do so unconditionally; in particular, he does not say that Christians are called to perform military service.[18]

As one more indication of the politics of God that Jesus represented, we can point to the reappearance of the symbol "king" used with respect to Jesus. There is not only the ironic inscription that the Romans put atop the cross, but the fact that Christians early on referred to Jesus as "Lord," a term normally used for the emperor. Christ is the Lamb of God but he is also Christ the King, now as before. And if Christ is the true king, what are the kings of this world?

16. John Howard Yoder, *The Politics of Jesus* (Grand Rapids, Mich.: Eerdmans, 1972).

17. On this point, see especially Gerhard Lohfink, "Jesus and Israel," in *Jesus and Community* (1982; repr., Philadelphia: Fortress Press, 1984), 7–29.

18. Yoder, *Politics,* 193–214, esp. 205.

Both the prophets and Jesus preached to communities that on the whole refused to heed them. That some people within those communities did heed them and did try to live by their words was critical for the survival of what would become Judaism and Christianity, but those followers existed as communities called out of the surrounding world and did not exercise political authority within it. When Israel regained political autonomy under the Maccabeans, a full-scale religio-political crisis ensued, but one whose full consequences were aborted by the Roman overthrow of the Maccabean kingdom. The establishment of Christianity after Constantine, on the other hand, was not short lived. We have been living with its consequences to this day.

Constantine, the Reformation, and the American Experience

I do not consider the Constantinian moment to be a catastrophe, as sometimes Yoder and Hauerwas have seemed to do. It was a moment full of both challenge and opportunity for the church, but what historical moment has not been? Above all, what else could one expect? All across the Old World in the centuries before and after Christ, great empires were institutionalizing religions that had originated as movements withdrawn from and often critical of political power structures. Asokan India had institutionalized Buddhism; Han China had institutionalized Confucianism; Sassanid Persia had institutionalized Zoroastrianism; so it was hardly unexpected that the Roman Empire would institutionalize Christianity.

The question was who would use whom? After the Axial Age, the claim to royal divinity (except in far-off Japan) was no longer believable; the next best thing would be to have an established church anoint a ruler as king by divine right, chosen by God. In the case of Christianity, the church could use the resources of the state to alleviate the condition of the poor and to build up a substantial Christian culture. On the other hand, the state could use the church to solidify its exploitative power and to brand potential rebels as heretics. But the very opposition to which establishment gave rise, above all the movement of monasticism that sought to recover the ethic of the early church when the established church was viewed as corrupt, was creative, giving rise to new social and spiritual forms that would serve well in subsequent centuries. To summarize what was going on we can say that the old archaic substructure in which king and god were fused continued in a new guise in the imperial establishment, but at the same time the creativity of communities accepting only the sovereignty of God continued to thrive in the very pores, so to speak, of that establishment.

Fast forward to the Reformation. The Protestant churches challenged the old establishment symbolized in the figures of emperor and pope, asserting the autonomy of the church, the priesthood of all believers, and a community based on a covenant with God, beyond the state. But in several ways Protestants compromised with state structures, producing new forms of establishment. This compromise occurred most obviously in Lutheran lands where the prince replaced the pope as the highest church authority. Where Calvinism predominated, the process was more complex. I think Philip Gorski is right that Calvinism was the chrysalis of the modern democratic state.[19] Geneva was already a republic, but Calvin revolutionized it (not without a Leninist touch—the execution of Servetus, for example) into a self-governing church in a self-governing state. The new covenant people was at first a "guided democracy," as was Israel under Moses, but Calvinist discipline created people who could take responsibility for themselves—religiously, politically, and, not insignificantly, economically. The result was that Holland, England, and, above all, New England became the demonstration experiments for modern political and social life.

The Reformation was, of course, more than Lutheranism and Calvinism. What George Williams called the Radical Reformation had its own authentic understanding of what it meant to be a covenant people, and its politics resembled what Yoder, himself a Mennonite, called the politics of Jesus.[20] Although the churches of the Radical Reformation were important witness communities in several parts of the world, they never embraced the state as the Lutherans and Calvinists did, but were not infrequently persecuted by it. The Counter-Reformation Catholic Church was also an important player in the religio-political space of modernity. It picked up a number of organizational techniques from the Protestants and intensified its disciplinary structures for both clergy and laity. Like the Lutherans and Calvinists it was not averse to being established in some of the new post-Reformation states, but its transnational presence gave it leverage in relation to the modern nation-state that Protestant churches seldom had.

In trying to understand the American experience, however, we must focus on Calvinism. Calvinists placed a particular stamp on modern nationalism, especially in England but even more so in New England, by taking their covenant theology so seriously that they thought of themselves as a chosen people, God's New Israel, fusing church and

19. Philip S. Gorski, *The Disciplinary Revolution: Calvinism and the Rise of the State in Early Modern Europe* (Chicago: University of Chicago Press, 2003).

20. George Huntston Williams, *The Radical Reformation* (Philadelphia: Westminster, 1962).

nation into a religio-political whole. It has often been pointed out that the Protestant Reformation paved the way for modern nationalism by breaking the hold of the international church and replacing it with state churches instead. "The glory of God was replaced by the glory of the nation; by a curious dialectic the Reformation paved the way for this development."[21] But in the American case it was not so much the replacement as the fusion of the glory of God with the glory of the nation that was most in evidence in colonial New England, and that to more than a small degree has remained ever since. Thus the conflation of church and nation that Hauerwas tends to blame on twentieth-century liberal Protestant theologians was there from the beginning of the European settlement on our shores.[22]

But the New England Congregationalist establishment, however important in the first phase of American nation-building, was not to be the truly formative religious influence on American national self-understanding. Rather it was the dissenting churches, first the Baptists and then the Methodists, who by the early nineteenth century not only represented the great majority of American Protestants, but also united with secularizing Deists such as Thomas Jefferson to oppose the very idea of establishment and create a liberal republic instead. What in terms of present-day talk of culture wars might appear to be an unlikely alliance was both effective and enormously influential in our subsequent history. Dissenting Protestants and Enlightenment liberals turned out to have surprisingly much in common.[23] Though their religious views could hardly be more different, they agreed on the importance of separation of church and state, and on the sanctity of individual belief. Both dissenting Protestants and Enlightenment liberals were deeply committed to individual autonomy as a central value; both were deeply suspicious of the state; both were more comfortable with voluntary associations in the civic sphere and individual entrepreneurship in the economic sphere than with bureaucracy or government direction. Both dissenting Protestants and Enlightenment liberals, and the alliance continues to

21. Francisco O. Ramirez and John Boli, "On the Union of States and Schools," in *Institutional Structure: Constituting State, Society, and the Individual,* ed. George M. Thomas et al. (Newbury Park, Calif.: Sage, 1987), 194.

22. Conrad Cherry, *God's New Israel: Religious Interpretations of American Destiny* (Englewood Cliffs, N.J.: Prentice-Hall, 1971).

23. James E. Block, in his important book *A Nation of Agents: The American Path to a Modern Self and Society* (Cambridge, Mass.: Harvard University Press, 2002), shows the deep affinity between Calvinist Protestantism and liberalism from the seventeenth century on. Both placed central emphasis on the agency of autonomous individuals. Without denying that there have been tensions between these two strands of the American tradition, Block shows how they have grown ever more closely intertwined throughout our history.

this day, believed in the idea of "strong society, weak state." This is the legacy that dominates American culture now as before, and it did not originate with twentieth-century liberal Protestant theologians—it goes far deeper than that. It is a classically liberal position, but those who today call themselves conservatives and vilify the term liberal hold it fervently. In fact, in America there has never been such a thing as conservatism, except marginally; all we have are varieties of liberalism.

Another thing that tended to unite secular liberals and dissenting Protestants was their belief in the virtue of the American nation (note: not the *government,* as Americans are wont to call the state) as a beacon of freedom, a liberator of other nations, as, indeed, a redeemer nation. The dark side of our history—slavery, genocide, terrorism[24]—has usually dropped below the radar screen in America's self-understanding. As George W. Bush said not long after 9/11: "Why do they hate us when we're so good?"

Church and World in the Liberal Empire

I have taken this excursus through moments in our history for one purpose: to understand better what Stanley Hauerwas is asking when he says, "Let the world be the world and let the church be the church," particularly when he has America in mind. I am suggesting that church and world are more deeply entangled than he seems to imagine, that the entanglement goes much deeper than liberal Protestant theology, and that it is even difficult to see where church leaves off and world begins in our country. It sometimes looks as if we have returned to the old archaic fusion and lost the axial chasm altogether. I want to pursue my inquiry by asking what the American "world" has become right now and where we are to find the "church" that is to be the church.

---

24. David Little, in a roundtable discussion on terrorism in a recent issue of *Harvard Magazine,* points out that the only place in international humanitarian law where the word "terror" appears is in two 1977 protocols that supplement the Geneva Conventions' protection of victims of armed conflict: "The civilian population as such, as well as individual civilians, shall not be the object of attack. Acts or threats of violence, the primary purpose of which is to spread terror among the civilian population, are prohibited." Jessica Stern then responded: "But what about the carpet bombing specifically with the aim of terrorizing the civilian population? Does that fit into our definition? What about dropping nuclear weapons on Hiroshima and Nagasaki? I think that has to fit into our definition, because it's very clear from the documents the purpose was to terrorize the civilian population." It would seem that the United States, now engaged in a "war on terrorism," not so long ago perpetrated the greatest acts of terrorism in human history. David Little and Jessica Stern in "Understanding Terrorism: A *Harvard Magazine* Roundtable," *Harvard Magazine* (January–February 2002): 39.

Edward Rhodes, in an important article, has come up with the best characterization of America's current world project: liberal empire.[25] Rhodes compliments the Bush administration for spelling out this conception with crystal clarity, although its roots go far back in our history.[26] The key documents are Bush's West Point address of June 2002 and his National Security Strategy document of September of that year.[27] In spite of the fact that in both documents Bush denies that America seeks "empire," what both documents describe is nothing if not a description of empire: America will strike any nation or any group that it deems dangerous, whenever and however it feels necessary, and regardless of provocation or lack thereof. America invites allies to join in these ventures but reserves the right to act with or without allies. No nation will be allowed to surpass or even equal American military power, and indeed other nations, including Russia, China, and India, are advised to limit or destroy any "weapons of mass destruction" they may have. Only the United States will have large reserves of weapons of mass destruction, apparently because only we can be trusted to use them justly. Although the National Security document several times uses the time-honored phrase "balance of power," it is unclear what that phrase can mean in a situation where we would have all the power and no one else would have anything to balance it with.[28]

Our enormous power will be used not only to inhibit the power of others but also to disseminate throughout the world what the National Security document calls "a single sustainable model for national success" (which it defines as "freedom, democracy, and free enterprise")

25. Edward Rhodes, "The Imperial Logic of Bush's Liberal Agenda," *Survival* 45, no. 1 (2003): 131–53.

26. I have given a brief sketch of that prehistory in "Seventy-five Years," in "Dissent from the Homeland: Essays after September 11," special issue, *South Atlantic Quarterly* 102, no. 2 (Spring 2002): 253–65.

27. George W. Bush, "Remarks by the President at 2002 Graduation Exercise of the United States Military Academy, West Point, New York," June 3, 2002, and "The National Security Strategy of the United States of America, September 2002," both available at the whitehouse.gov Website.

28. The American empire is not simply rhetorical, but quite material as well. Chalmers Johnson, in *The Sorrows of Empire: Militarism, Secrecy, and the End of the Republic* (New York: Metropolitan Books, 2004), points out that the United States has over 700 acknowledged military bases overseas, and probably over 1,000 bases if those not acknowledged are included. These bases are located in every part of the globe, are manned by a half million military personnel, and serviced by another half million civilians. The empire is ruled, outside the bases themselves, through client states, a kind of empire that predates the nineteenth-century European obsession with annexation. Because American rule is indirect we can deny we have an empire because "we have no territorial ambitions," that is, other than total global hegemony.

and what the West Point address defines as "the single surviving model of human progress, based on non-negotiable demands." In other words, all other nations had better look like the United States pretty soon, or else. That is what it means to be a liberal empire. Bush's position is not unprecedented. In his West Point address, Bush quotes General George C. Marshall's words to the West Point class of 1942, six months after Pearl Harbor: "We're determined that before the sun sets on this terrible struggle, our flag will be recognized throughout the world as the symbol of freedom on the one hand, and of overwhelming power on the other." But Rhodes points to a still earlier precedent: "This is Wilsonianism with a vengeance."[29] Bush is determined to make the world safe for (American-style) democracy far more forcefully than Woodrow Wilson ever envisioned.[30]

There is of course a deep, inner contradiction in the agenda of liberal imperialism, which it is Rhodes's main concern to point out: liberal democracy by definition is something people must choose; to attempt to enforce it by military violence undermines its very premise. That is one of several lessons we should be learning in our current occupation of Iraq. But for the moment I am trying to understand the cultural meaning of American liberal imperialism more than its policy consequences. A significant element in the Bush doctrine is his insistence, as at West Point, on "moral clarity." What moral clarity involves is clarity about right and wrong but above all about good and evil, and, make no mistake, our enemies are evil.

Americans who have grown up with comic books know what this kind of moral clarity is all about. There is the superhero who stands for "truth, justice, and the American way," and there is the evil genius who plans to destroy the city, the country, or the world.[31] In this scenario, Bush, in the Iraq war, was the superhero ("mission accomplished") and Saddam Hussein was the evil villain, so that, apparently, the capture of Saddam ("We got him") to many Americans meant that the whole thing was over and our troops could come home. But pitting the liberal empire against evil has much deeper cultural–religious roots than a mano a mano contest between a good Bush and an evil Saddam.

29. Rhodes, "Imperial Logic," 133.

30. While it is important to note that President Bush frequently invokes the central American symbol of democracy, it is quite another question whether his actions at home or abroad actually exemplify that ideal.

31. John Shelton Lawrence and Robert Jewett, *Myth of the American Superhero* (Grand Rapids, Mich.: Eerdmans, 2002). See also their *Captain America and the Crusade against Evil: The Dilemma of Zealous Nationalism* (Grand Rapids, Mich.: Eerdmans, 2003), an earlier version of which was published in 1973.

In America we live in the midst of a culture almost invisible to the educated elite, but very visible to perhaps a third or more of the American population: the culture of conservative Evangelical Christianity. Millennialism has been an element in Christianity from the beginning, though its fortunes have waxed and waned over the centuries. Millennialism was a prominent feature of early Protestantism and in America has never slipped far below the surface. It is very much alive today. In 2003, *Armageddon*, the eleventh novel in the "Left Behind" series, was published.[32] In eight years, this series has sold fifty-five million copies. It is, as the title of the eleventh book in the series indicates, concerned with the end times. I cannot spell out in detail this particular version of millennialism with its extraordinary resonance in today's America, though most readers of this Festschrift will have a sense of it. All I need to do is point out that the end times with which the series is concerned involve the final battle between good and evil, Christ and Antichrist, Christ and Satan. It is in this context that I think we have to understand the constant use of the words "evil" and "evildoer" in Mr. Bush's rhetoric since 9/11.

The most breathtaking reference to evil first appeared right after 9/11 in Bush's remarks at the National Cathedral on September 14, 2001, when he said it is our responsibility to history to "rid the world of evil," a pledge reiterated in the National Security Strategy document a year later. Mr. Bush has frequently referred to himself as a born-again Christian, but what version of Christianity would envision that human beings can "rid the world of evil"? For example, it is hard to imagine a Catholic making such a claim. But in the present atmosphere of conservative Evangelical Christianity, such a claim makes sense if it is put in the context of the end times. In that context, it is not Bush as mere human being who will rid the world of evil, but Bush as one chosen by God who will undertake that task. We have heard much of Bush's sense that he was called by God to the presidency, such as the "defining moment" before the 2000 election, described in his campaign autobiography, when he heard a sermon about Moses being called by God to lead his people out of Egypt. From this sermon, Bush concluded that God had called him to be president of the United States. And as with Moses, it is not only the leader but also the people he leads who are chosen. In his 2003 State of the Union address Bush spoke of "our calling, as a blessed country, to make the world better."[33]

---

32. Tim F. LaHaye and Jerry B. Jenkins, *Armageddon: The Cosmic Battle of the Ages* (Carol Stream, Ill.: Tyndale House, 2003). See Joan Didion's review, "Mr. Bush & the Divine," *New York Review of Books*, November 6, 2003, 81–86.

33. See the useful discussion of "Bush's Religious Language" by Juan Stam, *The Nation*, December 22, 2003, 27.

So here we are again, in spite of our extraordinarily ambiguous history, as God's chosen people, called to rid the world of evil in the end times. One could speak of a new Constantinianism, for America is the center of a world empire and its leader is God's choice. If that is the world in which we in America currently live, what does it mean to let the world be the world? Even more to the point, how in this situation can the church be the church? Do most American Christians look with horror on the assumption that our nation and our leader are divinely ordained? Some do, but there is reason to think that most are in perfect agreement with these extraordinary claims. A recent survey found that, though most Americans disavow the word "empire," they do affirm what Carl Bowman calls "American eminence." His American Eminence Index is based on the level of agreement with the following propositions:

Without America's leadership, the world would rapidly decline.

America is a force for good in the world.

Americans must lead the world into the 21st century.

The U.S. should remain the world's dominant military power.

America's culture is superior to most other cultures.

The world would be better off if more nations embraced American values.

America should pursue its own agenda even if the United Nations opposes it.[34]

And where is the church with respect to this index? Persons for whom "religion is very important" have "much higher views of American eminence" than others. But among religious persons there are significant differences:

Protestants, in general, have a more eminent view of America's global role than Catholics, and Christians have a stronger view than non-Christians or secular Americans. When the Protestant camp is divided into evangelicals and non-evangelicals, the Americanist views of the former stand out. Indeed, preliminary findings suggest that evangelicalism is the single largest predictor of a strong view of American eminence. . . . Evangelicals are much more inclined to believe that the world would be better if people of other nations could simply be more like us.[35]

34. Carl F. Bowman, "Survey Report: The Evidence for Empire," *The Hedgehog Review* 5, no. 1 (Spring 2003): 79.
35. Ibid., 80.

I don't want to exonerate the liberal Protestant theologians from Hauerwas's charges that they took the church for granted and often in effect abandoned it in an effort to improve the nation. But the fact that they did consciously what conservative Protestants were doing unconsciously at least gave them the possibility of critical distance and reappraisal. It would be hard to imagine Reinhold Niebuhr or his brother embracing the call for America to rid the world of evil, nor is it their successors who are most vociferously doing so, though some of the intellectually sophisticated defenders of the "war on terrorism" as a just war come very close. And Catholic voices have not been entirely absent in praise of the righteous empire and its global mission. But I think it undeniable that it is bedrock, popular Evangelical Christianity that has most uncritically embraced the new Constantinianism. And if that is the church, then what does it mean to let the church be the church in today's America?

That we live in a society that recapitulates the archaic fusion of religion and state in a way unique among modern nations (Japan excepted) is a challenge to all of us, both as Christians and as Americans. This challenge is not new. I think I first experienced it viscerally when John Kennedy was assassinated and the nation experienced three days of utter shock and horror. I thought at the time, "The king is dead; this is not a secular response," even though I participated in it. I think I would probably be in agreement with Stanley if he said: "Now more than ever we need the politics of Jesus, specifically some kind of linkage between the Mennonite and the Catholic traditions." The problem is how do we instantiate such a politics today in a society that seems once again to confuse God and king.

7

Hauerwasian Hooks and the Christian Social Imagination

Critical Reflections from an African Perspective

Emmanuel M. Katongole

My "work" . . . has been an attempt to make connections, to find the hooks, not only between scientists and theologians, but also between philosophy and theology, between the "past" and the "present" of our own lives, between the everyday and God. To discover "hooks" you first have to look and, just as important, you must be prepared to be surprised. Moreover, the endeavor to make connections is never finished because there will always be something else that needs to be said. What was "hooked" at one time can become "unhooked"' at another.

—Stanley Hauerwas[1]

Writing an essay in honor of someone from whom you have learned everything you know about theology and ethics can be a tricky busi-

---

1. Stanley Hauerwas, "Hooks: Random Thoughts by Way of a Response to Griffiths and Ochs," *Modern Theology* 19, no.1 (2003): 90.

ness. Apart from the feeling that such an essay cannot provide any new insights, there is also the fear of embarrassment, in that the essay may just confirm what a bad student one has been. But since for me Stanley Hauerwas has been more than just a mentor, but a wonderful friend, writing this essay is a joyful acknowledgment of the gift that Hauerwas and his work have been. I can find no better way of acknowledging this gift than to remember how it all started, namely, how I got hooked by Hauerwas in the first place. I use the language of being "hooked" because I think that is exactly what happened, given the fact that I was led into Hauerwas's work almost against my will. Moreover, as the epigraph shows, Hauerwas himself has admitted that finding hooks is indeed what his work is all about. And that a Catholic priest from Uganda (one moreover who wanted to be a philosopher) now finds himself a theologian and professor of world Christianity is itself a good example of the type of hook Hauerwas's work makes possible.

I also hope that my story will confirm that to be hooked by Hauerwas is to be unhooked in a number of ways and to find oneself in an odd space—at the margins—of the dominant cultural ways of looking at and dealing with the world. This "unhooking" is what makes Hauerwas a dangerous hook, but also, at least for me, an interesting and exciting one. His work forces me to think about the challenge of theology and ethics not in terms of being relevant to the world, but primarily in terms of the possibilities of new visions, new imaginations of the world. The need for a distinctly Christian social imagination is made particularly urgent today by the recent growth of Christianity in the non-Western world, Africa in particular. Thus, after sketching the story of my initial engagements with Hauerwas, I devote the rest of the essay to a discussion of the importance of such vision and imagination for telling the story of world Christianity, and for assessing the current prospects of Christianity in Africa.

On Being Hooked by Hauerwas

When I won a scholarship to Leuven in the summer of 1991, it was to study philosophy. It was therefore with great reservation that I started reading Stanley Hauerwas's theological essays in the fall of 1992. In a class on analytic philosophy I had just read Harry Frankfurt's small book *The Importance of What We Care About* and had found some of its insights on moral transcendence quite interesting.[2] I was therefore thinking of writing my MA thesis on the topic of moral transcendence

2. Harry G. Frankfurt, *The Importance of What We Care About* (Cambridge: Cambridge University Press, 1988).

in light of some aspects of African culture, and so had gone to ask Professor Frans De Wachter to be my thesis advisor. Although De Wachter thought the topic was potentially interesting, he nevertheless felt that the "African culture" in the title put it beyond his competence as advisor. He suggested that I think of a topic that might be (as he put it) "closer to us." His reply caught me off-guard, for I did not have any other topic on the top of my head, certainly not one that was "closer" to mainstream European philosophy. I had just assumed, given Belgium's historical links with Africa, a topic that had to do with the "African worldview" would not sound so strange at the Katholieke Universiteit Leuven Higher Institute of Philosophy.[3]

Seeing that I was at a loss, De Wachter asked if I knew the work of Stanley Hauerwas, and he remarked casually that Hauerwas seemed to be doing something interesting in the area of ethics. I had never heard of Hauerwas, but that afternoon, sitting at a library computer, I was amazed at the number of essays and books that showed up under his name. Since almost none of these were available at the Institute of Philosophy library, I was forced to make the journey to the department of theology library, where I read as many of Hauerwas's essays as were immediately available.

When I met with De Wachter a few days later, I had made up my mind. Stanley Hauerwas's reflection and writing were indeed interesting and provocative, but they were too "theological" for me. I had come to Leuven to do philosophy, and so for my dissertation I wanted to work on a philosopher, or some topic more recognizably philosophical. De Wachter, however, encouraged me to see that it would perhaps not be a waste of time to discover the "philosophical underpinnings" that sustained Hauerwas's provocative work in Christian ethics. Reluctantly, I followed his recommendation, not sure how or where the writing of an American theologian would lead me in either my PhD ambitions in philosophy, or my more particular interest in African studies.

As I plowed through Hauerwas's work to discover its philosophical underpinnings, I found his style of writing to be extremely engaging, and a great deal of what he said regarding Christian morals reflected my own experience of the moral life. The sense of communal identity; an appreciation of virtue; a respect for tradition and authority; and on the whole, a view of the universe as pervaded with spiritual and symbolic meaning—all Hauerwas notions—were part of the moral heritage

3. It had been, after all, a Belgian White Father missionary, Fr. Placide Tempels, who had inspired the modern discussions about the nature and possibility of African philosophy by his seminal essay in *La philosophie bantoue* (Elizabethville: Lovania, 1945); translated by Rev. Colin King as *Bantu Philosophy* (Paris: Présence africaine, 1969).

that, as an African, I simply took for granted. However, the familiarity I found in Hauerwas's work was also what worried me about what he was trying to do. Given my philosophical background, I had learned to view these experiences of the moral life—stories, practices, traditions, customs—as simply background, mere content to be transcended on the way to the moral and rational point of view. And so, even as I found Hauerwas's account of the moral life true to experience, I felt it was too down-to-earth, too concrete, kind of "tribal."

Then I read Gustafson's critique of Hauerwas's work. Gustafson had noted that Hauerwas's emphasis on narrative could not but result in a form of theological fideism whose social effect would be to force Christians to withdraw from the complexities of public life into a tribal ghetto.[4] I took this charge seriously, for as an African I had learned to be on constant guard against "tribalism," which seemed to be an ever-present reality, and which not only threatened peace and stability in Africa, but also was connected to primitive and backward forms of life. In fact, the whole of my educational background, including the philosophical and theological training in the seminary, was premised on the need, both explicit and implicit, to advance from the bondage of tribal backwardness into the civilization of modernity and the nation-state. I am sure my desire to study philosophy—a discipline that promised to lead to the discovery of the very nature and essence of reality—must itself have been somehow influenced by this conditioning. I was not excited about studying a theologian in the first place; now I became even less enthusiastic about the prospect of studying one that espoused a sectarian and tribalist perspective.

These concerns were part of the considerations I had on my mind when, after the masters thesis, I proposed to shift my focus from Hauerwas to Kant. As far as I was concerned, with the notions of moral character, vision, narrative, and community, I had discovered the philosophical foundations of Hauerwas's work, and the rest, for example, his stress on the church as a community in which these notions operated, were "merely" its theological content.[5] Accordingly, I mentioned to De Wachter that for my PhD research I needed to move on to what I thought of as "the more philosophically challenging" issues of moral rationality in Kant. To be sure, I also believed that since the Kantian tradition provided the ethical impetus behind colonialism and a great deal of the

---

4. James Gustafson, "The Sectarian Temptation: Reflections on Theology, the Church, and the University," *Proceedings of the Catholic Theological Society* 40 (1985): 83–94.

5. Emmanuel Katongole, "The Agent's Perspective: A Study of Stanley Hauerwas' Moral Philosophy" (master's thesis, Higher Institute of Philosophy, K.U. Leuven, June 1993).

modernizing rhetoric in Africa, working on Kant would be a step closer to understanding the challenges that face African societies.

De Wachter, however, insisted that I stay with Hauerwas's work and respond to the critical issues that arise out of a narrative-based account of ethics such as Hauerwas was providing.[6] When in the summer of the same year (1993) I had a chance to meet Hauerwas for the first time, I shared with him a copy of my master's thesis and told him about my Kant proposal. He did not seem impressed. "Emmanuel," he said in his usual half-joking, half-serious manner, "the best way for you to take Kant seriously is to stay clear of him." Still, I was not sure. Matters were, however, decided for me when I returned to Belgium in the fall and learned that I had only two more years of scholarship. I could not embark on a completely new research project. I was stuck with Hauerwas. Now I had no choice but to read closely even those sections of Hauerwas's work that in the master's research I had overlooked or simply glossed over as "mere theological content."

As I found myself in this odd situation of working on a theologian for a PhD in philosophy, I just tried to make the best of it. And so, for the next three and a half years of my stay in Leuven, I shuttled back and forth between the Institute of Philosophy and the theology department libraries. I even enrolled for a part-time master's in religious studies, and was accordingly assigned a desk in the theology library, where I spent a lot of time. My fellow theology students wondered whether I was still a philosopher or if I had finally seen the light and converted to theology. Even though I did not think of what I was doing in terms of conversion, I was not sure that what I was doing counted as interdisciplinary studies either, since Hauerwas's work was never considered part of the theological mainstream. I just tried to make sense of what Hauerwas was saying and in the process found myself unable to fit into the disciplines of philosophy or theology. I was working at their margins, never fully belonging to either discipline.

6. It was only at the formal dinner following my doctoral defense that De Wachter confessed why he desperately wanted me to work on Stanley Hauerwas. He had read a couple of Hauerwas's essays and found his claims both provocative and outrageously wrong. He needed, as he put it, "ammunition with which to counteract the misleading claims" that Hauerwas was making about ethics. He hoped that my research would come up with such ammunition. However, as he confessed at the dinner, working with me had only succeeded in winning him over, if not so much to Hauerwas's side, then at least to an appreciation for the tradition-based nature of the moral life. De Wachter's confession was particularly telling, and confirmed how we quite often find our lives inscribed in narratives not of our making, but in the process of negotiating those limitations, we may discover that our lives and the lives of others have been permanently transformed, hopefully, as in this case, for the better.

I have taken time to tell this story because in many ways it was the experience of being an "outsider" (both to European civilization and to the disciplines of theology and philosophy) that helped me appreciate how deeply political Hauerwas's work was. The formation of Christian character, Hauerwas had noted, does not take place in isolation but is made possible through the stories, symbols, interactions, and everyday practices that are available to one as a member of a community. The church is precisely such a community—a story-formed community— which in turn forms Christians into characters who reflect the story of God. As I struggled to make sense of this claim, I began to realize its truth in relation to other forms of politics. All politics, it was now clear, are based on stories that involve assumptions about the nature of the world and that, in turn, form particular expectations, identities, and characters that reflect those assumptions.[7]

Once I made this connection, I realized how relevant Hauerwas's work was for understanding the social–political challenges in Africa. The discovery came as a wonderful surprise, since one of the major reservations I had in working on an American theologian for my PhD had to do with the fear that such a theologian would not advance my understanding of the challenges facing Africa. But with the connection between stories, identity, and politics, I was now beginning to see that behind the problematic state of politics in Africa are stories. These stories involve assumptions about Africans and African societies, and in turn they shape African societies and Africans into patterns of hopelessness and violence. Accordingly, I was beginning to suspect that the problem of "tribalism" in Africa was not, as I had been made to understand, grounded in the natural or cultural differences of African peoples. It had greatly to do with the stories through which the nation-state politics had imagined and continues to imagine African societies.[8]

At the same time, I was now able to see more clearly the political motivations behind the charges of "tribalism" and "sectarianism" that Gustafson and many others were raising against Hauerwas's work. Apart

7. For a more extensive treatment of the relation between stories and politics, see my *Beyond Universal Reason: The Relation between Religion and Ethics in the Work of Stanley Hauerwas* (Notre Dame, Ind.: University of Notre Dame Press, 2000), 214–51.

8. The case of Rwanda provides a most compelling confirmation of this claim. Much has been written about the genocide of 1994. What is particularly striking in trying to understand this horrific event is how, in light of the hermetic story told by European colonialists, the pre- and later postcolonial state of Rwanda became two different "tribes"—Hutu and Tutsi—united in their animosity toward each other. For an excellent discussion of the role of the hermetic story in the formation of Hutu and Tutsi as political identities, see Mahamood Mamdani, *When Victims Become Killers: Colonialism, Nativism, and the Genocide in Rwanda* (Princeton: Princeton University Press, 2001).

from the fact that these charges rested on questionable philosophical foundations, they arose from a serious concern that the position Hauerwas advances cannot but marginalize the church from the dominant political imagination shaped by the story of Western liberal democracy.[9] But that is precisely what I was finding to be most therapeutic about Hauerwas's work, namely, the invitation to step outside the dominant political imaginations and formations and to realize how the world can and does look different. In fact, in view of this invitation I was beginning to see that the primary challenge of Christian social ethics in Africa was not how or if the church can contribute to securing the ever-illusory promises of democracy, human rights, and development—contributions that assume the political imagination of nation-state politics. The challenge was one of providing different stories, which reflect a different vision of the world and a different way of being in the world. It is this primary interest in political imagination that has continued to shape my own theological preoccupation. What my own experience at the margins of philosophy and theology may have helped to confirm is the fact that the hope and resources for an alternative social imagination are discovered and cultivated not on the back, so to say, but at the margins or within the cracks, of the dominant stories that shape the dominant social–political imaginations.

More recently Hauerwas has provided a more extensive argument in this direction in the context of his 2001 Gifford Lectures. And so, to get a better handle on the political force of Christian convictions, and how these offer a novel way of looking at and being in the world, it might be helpful to capture in brief outline the central argument of *With the Grain of the Universe*.[10]

The Church as Social Interruption

In *With the Grain of the Universe* Hauerwas undertakes to overcome what John Milbank has characterized as Christian theology's "false humility"(16)—the tendency by Christian ethics to allow its social contribution to be shaped and defined by the secular disciplines of political science, economics, and sociology. It is this tendency that gives rise to the project of natural theology, which in effect amounts to an attempt to divorce Christian claims about the world from the concrete prac-

---

9. See Katongole, *Beyond Universal Reason*, 189–213.
10. Stanley Hauerwas, *With the Grain of the Universe: The Church's Witness and Natural Theology* (Grand Rapids, Mich.: Brazos Press, 2001). References to this text will appear parenthetically within the body of my essay.

tices, characters, and stories in which those claims are embodied; such claims can then be displayed as the truth of anyone. In *With the Grain of the Universe*, Hauerwas sets out to show that the project of natural theology is misconceived. Natural theology, he argues, "divorced from a full doctrine of [and practice of] God cannot help but distort the character of God and, accordingly, of the world in which we find ourselves" (15). Simply stated, Hauerwas's response to natural theology is shaped around three interconnected arguments.

First, Hauerwas notes that Christians do in fact make claims about the world. The truth of these claims, however, cannot be separated from training in Christian discipleship and therefore cannot be known unless embodied in faithful lives. Only through such lives is one able to see concretely what it means to conceive the world differently. Witnesses are thus necessary, and Hauerwas uses three crucial witnesses—John Howard Yoder, John Paul II, and Dorothy Day—to advance the argument of *With the Grain of the Universe*.

Second, the fact that claims of truth require embodiment shows that Christian claims about creation, the resurrection, and so on are not simply located within a social reality that is neutral or independently given. Such claims constitute their own unique social reality. Hauerwas quotes Yoder:

> The point that apocalyptic makes is not only that people who wear crowns and who claim to foster justice by the sword are not as strong as they think—true as that is. . . . It is that people who bear crosses are working with the grain of the universe. One does not come to that belief by reducing social process to mechanical and statistical models, nor by winning some of one's battles for the control of one's own corner of the fallen world. One comes to it by sharing the life of those who sing about the Resurrection of the slain Lamb. (17)

Third, this passage makes clear that for those who profess the cross and resurrection of Christ, the world does indeed look different. Accordingly, the decisive social force constituted by belief in the cross and resurrection is not a force that sustains or stabilizes the politics of the day, nor is it one that lends itself to negotiating the world as it is currently defined; rather, the decisive social force of such belief is the formation of unique characters and patterns of life that interrupt the politics of the day. Thus, for Yoder, the life, death, and resurrection of Christ, as the most decisive event in history, calls into existence a people committed to a life of self-giving and nonresistant love (219). Similarly for John Paul II, affirming the truth that the Redeemer of humanity, Jesus Christ, is the center of the universe and of history makes the Christian a potential martyr (227–30).

This brief overview of *With the Grain of the Universe,* sketchy as it is, helps to make obvious the political import of Christian claims. What also becomes evident is that for Hauerwas this political import resides primarily not in recommendations to secure justice, democracy, or peace within liberal politics, but in concrete communities capable of forming patterns of life that reflect a different knowledge and different desires from those formed by nation-state politics. Once this essential political nature of Christian claims is recognized, Christianity offers more than guidelines or assistance for how Christians can cope with the existing social–political realities. It ushers in a new future, a revolutionary future, according to Herbert McCabe, in which "we do not merely see something new but have a new way of seeing; in which something is produced that could not be imagined in the old terms and that changes our whole way of envisaging what has gone before."[11] What the argument of *With the Grain of the Universe* helps confirm is that one comes into contact with this revolutionary future by "sharing the life of those who sing about the Resurrection of the Slain Lamb." In other words, the church does not simply preach about or help to usher in this revolutionary future. The church *is* the revolutionary future, or according to Richard Hays, "God's demonstration plot" of a new future, a new social imagination concretely embodied.[12]

The Next Christendom: A Tale of Two Christianities

Hauerwas has taught me that the challenge of Christian social ethics is primarily one of social imagination. As it turns out, contrary to the initial fears I had about studying the works of an American theologian, this lesson has everything to do with my long-standing interest in the challenges facing Africa. The extent to which these challenges concern social imagination is particularly evident in Philip Jenkins's book *The Next Christendom.*[13]

11. Herbert McCabe, *What Is Ethics All About?* (Washington, D.C.: Corpus Books, 1969), 77. McCabe's observation is part of his extended argument concerning ethics as language. In order to learn to speak a language, one needs to participate in the community in which that language is spoken. If Jesus as the Word is the self-communication of God and the meaning of human history, then in order to learn to speak in this manner one would need to participate in that new society of which Jesus is the harbinger and inaugurator.

12. Richard B. Hays, *The Moral Vision of the New Testament: Community, Cross, New Creation; A Contemporary Introduction to New Testament Ethics* (San Francisco: Harper-Collins, 1996).

13. Philip Jenkins, *The Next Christendom: The Coming of Global Christianity* (Oxford: Oxford University Press, 2002).

Jenkins offers a good indication of the shifts taking place within world Christianity that are helping to make the global South, Africa in particular, the new center of gravity of the Christian faith. While the number of Christians is rapidly shrinking in the global North and West, Jenkins observes, phenomenal growth is taking place in the global South:

> [By] the year 2025, . . . there would be around 2.6 billion Christians, of whom 633 million would live in Africa, 640 in Latin America, and 460 million in Asia. Europe, with 555 million, would have slipped to third place. Africa and Latin America would . . . account for half the Christians on the planet. By 2050, only about one-fifth of the world's 3 billion Christians will be non-Hispanic Whites. (3)

With such and similar projections, Jenkins shows not only that Christianity is experiencing exponential growth in the global South, but that Africa is at the center of this boom. For an African theologian this should be very good news; it confirms that Africa's hour of faith and confidence in the gospel is finally here.[14] In fact, with the growing confidence in the prospects of Christianity in Africa, the Catholics among us can begin to entertain hopes for an African pope.[15]

There are, to be sure, quite a number of aspects, apart from the overwhelming statistical evidence, that one finds instructive in Jenkins's study and that seem to bolster confidence in a southern Christianity. For instance, against a postcolonial sensitivity that tends to dismiss Christianity in the South as the arm of Western imperialism, Jenkins defends the trends shaping southern Christianity as "genuine" Christianity, effected at the intersection of biblical translation and the adaptation to local tradition and thought-patterns (108–24). Jenkins also provides helpful indications of the reasons behind the "success" of Christianity in the South. Specifically, he notes how in the wake of failed politics, the new churches provide functional alternative arrangements for health, welfare, and education (73). As Jenkins notes: "To be a member of an active Christian church today might well bring more tangible benefits than being a citizen of Nigeria or Peru" (76). Thus, according to Jenkins's observation, what we experience in the South is not the usual expectation of a "spiritual" (pie in the sky) gospel, but a confident, fully embodied Christian expression whose influence is reflected in the social, political, and economic spheres of life.

---

14. See, for instance, Kwame Bediako, *Christianity in Africa: The Renewal of a Non-Western Religion* (Maryknoll, N.Y.: Orbis, 1995).

15. For my extended reflection on the chances of an African pope, see "Prospects of Ecclesia in Africa in the Twenty-first Century," *Logos* 4, no. 1 (2001): 178–95.

Although these and many other aspects make *The Next Christendom* an instructive study, I find its underlying assumptions and objectives questionable. The way Jenkins describes both "the Coming of Global Christianity" and its dominant Pentecostal expression in the global South reflects the story of a Christianity that has long given up on the need to interrupt the dominant political imagination and thus to witness to a new future. One of Jenkins's primary assumptions is that of a neat North and South axis around which the story of world Christianity is told, providing for the many contrasts that Jenkins offers between the southern and the northern versions of Christianity. I have no doubt that as a professor of history and religious studies, Jenkins sees his task as descriptive, and that therefore his work simply describes the trends and the world as they are, and not as they *should* look. However, by assuming the categories of "North" and "South" as the lens through which the story of world Christianity is read, he cannot help but underwrite an account of Christianity that simply reflects the existing social, economic, and political constellations. This lens is what gives rise in Jenkins's work to two distinct faces of Christianity that have nothing or very little in common. For instance, in describing the growth of Christianity in the global South, Jenkins notes: "Christianity is thriving wonderfully among the poor and persecuted, while it atrophies among the rich and secure" (220). He also notes that in terms of theological and moral orientation, the members of a southern-dominated church are likely to be more conservative, "stalwartly traditional or even reactionary by the standards of the economically advanced nations" (7). In these and many other contrasts in the book, Jenkins depicts not only the trends shaping Christianity in the global South, but also how radically different this Christianity is from "our" northern version of Christianity.

Jenkins is aware that the social, economic, and cultural differences between the North and the South have contributed to the invisibility of southern Christianity. He notes: "For whatever reason, Southern churches remain almost invisible to Northern observers" (4). My concern is that the use of the categories "North" and "South" as the lens for telling the story of world Christianity cannot but further the distancing of southern Christians from their northern counterparts. This distance is already evident in such examples as the 1998 Lambeth Conference. After the defeat of the statement on homosexuality, primarily with the near-unanimous voice of Asian and African bishops, the famous liberal American bishop John Spong declared that "the African bishops have moved out of animism into a very superstitious kind of Christianity." "I never expected," he noted, "to see the Anglican Communion, which prides itself on the place of reason in faith, descend to this level of irrational Pentecostal hysteria" (121).

Jenkins's own descriptions of Christianity in the South, shaped by the assumptions of modern sociology of religion, betray a similar distancing. He, for instance, notes: "As Southern Christianity continues to *expand* and *mature* it will assuredly develop a wider theological spectrum than at present, and stronger liberal or secularizing tendencies may well emerge" (8, emphasis added). Here and in many other places, the clear indication is that southern Christianity is simply the pale shadow of the more rational forms of Christian expression in the North, and as the former grows, matures, expands (all expressions that Jenkins uses), it will take on a more decisively northern appearance.[16]

It is accordingly obvious that if one uses the current definitions of the world as the lens through which the story of global Christianity is told, northern Christians will find nothing or little to learn from their southern counterparts. In fact, they will tend to see themselves as caught in an irresolvable competition and conflict of interests. There is, Jenkins notes, "increasing tension between what one might call a liberal Northern Reformation and the surging Southern religious revolution. . . . No matter what the terminology, however, an enormous rift seems inevitable."[17] The more, therefore, Christians in the North assume the story of their white, rich, liberal, democratic nations, the more they will view the growth of southern Christianity, which is made up predominantly of poor black or brown Christians, as a worrisome "darkening" of the Christian landscape, and even as a political threat. Jenkins not only describes this threat; he himself assumes it. Accordingly, one of the key aims of Jenkins's study is to draw attention to the "religious revolution" shaping up in the South, and to warn governments in the North about the potential of fanaticism latent in the "Christian Third World." He notes:

> Worldwide, religious trends have the potential to reshape political assumptions in a way that has not been seen since the rise of modern nationalism. While we can imagine a number of possible futures, a worst-case scenario would include a wave of religious conflicts reminiscent of the Middle Ages,

---

16. In his response to Donald Miller's *Emergent Patterns of Congregational Life and Leadership in the Developing World: Personal Reflections from a Research Odyssey* (Durham, N.C.: Duke Divinity School, Pulpit and Pew Research Reports, Winter 2003), Daniel Aleshire, executive director, Association of Theological Schools in the United States and Canada, betrays the same distancing. While describing the growth and dynamism of Christianity in the South as "yet one more face, of which there have been many, and of which there will be many more," he notes, "I am not sure how instructive they are for organized Christianity in North America, with its different history, different culture, and itself the heir of another powerful emergent religious sentiment" (26).

17. Philip Jenkins, "The Next Christianity," *Atlantic Monthly,* October 2002, 54.

a new age of Christian crusades and Muslim jihads. . . . In responding to this prospect, we need at a minimum to ensure that our political leaders and diplomats pay as much attention to religions and to sectarian frontiers as they ever have to the distribution of oilfields. (13)

With this pointed statement of Jenkins's thesis, it becomes clear why as an African theologian I find myself ill at ease within this story of "the Coming of Global Christianity," whose subtext is to warn "our political leaders and diplomats" about the religious revolution in the South.

To be sure, there might be a lot that is worrisome about the trends shaping Christianity in the global South, Africa in particular (see below). I am not sure, however, that the "Christian Third World," as Jenkins calls it, will ferment a new Counter-Reformation, a new Council of Trent,[18] one that will pose the greatest challenge to the "McWorld" (6). What I find particularly disturbing, however, is the fact that the objectives of *The Next Christendom* are to ensure that no such challenge emerges out of global Christianity. That is why not only Christians in the South, but Christians generally should read *The Next Christendom* with a critical eye.

I am suggesting that *The Next Christendom* is bad news for Christians not simply because it assumes the existing North–South dichotomies shaped by the economic and political realities of late capitalism, but because it seeks to secure this current vision of the world against any interruption. In this way, its assumptions and objectives obscure and even resist the possibility of any Christian social interruption. To be sure, Jenkins is aware, as we have seen, that "religious trends have potential to reshape political assumptions and imaginations." But, according to Jenkins, this reshaping is what needs to be resisted. He notes that within the new Christian synthesis taking place in the South there might be many people for whom political loyalties might be secondary to religious beliefs, and "these are the terms in which people [will] define their identities" (11). Moreover, these identities may give rise to supranational affiliations and connections, which in turn give rise to a new cultural reference in which the "Christian world of the South could find unity in common religious beliefs"(11). It is precisely such a prospect that Jenkins finds troubling, for that would mean that in the twenty-first century, "religion [would] replace ideology as the prime animating and destructive force in human affairs, guiding attitudes to political liberty and obligation, concepts of nationhood, and of course, conflicts and wars."[19]

18. Ibid., 64.
19. Ibid., 55.

I doubt that the world Jenkins describes will come to pass, given that the dominant trends shaping Christianity in the South are themselves neatly located within the imagination of nation-state politics (see below). But the fact that Christianity has the potential to give rise to such transnational identities, associations, and communities is what Christians ought to find exciting. Such communities would not only embody a new future beyond the current North–South, rich–poor, liberal–conservative polarization; they might form new identities and visions of life beyond our usual racially colored visions. In noting the shift in world Christianity, Jenkins says that the majority of believers will be neither white, nor European, nor Euro-American and adds that "soon the phrase a 'White Christian' may sound like a curious oxymoron" (3). Although Jenkins means to warn us about this future, I hope it comes to pass, and soon. Of course, I do not mean to suggest that white folks should cease to be Christians; rather, I want to draw attention to the need we have for imagining world Christianity in terms of communities in which such labels as "white," "black," "Northern," "Southern," "African," "American," and so on have ceased to be the primary identities in which we view ourselves and the world.[20] Such Christian communities not only would embody a radical sense of catholicity, but would give rise to a new Christendom in the sense of the *Republica Christiana*—"an overarching unity and a focus of loyalty transcending mere kingdoms or empires"(10). Such radical communities are the bearers of a revolutionary future, one however that reflects God's never-tiring effort of bringing together a new assembly (or *ecclesia*) in which the old identities of Jew, Greek, male, and female have faded in the light of a new loyalty arising out of a common baptism (Gal. 3:27–28).

Such a revolutionary future does not come about by sheer numeric projections. It happens in the form of concrete communities that have learned to view the death and resurrection of Christ as the most decisive event in history, an event that interrupts the story of the McWorld. This interruption embodies an alternative vision of the world and, accordingly, new habits and patterns of living within it. To the extent that *The Next Christendom* both assumes the current social–economic realities and seeks to protect them from any such interruption, I find it disappointing. I find equally problematic, and for the same reason, the dominant trends of Pentecostalism shaping Christianity in the global South, particularly in Africa.

20. For a more elaborate discussion on this topic in the context of Christian worship, see my "Beyond Racial Reconciliation," in *The Blackwell Companion to Christian Ethics*, ed. Stanley Hauerwas and Sam Walls (Malden, Mass.: Blackwell, 2004), 68–81.

Pentecostalism, Modernity, and Political Imagination in Africa

In *The Next Christendom*, Jenkins rightly notes that Pentecostalism is fast becoming the dominant Christian expression in Africa.[21] Pentecostalism is a wide and complex phenomenon that defies any easy generalization. This is particularly true of Pentecostalism in Africa. There are, however, a number of elements—the call to be "born again," emphasis on the gifts of the Holy Spirit, healing, expectation of miracles, signs and wonders, charismatic expression, and so on—that cut across many Pentecostal churches in Africa. The more closely one examines these elements, as well as the influence they exercise within the mainline churches, the more one discovers that far from providing a critical challenge to the dominant political culture, these elements simply locate Pentecostalism at its center. That is why, at least in terms of political imagination, the "Christian Third World" is not markedly different from its northern counterpart.

This conclusion may sound surprising in light of Jenkins's work, especially since, as I noted above, one of the goals of Jenkins's study is to display how radically different the emergent forms of Christianity in the global South are from the northern version of Christianity. In particular, he notes the medieval outlook and premodern sensibilities that characterize the churches in the South. The new churches, Jenkins notes,

> preach deep personal faith and communal orthodoxy, mysticism and puritanism, all founded on clear scriptural authority. They preach messages that, to a Westerner, appear simplistically charismatic, visionary, and apocalyptic. In this thought-world, prophecy is an everyday reality, while faith-healing, exorcism, and dream-visions are all basic components of religious sensibility. For better or worse, the dominant churches of the future could have much in common with those of medieval or early modern European times. On present evidence, a Southernized Christian future should be distinctly conservative. (8)

Given such a description, it may come as a surprise to realize that for many Africans Pentecostalism nevertheless represents a form of modernity. This is an important observation that helps to confirm that in many ways the Pentecostal synthesis in Africa locates itself within the dominant political imagination in Africa and quite often reproduces its

21. Jenkins, *The Next Christendom*, 7, 67, passim. See also Miller, *Emergent Patterns;* Mika Vähäkangas and Andrew A. Kyomo, eds., *Charismatic Renewal in Africa: A Challenge for African Christianity* (Nairobi: Acton, 2003); Paul Gifford, *African Christianity: Its Public Role* (Bloomington: Indiana University Press, 1998).

patterns, more strikingly, its modernity, as well as its illusory promises of success and prosperity.

It would be productive to engage a full-scale exploration of the imagination that sustains nation-state politics in Africa, but it is sufficient here to note that since its introduction, the nation-state and its politics have been viewed as the purveyor of modernity in a continent otherwise stuck in primitive cultural, social, and economic conditions. Founded on the colonial imagination of Africa as a Dark Continent, the modernity of the nation-state has involved the need to break from Africa's primitive past in order to secure civilization and progress, which nation-statehood represented. In many ways the attempt to secure modernism, progress, and development is part of the rhetoric of postcolonial African leaders, as with each new developmental theory they promise to lead their countries from backwardness (and thus poverty) to modernization (and thus prosperity). Accordingly, the need to "break from the past" so as to be able to "progress" is the subtext that drives nation-state politics in Africa.

What is also noteworthy about nation-state politics in Africa is the fact that African politics, built on the need to break with the past, tends to understand itself and to operate not in terms of enduring structures, but in terms of serving the needs of the Now. This politics of the present is perhaps not surprising since the nation-state's own existence is never fully secured (witness the endless number of coups); it is also simply pragmatic insofar as the requirements for what Africa needs to do in order to progress keep shifting. And so, in its attempts to be relevant to the Now, nation-state politics has to reinvent itself constantly through ever-new ideologies, programs, and prescriptions—modernization theory, liberalization, privatization, globalization, structural adjustment, new world order, and so on.[22] In this respect, the politics of a modern Africa not only requires constant adjustability, but also forms a culture in which the desire to escape the past, the need to be relevant to the present, and the illusory promises of instant progress and prosperity are at home.

African Pentecostalism shares this imagination; moreover, it advances it, which might be one reason for its broad appeal and popularity. In her study of Pentecostalism in Ghana, Birgit Meyer has rightly noted that the notion of rupture forms the key to understanding Ghananian Pentecostalism.[23] In this connection, Meyer notes that Pentecostal dis-

22. See my "African Renaissance and the Challenge of Narrative Theology in Africa," in *African Theology Today,* ed. E. Katongole (Scranton: University of Scranton Press, 2002), 207–20.

23. Birgit Meyer, "Make a Complete Break with the Past: Memory and Post-Colonial Modernity in Ghanaian Pentecostalist Discourse," *Journal of Religion in Africa* 28, no. 3 (1998): 316–49.

course about the rupture allows the born-again Christian to approach the ideal modern, individual identity:

> The appeal to "time" as an epistemological category enables pentecostalists to draw a rift between "us"' and "them," "now" and "then," "modern" and "traditional" and . . . takes up the language of modernity as it spoke to Africans through colonialization, missionization and, after Independence, modernization theory. Indeed, a clear analogy exists between the pentecostalist—and, for that matter, the Protestant in general—conceptualization of conversation in terms of a rupture with the past and modernity's self definition in terms of progress and continuous renewal.[24]

The analogy between Pentecostalism and modernity's language is not new. In fact, as Meyer notes, even within the missionary churches, Protestantism was in many ways "the flip side of becoming modern in social, economic, and political aspects."[25] The missionary churches, however, maintained that conversion implied crossing the boundary between heathenism and Christianity once and for all; Pentecostal churches, on the contrary, continually dwell on this boundary.[26] In this way, the past is represented as an autonomous entity that is able to haunt a person even after he or she has been born again. It is thus important to keep on fighting Satan, who is believed to be operating in the guise of traditional spirits and practices. The past is a source of personal disturbance; it haunts people and stands in their way of making progress.

Meyer's analysis is helpful in understanding the appeal of Pentecostalism in Africa. First, it helps to explain the elaborate discourse on the devil and demons within African Pentecostalism, as well as the related focus on healing and "deliverance" as practices through which the demonic past is exorcised. Deliverance sessions and rituals lead people to realize that they are in the grip of the past (represented as a fearful thing out of control) and that they can gain control over their individual lives—and indeed become modern individuals—only by untying all the links connecting them with their past.[27] Thus, healing is popular within Pentecostalism not just because it relates to the African primal worldview, nor because it answers a real need in "communities of affliction," which have no ready access to modern medicine.[28] Pentecostal healing also fits

24. Ibid., 317.
25. Ibid.
26. Ibid., 322.
27. Ibid., 339.
28. On healing in Pentecostalism and its relation to the African primal worldview, see Cephas Omenyo, "Charismatization of the Mainline Churches in Ghana," in Vähäkangas

in well with, and at the same time helps advance, the political–cultural expectation of the need to "break with the past."

Meyer's analysis also helps us understand another key aspect that the Pentecostal–Evangelical synthesis shares with the dominant political culture in Africa, namely, the preoccupation with the Now. In this respect, as she rightly points out, the goal of deliverance is for the born-again "to be able to locate [himself] in the present through a process of continuous renewal. . . . Freedom is imagined to be achieved at the expense of history, by destroying all links with 'the past.'"[29] If traditional theology, at least the Catholic version of it, understands being saved as a process, one moreover whose goal was to reconstitute the believer by making him or her part of a unique community (the church) grounded in a long history, the aim of Pentecostal deliverance is to make available the benefits of salvation in the present. As Meyer notes: "The new identity of the born-again Christian is not simply built on memory as such, but on the rejection of all the links revealed by it. This new identity does not emphasize social ties, but rather the independent, modern individual who does not need to find positive roots in 'the past' in order to be guided on the way towards the future" (339–40). Accordingly, a very thin ecclesiology characterizes much of the emergent Pentecostal–Evangelical Christianity. Jessi Mugambi makes this point clearly:

> All that the prospective proselyte is expected to do is to accept the word . . . and "instant salvation" will be dispensed. The "fast food," "quick fix" culture is integral to these evangelistic campaigns. There is no ecclesial obligation on the part of the preachers to nurture the novices in the new faith. There are no ecclesial structures for the new proselytes to join. . . . This casual approach to pastoral care leads to shallow ecclesiology, with neither tradition nor social structure.[30]

This shallow or thin ecclesiology is part and parcel of the Pentecostal emphasis on breaking with past. This emphasis is also related to another key popular doctrine within African Pentecostalism, namely, the theme of "blessings," which is characterized in part by the language

---

and Kyomo, *Charismatic Renewal in Africa*, 23. On "communities of affliction," see Laurenti Magesa, "Charismatic Movements as 'Communities of Affliction,'" in Vähäkangas and Kyomo, *Charismatic Renewal in Africa*, 30. Magesa describes the various charismatic movements and groups in Africa as communities of affliction because, "by and large, charismatic movements have arisen out of a drastically changed social, economic, religious, moral and spiritual order, an order that has happened to make very many people uncertain, unsettled, and threatened in their lives at all those levels."

29. Meyer, "Make a Complete Break," 329.

30. Jessi Mugambi, "Evangelistic and Charismatic Initiative in Post-Colonial Africa," in Vähäkangas and Kyomo, *Charismatic Renewal in Africa*, 124.

of signs, wonders, and miracles and is associated with the "prosperity gospel." The relation between Pentecostalism and the prosperity gospel is complex and requires a full study of its own. I do, however, find David Maxwell's analysis of the two doctrines—the doctrine of the Spirit of poverty, and the doctrine of talents—helpful in understanding why the prosperity gospel fits easily with the expectation of "being delivered from the past."[31] With the doctrine of the Spirit of poverty, Maxwell notes, preachers are able to explain poverty in terms of bondage with the past, from which one needs to be delivered.[32] With the doctrine of talents, they exhort the born-again to give since it is only when they invest their talents with God that they can expect God to ensure their own accumulation.

I have taken time to draw attention to Meyer's as well as Maxwell's essays because they help to highlight the fact that the notions and categories in which Pentecostal Christianity trades—deliverance from the past, a focus on immediacy, promises of success and prosperity—are not new. In fact, these elements form the standard cultural expectation that nation-state modernities have formed in Africa. Rather than providing a way to challenge these expectations, Pentecostalism reinvents them and makes them available in the form of a dominant religious spirituality of being born again.

Nowhere is this repackaging of nation-state modernism more evident than in Reinhard Bonnke's "Christ for All Nations" crusades, which attract hundreds of thousands of participants across Africa.[33] The crusades, which in Bonnke's own words serve as a sort of "Holy Spirit Evangelism in Demonstration,"[34] are characterized by nightlong sessions of prayer and healing, interspersed with Bonnke's charismatic preaching. In his sermons, Bonnke expounds his popular theme—Africa shall be/is being saved—and offers promises of deliverance, miracles, and blessings as confirmation. To be sure, Bonnke is not the only evangelist who constantly revisits these themes, which reflect the influence of the prosperity gospel. As Gifford and others have noted, the prosperity gospel characterizes

31. See David Maxwell, "Delivered from the Spirit of Poverty? Pentecostalism, Prosperity, and Modernity in Zimbabwe," *Journal of Religion in Africa* 28, no. 3 (1998): 350–73.

32. The teaching can be summarized as follows: "Africans are poor, not because of structural injustice, but because of a spirit of poverty. Even though they are born again, only their soul has in fact been redeemed. Ancestral spirits, along with their pernicious influence, remain in their blood. These ancestors were social and economic failures during their own lifetimes. Misfortune is passed from generation to generation via demonic ancestral spirits." See Maxwell, "Delivered from the Spirit of Poverty," 358.

33. See http://www.cfan.org.

34. Paul Gifford, "Africa Shall Be Saved: An Appraisal of Reinhard Bonnke's Pan-African Crusade," *Journal of Religion in Africa* 17, no. 1 (1987): 64.

many of the charismatic churches in Africa.[35] Bonnke simply represents a strikingly obvious example. In light of the foregoing discussion, it is easy to see how the version of Christianity that makes Bonnke and similar charismatic preachers popular in Africa is one that promises a "redemptive uplift" that simply reflects the aspirations of a modern, prosperous Africa.[36] The Jesus one meets in Bonnke's crusades is not a Jesus who questions and challenges the social and political structures of the time, but one who helps the Christian to be among those who benefit from these structures. This Jesus is a supernatural wonder-worker whose death has won (once and for all) the blessings that those who are born again enjoy; such blessings allow the recipients to become successful in a world shaped by the postcolonial carriers of modernity.

Once the matter has been put in this way, it becomes clear that Pentecostalism is not only helping to make Christianity a dominant cultural force in Africa; it is doing so by making Christianity "relevant" to the real-life issues and needs of believers in an African social–cultural milieu. It is, accordingly, misleading to refer to this Pentecostal–Evangelical synthesis as a form of "liberation theology."[37] On the contrary, the words of a Latin American theologian are a more apt description of the dynamics at work in African Pentecostalism. Asked about the high profile of Pentecostalism in Latin America, the theologian is quoted as saying: "Liberation theology opted for the poor, but the poor opted for Pentecostalism."[38] In many ways, this observation is true of Pentecostalism in Africa. Moreover, the remark not only highlights the current popularity of Pentecostalism but also entails a critical observation, namely, that whereas liberation theology tends to challenge, evaluate, and question the economic and political systems that render many people poor, no such possibility exists within Pentecostalism. Instead, here born-again Christians are encouraged to be among those who benefit from the economic and political order. But this means that even if Pentecostalism purportedly stays clear of any direct political involvement, it remains deeply and "dangerously" political. Gifford is thus right when he says of Pentecostalism:

> By focusing so narrowly on supernatural causes it diverts attention from the economic or political causes of so much reality—it hardly encourages critical analyses of the economic interests or forces shaping societies. With its emphasis on personal healing, it diverts attention from social ills that are crying out for remedy. Its stress on human wickedness and

35. Paul Gifford, *African Christianity: Its Public Role* (Bloomington: Indiana University Press, 1988), 39–44, passim.

36. Maxwell, "Delivered from the Spirit of Poverty," 354.

37. Omenyo, "Charismatization," 23.

38. Miller, *Emergent Patterns*, 6.

the "fallen" nature of "the world" is no incentive to social, economic or constitutional reform. By emphasizing personal morality so exclusively, it all but eliminates any interest in systemic or institutionalized injustice. By making everything so simple, it distracts attention from the very real contradictions in the lives of so many in [South] Africa.[39]

There are, no doubt, a number of positive aspects that the Pentecostal–Evangelical synthesis contributes to African Christianity—the lively services; a renewed interest in Scripture; the element of personal transformation; the nurturing of new ministries and leadership skills, particularly among the youth.[40] I do not wish to give an overly negative characterization of Pentecostalism in Africa. I simply want to highlight how, even with these positive elements, Pentecostalism locates itself within the political imagination shaped by nation-state modernities and thus fails to offer an alternative vision of society and human flourishing. This failure is alarming because once African Christianity in the form of the Pentecostal appeal is hooked onto the nation-state imagination and its illusory promises of prosperity, it will never have either the resources or the critical distance to challenge the violence and corruption inherent in African politics. On the contrary, as many indications suggest, once this political imagination and culture is assumed, the churches themselves take on the same patterns of violence, corruption, and "culture of eating" that characterize politics in Africa.[41]

Narrative Realism and the Christian Social Imagination

How then do we go on from here? We can accept the world as it is and try to provide ways in which Christianity can be relevant to such a

39. Gifford, "Africa Shall Be Saved," 86.

40. Even the fact that in a country like Uganda, Christian ministries constitute the single biggest employer (Gifford, *African Christianity*, 177) should be taken seriously in terms of the promises and challenges it provides for Christian social imagination. Overall, Miller's *Emergent Patterns* (1–24) provides one of the most positive assessments of the prospects of the Pentecostal–Evangelical synthesis in the developing world.

41. In *African Christianity*, Gifford provides ample evidence of this violence and corruption in relation to Christianity in Ghana, Uganda, Zambia, and Cameroon. The case of Zambia is particularly telling. The irony is that President Chiluba's attempt to declare Zambia a Christian state created a situation in which the economic realities of Zambia's political world came to be nicely reflected and reproduced within the Christian churches. See Gifford, *African Christianity*, 181–245. For my extended argument on nation-state performance on the church, see "Mission and Social Formation: Searching for an Alternative to King Leopold's Ghost," in Katongole, *African Theology Today*, 121–46. See also my "Kannungu and the Movement for the Restoration of the Ten Commandments of God in Uganda: A Challenge for Christian Social Imagination," *Logos* 6, no. 3 (2003): 108–43.

world. This is one form of realism, which accepts as given the realities
of the McWorld and of a postcolonial Africa and seeks to shape Christianity within these realities. This is the kind of realism that is assumed
both within Jenkins's *The Next Christendom* and within the dominant
Pentecostal–Evangelical synthesis shaping up in Africa. Although this
realism might appear "successful" in terms of statistical growth and
cultural relevancy, its visions of the world and of human flourishing
reflect little more than the dominant economic and political forces of
the day. We do not, however, have to accept this realism. In fact, we
can look to a different kind of realism, one that acknowledges that the
world, as it is, is the product of stories. Stories shape not just a vision
of the world, but concrete expectations and identities within the world.
Different stories do, therefore, shape different worlds. Accordingly, Christian stories and beliefs shape a unique world. It is this realism that
Hauerwas's work has been inviting Christians to take seriously as the
task for Christian social imagination. Even though my discussion here
has been theoretical, this form of realism is itself concrete. As Stanley
Hauerwas has shown, this realism exists in the form of concrete communities—churches—capable of forming visions, habits, and lives that
betray the imagination of a God bent on creating and re-creating the
world in a new fashion through the death and resurrection of his own
Son. Those who tell this story and "sing about the resurrection of the
slain Lamb," therefore, are the bearers of this new, revolutionary future.
Since I have been hooked by this type of realism, I expect that the story
of global Christianity cannot but be about such communities, drawn
from across the nations. I expect also that the focus of such a story
will be to highlight the signs, postures, and everyday witness by which
the communities called church are able to interrupt the reality of the
McWorld or of a postcolonial Africa.

8

Christian Civilization*

Robert W. Jenson

An Emperor's Plea

The time came when the Roman Empire, and the civilization of which the empire was self-consciously the guardian, needed the Christians. The emperor called to the bishops: "Come over to the palace and help us!"

Did Constantine believe the Christians' gospel? Or did he simply realize that the empire now held no other source of morale? Did he see the bishops as pastors also for him? Or were they only a possible cadre of administrators who might be less devoted to their own *libidines dominandi* than were those in place? Current scholarship leans to the more charitable view. Anyway, who but the Spirit knows such things about

---

*This paper is written in Stanley Hauerwas's honor. We have approved of one another for decades. At the same time, it has always been clear that we disagreed about something. Yet I, anyway, have never been sure quite what that was. Stan is a pacifist; I wish I could be. But what exactly is the difference even there? Therefore I thought I would write—somewhat off the top of my head—on a theme closely interwoven with Stanley's concerns, yet different from any of them, and see what he thought of it.

153

any human heart? And what difference does it make—except of course to the Spirit and Constantine?

The call had been a long time coming. The persecutions had begun with Nero and continued on and off for about two hundred and sixty years, longer than the United States has existed. There had been more than enough time to harden what must be called the foundational form of the church within the empire and of the churches descended from that church: a suspect minority network, sometimes tolerated and sometimes not, devoted for very salvation's sake to her own faith and discipline, and with little opportunity or aspiration to mold the other cultures around her. If that defines a "sect," then the church was a sect, and until Western Christianity disappears altogether—whether at the eschaton or by sinking giggling into the sea of unbelief—sectarianism will remain its foundation.

But what were the bishops, blinking in the unaccustomed approbation, now to do? As with Constantine, the question is not about their motivations, which we may without further investigation be sure were mixed. How, as a matter of moral fact, were they to respond? Saying "No" might have put their necks in jeopardy again, but they were used to that. But could charity have refused the empire's call for help? The call of all those peoples who no longer knew their right hands from their left? For my part, I think not.

Anyway, the bishops said "Yes." They expanded their pastoral care to include the new civil function—and then version—of Christianity. It soon became politically and economically advantageous to be Christian. Stubborn pagans like the old Roman senatorial class found themselves regarded as unprogressive—as horrid a thought then as now. And the predictable happened.

Floods of dubious converts first required more centralized and formalized systems of catechization and penance and then swamped them. Church discipline and state law converged, of course to the detriment of the former. Folk could no longer be sure that they were Christians—do I believe or do I just go to church because I was born in Hippo?[1] Deadly riots had regularly broken out in the empire over matters of general concern; now that points of doctrine were matters of general concern, they broke out about doctrine too, sometimes with organized squads of monks as shock troops. Magnificent liturgies and theologies appeared. Christendom had come into being.

---

1. The question is not made up; a motive of St. Augustine's theology of grace was pastoral care for a generation of believers who looked back at the previous generation and could find in their own lives no such evidences of faithfulness as persecution imposed upon this earlier generation.

There are those who regard "the Constantinian settlement" as a fall of the church, and Christendom as an exile. There are others who celebrate the first centuries of Christendom and/or its middle centuries at Paris and Oxford as golden ages. For my part, I lean both ways, depending. Writing, for example, on sacramentology, I, like every other alumnus of the liturgical movement, take the fourth-century liturgies as normative; or lamenting our sad ecclesial state, I invoke the ecumenical councils as what my church's assemblies should be like and are not. But then, contemplating the dismantling of Christendom that has occupied my whole life, I wish God would hurry up. And attending service, I often long for what Justin the Martyr described as a Sunday's doings in AD 150.

Then High Culture

Meanwhile, within this new order, something enabled by it but nevertheless distinct from it was happening: the Christian community was creating a new high culture. To be sure, the church had always been a culture. By a definition that seems plausible, a culture is a group of deliberate human practices and artifacts that mutually and independently of the momentary intents of their users make a functioning system of signs. The church—with her strikingly odd meal and bath, with her particularist holy writings, eccentric forms of leadership and countercultural discipline, and with a hundred other distinctive gestures and habits—of course always fit this definition. But she had not had high culture, that is, distinctive cultural practices cultivated not only in their communal functions but also for their own value.

But then, for example, Rome one day put up a triumphal arch for Constantine. Always frugal, the Romans reused some old carvings for the lower courses of the arch. They commissioned new work for other courses. The contrast of styles is truly startling. The old figures were made to be looked at, and even in their recycled state do indeed look very nice; the new ones stare back at you, indeed anticipate your gaze, and want to communicate. There were to be twelve centuries of Christian painting and sculpture.[2]

At the end of the fourth century, a Roman official named Prudentius retired to his estates, which was a very proper Roman thing to do.[3] He

2. Followed by brief brilliant periods of modern and then of modernist art, followed by nothing.
3. I owe appreciation of Prudentius's place in history to a lecture by Robert Lewis Wilken given at the Center of Theological Inquiry and due shortly to appear in the center's series of published public lectures.

was a Christian and went there to tend his soul, which was a proper Christian thing to do. But he did not found a little community for prayer, though no doubt he prayed. He did not sell all he had and give to the poor, though no doubt he was generous. What did he do? He wrote poetry, lots of it, explicitly Christian and deliberately high-style poetry, very little of it suitable for liturgy. No one had done that before, but many who followed would.

All cult is of course drama, indeed is drama's originating form. Thus also the liturgies of the church had always been dramatic in structure. But so far as we know, the Christians before Christendom had not bothered much about such things as the prosody of the scripts, or the appearance of the costumes or props—what sort of cups did they use for the wine?—or the sets or choreography. Now their dramas became self-conscious as drama, though not of course under that label, and a new and distinctive dramaturgy developed. The plates and cups and books and identifying costumes and processions were *cultivated*. Treatises would be written that were effectively drama criticism of the Eucharist.

As the liturgical movement used to say, church buildings are there to keep the rain off the liturgy. When these could be purpose-built, various forms appeared. Constantine adapted the basilica, that is, the utilitarian Roman meeting space, and built basilican churches where he thought it would help his agenda. Sometimes Christians took over abandoned pagan temples and filled in between the columns of the outermost row to make an enclosed space, thus by the by creating another form of Christian building. Christian gatherings around the relics of martyrs could use buildings much like the structures the Romans put up around tombs they expected to be visited, so that centralized rather than longitudinal places of worship were also built. From the play of these forms—and of course under many other influences—a new architecture developed. It would not be long before Justinian would stand within an unprecedented achievement of art and engineering and cry, "I have surpassed you, O Solomon!"—and if the cry is legend, the building is not and must be seen to be appreciated.

I could go on—or anyway someone who knows more than I could go on—for there are jurisprudence and medicine and civic ceremonial and a hundred things that could be noted. But perhaps more is not needed.

And Then the Barbarians

Then the barbarians came. Barbarians have invaded civilized areas since there have been civilized areas. One way or another, the same thing has usually happened: contact with civilization eventually inspires desire not just for booty but for things that cannot be carted off but have to be learned or imitated, for an elegant life and for beautiful language and impressive buildings and for operas and circuses. Even if they decimate their victims and their works, the barbarians sooner or later are civilized by the remnant.

This time becoming civilized included becoming Christian. Thus there came to be not only a Christian culture within the remains of the old civilized empire, but a Christian civilization. When they took to calling the new barbarian empire that Charlemagne had built "Holy," it was because it aspired to be just that. In the vulgate of England, "like a Christian" meant "like a civilized human being" until well into the nineteenth century. Again one could go on.

We live during the final sack of that civilization. Notoriously, the barbarians have this time come from within, so that they are not civilized by what they destroy; they are barbarians not by lack of the good things but by "nostalgia for the muck." Perhaps Christian civilization always carried some seed of its own dissolution; I will return briefly to that point. In any case, Christian civilization is at an end, and we thus have the dubious privilege of looking back at it—dubious because we still belong ineluctably to it. And therewith we have the possibility and perhaps the duty of asking: "How shall we understand this incident in the church's history?"

The Warrant for Christian High Culture

Is there something within the structure of the gospel, and so of the gospel's community, that makes the creation of a Christian civilization possible? Certainly there is nothing in the gospel that makes such creation *mandatory;* the Western church thrived for centuries without any such thing, and nothing comparable has yet happened in Africa or Asia.

If there is nothing in the gospel that makes Christian civilization possible, then of course the making of such a civilization, whatever its benefits by the way, could be enabled only by some perversion of the gospel. Then Christian civilization would have to be seen as a sort of embodied heresy, however beneficent its side effects. In these days of disillusion, some say it was just that.

To the contrary, however, I want here to make an experimental and sketchy argument for the theological possibility of Christian civilization. There are two steps to be surmounted. First, I must show that the church has some reason to *cultivate* her culture, to create a high culture. Second, I must argue that, at least at some historical junctures, the church can have reason to share this culture beyond her borders, to be the culture of a civilization.

A problem with the second step should already be noted. The church must always know and show forth that she is one thing and the world is another, which includes that she is one thing and any civilization is another. When the church is one culture and the surrounding civilization is another, the cultural difference is a part of the distinction between church and world; and since cultural differences are not easily overlooked, neither is the difference between church and civilization. When the church and the surrounding civilization are the same culture, the distinction between church and world becomes sociologically much more precarious. Among other things, pastoral supervision of baptism comes to bear an immense—perhaps impossible—burden.

So for that first step: the church has a stake in a high version of her culture. To surmount it, we need further definition of culture. Modern reflections provide three definitions of "culture," which I will treat as three unpackings of one concept. First, a culture is that part of a group's mutual behavior that is maintained by teaching rather than by genes and physical ecology alone. Second, a culture is that part of a group's mutual behavior that can be abstracted from those doing the behaving, as a mutually constituting system of signs. Third, a culture is what a group does with nature as presented to it.

Let me then propose that a "high" culture is simply one version of a group's culture, a version that has been *carried further;* it is that culture intensified. If this definition is accepted, a sense of "high" can be fitted to each of the above definitions.

A culture is what a group does to transform nature. Its high version will then be constituted by doing more of this work. Thus, for example, Western music derives its penchant for a beat from dance, and one archetype of dance is sexual intercourse, the beat of which thus permeates our music. The beat of rock modifies the sexual beat very little (I well remember the first time Blanche and I, as house parents, watched adolescent girls watching Elvis Presley on TV); the beat of, say, a minuet is a more allusive mimesis, which at once sustains the reference and delightfully veils its character; the polyrhythms of the last generation of jazz drummers went a step further into subtlety; and *The Rite of Spring* plays one blatant musical orgasm over another, just so to create an immensely subtle, rhythmic complex, transforming fertility-stomping—already a cultural transformation of its prototype—into dance requiring the most severe training. Sophisticated rhythm is not less the working-over of nature's sexual beat than is rock; it just works it over *more,* to make it tricky and more subtly evocative.

A culture is a system of signs. Its higher versions will then have syntax and semantic possibilities that make a more complicated web of mutual reference and deference. Those disposing of, for example, higher linguistic culture will be able to say, "On the other hand I would have thought . . . ," rather than just "Wrong!"—which is not to deny that "Wrong!" would often be preferable. Those who lament "elite discourses" should try sometime to explain what an "elite discourse" *is* to freshmen lacking such a thing.

A culture is that part of a group's behavior that can be transmitted only by teaching. Its higher versions will then be the ones that take longer to teach and learn. For example, it took Velázquez long study before he knew how to compose a group portrait, and further study to prepare each new commission; and it takes the viewer almost as long to see Velázquez's work well enough to see why one should bother to see it—to be sure, persons of the sort who used to be revered as connoisseurs are quicker at this, but becoming a connoisseur in the first place takes the longest study of all. It takes little instruction to hang a urinal on the wall, and exactly none to get the point, there not being any—which is why Duchamp did it, but that is another topic.

So how about the church's culture? My suggestion is that the church indeed has a stake in the higher versions of its culture. Let it not be objected that according to Paul few of this world's cultivated are chosen. What Paul's converts were chosen *for* was a structure of mysteries that they could, in his view, appropriate only step by long and arduous step, under continuous training. For "the mature" he had a wisdom not to be reached from any peak of this world, and then within the church only by a progress of guided maturation. I could perhaps simply invoke Paul to the Corinthians at this point, and rest my case. But we will go on.

Consider the matter of teaching and learning. One cannot be born into the church; one can only be inducted into it. Therefore the convert has no antecedent access to the culture she is taking on: a whole new and at many points far from obvious system of signs must be conveyed by sheer teaching—when the church was more aware of this, months of discipline were regarded as just enough for a decent start. If you can teach previously clueless inquirers to participate in some "service of worship" in a week or two, the service is merely thereby unmasked as dubiously Christian. The baptized face a new culture of the church like a mountain in front of them, which they will be climbing till they die. Where the convert does not face such challenge, one must ask if it is the church he is entering.

As for the work to be done on nature, according to Scripture the needed work is nothing less than new creation. To be sure, we cannot ourselves so work on created nature as to achieve the new creation.

But the church's culture can very well be prayer for and anticipation of new creation's possibility, by being as much its own specific culture as it can manage.

What makes lower versions of the church's culture low is that too little work has been done on the nature in them; they embody too little longing for the ultimate cultural action of new creation. Bach shaped songs and dance forms to a sophisticated, even scholastic eschatology, and his work took time; the artisans who made the old cathedrals into liturgies in stone, paint, and glass did the same in their own way. Publishers churning out ditties for the youth choir, or commissioning cartoons for a Sunday school series, rarely dedicate time so richly.

Finally, as to the church's system of signs, it may be objected that the gospel is simple. Should the gospel not then be communicable within a simple web of signs? Well—"Yes" and "No." "Jesus is risen" is indeed the gospel, and a very simple sentence. Moreover, saints of limited linguistic means do hear, understand, and live by it, regularly more faithfully than, those with more resource.

But believers who can do it are commanded to move from hearing the gospel to speaking it—or from viewing it to painting it and so on. Then the necessary culture abruptly ceases to be so simple. When I tell someone that Jesus is risen, what if she asks what "risen" means? It will then do no good to repeat the sentence; I must be able to move from the straightforward predication to interpretation and explanation. Now I must be able to negotiate the complex sign-web of the Old Testament, within which alone "risen" makes sense; be able to negotiate whatever sign-web the inquirer antecedently inhabits, within which alone she can for the moment construe sense; and all along be devising ways to knit these webs together. Thus if, for example, we both are Western, answering the simple query will enmesh me in the whole system of signs we call Western theology, arguably theoretical physics' one competitor in subtlety and ramification.

There is strictly theological reason for all this. The church exists to worship and proclaim the one true, that is, triune, God. In that the triune God is Father, Son, and Spirit in specific communication and specific mutual action, he is in himself a culture, and then of course an infinitely ramifying, that is, high, culture. Let us see this, and its consequences for the church, yet again through those definitions.

A culture is action to transform nature. The triune God has no nature antecedent to the mutual action of Father, Son, and Spirit. What it is to be God is given in the Father's eternal begetting of the Son and enlivening through the Spirit, in the Spirit's eternal liberating of the Father and the Son for one another, in the Son's eternal self-giving to the Father in the Spirit. Thus the triune God is nothing *but* culture, and just so is infinite culture, culture setting nature and transforming it and just so setting nature and so on in an eternal act.

A human culture is oriented to the triune God insofar as it is restless to find a home in him; which is to say, a human culture is oriented to the triune God insofar as it strives to conform to the sheer culture that God is, strives to be as much culture as finite and sinful persons can manage. This striving is true of all cultures; it is, indeed, because God is a high culture that there is human culture at all, and the West's current revolt against its high culture is an epiphenomenon of its revolt against God. The church's culture, however, is commanded to shape itself as deliberate yearning for the culture God is.

A culture is a mutually determining web of signs. By classic doctrine, a "person" of the triune God is a "subsistent relation." That is, there is nothing to any one of the three prior to or apart from his special reference to the other two, apart from "begetting" or "being begotten" or "proceeding." In the present context, we may translate this doctrine: each of the three is a sign of the other two, and is actual at all, to be that sign, only in that he is, antecedently and in turn, signed by the other two. Thus there is no end to the variety and multiplicity of mutual reference within God—Derrida's doctrine that a culture's signs refer only to each other, and that endlessly, is pretty obviously false about human languages, but fits God quite well.

The church will be perfected as it is "deified." In this context, we may say that the church's web of signs will be perfected as it meshes with the web that God is. Our words will never suit the Father as *the* Word does, but they will eternally be brought more closely into that discourse. The church is thus mandated to set its mind on the web of meaning that is above: within the limits open to fallen creatures, its language and visible artifacts and music and choreography are to suggest the richness and subtlety of the sign-system that God is.

A culture is maintained not by genes and ecology alone but by teaching. The triune God descends from no one and is his own ecology. Thus his life is nothing but teaching: the Son says nothing but what he has heard from the Father; the Spirit elucidates and enforces only what the Father has taught the Son; the Father, the Teacher untaught, says nothing but by the Son and the Spirit.

The church of this God lives by hearing in the Spirit what the Father teaches the Son. It hangs for life and death on every bit of *torah*—"instruction"—that comes from the mouth of God. As with any community, the church's move from hearing instruction to speaking it is the moment of possible self-betrayal. Dumbed-down catechesis, music, and liturgical form that require no initiation, preaching that not only presumes but cultivates a short attention span, all betray the One whose teaching they pretend to bring.

So—Prudentius and the anonymous sculptors of Constantine's arch and the codifiers of Justinian's code and all the busy workers of Christian high culture were on a right track. Cultivation of high culture within the church is a possible and in the long run perhaps necessary thing to be done.[4] Now for step two.

The Warrant for Christian Civilization

Christian civilization was then the sharing of high churchly culture with a civilization that, however wrapped up with the church, was not the church. By the church's own insight into what is good, was that a good thing for the church to do?

The church is not herself a civilization, because she is a *polity,* and a civilization is not. The church is the segment for this age of the single and unitary city of God, whereas a civilization may encompass dozens of polities or none at all.[5]

A polity is a public space for moral deliberation of the community's future. Polities differ according to who is admitted to this space—the many, the few, a monarch and his mistress, a class of permanent politicians as now in the United States—but all are forums for moral debate and decision by those allowed to be responsible for the community's future: What, if anything, justifies our community's use of force against others? What shall we teach our children? How shall we distribute the costs of community? A civilization, on the other hand, is not morally in its own hands; its future is indeed—at least partly—shaped in the way Marx, or the recent Annales school of historians, or some capitalist theorists have thought all human community is shaped.

Therefore if the church shares her cultural treasures with a civilization, she shares them with an entity that does not control her own use of them. The church takes the risk that instead of despoiling the Egyptians, she is inviting Egyptian chaos to despoil her: to make of her freedom, libertinism; of her art, blasphemy; of her debunking of myth, nihilism. Should she take that risk?

Insofar as the creation of the late Christian civilization involved choice—which probably, of course, it did only minimally—I think the late antique and early medieval Christians made the right choice for their

---

4. It might be objected here that the church should not contemplate a long run. I think it must. Can this be a point of difference with Stan Hauerwas?

5. Behind Augustine's Latin *civitas* was, of course, *polis.*

time and place, even considering the risks. For even if civilizations are not self-directed, neither can Christian theology say they are directed wholly by impersonal force, that God has left himself without witness in their histories. Whether as common grace or natural law or general revelation, or Barth's "little lights," Christianity has recognized the Word spoken also outside the divine polity. When the barbarians say, "Teach us to sing," can the church say "No"? I think not. I think the church has at that point to turn the risk-management over to God.

Moreover, in a situation where the church lives amid desperate would-be sharers of her high culture, can the church in fact develop and maintain that culture within herself while insisting on this culture being only for herself? Again I think not.

I will conclude with a rhetorical question, whose probative value will, I suppose, be mostly for the otherwise convinced. This paragraph and the next are written just after attending a brilliant performance of Beethoven's *Missa solemnis.* The work and its continued performance are a prime case of Christian civilization. Beethoven's relation to Christian faith was fractured and idiosyncratic, and the audience in Avery Fisher Hall was surely in large part drawn by the ensemble and conductor. Yet Beethoven did set the Mass with precise sensitivity to the texts even while exploiting them to his own purposes, and one hundred and eighty-two years later a New York audience was enraptured.

The music is unparalleled and indeed unthinkable outside Christian civilization. As a whole it is relentlessly propelled, with improbable climax upon climax, toward a goal anticipated by the music's tonality and phrasal structure yet never explicitly realized. But then the storm pauses for the *Benedictus,* a delicate musical evocation of christological meditation. Did Beethoven trust the promise of the kingdom, or contemplate Christ's beauty? Who finally knows? What is clear: his art was shaped and driven by a cultural memory of Christian eschatology and devotion. The question is: Would we really want there to be no such music, to spare the church's purity?

This second step has been much more briefly discussed than the first. We dwelled with aspects of Christian high culture, and here have hastened. I do not know whether this is because the argument is weak, its author is weak, or nothing further is needed.

Part 3

A City on a Hill . . .
and the Church(es)

9

Representing the Absent in the City

Prolegomena to a Negative Political Theology according to Revelation 21

Bernd Wannenwetsch

In the beginning God had planted a garden for humanity to live in (Gen. 2:8). In the end he will give them a city. In the New Jerusalem the blessings of paradise will be restored, but the New Jerusalem is more than paradise regained. As a city it fulfills humanity's desire to build out of nature a human place of human culture and community.

—Richard Bauckham[1]

After periods of neglect, it has again become popular to stress the political dimension of the Christian hope as symbolized by the Heavenly City. As

---

1. Richard Bauckham, *The Theology of the Book of Revelation* (Cambridge: Cambridge University Press, 1993), 135.

Richard Bauckham and others since Karl Barth, most notably among them Stanley Hauerwas, have reminded us, the final destination of humankind is a life of beatitude that assumes a political form—not ecclesial or simply social but explicitly political.[2] Hence, theologians have become keen to stress the analogical value of human politics and polities. The cities of this earth are, after all, analogues of the eschatological dwelling place. Though they are *only* analogues, the current emphasis is on affirmative implications of this relationship: earthly cities, however broken and fallen, are *still* analogues that must be respected for what they are and cared for in deliberate political engagement and involvement.[3]

Although this trend can be seen as reconnecting with the tradition that is invoked in Jeremiah's letter to the exultant exilic community in Babylon—"Seek the welfare of the city where I have sent you" (Jer. 29:7 NRSV)[4]—it will be genuinely Christian only as long as it does not lose touch with another tradition of Christian political thought: the tradition of de-citifying the city.

De-citifying the City

"De-citifying" (not to be confused with "de-civilizing") I use as shorthand for the threefold need to defortify, demythologize, and desacralize the earthly city by stripping it of exactly those traits that represent its most profound self-understanding: its *civic pride*.[5] To speak of the city in this way is to think of it not simply in terms of a structured and governed communal dwelling place but as the ultimate expression of civilization and the icon of human sociality. Rome, for example, even when it was a long-established empire that reached out to the *oikoumene*, still prided

2. Karl Barth, "The Christian Community and the Civil Community," in *Against the Stream: Shorter Post-War Writings 1946–52* (New York: Philosophical Library, 1954), 19; Stanley Hauerwas, *In Good Company: The Church as Polis* (Notre Dame: University of Notre Dame Press, 1995).

3. Eberhard Jüngel, *Reden für die Stadt: Zum Verhältnis von Christengemeinde und Bürgergemeinde* (Munich: Kaiser, 1979), 28.

4. Scripture quotations are from the New Revised Standard Version (NRSV) unless otherwise noted.

5. Though the American sense of civic pride is rather nonurban in origin and emphasis, Stanley Hauerwas's contributions to political theology belong, if anywhere, to this tradition of de-citifying the city. To the extent that the deconstructive thrust of his writings has resulted in the charge that he is disinterested in actual politics and political engagement, the following considerations may shed some critical light by demonstrating that a genuine theological engagement of politics should be *precisely negative*, representing what is absent rather than what is present.

itself as a city—*the* city, of course. Unmindful as it was of any criteria of size for a city to function as a city, it imperiously presented itself as such when offering "citizenship" to other nations. The city of Rome was not so much the capital of an empire; rather, the empire was seen as a virtually infinite stretching of the city walls that offered *Pax Romana* to those forced inside.[6] Correspondingly, we find the apocalyptical visionary on the island of Patmos portraying the demonic imperial power as a city—Babel/Rome—precisely because of its claim and status as an all-encompassing scheme of human sociality.[7] John's vision of a city that "comes down from heaven" (Rev. 21:2) is the strongest reminder that the cities we have are not only analogous to the Heavenly City but also in opposition to it.

This opposition is made obvious through the use of a whole range of antitypes. The New City comes dressed as a "bride" (21:2), as opposed to the great whore Babel, who is dressed in purple and scarlet and drunk with the blood of the saints (17:4–6). Whereas Babel/Rome's empire was based on violence and death—bringing death to others as well as fearing death for itself[8]—the New City will be marked by the absence of death and crying and pain (21:4). While Rome's habit of "giving" was actually a means of sustained oppression, in the New City the water of life will be given to the thirsty "without cost" (v. 6).

No theologian better understood this critical relation than Augustine of Hippo, who spoke of the Celestial City during the present age as living "like a captive and a stranger in the earthly city, though . . . it makes no scruple to obey the laws of the earthly city, whereby the things necessary for the maintenance of this mortal life are administered."[9] Yet the wisdom of this tradition of Christian political thought lies not so much in its insistence on an ambiguous relation of the two cities as in the insight that this ambiguity results from their *actually touching*

6. As Tacitus has a Caledonian chieftain comment: "[The Romans] rob, butcher, plunder . . . and where they make a desolation, they call it 'peace.'" *Vita Agricolae*, ed. Ogilvie and Richmond (Oxford: 1967), 30; see also the essays in R. A. Horsley, ed., *Paul and Empire: Religion and Power in Roman Imperial Society* (Harrisburg, Pa.: Trinity, 1997).

7. The goddess Roma was worshipped in the cities of the province of Asia to which the seven letters of the book of Revelation are addressed. Bauckham, *Theology of the Book of Revelation*, 126.

8. According to Augustine's account in *City of God* 2.18.

9. *City of God* 19.17. Augustine's apologia rests on a distinction between two *civitates*, a model widely accepted in both Stoicism and Neoplatonism. But whereas in those philosophies actually existing political communities are viewed as imperfect realizations of the cosmic ideal *civitas*, Augustine turns this relationship into an antithesis. The *civitas terrena*, which is determined by self-love, is poles apart from its heavenly counterpart, the *civitas caelestis*, which is governed by *agape*. The difference is qualitative, not quantitative; categorical, not relative.

one another and that a genuine theological perception cannot therefore assume a relation of perfection/proxy values, as in idealist configurations of a cosmic "ur-city" and its earthly representatives. Whereas the prevailing oriental cosmology pictured a heavenly city hovering over its earthly representatives, always at some remove, the seer on the island of Patmos envisions a city actually coming *down* from heaven, thus eliminating the parameters of both political idealism and quietism from Christian discourse. What does it mean to say that the cities are touching one another? Rather than establishing a reassuring equilibrium and equidistance, this relation will be characterized by judgment and hope. In this age in which the Heavenly City lives as captive and stranger to the earthly, it can have no *stabilitas loci*. It "touches down" rather than "settles down." It intersects rather than occupies. It cannot leave the earthly city unaffected. But the way in which it affects it is precisely as judgment and hope—not as a model, blueprint, or actual "betterment," but neither as blunt annihilation nor disdain.

What is of lasting analogical value is the city as dwelling place, the ordered structure of communal life that offers government and participation; what must be uncovered and countered in a theological vision is the city as idol. De-citifying the city therefore means to strip human communal dwelling places of their status as idols by helping the city toward a healthy secularity. Of course, "secularization" of this type is not to be confused with what sociologists usually refer to under this label. The theologically envisioned secularization of the city is not a process whose dynamics are an inbuilt feature of modernity; it rather requires what Oliver O'Donovan has called "critical ascesis" that feeds on nothing less than eschatological faith.[10]

This eschatologically shaped critical ascesis is summed up in Hebrews 13:14: "Here we have no lasting city, but we are looking for the city that is to come." By instinct, we tend to read this "forward," from our own cities toward the future one: all that is good with ours will be even better then, and what is bad, frail, and fragmented will be made good, strong, and whole. But the saying can also be read backward: as we are looking for the city that is to come, we *come to understand* that the city we dwell in cannot last. As the particular shape of Christian political hope reveals, the more the earthly city busies itself in organizing its own endurance, the less success it will have. Yet what is more

10. Oliver O'Donovan, *Common Objects of Love: Moral Reflection and the Shaping of Community* (Grand Rapids and Cambridge: Eerdmans, 2002), 44. "'Secularity' is irreducibly an eschatological notion; it requires an eschatological faith to sustain it. . . . An unbelieving society has forgotten how to be secular" (42).

natural for any city than the desire for stability and security in the here and now, as well as in the future?

The context of the verse in Hebrews illuminates the political icono-clasm of the Christian hope. The statement about not having an endur-ing city here is motivated by the reference to Jesus's sacrificial death "outside the city gate" (v. 12): "Let us, then, go to him outside the camp, bearing the disgrace he bore. For here we do not have an enduring city, but we are looking for the city that is to come" (v. 13 NIV). What a blow to urban civic pride: the one crucial event in the history of mankind, its actual turning point, was meant to happen *outside* the city. And when it was accomplished, the concomitant signs of Jesus's death were the extinguishing of the lights that illuminate the city's grandeur, the tearing of the temple curtain, and the shaking of the city walls (Matt. 27:45–51ff).

Yet this darkening, tearing, and shaking does not *merely* deconstruct the city; at the same time it carries the promise of the "future one." The torn curtain that no longer separates the holy of holies from the rest of the temple indicates that unrestricted access to the most holy God has been accomplished; the earthquake that shatters the walls breaks open the tombs of "many holy people," who are seen within the city after Jesus's resurrection. There is no promise of the new without judgment on the "old order of things" (Rev. 21:4 NIV). But in the vision of the New Testament, there is also no deconstruction of the old that does not itself bear the shape of hope and promise of the new.

The Heavenly City is not simply the *other* city; it is also and primarily the *New* City, the *New* Jerusalem. While the aforementioned oriental model focused on spatial imagination, the perspective of the prophetic tradition has a temporal quality. The Celestial City is new insofar as it comes from the future. Its coming down from heaven does not neces-sarily imply a spatial interpretation of "from the skies" but rather points to an emanation from God's eternal presence. The contact point is God's *kairos* breaking into the *chronos,* an event that simultaneously disrupts the patterns of the reigning *chronos* with its adversarial spatial logic, in which claims are continuously set up and boundaries negotiated.

How then can a construal of the political bear witness to the escha-tological and judgmental quality of the New City? In other words: How can the future impinge on our present without being construed as a project of annihilation? How can the hope in the Future City impinge on our present one without being construed as a project of its better-ment? And how can the judgment of the Future City on our present one be conceived as something other than a final annihilation of what is good about it?

From the perspective that Revelation 21 invests us with, the primordial problem with political idealism is not that it presents us with ideals that are hard to realize or whose implementation necessitates doing violence to the material to make it fit the concepts; rather, political idealism represents an impoverished notion of the things to come.[11] It is a forswearing of newness. We can note a certain "apophaticism" in the imagery employed in the book of Revelation, which presents more of a contrast of the Eschatological City with earthly political rule than a comparison of the two.[12] But in this contrast, earthly rule is not simply transposed into a categorically different—that is, apolitical or antipolitical—entity. Rather, the new rule remains political, but marked by the "presence of the absence" of dominant features of earthly political rule such as separatism, self-preservation, and civil religion. This absence ought not be characterized as simple; rather, it is absence as known to the saints—present as awareness of its removal.[13] The New Jerusalem brings not the annihilation of history but its consummation, not the abolition of the political but its transformation, a New Earth that is recognizable as earth, a New City that is recognizable as city.

Negative Political Theology

If we wish to stay true to the double characterization of the New City as judgment and hope for the earthly city, we will be well advised, I suppose, to envision a kind of "negative political theology"—a theology of the *presence of the absence*. Such a perspective will not—as does the predominating discourse of "compatibility"—aim at identifying individual traits that exist in both cities so as to establish degrees of compatibility and noncompatibility; rather, it will have to focus on precisely those moments of political rule that are portrayed as being absent in the New City. And it will have to focus on the way in which that absence can be represented: presented to the earthly city through the witness of those who know themselves to be citizens of the New City while still living in the old. A negative political theology of the "presence of the absence" will interpret the newness of the city that is to come in the form of its hid-

11. Hannah Arendt, *The Human Condition* (Chicago: University of Chicago Press, 1958), 220–30.

12. Bauckham, *Theology of the Book of Revelation*, 43.

13. Cf. Augustine, *City of God* 22.30, where he characterizes the life of citizens in the New City as "oblivious of sin, oblivious of sufferings, and yet not so oblivious of its deliverance as to be ungrateful to its Deliverer."

denness under the form of the church: as a gift and object of faith—not invisible but visible to the eyes of faith, not without effect but effective in nonprojectable ways.[14]

I have gained the notion of a negative political theology directly from a reading of Revelation 21. A concept of this kind will almost force itself upon our reading if we pay due attention to the three core symbols of political rule that this text presents as being characteristically absent in the Celestial City:

1. shut gates in the city *wall* (v. 25);
2. a need for lighting (*sun and moon*) to reflect the grandeur of the city (v. 23);
3. a *temple* at/as the center of the city (v. 22).

What I take these symbols to address is the iconic quality of the earthly city as a defined space that organizes social identity by virtue of the security that it bestows on its inhabitants in a threefold sense:

1. a sense of "being inside" provided by the *wall* and its gates, which separate "our place" from the hostile outside world
2. a sense of a cosmologically (*sun and moon*) warranted eternality that is reflected in the myth of "foundation"
3. a sense of being comfortably fixed in space through the presence of the *temple* at the city's center.

Before we venture a more detailed analysis of each individual sense in terms of the proposed negative political theology, I must, of course, grant that ultimately the New City will *not* be characterized by absence but by presence: the immediate presence of the Lord, which makes the absence of the three symbols meaningful and hopeful in the first place. The repeated structure in which the absence of these symbols is expressed follows the pattern of "there will be no . . . as the Lord will be . . ." What is made superfluous is not what these symbols usually address in terms of elemental human desire—protection, eternality, divinity—but precisely their character as *means of acquisition* of these goods and as poor surrogates for the immediacy of gift as it is coterminous with God's presence filling the city. Hence, in regard to the goods that these three symbols-in-absence signify we must employ the following qualifications:

14. See my "Ethics and Ecclesiology," in *Oxford Handbook of Theological Ethics*, ed. Gilbert Meilaender and William Werpehowski (Oxford: Oxford University Press, 2005).

1. The New City from heaven *is* to be a peaceful, protected place; yet its peace results from the sheer absence of threat and fear and not from the employment of protective measures that operate on the basis of separating an inside from an outside.[15]

2. The New City will indeed be "without end," but its eternality is not based on a mythical foundation that guarantees its indestructibility in history by virtue of its extrahistorical origin. As the fulfillment and end of history, the city will be a truly *New* Jerusalem, not a revived *ur-city*, since it arrives "from heaven" and not from the depths of a mythical *Urgrund*.

3. In the New City there will be veneration of divine majesty, but not as religion or *civil religion*. The eschatological singing of God's praise will no longer be intelligible in terms of *re-ligare, Rück-bindung*, the binding of one's own fate and the fate of the city to a deity whose presence must be visualized and localized, fixed in space and domesticated for continuous service for the city. Rather than being a god in a temple at the center of the city, God will be its temple. God's presence will fill the whole of the city. Rather than himself being localized *within* the city, God's presence will actually *make* the city a *locus*, a true place.

We shall now look at the three motifs in more detail.

No Shut Gates: Belonging without Exclusion

The seer's vision portrays the New City as possessing a city wall with gates that never close (v. 25). The city will have no need of protective measures, since the distinction between inside and outside will have lost its foundational role for the political life inside. Like Augustine's use of Rome's gate of Janus, a gate closed only in times of peace and therefore not closed for the two-hundred-year stretch between 235 and 31 BC, John's vision may also have been intended to display an antitype.[16] While the twelve open gates of the New City, named after the twelve tribes of Israel, indicate eternal peace, the long-open gate of Janus denotes a perennial state of war.[17]

It was indeed an established belief in Greco-Roman antiquity that war should not be considered something exceptional or problematic:

---

15. Augustine, *City of God* 19.10: "There the virtues shall no longer be struggling against any vice or evil."

16. *City of God* 3.9–10.

17. As in Ezekiel's vision of the new temple, 48:31.

"War is both father and king of all; some he has shown forth as gods and others as men, some he has made slaves and others free," as Heraclitus declares.[18] And Hesiod in his poem *Works and Days* celebrates Eris, the goddess of discord who is responsible at the same time for the Trojan War and prosperity within society, implementing strife as the central form of action: "This strife is wholesome for men. For a man grows eager to work when he considers his neighbor, a rich man."[19] Although in the earlier rural setting of Greek societies inner social unity and balance were guaranteed by Dike and Eris (the gods of discord and vengeful justice who expelled transgressors of the inner law of society), the later ethos of the Greek city-state was apparently more peaceful—but only apparently. As we learn in Aeschylus's tragedy *Eumenides*, Eris has now developed a peaceful personality: "Our rivalry (*eris*) in doing good is victorious forever."[20] The vengeful and violent Erinyes are transformed into the gentle and fruitful Eumenides, who tame the internal rivalries of society. Yet this inner peace is really only violence transformed into a structural phenomenon that takes its balance from enmity turned toward the outside world. Civil war will be overcome by common love *and* unanimous hatred: "I pray that discord, greedy for evil, may never clamor in this city. . . . But may they return joy for joy in a spirit of common love, and may they hate with one mind; for this is the cure of many an evil in the world."[21]

The political ontology that is spelled out here is clear: the internal unity, balance, and peace of a society are guaranteed either by a rigorous politics of inner exclusiveness (vengeful expulsion of threatening elements) or by warfare with people outside. Either way, the identity of the political entity rests on an agonistic base and must be reassured by violent means within or outside the polis. We can see a revival of this pattern in modern political thought, where, as in contractual theories from Hobbes onward, the material base of politics is seen in the origi-

18. Fragment 53. Quoted according to *Hippolytus Ref. IX, 9, 4*, in G. S. Kirk, J. E. Raven, M. Schofield, *The Presocratic Philosophers: A Critical History*, 2nd ed., with a selection of texts (Cambridge: Cambridge University Press, 1995). For the following interpretation of the classical ontology of strife see Wolfgang Palaver, "Europe's Political Economy: A Discussion of Its Economic and Political Theologies," in *Peace in Europe—Peace in the World: Conference of European Justice and Peace Commissions*, ed. W. Palaver (Wien: Südwind-Verlag, 2001), 69–84.

19. *Works and Days* 20ff, rearranged order. Quoted from Hesiod, *Homeric Hymns, Epic Cycle, Homerica*, trans. Hugh G. Evelyn-White (Cambridge, Mass.: Harvard University Press, 1995).

20. Aeschylus, *Eumenides*, in vol. 2 of *Aeschylus in Two Volumes*, ed. H. Lloyd-Jones (Cambridge, Mass.: Harvard University Press, 1983), lines 974–75.

21. Ibid., lines 977–87.

nal state of strife that provokes the genesis of a political culture. With various degrees of subtlety, this inside–outside pattern has been used to define and structure the life of cities up to the present: from the polis as originally depicting an ancient warrior camp that literally embodied the inside–outside distinction by way of political and cultural modes of segregation (townships, ghettos, enclaves) up to the precision with which, for example, North American suburban life must fit its location into the proper band of salary and social prestige.

Read against the backdrop of the Greco-Roman/modern belief in "original violence" (R. Girard) as the breeding ground of politics, the vision of gates that are never shut appears not only different but *fundamentally* different. We need to take notice, however, of the fact that Revelation 21 still reckons with the existence of a wall. It does not follow Zechariah 2:1–5 in its portrayal of the Eschatological City as unwalled ("because of the multitude of people and animals in it") with God as a "wall of fire all around it." This reference to a wall seems to indicate, again, the significance of place. By virtue of its wall, the New City is recognizable as a *locus,* a defined and circumscribed space, not an amorphous open country that consists of nothing but horizon. As Oliver O'Donovan has emphasized, (a sense of) place is essential for human social dwelling, as "mediating a possibility for human life in community." Such a sense allows the kind of proximity that is not dependent upon blood ties but establishes neighborliness as it is paradigmatically narrated in the parable of the good Samaritan.[22]

We have spoken of Revelation 21 as overcoming the inside–outside ideology that so dramatically marks earthly political life. Yet upon closer reading, its New City still seems to be envisioned as having an "outside": "Nothing unclean will enter it, nor anyone who practices abomination or falsehood" (v. 27). The divergence from the ancient/modern pattern must be at this point: those who remain outside have not been pushed or kept outside by measures of exclusion or defense. Rather, it is simply said that they will not enter. Their assumed course of action will be as obvious to themselves as to everyone for what it is: an essential non-fit with the city. Hence, we are presented with a twofold reconceptualization of locus/space and inside–outside. With the employment of the former, the latter distinction is robbed of its *foundational* status, as it can no longer serve as the constitutive principle of civil and political life. The imagery of city gates that never close is a token of eschatological irony that parallels another in John's vision, where it is said that the believ-

22. Oliver O'Donovan, "The Loss of a Sense of Place," in *Bonds of Imperfection: Christian Politics, Past and Present,* ed. Oliver O'Donovan and Joan Lockwood O'Donovan (Grand Rapids, Mich.: Eerdmans, 2004), 304; 316–20.

ers will "rule" (*basileuein*) with God, though there will be no one who is ruled. In both cases the vision is one of structure and order without compulsion or hierarchy. As Richard Bauckham puts it: "The point is not that they reign over anyone: the point is that God's rule over them is for them a participation in his rule. The image expresses the eschatological reconciliation of God's rule and human freedom."[23]

No Sun and Moon: Glory without Foundation

And what of the political significance of the absence of sun and moon in the New City? The reason for this absence is, of course, positive: in contrast to the old city, the New City will shine from within, God himself being its light. Yet the (formally) negative aspect is also hopeful. The New City, by implication, will not need the lighting that shines on the city's glamour and grandeur, casting into spectacular relief its arches of triumph and statues of defenders, dancing off the burnished surfaces of the monuments of its founder(s). In the old city, just as the cosmic lights in their enduring dynamism guarantee permanence in time, so the symbols that reflect their light stand as tokens and promises of permanence. "Even the state knows no more powerful unwritten laws than the mythical foundation which guarantees its connection to religion, its growth out of mythic ideas."[24] This quest for permanence accounts for the common practice of cities deifying their founders and establishing cults that commemorate the original myth as a token of perennial security. Thus Romulus, the founder of Rome, was said to be a descendant from the god Mars and a vestal virgin, and after his miraculous disappearance in a storm he became venerated by the Romans as the major godhead Quirinus, ranking close to Jupiter and Mars.[25]

The theological problems with these stories of the cities' mythical beginnings are not exhausted, however, in their deification of founders and their beguiling of believers with a false sense of security. Such tales also rule out belief in the social quality of creation, presuming instead original disorder within which the founders of cities or republics are cast as the bringers of order. These tales thus portray the political entity's

---

23. Bauckham, *Theology of the Book of Revelation*, 142.

24. Friedrich Nietzsche, *The Birth of Tragedy*, trans. Ian C. Johnston (2000; rev., Nanaimo, British Columbia: Prideaux Street Publications, 2003), chap. 23; available online at http://www.mala.bc.ca/%7Ejohnstoi/Nietzsche/tragedy_all.htm.

25. Cf. the contrast that Augustine marks in his *City of God* (22.6) between Rome, which "loved its founder, and therefore believed him to be a god," and the church, which "believed Christ to be God, and therefore loved him." For the Roman myth see also Carlos Parada, Greek Mythology Link, http://homepage.mac.com/cparada/GML/Romulus.html.

origin as a result of a *lonely* will's act of violent victory. As Rome's foundational myth reveals, the act of founding was already coterminous with demarcating boundaries: Romulus's building of a wall and killing of his twin brother.[26] Mocking the "lowly walls" by leaping across them, Remus committed two unforgivable sins: he not only ignored the foundational role of the wall, with its inside–outside logic, but also spurned the pride that it shelters. Insisting that there can be only one founder, the myth makes a strong case for denying any original societal character to cities.

If the book of Revelation, to the contrary, emphasizes the absence of a foundational myth in the absence of lights to shine on its monuments, it prepares the way for the powerful rival political ontology that Augustine fleshed out in conscious opposition to Rome's. From this perspective, a political society does not come into being through the triumphant will of a founding figure (whether individual or communal) but through the socially formative power of love: "A people . . . is a gathered multitude of rational beings united by agreeing to share the things they love."[27]

While the founder's myth envisions the birth of civilization from the maternal womb of primal discord—Romulus and Remus were said to have turned to the founding of Rome and quarreling about the founder's right since, having vanquished their enemies, they had no one to quarrel with except themselves—the Augustinian tradition assumes that there can be a *zoon politikon* because man is created a social animal from the outset. And while Rome's foundational myth casts programmatic silence on the existing villages on the seven hills as the *materia* of the political unification achieved, the theologian's idea accounts for human diversity and plurality from the outset. As Jean Bethke Elshtain puts it: "No single man can create a commonwealth. There is no ur-Founder, no great bringer of order. It begins in ties of fellowship, in households, clans, and tribes, in earthly love and its many discontents. And it begins in an ontology of peace, not war."[28] It seems wholly in line with the repudiation of the ancient logic of a lonely founder that John of Patmos's vision implies a multitude of "founding figures," with the walls of the New City resting on the foundation of the twelve Apostles (v. 14) and the gates associated with the twelve tribes of Israel (vv. 12–13). Corresponding to this emphasis on original multitude, the future vi-

---

26. Cf. the parallel Augustine draws between Romulus and Cain, both of whose stories interweave the acts of city founding and fratricide, *City of God* 15.5.

27. Augustine, *City of God* 19.24: *Populus est coetus multitudinis rationalis rerum quas diligit concordi communione sociatus.* English translation according to O'Donovan, *Common Objects of Love*, 20.

28. Jean Bethke Elshtain, *Augustine and the Limits of Politics* (Notre Dame, Ind.: University of Notre Dame Press, 1995), 97.

sion sees the city inhabited not merely by hordes of individual human beings or congregations of believers but by a *multitude of peoples:* "The nations will walk by its light" (v. 24).

Just as the vision repudiates the foundational myth of a political *creatio ex nihilo,* so too it rejects the annihilation of plurality. Indeed, what seems even more remarkable than its sheer affirmation of multitude and plurality is what Revelation 21 says of the lasting significance of the cultural heritage of the various peoples: "And the kings of the earth will bring their glory into it. . . . And they will bring the glory and the honor of the nations into it" (vv. 24–26 NASB). This passage is striking. In the previous verse, the reason for the absence of sun and moon is made unambiguously clear—"for the GLORY of God is its light" (v. 23)—so it is all the more noteworthy that here this light is not depicted as eclipsing any other light. God's shining glory that fills and illuminates the New City does *not,* in retrospect, render dark, meaningless, and void what was good and healthy in human civilization. Again, this vision seems to resonate with Augustine's definition of a people as coming into being through socially formative, or political, love, insofar as such love does not mean simply "affection for one another" but common love of *things* to share in.[29] In Augustinian terms, we may associate the "glory and honor of the nations" with all these patterns of cultural and political life that have *not* been born of self-love but, whether knowingly or not, have been positively echoing and responding to God's providential grace in the presence of political authority.[30] "The nations will walk by its light," and "kings . . . will bring their glory into it." As the mention of the kings seems to suggest, the New City will not annihilate political authority but consummate it under "the throne of God and the Lamb" (22:3), when those who "serve God" will "reign" with him (22:3–5).

Of course, this affirmation of political rule, culture, and heritage goes along with a series of sharp contrasts. Whereas Rome/Babylon's wealth was *extorted* from all the world, in the New City the kings of the earth are said to *bring* their glory into it—of their own free will.[31] And unlike the glory of the city that is reflected in the *external* splendor of monuments of triumph, that is defined by defeat and destruction of other claims of glory, that is demarcated by high city walls and protected by

---

29. Cf. O'Donovan, *Common Objects of Love,* 26.

30. Though I think this a viable reading of the biblical text in Augustinian terms, I would be less confident to find strong repercussions of John's notion of the "glory of the nations" in Augustine's own actual account. We may see a hint, at least, in his granting that the earthly city's desire for peace "cannot justly be said to be evil, for it is itself, in its own kind, better than all other human good." *City of God* 15.4.

31. Bauckham, *Theology of the Book of Revelation,* 131.

partisan gods, God's radiant glory allows others to shine as well: as a light from *within*. The city gates allow entry to that kind of civic glory and splendor that does not claim to shine from its own inner power, as celebrated in foundational myths and protected through military and other defense mechanisms such as civil religion. Though the human city is not destined to shine for itself, the negation of this idea—represented in the lack of a *need* of external lighting—does not entail denying that by virtue of God's providential care there can be a kind of honor and glory of the nations that is compatible with the New City, precisely as it is willing and able to receive its illumination from within through God's own radiant presence.

No Temple: Worship without Religion

> The throne of God and of the Lamb will be in [the city], and his servants will worship him; they will see his face, and his name will be on their foreheads.
>
> —Revelation 22:3–4

The New City will feature a throne, but no temple. Although its life is portrayed as one of joyful veneration and worship, its most striking characteristic is its immediacy. Worshipping will be a matter not only of "tasting and seeing the *goodness* of the Lord" but of seeing the Lord *himself*—his "face," whose radiant glory would have consumed any human onlooker (Exod. 33:20) this side of the New City's gates. And what had been granted only to Israel's high priest, and only once a year—to wear the name of the Lord on his forehead when entering the holy of holies—will become the eternal privilege in the New City, enjoyed by all of "his servants."

This immediacy of divine communion is reflected in what may be the most astonishing absence in the New City: the absence of a temple. This feature appears all the more stunning in light of the fact that visions of a renewed temple were a typical pattern of Jewish contemporary eschatological writing. The so-called Temple Scroll from Cave 11 in Qumran gives an outline of the New City and temple as revealed to Moses by God—thereby suggesting the divine sanction of the temple denied in Torah itself.[32] While the portrayal of the New City follows a whole range of Old Testament models (Isa. 52:1; 54:11–12; 60:1–22; Ezek.

---

32. Christopher Rowland and Judith Kovacs, *Revelation: The Apocalypse of Jesus Christ*, Blackwell Bible Commentaries (Oxford: Blackwell, 2004), 221.

40:2–5; 47:1–12; 48:30–34; Zech. 14:6–21), it is precisely the absence of the temple that marks the novelty. Though prophets could name the New Jerusalem "The Lord is There" (Ezek. 48:35) and envision God's presence as filling the whole of the city *as in the temple,* none of them went as far as declaring the temple itself superfluous in the eschatological dwelling place.[33] It even seems as though the vision of the absent temple comes as a surprise to the seer himself: whereas in 16:17 John hears God speak "out of the temple, from the throne," in 21:3 the mediation of the temple has become superfluous and the voice from the throne is heard immediately.

A common approach in interpreting the absence of a temple is to dwell on the point that divine presence is finally revealed to be in no way dependent on buildings. Yet the politically crucial point is hardly grasped by the dichotomy between "static" (building) and "dynamic" (community);[34] the problem that Revelation envisions with the temple is not a lack of dynamism but the kind of dynamism that aims at the provision of protection and identity associated with organized and administered religion in which everything—human and divine—is in its place, and the place of the holy is exactly circumscribed, thoroughly known and administered to. A strong hint in this direction can be seen in the fact that John's portrayal of the New City is based on the plan of the tabernacle (21:16, cf. 1 Kings 6:20). Although Richard Bauckham concludes that "as a result, the city itself becomes a temple,"[35] this conclusion seems to miss the point. The text actually reads "the Lord God Almighty and the Lamb are its temple" (21:22 NIV). With these words, the temple is actually made superfluous, not merely stretched toward the limits of the city walls.

Although the city's measurements and its perfect cubic shape mirror the holy of holies in the temple, the imagery is not a *pars pro toto* for the temple as a whole; rather, it represents an odd stretching of the holy of holies to embrace the whole of the city as a sign of the eschatological supersession of the temple principle itself. God's immediate presence will mark the New City just as it marked the holy of holies in the temple and will make obsolete the temple principle of delimiting a predetermined space of God's special presence on a gradualist model. This concept included the demarcation of the holy of holies not only from the holy but also from the forecourts and eventually from the *profanum*—the "profane," as the outside of the temple. With the New City's abolishing

33. Bauckham, *Theology of the Book of Revelation,* 136.

34. Christopher Rowland, *Revelation,* Epworth Commentaries (London: Epworth, 1993), 157.

35. Bauckham, *Theology of the Book of Revelation,* 136.

of the temple will come also the nullification of a pattern of separation that narrowly circumscribed divine presence, excluding all those, such as women and proselytes, who were relegated to the forecourts.[36]

Though the inclusiveness of the New City's population—which spans all nations, sexes, and social classes—is not a denial that there will be those who will not enter it (v. 27), the judgment will not be drawn from a known and organized topography of God's presence but will be left to the revelatory opening of the Lamb's book of life, where all the names are written. Thus what the absence of the temple envisions is a political form of life that allows worship without religion, a "serving the throne" without the compartmentalizing and exclusion of human beings that goes hand in hand with the domestication of the divine for the sake of the sense of security without which humans find it so hard to exist.[37]

If this interpretation has any validity, it may also help us better understand the role of the church in its earthly pilgrimage. The often noted "imprecision" of Augustine's portrayal of the church in relation to the Celestial City—not quite the same, but intimately related nevertheless—is a healthy one, it seems, when viewed against the backdrop of the church's central practice of worship. While inevitably entangled in "religion," in the organizing of "secure" modes of encountering God from the back, as it were, the journey of the church toward a city without a temple suggests that the church's worship is based on the promise of ultimately seeing God's face, which will make superfluous all the husks of religion.

Though not exempt from this profoundly critical relation that suggests the need for worship versus worship *within* worship, the Christian practice of praising and serving God is at the same time invested with the actual tasting of the absence of the temple principle in that the "real presence" of its Lord (as *totus Christus,* though not yet *in toto*) is offered to all those who feast at the Lamb's table. In eating and drinking the body of its Lord, the church is in fact made instantly present to the heavenly kingdom that comes out of the future. Yet as for the church's liaison with religion that cannot be wholly overcome this side of the New City, we must speak of a certain hiddenness of the City of God, not only under the earthly city but also under the church. Although we may find this hiddenness deplorable at first sight, it is essentially a hopeful

36. A prefiguration of this motif may be seen in Rev. 11:1–2, with its summons "go and measure the temple . . . but exclude the outer court . . . because it has been given to the Gentiles [who] will trample on the holy city" (NIV).

37. Bonhoeffer's musings in regard to a future Christianity without the "garment" of religion seem to point in a similar direction: "What do a church, a community, a sermon, a liturgy, a Christian life mean in a religionless world? How do we speak of God—without religion?" *Letters and Papers from Prison,* enlarged edition, ed. E. Bethge (London: SCM, 1971), 280.

hiddenness. Since the church is the community that is granted instances of God's real presence as a gift, it will certainly have to bear witness to that presence before the earthly city. Yet because of the necessity of the church's self-distinction from the New City—as suggested by its own degree of reliance on the temple pattern—the way in which this witness is to be primarily conceived may well have to assume the mode of a "negative political theology": of making present the *absent*. Before we attempt to identify patterns of the church's ongoing engagement in such witness (although perhaps not conceptualized in this way) I wish to sharpen the critical contours that we have gained from our reading of Revelation 21, in terms of de-citifying the city, by contrasting it with another notable critic of "the" city, Friedrich Nietzsche.

Heaven's Bride and Zarathustra's Ape

A reading of a vivid episode in Nietzsche's *Zarathustra* will reveal some stunning similarities in diagnosis—and some fundamental differences in treatment.[38] When Zarathustra's wandering through the territory of "many peoples" is drawing to its end and the great commentator is about to return to his cave, he unexpectedly finds himself in front of the gate of the GREAT CITY. As Nietzsche's own use of capitalized letters (in the German edition) suggests, there is much more at stake here than with the "diverse cities" he has wandered through to this point. With the GREAT CITY he is facing the quintessential nature of civil life as it presents itself to him in his time.[39] The episode unfolds as he is suddenly confronted by a "frothing fool" who is referred to as "Zarathustra's ape," for the fool mimics some of the protagonist's expressions as well as his wisdom. From the mouth of this fool the wise man receives a dire warning:

> O Zarathustra, here is the GREAT CITY: here you have nothing to seek and everything to lose. Why do you want to wade through this mud? Take pity on your feet! Rather spit upon the gate and—turn back! (195)

The fool emphasizes his warning through a graphic portrayal of the GREAT CITY's deplorable character, where "all lusts and vices are at

---

38. *Thus Spoke Zarathustra*, trans. R. J. Hollingdale (London: Penguin, 2003). Quotations and page references in the text refer to this edition, with additional capitalization of "GREAT CITY" according to the German original.

39. Nietzsche may have been aware of the characterization of Babel as the "great city" in Rev. 18:19 pass. Revelation 11:8 speaks of the "great city" as the one "which is figuratively called Sodom and Egypt, where also their Lord was crucified."

home" (196). Every ancient claim to greatness—intellectual and emotional—is now found in a state of corruption: great thoughts are "boiled alive and cooked small"; "great emotions decay," and "only little, dry emotions may rattle"; the sprit is "slaughtered," and the souls are "hanging like dirty limp rags" (195–96).

It is the sudden and sharp focus on the listing of "all vices" that I take to be the *cantus firmus* of the whole portrayal:

> Do you not see the souls hanging like dirty, limp rags?—And they make newspapers also from these rags! Have you not heard how the spirit has here become a play with words? It vomits out repulsive verbal swill!—And they make newspapers also from this verbal swill! (196)[40]

At this point the actual greatness of the GREAT CITY is revealed. This greatness consists in the city's unlimited capacity to turn its own abundant vices into virtues—through publicity. In this city there is not a single vice that cannot be made into a public sensation—appalling perhaps, but interesting nevertheless; perverted perhaps, but consoling for this very fact. We do not have to look far, I guess, in our own mass media culture, with its persistent flow of reality shows and soul-baring daily talk shows, to see the topical value of this portrayal. What Nietzsche foresaw at a time when the patterns of publicity were still in an embryonic stage has become only all too obvious in contemporary Western societies. The experience of civil life is organized around a virtual space called "public" that is busily filled and refilled with publicity events and constantly illuminated by the big neon lights of media interest. This experience reminds us again of the means of lighting that John of Patmos's vision described as being characteristically absent in the Celestial City. Of Zarathustra's GREAT CITY we may say that even though floodlights have replaced sun and moon as ancient symbols of its splendor, they nevertheless uphold and reinforce the civil purpose of the ancient lights by illuminating the grandeur of the city. The modern floodlights of publicity are meant to achieve this effect by assuring people that nothing can be essentially wrong with the city since all sorts of concerns are constantly talked about in public, and public opinion rules.

Yet the anonymity of public opinion in a mass society makes the faceless ruler a tendentious tyrant.[41] Zarathustra's ape offers a similar concluding analysis. Whether people shut themselves off from one an-

---

40. Slightly rearranged according to the German original.
41. Cf. David Riesman, *The Lonely Crowd: A Study of the Changing American Character* (1953; repr., New Haven: Yale University Press, 2003); Arendt, *The Human Condition*, 40.

other by building walls or tear down the walls between them by force, they seem to be unaware of what they are doing:

> They pursue one another and do not know where. They inflame one another, and do not know why. . . . They are cold and seek warmth in distilled waters; they are inflamed and seek coolness in frozen spirits; they are all ill and diseased with public opinion. (196)

Publicity, hailed as the saving grace that turns vices into virtues, is itself revealed at the end of the day as a disease rather than a cure. If people orient their behavior and organize their social relations in antecedent obedience to the imperatives of the public square, where seeming and appearing are more important than being and truth, they merely rearrange the inside–outside logic of the ancient warrior polis.

To place this point within the horizon of our three symbols of absence in Revelation 21: the technological progress from the "sun and moon" that shine on the triumphal arches to the big neon lights that illuminate the public square has *not* made superfluous the wall and its gates. It has only changed the rhythm of the closing and opening of the gates from a day- and nighttime pattern to an arbitrary irregularity. Unpredictability being the lifeblood of publicity, anyone can become public opinion's villain at any moment. It is almost as if John of Patmos foresaw this point in introducing another apocalyptic figure: the "beast from the land," the "false prophet"—the propagandist of the empire whose business is to conceal by his impressive appearance the actual disappearance of free speech under the reign of the beast from the sea.

And what may we say about the third absent symbol in this respect, the temple? Can it also be said to be accounted for in Nietzsche's portrayal of the GREAT CITY? Having noted the implicit parallels so far, we should perhaps not be too surprised to find Zarathustra's ape addressing this symbol as well. Approaching the "temple," as it were, first from a moral point of view, he notes that for all its assembled vices, the GREAT CITY is not without virtuous people. The virtue at hand, however, is of a thoroughly bureaucratic nature, "with scribbling fingers and behinds hardened to sitting and waiting, blessed with little chest decorations and padded, rumpless daughters" (196). Even when explicitly religious terminology is adopted, the bureaucratic or even mendicant overtones prevail: "There is also much piety here and much devout spittle-licking and fawning before the God of Hosts. . . . 'I serve, you serve, we serve'—thus does all adroit virtue pray to the prince: so that the merited star may at last be fastened to the narrow breast" (196). In a city that is organized around the patterns of publicity, religion cannot be anything but civil religion in its bluntest form of offering devotion to the godhead in return for protection and blessing. The floodlights of publicity turn devotion into calculus, since the devoted assembly can never keep its gaze on God alone but will at the same time have to reflect on the effect that its own devotion has in the public arena.

Even Zarathustra's ape knows that civil religion, the only religion that the GREAT CITY knows, cannot but eventually miss God—"The God of Hosts is not the god of the golden ingots"—but it is nevertheless stuck with its "mendicant virtues": "the prince proposes, but the shop-keeper—disposes!" (196).

Such a reading of Nietzsche's portrayal of the city almost makes it believable that he somehow modeled it according to the three symbols of absence in John's vision. Yet his focus on publicity as the new icon of city-ness has afforded us a sharper account of how the identity poli-tics of the GREAT CITY articulates itself in modern times. It has also helped us bring into sharper relief how the interaction between current modes of responding to the three symbols—wall, sun and moon, and temple—must be understood, that is, how the GREAT CITY finds its triadic unity in these patterns. Is Nietzsche, in his account of city-ness, therefore a prophetic voice, congenial to the Christian tradition as it emerged from Patmos?

To some—analytical—degree Nietzsche is such a voice, but not fully, as we shall see when we now turn to observing the way in which Nietzsche makes his Zarathustra respond to the sympathetic portrayal of the ape:

> "By all that is luminous and strong and good in you, O Zarathustra! spit upon this city of shopkeepers and turn back! . . . Spit upon the city . . . of the importunate, the shameless, the ranters in writing and speech, the overheated ambitious: where everything rotten, disreputable, lustful, gloomy, overripe, ulcerous, conspiratorial festers together—spit upon the GREAT CITY and turn back." But here Zarathustra interrupted the froth-ing fool and stopped his mouth. "Have done!" (cried Zarathustra), "Your speech and your kind have long disgusted me! Why did you live so long in the swamp that you had to become a frog and toad yourself? . . . Why did you not go into the forest? . . . I despise your contempt; and since you warned me, why did you not warn yourself?" (196–97)

The wise man's rebuke seems surprising and a little unfair, all the more so since he actually shares the ape's negative verdict on the city, as he will reveal later on. But his point is well taken. Even as its most caustic critic, the ape still belongs to the GREAT CITY. He has not fled its vices but remains within its portals. His critique is turned into a warning that he issues to the outside world—delighting in the sensation that the detailed account of the city's decadence is meant to cause in the addressed.

Notwithstanding the question whether he would or would not have ventured such a critique to those inside the city, the decisive point seems to be this: via publicity, the GREAT CITY is capable not only of turning vices into virtues but also of integrating any critique into its own patterns by "making a newspaper of it," so to speak. Turning critique into the exchange value of information or sensation, the GREAT CITY incorporates any critique into its own substance, not through repentance, of course, but by declaring it yet another matter of discussion. Thus, just as independent nations would have to be turned into "Rome" by being "invited" into Rome's citizenship, the critic in the GREAT CITY of our time will be systemically domesticated in that the rule of publicity causes him to strategize his critique in order to "score" in the public realm, to "influence" public opinion, and so on.

Nietzsche's episode draws to a dramatic close where the messianic overtones are as obvious as is the difference from the way of the Christian Messiah. What is to be done with the GREAT CITY? How should one respond not only to the warning but to the presence of its very object?

> Thus spoke Zarathustra; and he looked at the GREAT CITY, sighed and was long silent. At length he spoke thus: "This GREAT CITY, and not only this fool, disgusts me. In both there is nothing to make better, nothing to make worse. Woe to this GREAT CITY! And I wish I could see already the pillar of fire in which it will be consumed! For such pillars of fire must precede the great noontide. Yet this has its time and its own destiny. But I offer you in farewell this precept, you fool: Where one can no longer love, one should—*pass by*!" Thus spoke Zarathustra and passed by the fool and the GREAT CITY. (198)

After a Jesus-like pattern of keeping silent, sighing, and then pronouncing woe, the wise man's conclusion is unambiguously clear: have nothing to do with this city; spit on it and pass by. When the city is beyond love, for all its vices and presumption, one can only leave it alone, leave it to the dynamics of decay, destruction, and final consumption. Perhaps it will be reborn from the ashes like the phoenix.

Though we grant that Zarathustra's response of simply passing by the city and returning to his cave is unthinkable in any Christian political theology that needs to uphold both judgment and engagement, we must acknowledge Zarathustra's main critical point as leveled at the fool. Neither solidarity ("staying") nor criticism ("warning") nor engagement ("better") will do. No matter how much solidarity is undertaken, nor how critical or engaged one is, those who remain in the swamp cannot but become "frogs and toads" themselves. Over against such well-meaning activist attitudes that obviously underestimate the idolatrous undertow of the city, Nietzsche's sage is right to assume the necessity of a critical vantage point from *outside* the city if one wants to be unaffected by its corruptive power.

Yet the cave to which Zarathustra himself returns remains a *mere outside*. Christians can hardly settle for an existence that cares above all about being unaffected.[42] What is needed in terms of an outside, a critical distance from the GREAT CITY, is not a cave, a withdrawal to an unaffected pre- or anticivic life, but rather another citizenship, a different sort of citizenship. What is needed is a belonging to another city—a city that is not defined by walls that separate it from any other but is capable of turning to another city without invading it.[43]

With the New City that John of Patmos saw there is an outside that is not defined by distance from the earthly city and by a shying away from its inside. The particular "outside" that dwelling in the New City provides for those on the Christian pilgrimage through faith and hope, for those in the anticipatory community of the church as "fellow citizens with God's people" (Eph. 2:19 NIV), is in fact capable of existing "inside" the earthly city. Whereas for Nietzsche's sage it is *presence* that motivates contempt of the GREAT CITY—the actual presence of vices and pseudo-virtues, which renders love impossible—according to John's vision, the deconstruction of the city is a hopeful possibility that arises from the *absence* of the three symbols of city-ness as defined by the New City. Of course, Revelation 21 is predominately concerned with *another presence*, the all-encompassing presence of God that warrants the absence of wall, sun and moon, and temple in the first place.

Yet the unique and dialectical relation that Christian political theology assumes to the earthly city, a relation that is exhausted neither in activist modes of solidarity, criticism, and engagement nor in a blunt countercultural negation of civil life as such, rests on a peculiar inversion of absence and presence. The genuine and unique Christian stance toward and within the earthly city is possible only insofar as the hidden city within the city makes present the absence of the three symbols of city-ness as addressed in John's vision of the New City. This side of the final judgment we shall hardly see a city that can do without the

---

42. Dietrich Bonhoeffer, *Ethics*, ed. E. Bethge (London: SCM, 1955), 209–16.

43. "If they were to dissociate themselves from Babylon and its corrupting influence on their own cities, they needed not only to be shown Roman civilization in a different light from the way its own propaganda portrayed it; they also needed an alternative. If they were—metaphorically—to 'come out of' Babylon (18:4), they needed somewhere to go, another city to belong to" (Bauckham, *Theology of the Book of Revelation*, 129).

presumptuous triad of wall, sun and moon, and temple. Every city on this earth will seek (though not gain) security in separatism, identity politics, and civil religion. Yet in spite of its delusive character, we need not and must not flee or seek to destroy the earthly city, since in the midst of the GREAT CITY lives the church as a hidden city that makes present—that literally "presents"—to the earthly city the holy absence of these patterns, an absence to be perfected in the New City.

For all its critical thrust, the de-citifying of the city that Christian political theology envisions as a task is ultimately but a reminder of the city's own future, in which publicity will give way to a public that is God's presence among his people.

"Trying On" the Absent: Negative Political Theology as Invitation to the New City

As I move toward conclusion, I would like to draw our attention to a few concrete examples that demonstrate the political theology whose pattern I have described in terms of "de-citifying" the city, for this theology is not a theoretical program. Some hints may suffice to indicate its concrete political impact, which has proved its power to change the perception and shape of the earthly city more than once. The examples are, again, structured according to the three symbols in absence.

1. *Inverting the wall: Church asylum.* The inside–outside pattern, which is as old as the first cities—"polis" originally signified a fortified settlement of warriors—was broken up through the church in a threefold way.[44] First, the Christian community overcame the "outside" definition that had kept Gentiles from approaching the "inside" of God's elect people: "So he came and proclaimed peace to you who were far off and peace to those who were near. . . . So then you are no longer strangers and aliens, but you are citizens with the saints and also members of the household of God" (Eph. 2:17–19). Second, the church overcame the "inside" definition that Roman citizenship required in terms of an absolute and unquestioning loyalty to the city and its gods by deliberately adopting the term *paroikoi*, resident aliens, as a genuine mode of self-reference. Since for the fellow citizens of God's people there can be only *one* full citizenship—the celestial *politeuma*—the civil existence of, say, a Roman citizen had to be redefined in a distancing way that refused the claim to complete inside-ness without remainder. Third,

44. See my *Political Worship: Ethics for Christian Citizens* (Oxford: Oxford University Press, 2004).

there was a characteristic way in which the church would provide an "inside" *within* the city for those who were destined to be kept "outside": the extension of Israel's system of asylum cities into the practice of church asylum.

2. *Outshining sun and moon: Mediated political representation.* What did it mean for the city's political mode of self-reference when the inherited pattern of drawing confidence and pride from cosmological analogies or foundational myths was confronted with a community in the midst of the city that insisted on the singularity of one identity marker: Christ?[45] ("For no one can lay any foundation other than the one that has been laid," 1 Cor. 3:11.) What difference did it make that the crucial point of reference was now not to a founding myth *within* the city but toward a historical event that happened explicitly "outside the city gate" (Heb. 13:12)? If the radiant face of Christ, the slain lamb, is the light of the New City, replacing the natural lighting that illuminates the city's triumphal avenues, then the historic abolition of the ancient emperor's cult becomes intelligible as representing a general thrust toward a redefinition of political authority in theory and practice. This redefinition, as it is reflected in Romans 12 and 13, made not representation but judgment the political act par excellence.[46] Though representation was not simply ruled out altogether as in a Rousseauean perspective, it was now understood in a characteristically mediated way, whereby the ruler represented neither God nor the people in any immediate sense but rather God's rule according to God's own establishing of the *ministerium politicum.*[47]

3. *Walking the temple: Stational liturgies.* It is interesting to note that Christianity, when rising to power in the Roman Empire, did not simply destroy pagan temples and build churches in their places; it also developed a characteristic form of worship that was particularly suited to big cities. This type of liturgy embodied the Christian challenge to the temple principle of localizing God's presence in a stable, artifactual unit. The so-called *stational liturgies*—eucharistic processions that led through streets and public places to one of the churches in the city—were a way in which Christians "conquered the city," as John F. Baldovin characterized

45. "There is really no human activity in which human virtue approaches more closely the divine power of the gods than the founding of new civil entities *(civitates).*" Cicero, *Republic* 1.12.

46. Oliver O'Donovan, *The Desire of the Nations* (Cambridge: Cambridge University Press, 1997), 120–57.

47. See my "Members of One Another: Charis, Ministry, and Representation. A Politico-Ecclesial Reading of Romans 12," in *A Royal Priesthood? The Use of the Bible Ethically and Politically,* ed. C. Bartholomew et al. (Carlisle: Paternoster; Grand Rapids, Mich.: Zondervan, 2002), 196–220.

this phenomenon in his seminal study.[48] At the same time, the mobile format of these liturgies emphasized the church's self-understanding as a pilgrimage to the Eternal City. Hence, the contrast with an urban culture, with its static places of worship at the center, was now being imprinted on the city itself, whose spatial structure was translated into a (temporary) flux. Though the city's desire for a stabilizing civil religion would—and not without partial success—try to capitalize on even this new form of liturgy, its inherent viatorian nature was nevertheless perceived as a disconcerting factor. The political danger of this kind of unsettledness was soon recognized by the men in power, who tried to quell it through legislation.[49] A church on pilgrimage to the New City would perhaps not be wholly immune from the call for a religious underpinning of civil life, but it would at least understand its prophetic mission as a constant challenge to the "temple," both in the city and in the church itself.

These brief examples of the church's concrete presentation of the three absences display the "negative political theology" that I have outlined on the basis of a reading of Revelation 21. Note, however, that we did not take our cues from the absence of negative human core experiences that are noted in the portrayal of the New City: "There will be no more death . . . or crying or pain" (v. 4 NIV). To dwell on these tokens would have been to imagine the eschatological future *via negativa:* by contrasting it with negative aspects of the present life and overstretching these experiences, as it were, into their opposites.

What we found more disconcerting and exciting was the absence of features that represent things that usually matter positively to us: protection, identity, religion. In meditating on the significance of their absence in the New City, we have been offered a particular and genuinely theological way of understanding both the glory and the predicament of earthly cities, insofar as they tend to define civil life through protective measures, identity politics, and civil religion instead of seeking their true glory and honor in the "light for the nations."

The analyzed predicament of the city does, however, also project back critically on certain modes of the theological construal of the New City's import for the earthly one. John of Patmos's emphasis on the absent sheds critical light on a Christian participation in utopian or other idealist projects that seek to grasp the consequence of the eschatological vision for the present by actually *representing the present* rather than

48. John F. Baldovin, SJ, *The Urban Character of Christian Worship: The Origins, Development, and Meaning of Stational Liturgy,* Orientalia Christiana Analecta 222 (Rome: Pontifical Institute of Oriental Studies, 1987).

49. Ibid., 268.

the absent. For all their varied provenances, these accounts converge in taking their cues from the "positive" features of John's vision. They typically revolve around those features that are expressed as present rather than absent in it, whether, for example, in modes of representing the "throne" and the believers' ruling through the imposition of a theocratic form of government, or in the attempt to approximate the New City's aesthetic splendor through an abundance of visual delights built into places of worship.

While it bears a certain irony that utopian programs aimed at *representing the present*—the positive features of the New City—often seem to end up portraying more their own authors' political prerogatives than John's,[50] such programs are structurally closer to accounts that focus on the *presence of the negative* than to our suggestion of *representing the absent*. In Nietzsche's Zarathustra, we found two very different attitudes—the ape's attitude of perennial critical engagement and the master's attitude of fatalist despising—united in their fixation on the overwhelming presence of the GREAT CITY's vice. Both attitudes were aimed at the erasure of the negative, through moralist programs of purification or a "final" purification out of the ashes. In contrast to these futile alternatives, the church can be said to be engaged in a kind of "trying on" of the life in the New City that can do without inside–outside logic, mythical foundation, and (civil) religion. Representing the absent certainly entails a token of humility over against utopianism or fatalism. But at the same time, it invites an understanding of our cities' predicament that, compared with these alternatives, is rather merciful. It is merciful in that it does not focus on the cities' vices per se but supports an understanding of them as mere consequences of the not-yet absence, the not-yet-willed or -tasted absence of those patterns that the New City will eventually make superfluous. By the same token, negative political theology, in reflecting on the church's political role as representing the absent, as "trying on" a life in the absence of these patterns, will eventually amount to an invitation into the New City itself.

50. For example, Joachim of Fiore's *figura* entitled *Dispositio novi ordinis pertinens ad tercium statum ad instar novi Hierusalem* offers a detailed plan of the New City, including interesting specifications such as assigning to the religious the place at the top and to those who are married the bottom. See the illustration and explanation, among other discussions of utopian projects based on Revelation 21, in Kovacs and Rowland, *Revelation*, 228ff.

10

The Belligerent Kingdom*

Or:

Why Authentic Christianity Is Even More Politically Incorrect Than Hauerwas Acknowledges

H. Tristram Engelhardt, Jr.

St. Constantine the Great and Charlemagne at the Airport

Some time in the early 1990s, I found myself in an airport with Stanley Hauerwas. Joyfully, he greeted me: "Hey, *merdae caput,*[1] I hear you're a

---

*About my title: Christ describes his followers as violent: "From the days of John the Baptist until now, the kingdom of heaven is being forcibly entered and violent men seize it" (Matt. 11:12). To enter the kingdom, one must do violence to one's passions. In addition, Christian belligerence contends against arguments and "every pretension that sets itself up against the knowledge of God" (2 Cor. 10:5). Hauerwas acknowledges that "God's peaceable people cannot but appear to the world as 'violent people' just to the extent that they challenge the normality of violence," *With the Grain of the Universe: The Church's Witness and Natural Theology* (Grand Rapids, Mich.: Brazos Press, 2002), 227. Hauerwas passes over in relative silence the profound provocation from traditional Christianity's proclamations of the sinful character of both homosexual acts and homosexual marriage, as well as the impossibility of Christian priestesses. Traditional Christianity brings the very fabric of the dominant, post-Christian, post-traditional, secular ethos into question: its views regarding not just war, but the full fabric of life from sexuality, reproduction, marriage, asceticism, and chastity to dying and death.

1. Those acquainted with Stan Hauerwas know he addressed me not in Latin but in colloquial Anglo-Saxon. In a collection of esteemed essays such as this, I adopt the tra-

Christian!" I acknowledged with enthusiasm that, after a life spent as a wayward Vaticanian,[2] I had joined the right-believing, right-worshipping Christians. To my unexpected reply he responded: "That's wonderful," adding that at least we were on the right side of the Enlightenment,[3]

---

ditional device of placing such ejaculations in the Latin. Before Hauerwas suggests that this refinement is not appropriately Texan, I note that an article appeared in the *Galveston Daily News* recounting the activities of a local Galvestonian, I. Grummus Merdae: "Merdae, who did summer work at the University of Texas Medical Branch several years ago for Dr. Inte Caco, is a graduate of Texas A & M University and the Cacati School in New York" (November 30, 1974, 5A). *Verbum sat sapienti.*

2. Hauerwas uses cultural provocations of the rather straightforward English equivalent of *merdae caput*. I prefer doctrinally instructive provocations, such as "Vaticanian" (as employed by the late Orthodox Christian theologian Father John S. Romanides), to underscore the important beliefs that separate Christians from one another, such as the significant deviations from traditional Christianity that mark the Vatican church in its construal of Peter's primacy as one of universal jurisdiction and, worse yet, of infallibility, thus failing to appreciate St. Peter's primacy as that of the first among equals, which office continues to be rightly exercised by the contemporary successor in St. Peter's primacy, namely, Bartholomew I of Constantinople. (Lord, may the time come soon when holy Texas arises, is restored to her rightful boundaries, and Santa Fe becomes the fourth Rome, that diocese possessing the primacy of guiding in loving care all right-believing churches.) See H. T. Engelhardt, Jr., *The Foundations of Christian Bioethics* (Lisse, Netherlands: Swets & Zeitlinger, 2000), 293–94. The term "Vaticanian" also helps to reserve "Catholic" for the Orthodox Catholic Church. Strictly speaking, the Romans are those loyal to the second Rome, the first among the remaining right-believing patriarchates. *Roum* or Roman in the Levant still identifies Orthodox Christians, those true to the original Christianity of the ancient Christian Roman Empire (and who among other things are not Monophysites). Pace Hauerwas, all of this is to say that it is important to be clear as to the *ecclesia*, the church, of which one is a member.

3. The distinctive character of Hauerwas's work must be appreciated within the history that produced the Western Christianities. Otherwise, one cannot understand why he would consider the church an extended argument or think of theology in a narrative mode (i.e., rather than to recognize the church as united in an unbroken experience of the Holy Spirit).

Hauerwas is both at peace in and critical of churches transformed by the Enlightenment. Surely there were numerous Enlightenments (German, French, English, Scottish, Italian), each compassing complex sets of events, setting in train multiple influences on Protestantism and Roman Catholicism. In particular, Immanuel Kant (1724–1804; one might think of Kant's *Die Religion innerhalb der Grenzen der blossen Vernunft* [1793]) contributed to a final Protestant Reformation, completed by G. W. F. Hegel (1770–1831). Kant attempted to reduce Christianity to its moral significance, and Hegel attempted to reduce Christianity to its cultural meaning (its narrative writ large). This metastory can undoubtedly be told in different ways. See J. B. Schneewind, *The Invention of Autonomy* (New York: Cambridge University Press, 1998); Hans Blumenberg, *Die Legitimität der Neuzeit* (Frankfurt/M: Suhrkamp, 1976); and Charles Taylor, *Hegel* (Cambridge: Cambridge University Press, 1975). The result is that mainline Protestantism was radically recast in the nineteenth and twentieth centuries, as was the Roman church after Vatican II. Hauerwas both protests and affirms the results of this history.

not having problems with the priestly ministry of women that beset the Vaticanians (my characterization, not his). Wryly I responded: "What do

---

The roots of the problems of contemporary Western Christianity lie at its very beginning. Western Christianity was influenced by Neoplatonic and other views that, early on, supported movements to impose clerical celibacy. One might think of pleadings to that effect made by Western clerics at Nicea I (AD 325), the first ecumenical council; see Socrates Scholasticus, *The Ecclesiastical History*, bk. 1, chap. 11, and Sozomen, *The Ecclesiastical History*, bk. 1, chap. 23. In Augustine's North African church, the Third Council of Carthage (AD 418) forbade married priests and deacons from having carnal conversation with their wives; see Saints Nicodemus and Agapius, *The Rudder of the Orthodox Catholic Church* (Chicago: Orthodox Christian Educational Society, 1957), canons 3, 4, 33, pp. 606–7, 624; in other lists, the last canon is given as 25 or 28. This prohibition was condemned by the universal church. See the Quinisext Council or Council in Trullo (AD 692; *The Rudder,* canon 13, p. 329). Western Christianity was also dramatically influenced by Augustine of Hippo's peculiar positions regarding original sin, prevenient grace, truth-telling, and the *filioque,* to name only a few. Of equal impact were novel interpretations of Aristotle. See David Bradshaw, *Aristotle East and West: Metaphysics and the Division of Christendom* (New York: Cambridge University Press, 2004). These changes took root in a church already changed by the Carolingian renaissance. For an account of the role played by Charles the Great, his court, and their successors in recasting Western Christianity, see John Romanides, *Franks, Romans, Feudalism, and Doctrine* (Brookline, Mass.: Holy Cross Orthodox, 1981). When Western universities emerged in the thirteenth century, philosophers were no longer regarded as primarily ascetics, as those who wholeheartedly pursued wisdom. Theologians were no longer those who experienced God, but those whom Hauerwas takes for granted as theologians: academicians, who came to regard theology as a tradition of argument and doctrinal development. The recognition of this radical departure of the West from the church of the first seven councils led to the ninth ecumenical council's (i.e., Constantinople V, 1341, 1347, 1351) affirmation of St. Gregory Palamas and his account of theology. Western Christianity had created a set of defining theological difficulties, philosophical puzzles, and doctrinal deviations. The result for the West was dramatic. See, for example, Michael Buckley, *At the Origins of Modern Atheism* (New Haven: Yale University Press, 1987).

When the Protestants protested, they defined themselves against and in terms of the church they sought to reform, leading to a new set of philosophical and theological puzzles, including novel claims about the Bible. Their solutions were not drawn from the church of the first seven ecumenical councils. The result was a hodgepodge Christianity, a mosaic of isolated solutions to isolated problems fraught with contradictions, making Christianity generally implausible. The Enlightenment emerged as a philosophes' rebellion against the philosophical and theological contradictions and problems of Western Christianity; see Peter Gay, *The Enlightenment* (New York: W. W. Norton, 1966). In this sense, as Gianni Vattimo argues in *After Christianity,* trans. Luca D'Isanto (New York: Columbia University Press, 2002), the secular West is Christianity (one must read here Western Christianity) secularized. The bottom line for Protestantism and post-Vatican II Roman Catholicism is that they represent Christianities profoundly transformed by the Enlightenment, which occurred in response to the philosophical, theological, and political difficulties generated by the Western Christianity of the first two-thirds of the second millennium. The bottom line for Hauerwas is that he cannot clean up the mess of contemporary Christianity while severed from the church of the first seven councils. Things only get more confused as he attempts piecemeal to criticize and remedy the Kantian collapse of Christian ethics into

you mean 'we,' Kemo Sabe?[4] I'm surely on the right side of the Enlightenment.[5] It seems you're not. I'm even on the correct side of the Renaissance. Don't forget, Stan, most of contemporary Western Christianity's

---

a universal ethics. He thinks it is enough to respond in terms of a narrative critique and
account of Christian history. See, in particular, Stanley Hauerwas, *The Peaceable Kingdom*
(Notre Dame, Ind.: University of Notre Dame Press, 1983), 61–64.

4. This involves an allusion to the radio program "The Lone Ranger," which began in
1933 and was continued in a television series. His faithful companion Tonto addressed
the Lone Ranger as "Kemo Sabe." This term may refer to a boy's camp in Michigan, or it
may mean "friendly Apache," "soggy bush," "trusty friend," or even "one who is white."
Among some Alaskan native peoples who have been Orthodox Christian for two hundred
years, "white man" is used to identify Protestants and Roman Catholics. In this case,
"Kemo Sabe" indicates a point of disagreement between me and Hauerwas, with me on
the side of Orthodox Christian Alaskans.

Hauerwas has introduced a "Tonto" principle: "The story goes that one time the Lone
Ranger and his faithful Indian sidekick, Tonto, found themselves surrounded by twenty-
thousand Sioux. The Lone Ranger turned to Tonto and asked, 'What do you think we
ought to do, Tonto?' Tonto responded, 'What do you mean by "we," white man?' . . . The
'Tonto' principle means that we cannot avoid asking Alasdair MacIntyre's questions,
'Whose justice? Which rationality?'" Hauerwas, *After Christendom?* (Nashville: Abingdon,
1991), 133. Saying "Kemo Sabe" elliptically invoked the Tonto principle to remind Stan
that one must always ask, Which church? Whose Christianity? What particular sense
of right worship and right belief? Getting it right as a Christian requires understanding
how properly to ask and answer these questions so that one unites oneself in the body of
Christ, which is the church, so as to discharge the obligation of being one, as the Father
and the Son are one (John 17:22). As to the appellation "Tonto," there is evidence that it
did not mean, as the Spanish would require, "a stupid or silly person, fool, or clown." Be
that as it may, my use of the term "Kemo Sabe" is far less problematic than Hauerwas's
use of "Tonto": a strike in favor of political correctness.

5. Traditional Christian views of the world are in many ways much closer to those
of Orthodox Judaism than to those of Roman Catholicism and the Protestant churches.
Traditional Christianity and Orthodox Judaism are on the right side of the Enlightenment (though the cleft started earlier: after Jerome and St. Ambrose, the Western church
began to deviate on the issue of suicide). For example, once while listening to a Reform
Jewish rabbi defend the allowability of physician-assisted euthanasia, I found myself
standing in the back of the lecture hall next to an Orthodox Jewish friend who said: "Tris,
before that son of Kant and the Enlightenment gives his exegesis, please tell me the real
meaning of the passage he is reading." The passage concerned the ship transporting
captives from Palestine after the fall of the second temple; when they discovered they
would be sold into bordellos, the captives leapt into the water; see *A Rabbinic Anthology*,
ed. C. G. Montefiore and H. Loewe (New York: Schocken Books, 1974), 265. My friend
continued: "Did they commit suicide?" I responded: "Absolutely not; they leapt into the
hands of God. Anyone may do that to avoid seduction or rape, as have many saints, even
Orthodox in the twentieth century." My friend then said: "Yes, you and I understand that,
but not that son of Kant!" For a twentieth-century example of a holy Father leaping to
seemingly certain death to avoid seduction, see the life of Augustinus the Russian (d.
1965), in Engelhardt, *Foundations of Christian Bioethics*, 328, 329, 347. Augustinus was
miraculously preserved. Hauerwas may not have been preserved from the seduction of
modernity. God help us all.

problems are rooted in the West's radical recasting of Christianity that began even before Charles the Great (a.k.a. Charlemagne) set in train his mini-Renaissance (and established a false Western empire over against Empress Irene of the second Rome).[6] All that led to a fundamentally different approach to theology (in short, 'My St. Constantine is far better than your Charlemagne'). As a result, in the West, theologians are no longer primarily holy men, but mostly passion-broken academicians like you and me." I then explained that I tried to live in continuity with the church of the first half-millennium.

At this point, I believe Hauerwas said something scatological (a safe bet). He tried to change the subject by asking if my wife and daughters were Orthodox. I told him my wife was, as were our two younger daughters.[7] "What do they think about all this?" he asked. I replied: "Stan, their only discussions have concerned when a menstruating woman may piously approach the communion chalice."[8] As I recounted, my two younger daughters had experienced a successful soft landing in the fourth century and were living in the light of St. Constantine the Great, Equal-to-the-Apostles.[9] Stan's expression was like that of someone who

6. Charles the Great may have attempted to make marriage with the Empress Irene. Contrary to some allegations, this was not the origin of the twentieth-century song, "Good Night, Irene." See J. B. Bury, "Charles the Great and Irene," *Hermathena* 8, no. 17 (1891): 17–37. It should be stressed that Irene as empress-regent did not rule in her own name but signed her name as Basileus, not Basilissa. She was the agent for the office of the emperor who is an icon of Christ.

7. For an account of my wife's conversion, see Susan Engelhardt, "Bless Me, St. Patrick, I'm Coming Home," *Again* 18 (June 1995): 18–19, and "From Rome to Home," in *Our Hearts' True Home*, ed. Virginia Nieuwsma (Ben Lomond, Calif.: Conciliar, 1996), 61–71.

8. See St. Dionysios of Alexandria, canon 2 (718), and St. Timothy of Alexandria, answer 7 (893), in Nicodemus and Agapius, *The Rudder*. In my household such discussions have abated. My wife and Orthodox daughters were for that matter always submissive to the mind of the Fathers. Far be it from me to note that my wife is too old to have practical interest in these matters. My two Orthodox daughters, on the other hand, have been either pregnant or nursing children for over half a decade each. The concerns of the latter are primarily expressed in my daughter the presbytera Dorothea making sure that her daughters let her nephews approach the communion chalice first, so as to acknowledge the headship of Adam in the family and in the church.

9. Hauerwas's use of "Constantinian" as a moral and theological invective can be understood if one recognizes Hauerwas's work as both crucially influenced by and cardinally in reaction against the Enlightenment transformation of Protestantism in the nineteenth and twentieth centuries. On the one hand, he wishes to reject the universalist claims of Enlightenment morality. On the other hand, he embraces the Enlightenment's rejection of clericism and church power (which, not unexpectedly, resonates with Anabaptist and free church movements). Hauerwas's Christianity is quintessentially American (oh, forgive me, Texan). The difficulty is that authentic Christianity is not a Western religion, but an Eastern religion. God in his sovereignty chose Israel; Christ was born in Palestine; and the vision of the authentic Christianity of the Apostles and the Fathers is radically other

confronts for the first time Stan's own ejaculations in Anglo-Saxon: *merdae caput,* etc. Our planes took us our separate ways.

---

than that of a Texan who, at the end of the twentieth and beginning of the twenty-first century, is as suspicious of ecclesial power as of state power, leading to a deep reluctance to identify church with a particular assembly with particular commitments to right worship and right belief. Thus Hauerwas (at times with Willimon) identifies Constantinianism both with a state-imposed religious viewpoint, and with a moral understanding effectively achieved in society by Christian communities. He thus seems to speak against Christians acting together "to ensure social order in the name of Christ." See Stanley Hauerwas and William Willimon, *Resident Aliens* (Nashville: Abingdon, 1989), 17. Hauerwas and Willimon describe the Fox Theater in Greenville, South Carolina, opening on Sundays in 1963 in defiance of local blue laws. They then state that the loss of "the notion that the church needs some sort of surrounding 'Christian' culture to prop it up and mold its young is not a death to lament. It is an opportunity to celebrate. The decline of the old, Constantinian synthesis between the church and the world means that we American Christians are at last free to be faithful in a way that makes being a Christian today an exciting adventure" (18).

Hauerwas (with Willimon) fails to distinguish between (a) a government imposing "a domesticated gospel" that would accord with some American version of a loosely conceived Christian framework and (b) the peaceable pressure Christians can place on society (e.g., through boycotts) to protect children from a neopagan culture. The mass secularization of youth in western Europe and North America indicates that the collapse of the "Constantinian" informal control of community life and education has in fact led to the salience of numerous subtle devices to seduce the children of Christians. To survive in a seductive secular culture like America's, one must have a stronger sense of what it is to be a Christian than that possessed by either Methodists or Roman Catholics. See, for example, Kenneth C. Jones, *Index of Leading Catholic Indicators* (Fort Collins, Colo.: Roman Catholic Books, 2003). One must have the kind of commitment to maintaining religious integrity and giving witness, even to death if necessary, sustained by Orthodox Judaism. But there is nothing wrong with trying in addition to defang some of the attacks of a hostile culture. Reading the account by Hauerwas and Willimon, I wonder if they were trying to raise children on a planet different from where my wife and I found ourselves.

Hauerwas also identifies Constantinianism with the view that discursive rationality can disclose Christianity as a truth apart from truthful witness: "As a result of the attempt to make Christianity anyone's fate, the truth that is God is assumed to be available to anyone, without moral transformation and spiritual guidance" (*With the Grain of the Universe*, 36). This characterization of Constantinianism has nothing to do with the theology or religious culture of Constantine or Constantine's time. It is rather a view that grew out of the Western faith in reason rooted in the peculiar developments of Western Christianity noted above. Hauerwas elsewhere in the same text qualifies his account of Constantinianism (221).

It is hard to underestimate St. Constantine the Great's importance for Christianity: by giving Christians freedom to worship in peace and security, he allowed Christianity to be expressed in its fullness. It is also difficult for a traditional Christian to appreciate the hesitation of many in recognizing the positive importance of St. Constantine. After all, Christians are asked by St. Peter to honor even a pagan emperor (1 Pet. 2:17). St. Paul when speaking of a pagan Roman government informs the Christians in Rome: "Let every person be subject to the governing authorities; for there is no authority except from God, and those authorities that exist have been instituted by God. Therefore whoever

My debt to Stan Hauerwas is deep. From him I learned a lot. He is a good and very generous, affective friend. Now we finally share the common task of witnessing that the Messiah of Israel has come, Jesus Christ, the Son of the living God, who has risen from the dead. As Stan realizes, this is the most politically incorrect and disturbing of truths. It threatens to break all who hear it out of their taken-for-granted accommodations to the world, to the flesh, and to the devil. I am here Stan's Amen Charlie. Traditional Christians find themselves in a community publicly at odds with the surrounding post-traditional, post-Christian society. Set off against a hostile culture and aimed at union with God, Christianity is not an individually oriented, self-help path to salvation. Christians are called to live, struggle, and worship in a community that is unlike other communities; it is the body of Christ (Eph. 5:30).

We confront a moral and metaphysical pluralism. Because there is a lack of common agreement about the foundations of morality, or with respect to who is in authority to resolve controversies,[10] moral (e.g., the morality of sexual acts outside of the marriage of a man and a woman) and metaphysical (e.g., the status of the embryo) controversies go on and on, as Alasdair MacIntyre has rightly noted.[11] Before my conversion, Stan would have agreed that he and I were moral strangers (albeit affective friends). We disagreed about the foundations of morality. Now that we both call ourselves Christians, one might hope that we could finally be moral friends as members of one moral community, united in a common agreement about what human life, the family, and community, indeed the universe are about. Alas, as Stan and I went to our different departure gates that day, it was clear that such was not the

---

resists authority resists what God has appointed" (Rom. 13:1–2). If Christians can speak in such affirming fashions of pagan emperors who would persecute Christians, think of how they ought to respond to an emperor who as a Christian assured the growth of the church and the conversion of millions. It is for this reason that the church sings at the *litya* of Vespers for the feast of Saints Constantine and Helena: "As is meet, we celebrate thy memory, O Constantine, equal of the apostles, thou foundation and boast of all kings; for, illumined by the rays of the Spirit, thou didst enlighten the whole Church of Christ, gathering together assemblies of the faithful from everywhere in the city of Nicea. . . . Wherefore, we who celebrate thy memory entreat thee with faith: ask thou cleansing of transgressions for our souls." See *The Menaion of the Orthodox Church*, trans. Isaac Lambertsen (Liberty, Tenn.: St. John of Kronstadt, 1996), vol. 9, 178.

10. For an account of moral friends and moral strangers in terms of when individuals are united in a community able to resolve their controversies by appeal to common premises and rules of evidence, or by appeal to a commonly recognized authority, see H. T. Engelhardt, Jr., *Foundations of Bioethics*, 2nd ed. (New York: Oxford University Press, 1996), chaps. 1–2.

11. Alasdair MacIntyre, *After Virtue* (Notre Dame, Ind.: University of Notre Dame Press, 1981), 1.

case. In particular, we did not agree about the nature of the church to which we both recognized we are called to be members.

Separated by Christ

Hauerwas and I are separated by the present, the past, and the connection between the two. I find myself living in a life-world fully at one with St. Basil the Great (AD 329–379), St. John Chrysostom (AD 354–407), St. Gregory the Theologian (AD 329–390), St. Photios the Great (AD 820–891), St. Symeon the New Theologian (AD 949–1022), St. Gregory Palamas (AD 1296–1359), St. Mark of Ephesus (AD 1392–1444), St. Herman of Alaska (AD 1757–1836), and St. John of San Francisco (AD 1894–1966). Like other Orthodox Christians, I strive to live in the *phronema*, the mind of the Fathers, a context that to outsiders is strikingly untouched by the Western experience of the Renaissance, the Reformation, and the Enlightenment. In contrast, Western theologians, including Stanley Hauerwas, live in a discipline whose style of thought is defined by a conversation and community of thought immediately shared with recent academic theologians such as Reinhold Niebuhr, Karl Barth, Paul Ramsey, James Gustafson, and John Howard Yoder. This community's center of gravity is in the present so that the Fathers of the first millennium no longer live immediately in its conversations. For members of this community, the Fathers are in the past; the Fathers are no longer present; the Fathers are no longer at firsthand. The Fathers' presence is mediated through layers of subsequent commentators. Moreover and most importantly, theology has become for members of this community primarily a matter of academic analysis, examination, and dispute, rather than a common experience in the heart open to God. Hauerwas and I are separated by different experiences of what it is to live in the body of Christ, the church.

Hauerwas claims that "the church is the extended argument over time about the significance of that story [of Christ] and how best to understand it."[12] For him the church as a community is sustained in an ongoing reflection and narrative regarding the significance of the narratives concerning Christ. The church becomes the bearer of, and not just the adventitious producer of, an academic metanarrative otherwise known as Christian theology (at least as theology has come to be understood in the West). The higher truth of the church is in this circumstance in danger of becoming theology academically construed.[13]

---

12. Hauerwas, *The Peaceable Kingdom,* 107.
13. For the Roman church, theology becomes integral to the magisterium and is understood as a robustly scholarly undertaking. "Through the course of centuries, theology

Among many things, this means that the church is not the community that allows one to share a common theological "Now" with St. Basil the Great, and with relatively unlettered holy Fathers of recent times such as Paisios of the Holy Mountain (1924–1994).[14] The church is not a common experience sustained in a shared appreciation of and engagement in baptism, chrismation, the Eucharist, and the other mysteries that bind the members of the church as the "assembly of the saints," to quote Emperor Constantine the Great in his paschal oration (AD 324). For the Christianity of the first millennium, the church itself would not have been thought of as an extended argument: the church is the body of Christ. Countless heresies break upon the peace of her members, pressing them unwillingly into arguments, as they strive to remain in unity with the unbroken truth of the Apostles and the Fathers.[15] But the unity of the church is achieved in the Holy Spirit. It is a work of God. It is a miracle.

This brief examination of one element of Hauerwas's work addresses some of his reflections about community, church, and the nature of Christianity. My goal is not to be systematic or exhaustive, but rather heuristic and provocative. Recapturing a proper understanding of church is a prime contemporary challenge. Hauerwas and I are separated on what this should mean. I embrace a sense of church from that time which for Stan Hauerwas is terrible—the splendor of Christendom, the age of the ancient Fathers, set in the light of St. Constantine the Great. Where Hauerwas sees a new (and wrongly directed) Christendom emerging with St. Constantine's reign, I see apostolic Christianity finally given its opportunity to flourish relatively secure from persecution and in the light of a large-scale pursuit of the counsels of perfection.[16] My purpose

---

has progressively developed into a true and proper science." See the "Instruction on the Ecclesial Vocation of the Theologian," *Origins* 20 (July 5, 1990): 120.

14. See, for example, Geronde Paisios, *Hagioreitai Pateres kai Hagioreitika* (Thessaloniki: Holy Monastery Monazouson, 1993); and Priestmonk Christodoulos, *Elder Paisios of the Holy Mountain* (Holy Mountain, 1998).

15. As the Fathers of the seven ecumenical councils declared in AD 787: "To make our confession short, we keep unchanged all the ecclesiastical traditions handed down to us, whether in writing or verbally. . . . For we follow the most ancient legislation of the Catholic Church. We keep the laws of the Fathers. We anathematize those who add anything to or take anything away from the Catholic Church. We anathematize the introduced novelty of the revilers of Christians." See the "Decree of the Holy, Great, Ecumenical Synod, the Second of Nice," in *Nicene and Post-Nicene Fathers*, 2nd ser., ed. Philip Schaff and Henry Wace (Peabody, Mass.: Hendrickson, 1994), vol. 14, 550–51.

16. The age of Constantine was also an age of the flourishing of monasticism, an age in which people were willing wholeheartedly to follow Christ's injunction: "Go, sell your possessions and give to the poor, and you will have treasure in heaven" (Matt. 19:21). This is a hard saying for Protestants.

is to show that here, as elsewhere, Hauerwas has led us to confront a core issue in the definition of ourselves: the meaning of church.

The Church as the Body of Christ

Hauerwas has creatively explored the character of human community, especially Christian community, under the metaphors of the peaceable community[17] and the community of character.[18] However, he does not explore in depth what it is to have the church as community. On the surface, it appears that the ambivalence lies in his indecision as to how Protestant or how Roman Catholic he really wishes to be (it seems never to have dawned on him to consider Orthodoxy). Consider his answer to his own question, "Do I write as a Catholic or as a Protestant?"—namely: "I do not believe that theology when rightly done is either Catholic or Protestant. The object of the theologian's inquiry is quite simply God—not Catholicism or Protestantism. The proper object of the qualifier 'catholic' is the church, not theology or theologians."[19] The difficulty is that theology must be formed in catholicity. Theology is at its roots a rightly ordered, prayerful relationship with God. The church does not exist abstracted from right worship and right belief but lives in doxologizing and theologizing God. The church unites her members in her *ecclesia,* the assembly of the faithful, which assembly is united in the body of Christ only insofar as it maintains right worship and right belief. The councils of the first millennium focused on excommunicating those who believed, worshipped, and acted wrongly. In the ancient church—as in devout monasteries today—only those who could join in the mysteries could remain in the nave of the church once the Liturgy of the Faithful began. Hauerwas neglects the grounds for communion.

With almost all of the West he has lost the cardinal appreciation that theology is in its roots an empirical science grounded in a noetic experience of God that rises out of rightly directed worship.[20] Thus the force of Evagrios the Solitary's (Evagrios of Pontus, AD 345–399) famous axiom:

17. Hauerwas, *The Peaceable Kingdom.*
18. Stanley Hauerwas, *A Community of Character: Toward a Constructive Christian Social Ethic* (Notre Dame, Ind.: University of Notre Dame Press, 1981).
19. Hauerwas, *The Peaceable Kingdom,* xxiv.
20. The church of the first seven councils understood and understands that the Christian life should lead to *theoria,* to seeing God, thus taking seriously the sixth beatitude: "Blessed are the pure in heart, for they will see God" (Matt. 5:8). This church understood and understands that it was the ancestral sin of Adam that closed the heart to God, and it is the grace of a Christian life that can open it. See, for example, John Romanides, *The Ancestral Sin,* trans. George S. Gabriel (Ridgewood, N.Y.: Zephyr, 2002).

"If you are a theologian, you will pray truly. And if you pray truly, you are a theologian."[21] Hauerwas also fails to note that, as a consequence, the community of believers, which is truly the church, is that of which "catholic" is appropriately predicated. It is the church, the assembly united in right worship, that preserves right belief through the indwelling of the Holy Spirit; the Spirit grounds the church's theology, so that her assembly is full, complete, whole, and catholic.[22] As an Orthodox Christian, I can understand Hauerwas's ambivalence about choosing between Roman Catholicism and Protestantism. After all, the truth lies with a *tertium quid* (i.e., Orthodox Christianity), an unbroken tradition at one with the Fathers, of which Roman Catholicism and Protestantism have preserved only fragments.[23] Orthodoxy recognizes the enduring commitments required to be in unity with the ancient Christian church alive today, which is the same yesterday, today, and tomorrow (Heb. 13:8).

Hauerwas seems to have flirted with Roman views. Having grown to his scholarly strength as the Roman church was taking on a Protestant character in the wake of Vatican II, Hauerwas may have experienced the Romans as a credible third way between the Protestants and the Roman Catholics of yore. Vatican II had clearly rejected Boniface VIII's *extra ecclesia nulla salus*.[24] At least until Cardinal Ratzinger's *Dominus Iesus*,[25]

---

21. Evagrios the Solitary, "On Prayer," in *The Philokalia*, ed. Saints Nikodimos and Makarios, trans. G. E. H. Palmer, Philip Sherrard, and Kallistos Ware (Boston: Faber and Faber, 1988), vol. 1, 62.

22. The declarations of faith as well as the canons of the first seven ecumenical councils focus on uniting right-believing Christians in one identifiable living church.

23. While at Notre Dame, Hauerwas characterized himself as a high-church Mennonite. "I am, after all, a (Southern) Methodist of doubtful theological background (when you are a Methodist it goes without saying you have a doubtful theological background); who teaches and worships with and is sustained morally and financially by Roman Catholics; who believes that the most nearly faithful form of Christian witness is best exemplified by the often unjustly ignored people called Anabaptists or Mennonites. In short my ecclesial preference is to be a high-church Mennonite," Hauerwas, *A Community of Character*, 6. As to the issue of Southern Methodist, I can understand his emphasis on "Southern" in the parentheses. My mother's mother told me of the tragedy when a family member married a Northern Baptist. O tempora! O mores! Ecclesial commitment is a serious matter.

24. The Romans once declared there to be "One holy Church . . . outside of which there is neither salvation nor remission of sins. . . . Furthermore we declare, state, define and pronounce that it is altogether necessary to salvation for every human creature to be subject to the Roman pontiff." See Boniface VIII, "Unam sanctam" (November 18, 1302), in *Documents of the Christian Church*, ed. Henry Bettenson (New York: Oxford University Press, 1963), 159, 161. "Unam sanctam Ecclesiam . . . extra quam nec salus est nec remissio peccatorum. . . . Porro subesse Romano Pontifici omni humanae creaturae declaramus, dicimus, diffinimus omnino esse de necessitate salutis." *Enchiridion Symbolorum definitionum et declarationum de rebus fidei et morum*, ed. Henricus Denzinger (Freiburg: Herder, 1965), secs. 870, 875; pp. 280–81.

the take-home message seemed to be that one could choose among different "Christian" communities as more or less adequate realizations of the Christian church. The church did not appear to require an assembly united in right worship, right belief, and one chalice. For this reason, Hauerwas can worry about whether Karl Barth was sufficiently "catholic" and then opine: "Barth is not sufficiently catholic just to the extent that his critique and rejection of Protestant liberalism make it difficult for him to acknowledge that, through the work of the Holy Spirit, we are made part of God's care of the world through the church."[26] Here "catholic" has to do the work of a concern for the world, which in liberal Protestantism came to be mediated by a state strong enough to engage not only in welfare programs but also in waging total war.[27] To compass all of this service, the "catholicity" of the church becomes a mark that identifies a largeness of tent, not the wholeness of right worship and right belief that unites the church over space and time with the church of the Apostles and the Fathers.

Hauerwas identifies the church with a community committed to the proclamation of the gospel and a care for the world (not to mention with narrative and extended argument about Christ and his message) but not with transforming holiness. Among the difficulties is that there are thousands of Protestant sects proclaiming the gospel, caring for the world, and arguing about Jesus in a great multitude of ways. There is a legion of witnesses to different truths.[28] It was clear to me in the airport that either Hauerwas is unclear as to how he wishes to understand the truth of the church, or else his sense of the church's truth is radically incompatible with the church of the seven councils, or both. For Hauerwas the unity of the church, the being of the *ecclesia*, the assembly of those who confess Christ is not found and expressed in a unity of right worship or right belief. For Hauerwas the members of the church do not appear to need to agree about what it means for Jesus to be the Christ. In this circumstance of robust theological and ecclesiological pluralism, what can it mean to speak of the church, indeed, of Christ's church?

25. Congregation for the Doctrine of the Faith, *Dominus Iesus* (Vatican City: August 6, 2000).

26. Hauerwas, *With the Grain of the Universe*, 145.

27. Consider Adolf von Harnack's address on September 29, 1914: "What we have won already and what we still must win" (Was wir schon gewonnen haben und was wir noch gewinnen müssen). See *Rede am 29. Sept. 1914*, ed. Zentralstelle für Volkswohlfahrt und Verein für volkstumliche Kurse von Berliner Hochschullehren (Berlin: Carl Heymanns Verlag, 1914).

28. When the witness of the spirit is legion, one must worry as to which spirits are speaking. See Mark 5:9.

In his account of church, Hauerwas trades, inter alia, on a strategically underdefined concept of the empirical and of the ideal. For example, he states:

> The people of God are no less an empirical reality than the crucifixion of Christ. The church is as real as his cross. There is no ideal church, no invisible church, no mystically existing universal church more real than the concrete church with parking lots and potluck dinners. No, it is the church of parking lots and potluck dinners that comprises the sanctified ones formed by, and forming the continuing story of Jesus Christ in the world. In effect, the church is the extended argument over time about the significance of that story and how best to understand it.[29]

In contrast, an Orthodox would have placed these observations in a different context, presupposing a different account of grace, church, and empirical knowledge. Consider:

> The people of God are an empirical reality, just like Christ at the crucifixion. Of course, one cannot appreciate who Christ is, the significance of the crucifixion, and the meaning of the redemption, save through a heart illumined by the Holy Spirit. In this very particular sense, the church is as real as his cross. There is no ideal church in that there is no church that falls short of the ideal (it is individuals who are more or less ideal, more or less sinful). The church is the very body of Christ, into which all are born by valid baptism, and within which Christians remain by persevering in right worship and right belief. The church is not concrete buildings with parking lots and potluck dinners. The temple where there is the assembly of the church, the body of Christ, is hallowed by the presence of that body, which is indeed a mystical body, a window to the transcendent presence of God. Church as the body of Christ is not just the continuing story of Christ in the world. It is through Christ being in the world that one can enter into the history of redemption that stretches from the incarnation to the second coming. It is in the church that we not only remember but also encounter the life of Christ, his saints, and his ever-present miracles. The church is not a continued argument about Christ over time, though the church as a sign of contradiction provokes contention. The church invites us into a place before and beyond arguments, the peace and unity of the presence of the Holy Spirit. It is here that we rightly experience and in unity understand.

This appreciation recognizes the church as a force and reality transcending space and history.

---

29. Hauerwas, *The Peaceable Kingdom*, 107.

In Hauerwas's text there is no indication that by "empirical" (the "empirical reality" of the cross and the church) he has in mind a noetic experience of the church as the body of Christ. His account of church is strikingly immanent and nonincarnational. Nor is it clear how much heresy (indeed, if any) should leave one in the parking lot outside the church and its potluck dinners.[30] Hauerwas argues, for example, that the church is "not some ideal of community but a particular people who, like Israel, must find the way to sustain its existence generation after generation."[31] Here a recognition is lacking that Israel was not united by its own works but through the uncreated energies of God. In this very significant passage, there is no acknowledgment that Christians, by dying to themselves and taking on Christ, can become a part of the body of Christ, a community that will in fact prevail unaltered until the restoration of all things (Heb. 13:8).

The extent to which Hauerwas's account of the church and the sacraments is nonsacramental is highlighted in his account of marriage. As Hauerwas puts it: "Christian marriage is not a 'natural' institution but rather the creation of a people who marry for very definite purposes."[32] The notion that marriage is a Christian creation, rather than a sanctification by the church through God's grace of a natural relation, sounds at odds with St. Paul's account in Ephesians. St. Paul seamlessly integrates marriage into the nature of the church itself: "'For this reason a man will leave his father and mother and be united to his wife, and the two will become one flesh.' This is a profound mystery [*mysterion*]—but I am talking about Christ and the church" (Eph. 5:31–32).[33] Hauerwas does not acknowledge that the church as the body of Christ is able to radically transform its members and in the process to sanctify and transform all of our everyday undertakings. It is not just that he lacks a catholic sense of liturgy (e.g., that right worship is a necessary condition for assembling in the church), an issue much more profound than a mere liturgical sense. He also fails to appreciate that the transformative power of the church, insofar as it is effectively liturgical, is embodied not merely in its narratives but most importantly and crucially in the uncreated energies of God. This nonsacramental character of Hauerwas's theology indicates how robustly Protestant his account of church turns out to be.

---

30. St. John the Theologian radically excluded heretics from the Christian potluck dinners of his age. "Do not take him into your house or welcome him. Anyone who welcomes him shares in his wicked work [of false doctrine]" (2 John 10–11).

31. Hauerwas, *The Peaceable Kingdom*, 107.

32. Hauerwas, *A Community of Character*, 189.

33. Let the reader be warned: a subtext here is the Orthodox recognition that, though natural marriage is contractual, the mystery or sacrament of marriage is not a contract, but an act of the body of Christ by which the couple is transformed.

This point becomes even clearer when Hauerwas lays out the "marks" of the church as the community where "the sacraments are celebrated, the word is preached, and upright lives are encouraged and lived."[34] Mention of the marks of the church as apostolic and catholic (in the sense of compassing the whole of right belief in continuity with the beliefs of the Apostles) is strikingly absent. The sacraments to which Hauerwas makes reference do not bring the recipient into union with the holy, in the sense of that power who can radically transform us, so that the church is indeed more than its parking lots and potluck dinners. The sacraments for Hauerwas appear to possess more of a narrative than a mystagogical force. They are not mysteries that open to us the reality of the unchanging presence and reality of Christ. Rather, the "sacraments enact the story of Jesus and, thus, form a community in his image."[35] For Hauerwas, within the church as a community sustained by narrative, the mysteries do not through the energies of God actually and factually render us holy.[36] His truncated account of the mysteries is not surprising. Again, this is one of the things that being a Protestant can be about. It is for this reason that, against Hauerwas and most Protestants, both Roman Catholics and Orthodox Christians are in agreement that "ecclesial communities which have not preserved the valid Episcopate and the genuine and integral substance of the Eucharistic mystery are not Churches in the proper sense."[37]

34. Hauerwas, *A Community of Character*, 189.

35. Ibid.

36. For Hauerwas, tradition is not the carrying on of the Holy Spirit so that the community remains united in right worship and right belief. "Tradition, as we use the term here, is a complex, lively argument about what happened in Jesus that has been carried on, across the generations, by a concrete body of people called the church," *Resident Aliens*, 72.

37. As the Roman church currently puts it: "Therefore, there exists a single Church of Christ, which subsists in the Catholic Church, governed by the Successor of Peter and by the Bishops in communion with him. The Churches which, while not existing in perfect communion with the Catholic Church, remain united to her by means of the closest bonds, that is, by apostolic succession and a valid Eucharist, are true particular Churches" (Congregation for the Doctrine of the Faith, "Declaration Dominus Iesus," section 17). Besides the Roman church, the churches with apostolic succession and valid Eucharist are for Joseph Cardinal Ratzinger, the prefect of the Congregation, only those of the Orthodox. See Ratzinger and Christian Geyer, "Es scheint mir absurd, was unsere lutherischen Freunde jetzt wollen," *Frankfurter Allgemeine Zeitung* (September 22, 2000): 51–52. This quotation from the Roman Congregation for the Doctrine of the Faith should not suggest an affirmation of Roman ecclesiology; rather, one should note Metropolitan Maximos's statement: "In some theological circles, the contemporary Orthodox Church is viewed as just one of many Christian 'denominations' (*Partikularkirche*). This is a misrepresentation of Holy Orthodoxy. Orthodoxy is not a denomination. It is the Church of the Apostles and of the Fathers. Its faith and ethos are those of the early Church. The doctrine of the

Hauerwas's account of the sacraments is closely tied to his near reduction of being holy to being charitable, hospitable, just, and pacifist: "The church . . . [is] called to be a holy people—that is, a people who are capable of maintaining the life of charity, hospitality, and justice."[38] Hauerwas's account does not recognize that the holiness of the Christian church is the real and palpable energy of God, which rightly locates and transforms charity, hospitality, and justice, and which is manifest, for example, when St. Paul is so changed that handkerchiefs touched to him can cure others (Acts 19:12). In particular, holiness is incarnate in that church rightly united in the prime liturgical act of communion. For this reason in the *epiclesis* of St. Basil's liturgy the church prays: "And as for us, partakers of the one bread and of the cup, do thou unite all to one another unto communion of the one Holy Spirit, and grant that no one of us may partake of the holy Body and Blood of thy Christ unto judgment or unto condemnation, but rather that we may find mercy and grace."[39] The Eucharist unites the church across time and space. In contrast, Hauerwas's holiness seems to come closer to the domesticated holiness of a post-Kantian Protestant who equates the holy with the moral, with an overlay of enthusiasm for the experience of God's awesomeness. Hauerwas indicates that he wants to say more, as when he speaks of the sacraments opening us up to the "wild presence" of God.[40] But just as one thinks he is about to take seriously the circumstance that love of neighbor can never be rightly achieved except in the light of a love of God rightly directed in true worship, he construes the love and peace of God in terms of the upright life and the pacifism that he sets centrally.

The central role Hauerwas gives pacifism in isolation from chastity and right worship is puzzling.[41] In failing to incorporate a substantive

---

Orthodox Church is the doctrine of the undivided Church, the doctrine of the Apostles, the Fathers, and the seven (or eight) ecumenical councils." See Metropolitan Maximos, "Turning Our Hearts to the Fathers," *Touchstone* 16 (July 2003): 43. Christ's church is without branches and with both lungs (there are, after all, Western Rite Orthodox), and that church is the church about which Bishop Maximos speaks.

38. Hauerwas, *The Peaceable Kingdom*, 109.

39. *The Liturgicon* (Englewood, N.J.: Antiochian Orthodox Christian Archdiocese, 1989), 292–93.

40. Hauerwas, *The Peaceable Kingdom*, 108.

41. On chastity, it should not be overlooked that St. Paul emphasizes that the community of Christians is not to include the *unrepentantly* sexually immoral. They are not to be invited to the potluck dinners. "With such a man do not even eat" (1 Cor. 5:9–11). As for right worship, the ancient church took seriously the injunction that Christians are called to be perfect, as the Father is perfect (Matt. 5:48), and to be one with the Father, as Christ is one with the Father (John 17:22). In this light, one can understand the ecclesiology of the Apostles and the Fathers, which one finds, for instance, recorded in the letters of St.

account of the holy, his pacifism is placed in an account of a church at odds with the ancient church, where concern with having blood on one's hands was understood in light of the requirement of right worship. I do not mean to quarrel with Stan Hauerwas's pacifism directly. I might be inclined to quote the admonitions of St. John the Baptist to the Roman soldiers, namely, that they should be satisfied with their wages and not pillage (nowhere does he say they should not wage war).[42] Nor am I

Ignatius of Antioch, who emphasizes that one comes into union with the Father through being in obedient union with a right-believing bishop, who sums up the wholeness, the catholicity of the church: "As then the Lord was united to the Father and did nothing without him, . . . so do you do nothing without the bishop and the presbyters." See "Ignatius to the Magnesians," 7.1, in *Apostolic Fathers*, trans. Kirsopp Lake (Cambridge, Mass.: Harvard University Press, 1965), 103. This union is first and foremost found in an actual and hierarchical eucharistic assembly: "See that you all follow the bishop, as Jesus Christ follows the Father, and the presbytery as if it were the Apostles. And reverence the deacons as the command of God. Let no one do any of the things appertaining to the Church without the bishop. Let that be considered a valid Eucharist which is celebrated by the bishop, or by one whom he appoints. Wherever the bishop appears let the congregation be present; just as wherever Jesus Christ is, there is the Catholic Church" ("Ignatius to the Smyrnaeans," 8.1–2, in *Apostolic Fathers*, 161).

Ignatius underscores that a Eucharist celebrated without the authority of the bishop (and it is clear from his letters that he means a nonheretical, that is, right-worshipping and right-believing bishop) is invalid. Hauerwas's account of a church lacks recognition of the essential centering given by right worship, the apostolic episcopacy, and the Eucharist.

42. The Gospels do not directly condemn waging war. For example: "He [St. John the Baptist] replied [to the soldiers], 'Don't extort money and don't accuse people falsely—be content with your pay'" (Luke 3:14). Christ cures the centurion's slave (Matt. 8:5–13) and Peter baptized the centurion Cornelius and his household (Acts 10:48), all without any suggestion that they should cease to discharge their bloody duties as Roman soldiers. These passages of the Scriptures are fully in concert with St. Paul's warning that those in authority do "not bear the sword for nothing" (Rom. 13:4). Some Texans dispute whether the original Greek indicated a sword or a pistol, but pacifism does not seem to be required.

Early Christian views regarding military service cover a wide range, and there is not enough of a record remaining to establish their unity. For an overview of the range of opinions, see Louis J. Swift, *The Early Fathers on War and Military Service* (Wilmington, Del.: Michael Glazier, 1983). Though Tertullian (AD 160–220) speaks against military service, he also explicitly acknowledges the presence of Christians in the twelfth legion (*legio XII fulminata*) during the campaign against the Germans and Sarmatians in AD 173: "If you will examine the letters of the most venerable emperor, Marcus Aurelius. In his letters he attests that the great drought in Germany was relieved by rain which fell in answer to the prayers of the Christians who happened to be in his army" (Tertullian, "Apology" 5.6, in *Tertullian: Apologetical Works*, trans. R. Arbesmann, E. J. Daly, and E. A. Quain (Washington, D.C.: Catholic University Press, 1962), 21–22. Even St. Cyprian (d. 258), considerably before the advent of St. Constantine the Great, appeals to the appropriate virtues and duties of soldiers in the defense of orthodoxy against heresy. "It is the duty of a good soldier to defend the camp of his commander against enemies and rebels; it is the duty of an illustrious general to guard the standards entrusted to his safekeeping." See *The Letters of St. Cyprian of Carthage*, trans. G. W. Clarke (New York:

disposed to speak of such great warrior saints as St. Alexander Nevsky (1220–1263), or of how St. Sergius of Radonezh (d. 1393) sent to Dmitry, prince of Moscow, the message that holy Russia would prevail over the Muslim invaders at the battle of Kovikolo Pole on September 8, 1380. The point is that Hauerwas's pacifism is not integrated into an account of how in holiness and purity Christians are called to approach God.

Miserabile factu: as I sat on the plane taking me away from Stan Hauerwas, it was apparent how different our life-worlds remained. We could not share the same chalice. If church is communion, we were not of one church. Indeed, I understood that we were separated by what church means, what that body of Christ is of which Christians are to be members. For Stan, it was not crucially important to worry, as the authors of the Nicene–Constantinopolitan Creed did in fact worry, about being a member of that actual, one, holy, catholic, and apostolic Church: that real, living, yet mystical community united in worship, belief, and the Eucharist over time and space.[43] That church, that *ecclesia*, that assembly is for Hauerwas, as it is now for many if not most in the West, not an actual assembly transformed by and united to Christ. He is painfully insistent on the dialogical, argumentative, and narrative rather than the hierological character of the church and of theology: church for him sustains a quasi-academic dialogue, as if to deny the metaphysical reality of the mystical body of Christ.

Newman, 1989), letter 73, 10.1, 59. The Fathers integrate the concern to turn the other cheek (Matt. 5:38–41), avoid violence, and keep one's hands free from blood by recognizing both (1) that taking human life tends to fall short of the mark, to harm the agent, and to be a stumbling block on the road to holiness, and (2) that soldiers should protect their country, even with deadly force if necessary, though this may harm their hearts (by involving a *hamartia*, an act that may not perfectly aim at God). It is for this reason that the Orthodox Church generally excommunicates even those who out of moral obligations take life in a just war. "Our Fathers did not consider murders committed in the course of wars to be classifiable as murders at all, on the score, it seems to me, of allowing a pardon to men fighting in defense of sobriety and piety. Perhaps, though, it might be advisable to refuse them communion for three years, on the ground that they are not clean-handed" ("Canons of St. Basil the Great," in Nicodemus and Agapius, *The Rudder*, canon 13, 801). After returning from war, they may be excommunicated for a period of time, not for punishment, but for therapy of their hearts. In this nonjuridical sense, sins can be involuntary and committed in ignorance.

43. Belief in the church has from the earliest periods been recognized as integral to being Christian. For example, a baptismal profession (ca. AD 215–217) attributed to St. Hippolytus requires the catechumen to respond affirmatively to the question: "Do you believe in the Holy Church?" Similarly, the der-balizeh papyrus (with origins in the second century) records in its creed a profession of belief in the "Holy Catholic Church." See *The Christian Faith*, ed. J. Neuner and J. Dupuis (New York: Alba House, 1982), 3. All evidence indicates such creeds identified a real assembly that understood itself to be united in right worship, right belief, and one communion.

T. S. Eliot, in *Sweeney Agonistes,* underscores that birth, copulation, and death are all the facts when you get down to brass tacks.[44] In subtle and often not-too-subtle ways, Hauerwas and I, after our encounter at the airport, were in disagreement about the meaning of these passion-laden elements and passages of human life. We were again moral strangers; we looked at Christianity in radically different ways from within fundamentally different communities. It was not just that I was part of a community about to enter a Lenten fast like that described by Egeria,[45] and now totally forgotten in the West. We were separated by divergent accounts of right worship and right belief, in great measure because we were separated by different understandings of church embedded in incompatible theological epistemologies and divergent sociologies of the holy. For all the important ways in which he has forced us to think about what it is to be a Christian at the beginning of the twenty-first century, Hauerwas has left his account of church undeveloped.

Being a Christian in a Post-Christian Age

Hauerwas has indicated how, by living with the grain of the universe, one is oriented to its Creator, though one is called to live against the grain of the moral and theological conceits of our age. Being a right-believing Christian is, as Christ warns us, to live against the commitments of the world (John 15:18–19). The nature of an enduring church as an assembly in right worship and right belief is a great puzzle and scandal for many contemporary Christians who (1) approach the Scriptures as merely a text that gives a point of departure for scholarship rather than offers an icon through which to see God (after all, the Scriptures are not revelation itself, but a record of revelation); (2) engage in discursive theological reflection, having forgotten that one must aim at actual illumination by God; and (3) use "church" as a vague umbrella term under which to gather various assemblies of disparate believers separated by fundamentally incompatible understandings of the moral and hierological significance of sex, reproduction, chastity, charity, suffering, dying, death, the church, and Christ himself. Hauerwas brings us directly and indirectly to confront this cardinal cluster of challenges, leaving us all the richer.

44. T. S. Eliot, "Fragment of an Agon," in *The Complete Poems and Plays 1909–1950* (New York: Harcourt, Brace, 1952), 80.

45. See Egeria, *Diary of a Pilgrimage,* trans. George E. Gingras (New York: Newman, 1970).

11

Ecumenisms in Conflict

Where Does Hauerwas Stand?

George Lindbeck

This essay is in part an apology. It is a long-delayed response to what Stanley Hauerwas has written to and about me over the years. To be sure, the imbalance in our exchanges is to some extent the result of an asymmetry in our areas of work. Up until twenty years ago, Stan and I had gone our separate ways. He had focused, as he has continued to do, on theology and ethics in relation to the contemporary American situation, and I had concentrated on history in other times and on ecumenism in other places. This division of labor was broken, however, by my *Nature of Doctrine: Religion and Theology in a Postliberal Age*, which was, and still is, peripheral to my main concerns but overlaps with his.[1]

---

1. George Lindbeck, *Nature of Doctrine: Religion and Theology in a Postliberal Age* (Philadelphia: Westminster, 1984). This book is peripheral because it is a less-than-necessary offshoot of the ecumenical practice of doctrinal "reconciliation without capitulation,"

Stan found the book helpful for his purposes and has been unfailingly fair and almost always favorable in his references to it and to other, shorter pieces on related topics.[2] In contrast, none of his output bears with comparable directness on my work (though indirect influences are not lacking). Yet that does not excuse my silence. I have been able to find only two references to him in what I have published: one is routine, and the other, unfair.[3]

---

which developed especially after Vatican II. It is a less-than-necessary offshoot because its aim is to make theoretically intelligible the possibility of what by some conventional standards is the self-contradictory practice of reconciliation without capitulation. Nothing of vital consequence for the practice hinges on the theories of religion and doctrine that the book expounds in its effort to persuade doubters that what is actually happening is indeed possible. The common-sense medieval axiom *ab esse ad posse valet illatio* (from being to possibility is a valid inference) is the premise, for just as *esse* takes precedence over *posse*, the practice is prior to and independent of the theory of its possibility. This approach, it will be observed, resembles Kantian transcendental deductions in that these latter are also investigations of the conditions of the possibility of an assumed reality. The difference is that the theories of religion and doctrine proposed in *Nature of Doctrine* as conditions of the possibility of doctrinal reconciliations without capitulation are not "transcendental": they are not said to be the necessary, nor the only, nor the best account of the possibility of the actualities under discussion.

2. Hauerwas first refers to me, as far as I know, in the nine admirable pages on my *Nature of Doctrine* with which he begins his *Against the Nations* (Minneapolis: Winston, 1985). He sent me a copy of the book together with a warm-hearted letter, which, to my shame, I never answered. I wanted to tell him of my reactions in detail, but never got around to writing them up. Much the same pattern has been repeated over and over again, even if less egregiously. The most recent instance is in my failure to thank Stan for two footnotes in *With the Grain of the Universe: The Church's Witness and Natural Theology* (Grand Rapids, Mich.: Brazos Press, 2001). In one of these, Stan says, to my pleased surprise, that a forgotten article I published forty-five years ago "was the first to show that [Reinhold] Niebuhr's work, in spite of his denials, could be construed in natural law terms" (134). In the other he defends at some length my now notorious suggestion that "the crusader's cry '*Christus est Dominus*' while cleaving the skull of the infidel falsifies the claim" (176). Fuller treatments of the debate over this point are in Reinhard Hütter, *Suffering Divine Things: Theology as Church Practice* (Grand Rapids, Mich.: Eerdmans, 2000), 191–94. Hauerwas goes further than such treatments, however, by arguing that the view of the self-involving character of religious discourse exemplified by the above suggestion is closer to Barth than critics have thought.

3. The "routine" reference is an acknowledgment in the preface of the 1994 German translation of *Nature of Doctrine* that Hauerwas and I have "affinities" (with no indication of what they are). The "unfair" reference, dating from 1990, seeks to distance me from "a disenchantment with Christendom" close to Hauerwas's that "led me . . . to hope for the end of cultural Christianity" so that "diaspora Christianity" could flourish. These two references are reprinted in a collection of my essays, *The Church in a Postliberal Age* (Grand Rapids, Mich.: Eerdmans, 2002), 199, and 2, cf. 7, respectively.

One reason I now consider the second reference unfair is an article Hauerwas sent me before it was published (and for which I don't remember thanking him), "What Could It Mean for the Church to Be Christ's Body," now in Stanley Hauerwas, *In Good Company*

Why This Question?

Ecumenism is the obvious topic on which to break the silence; it is important to both of us, but in very different ways. Hauerwas's ecumenicity is in some respects exemplary, and yet he has published scarcely anything about ecumenism as a movement or practice as far as I have been able to ascertain. The great bulk of what I have written, in contrast, is about or on behalf of these enterprises.[4] (This is especially true if one includes unpublished and often unsigned working papers and drafts of group reports.) Inevitably I find myself wondering where those who share Hauerwas's principles should stand on the issues that divide ecumenists and on which Hauerwas has not expressed himself. This essay speculates on the answer to this question.

The purpose is not to force Hauerwas or anyone else out of the closet, so to speak, but to help Hauerwasians, if I may call them that, to reflect on where they should stand when and if they get embroiled in the present ecumenical wars. Some of them are or will be involved whether or not they want to be, but not everyone. There may be better things for Hauerwasians to do than to expend large amounts of uncompensated time and energy on issues about which fewer and fewer people seem to care. Moreover, taking stands on ecumenical issues may compromise such Hauerwasians' usefulness to those they have been sent to serve. Our Lord himself remained silent when inopportunely questioned, and at times resorted to ambiguities in order to avoid declaring himself about matters on which he was sure to be misunderstood.[5] There may, in short, be good reasons, conscious or unconscious, for ecumenical disengagement, and this applies also to Stanley Hauerwas.

(Notre Dame, Ind.: University of Notre Dame Press, 1995). On the basis of this and other more recent writings, I see no clear disagreement between us on the question of Christendom and cultural and diaspora Christianity. This is not only because he has changed (or, at least, my view of him has changed), but also because I have been influenced by him. For example, his objection (in *Unleashing the Scripture: Freeing the Bible from Captivity to America* [Nashville: Abingdon, 1993], 155 n. 7) to a 1989 essay of mine ("The Church's Mission to a Postmodern Culture") seems to me on target. I still think, as I argued in that essay, that biblical literacy is culturally important, but I should have anticipated his counterevidence and added that, apart from the influence of faithful communal witness, widespread knowledge of Scripture in a society may be the opposite of beneficial.

4. As is explained in note 1 above, *Nature of Doctrine* belongs in this category. It is misinterpreted when its purpose of supplying theoretical warrants for ecumenical practice is disregarded, as has often been done.

5. "Render therefore to Caesar the things that are Caesar's, and to God the things that are God's" (Matt. 22:21) is a historically notable example. It has functioned as a warrant for the full range of church–state relations from theocracy to Erastianism, and has been used by both pacifists and nonpacifists in support of their respective causes.

Yet in view of what I have called Stan's ecumenicity, this disengagement is difficult for ecumaniacs like myself to understand. He described himself in 1981, during his Notre Dame period, as "a (Southern) Methodist of doubtful theological background . . . who teaches and worships with and is sustained morally and financially by Roman Catholics; who believes that the most nearly faithful form of Christian witness is best exemplified by the often unjustly ignored people called Anabaptists or Mennonites. In short my ecclesial preference is to be a high-church Mennonite."[6] This marriage of extremes no doubt helps to account for his ability to interest an astonishing range of students and readers from Eastern Orthodox to Pentecostals on both sides of the Atlantic and including secularists such as Jeffrey Stout of Princeton University. Stout calls him "the most prolific and influential theologian now working in the United States,"[7] and the two studies of his work from which I have learned the most are by Europeans, one a free church Swede and the other a Lutheran German.[8] This breadth of Hauerwas's appeal is one factor that makes his comparative silence about ecumenism puzzling.

Moreover, there are ambiguities in what little he does say. Naturally his occasional remarks change from one period to another, but even when they are close in time, they are confusing. Two passing comments from the late 1980s, for example, seem to agree in downplaying what ecumenists call Faith and Order (i.e., the search for the doctrinal and structural reconciliation of the churches), in favor of growth in unity through cooperation in what ecumenists call Life and Work. Not that Hauerwas uses this terminology; indeed, it is only in the first of the remarks I shall quote (and practically nowhere else that I have been able to locate) that he speaks in so many words of the ecumenical movement. He says that "the ecumenical movement can be seen not just as a theological necessity, but rather as the most significant political act the

6. Stanley Hauerwas, *A Community of Character: Toward a Constructive Christian Social Ethic* (Notre Dame, Ind.: University of Notre Dame Press, 1981), 6.

7. This quote is taken from an essay adapted from Stout's most recent book, *Democracy and Tradition* (Princeton: Princeton University Press, 2004), and published in *Commonweal*, October 10, 2003, 14.

8. Arne Rasmusson, *The Church as Polis: From Political Theology to Theological Politics as Exemplified by Jürgen Moltmann and Stanley Hauerwas* (Notre Dame, Ind.: University of Notre Dame Press, 1995), and Reinhard Hütter, *Evangelische Ethik als kirchliches Zeugnis: Interpretationen zu Schlüsselfragen theologischer Ethik inder Gegenwart* (Neukirchener: Neukirchener–Vluyn, 1993). Rasmusson's judgment that Hütter's book is "the best work about Hauerwas" (22) seems to me to remain true a decade later. Moreover, as a Lutheran, Hütter is sensitive to Hauerwas's seeming "semi-Pelagianism" (a term neither Hütter nor Hauerwas uses), especially in some of his earlier writings, and Hütter shows how this tendency can, with the help of Barth's pneumatology, be given an interpretation compatible with adherence to the Lutheranism he and I share.

church can perform for the world. . . . So the unity of the church—and we must remember that our deepest disunity is not between Catholics and Protestants, but between classes, races, nationalities, hemispheres, etc.—becomes the prerequisite of our serving the world as God's peaceable community."[9] The second comment is similar: we must not "forget that the most embarrassing divisions in the church are not between Catholic and Protestant, U.C.C. and Methodist, Presbyterian and Church of Christ, liberal and conservative, but among social and economic classes and between races and nationalities."[10] Except for the lack of an environmental emphasis, the rhetoric sounds like that of the World Council of Churches' JPIC (justice, peace, and the integrity of creation) programs, and suggests that Hauerwas's ecumenism is shaped by a political theology of the same general type as Jürgen Moltmann's.[11]

The continuation of the second quotation, however, makes it clear that Hauerwas's "theological politics," as it has been called, is quite different from Moltmann's political theology.[12] He says the church "must take its lead from those like Mother Teresa. From the perspective that would associate the church's social task with effectiveness, Mother Teresa is a deeply immoral woman. She takes the time to hold the hand of a dying leprosy victim when she could be raising money in Europe and America for the starving in India . . . because she knows that by exactly such care God will have the Kingdom come."[13] Anyone who writes this is not likely to have any more enthusiasm for Life and Work, at least in the form of JPIC, than for Faith and Order. Interdenominational cooperation in the service of human needs such as is represented by Life and Work simply cannot follow the example of Mother Teresa in our bureaucratic age because elementary financial responsibility requires all social action enterprises, whether religious or nonreligious, to pay attention to cost effectiveness in assessing their programs. If, then, neither of the two sides of what is normally thought of as Christian ecumenism meet with Hauerwas's approval, what is left? Is the movement toward unity, which he described in 1988 as "the most significant political act the church can perform in the world," a nondenominational or transdenominational affair rather than a matter of interchurch action?

9. Stanley Hauerwas, "The Sermon on the Mount," in *Concilium: A Council for Peace* (Edinburgh: T. & T. Clark, 1988), 42.

10. Stanley Hauerwas, "The Gesture of a Truthful Story," in *Christian Existence Today: Essays on Church, World, and Living in Between* (1988; repr., Grand Rapids, Mich.: Brazos Press, 2001), 105.

11. Rasmusson, *Church as Polis*, mentions the first of the above quotations as suggesting such a similarity (313).

12. The whole of Rasmusson's *Church as Polis* is an argument to that effect.

13. Hauerwas, "The Gesture of a Truthful Story," 105–6.

Fast-forward a dozen years to the Gifford Lectures of 2000–2001 (published as *With the Grain of the Universe*). In the last chapter, "The Necessity of Witness," Hauerwas amplifies his position, but without substantially changing it. He does not mention ecumenism by name even though much of the discussion would have been impossible without the ecumenical movement. The evils flowing from the church's disunity are stressed as never before, and the sense in which someone like Mother Teresa embodies a response to these evils is further clarified by the use of other examples, but what this implies for the concrete practice of ecumenism remains obscure.

His initial characterization of the evil of disunity has long been a commonplace in ecumenical circles (though I do not recall Hauerwas asserting it before): "Confident Christian speech has been compromised by the disunity of the church" (217). He goes beyond the commonplace in a long footnote, however, by borrowing first from Bruce Marshall, for whom, as Hauerwas puts it, "the unity of the church is a necessary condition for holding the gospel to be true." This church unity, which is necessary for truthful speaking, is neither ideal nor invisible, but a tangible communal reality in space and time. "The credibility of the gospel, therefore, depends not on its content alone but on the contingent communal shape of the communal history in which it is proclaimed" (that is, to parse the obvious, on the historically shaped creedal and organizational features of the confessional and denominational traditions in which the gospel is proclaimed). This sobering word is intensified by a second borrowing, also from a younger theologian, Ephraim Radner, for whom, Stan says, "The violence that the disunity of the church entails is . . . a problem at the heart of the Christian doctrine of God" (217–18 n. 26). In view of Hauerwas's consistent insistence that Christianity can be neither properly practiced nor preached by individuals apart from participation in Christian community, it follows from his agreements with Marshall and Radner that confessional and denominational divisions are among those things that make impossible confident and truthful witness to God. In contrast to the late 1980s, these divisions are not described as secondary. In the jargon of the ecumenical movement, Hauerwas no longer subordinates Faith and Order to Life and Work but by implication seems to say that the ecumenical search for the visible unity of the churches is, at the very least, an essential part of an authentically Christian struggle to overcome the divisions "among social and economic classes and between races and nationalities" within the church and, as a consequence, in the world at large.

Yet this change is not reflected in Hauerwas's response to the dire situation he has identified. Instead, he argues—by no means unpersuasively—"that John Howard Yoder and John Paul II are one in witness to the One who moves the sun and the stars and is to be found in a manger" (217). Others could have been chosen as exemplifications of this oneness, but these two "are theologically articulate." Their "witness has required them to say why the truth of what the church proclaims cannot be known as truth without witnesses" (218). It is in the oneness of this testimony to the God of Israel and of Jesus Christ offered by witnesses as ecclesially remote from each other as a Roman Catholic pope and a Mennonite theologian that the unity of the church becomes manifest even in the midst of its fragmentation. As the capstone of his argument, Hauerwas says: "What John Paul II and John Howard Yoder share over and above their differences is exemplified by a life that joins what they each hold dear. The name given to that life is Dorothy Day. . . . Because Dorothy Day existed, we can know that the church to which John Paul II and John Howard Yoder witness is not some ideal but an undeniable reality" (230). In brief, Hauerwas's reply to the uncertainty and inauthenticity of Christian proclamation that has resulted from, among other things, denominational and confessional divisions is that these evils, by the grace of God, have not wholly extinguished the visible unity of the church's testimony to Jesus Christ as this shines forth in the best of its members.[14]

So far so good, but it may still be asked why Hauerwas, when describing the shared concerns of the pope and Mennonite professor, omits all mention of ecumenism even though this was (and in the case of the pope, is) immensely important for both.[15] The answer is that the case for the visibility of the church's unity is independent of ecumenism. Practice precedes theory. Thoroughly visible unity in Christ may be massively present in the broken fragments of the church even when there are no eyes to see this (or, more prosaically, when there are no theologies that can make sense of it). This unity was present before ecumenism entered the scene. It is present whenever and wherever the Holy Spirit uses church practices, diverse and defective though these are in the different communions, to embody that unity visibly and identifiably in faithful lives. Some few of these lives (not necessarily the most holy and perhaps never consciously ecumenical ones) are empowered by the Spirit to testify to this unity in ways that are transdenominationally and transconfessionally recognizable. It is because of these lives that

14. The lists of saints, of preeminent public enactments of witness, vary greatly from communion to communion and sometimes contradict each other, but the overlap is nevertheless astonishing.

15. For the pope, see esp. the ecumenical encyclical *Ut Unum Sint* (1995), and for Yoder, "Ecumenical Responses," in *The Royal Priesthood*, ed. Michael G. Cartwright (Grand Rapids, Mich.: Eerdmans, 1994), 221–320.

it is possible to articulate theories (which are then tested in practice) about that search for fuller unity that is the ecumenical movement.[16] Less abstractly stated, the ecumenical developments that began about a century ago at Edinburgh (1910) are unimaginable apart from the growing recognition throughout the Christian family of the unity in Christ manifest in such witnesses as Mother Teresa and Dorothy Day (and Francis of Assisi, Theresa of Avila, Dietrich Bonhoeffer, etc.). In summary, Hauerwas need not include ecumenism as one of the strands in the bond uniting the witness of the pope and Yoder because the visible oneness in Christ of ecclesially separated witnesses is prior to ecumenism and a condition for its possibility.

Yet even though ecumenism is a logically dispensable part of Hauerwas's argument, it is a practically necessary precondition for his work; and that is why the question with which this essay deals is in order. His ecumenicity, as we earlier called it, would be impossible without the ecumenical movement. If the Roman Catholic opening to that movement at Vatican II had not taken place, he and Yoder would never have gotten to know each other while both were teaching at Notre Dame and he would have had neither the opportunity nor the incentive to span the apparently unbridgeable chasm between Catholic and Mennonite. Moreover, if he had tried, he would have had neither subject matter nor audience. His descriptions of neither John Paul II nor John Howard Yoder would have been possible before the 1960s, not only because the unity of their witness to Christ would have had a different character, but because Hauerwas, if he by some miracle had written of them as he did in 2000, would have received no hearing whatsoever, much less an invitation to be a Gifford lecturer. While it is true that ecumenism is impossible apart from witnesses who visibly enact the division-transcending unity that is in Christ, Hauerwas's lifework—his efforts to spread the recognition of such enactments and encourage their occurrence—is in part dependent on ecumenical developments. Their future and the future of his own concerns are intertwined. His apparent disengagement may be permissible in view of the division of labor that is a part of every communal enterprise, but it is imperative for the sake of his own work that some of those who share his outlook enter the ecumenical fray. That is why the question of where Hauerwas

16. By speaking of "theories" rather than "theory," I am here comparing the ecumenical movement to a research program in which a variety of theories of how to reach a given goal are "practiced," that is, experimentally tested. Viewed as a second-order investigation of first-order actualities, ecumenism itself, needless to say, also consists of practices that are open to (third-order) theorizing. See note 1 above.

or Hauerwasians should stand in the conflict is important for them and not only for ecumenists such as myself.

How Ecumenism Got to Where It Is Now

A bit of history is needed in order to understand the present-day ecumenical options. I shall start with the year in which my own ecumenical involvement began.

In 1950 there was general agreement, at least in France where I was then studying, on the goal of ecumenism and how to attain it. The goal is a visibly united church, but this goal will not be reached by the conversion of individuals or groups from one ecclesial allegiance to another. Rather it will take place in God's own time by means now largely hidden but that can be pointed to by such words as convergence, *rapprochement*, and integration. Each of the uniting bodies will have to change profoundly in order to enter into full communion, but they can do this, it is believed, without rejecting what is essential to their own identities.[17] The degree to which this quest will be successful before the eschaton God only knows, but to the degree that it is, the resulting ecumenical, catholic church will be richer and more variegated than anything we can imagine, and yet it will be genuinely one. This outlook is basically that of what can be conveniently named the "convergence" ecumenism that later became temporarily dominant.

Convergence ecumenism, insofar as it is understood as including Roman Catholics (and not only the Protestants and Orthodox who had organized the WCC [World Council of Churches] in 1948), was in its beginnings when I encountered it. Those who were open to it were few in number and, on the Roman Catholic side, were considered suspect by church authorities. Yves Congar, OP, author of *Chrétiens désunis*,[18] the first, and in some respects still the greatest, catholic ecumenical manifesto, was officially silenced in 1954, but his work set the tone for the discussions in which I was one of the student auditors. The air was electric with hope and excitement despite suppressive measures.[19]

---

17. See "reconciliation without capitulation" in note 1 above.

18. Yves Congar, OP, *Chrétiens désunis* (Paris: Cerf, 1937).

19. The characterization of convergence ecumenism in this paragraph and the previous one is indebted not only to *Chrétiens désunis*, but even more to Congar's autobiographical sketch of his ecumenical travels (and travails), "Appels et cheminements, 1929–1963," which is the preface to a collection of his essays, *Chrétiens en dialogue: Contributions catholiques à l'Oecuménisme* (Paris: Cerf, 1976), ix–lxiv. Translated by Philip Loretz as *Dialogue between Christians: Catholic Contributions to Ecumenism* (Westminster, Md.: Newman, 1966).

The next decades brought far greater progress toward that goal than those who were active in 1950 had dared to hope. Congar's trajectory may be taken as representative. His silencing was lifted; he greatly influenced Vatican II, became a cardinal, and is reported to have been the favorite theologian of Pope Paul VI. Convergence ecumenism came to dominate the ecumenical establishment (by which I mean those who to one degree or another are professionally engaged in ecumenism, whether as students, teachers, and bureaucrats or as active participants in relevant meetings, commissions, and assemblies). Three of the high-water marks of twentieth-century ecumenism reflect this dominance: the New Delhi statement on "the unity we seek" (1961), the conciliar *Unitatis redintegratio* (Decree on Ecumenism; 1964), and the Faith and Order document, *Baptism, Eucharist, and Ministry,* which, though not given its finishing touches until just before its publication in 1982, reflects in its substance agreements that had been reached a decade or more earlier. In short, it took only until around 1970 for convergence ecumenism to reach its apogee.

Since then, ecumenism has been in decline. Significant convergences on doctrinal issues have not ceased, as in, for example, the "Lutheran/ Roman Catholic Joint Declaration on the Doctrine of Justification" (1999), but these convergences tend to be the outcome of discussions already well advanced in earlier decades and are to be attributed more to institutional inertia than to continuing enthusiasm. Nonconvergence strategies for moving toward visible unity have also weakened. Beginning already at the WCC Uppsala assembly in 1968, the emphasis started to shift from the concerns of Faith and Order toward those of Life and Work. It is almost as if the social activism of the 1920s and 1930s, summed up in the 1925 Life and Work slogan, "Doctrine divides but service unites," were once again ecumenically triumphant. A major change from 1925, however, is that since Uppsala it is the unity of the world, not that of the church in service to the world's unity, that is more and more the direct goal. In the imagery employed by those in favor of the change, the paradigm is not the old "God–church–world" but rather "God–world–church." According to this new paradigm, Christians should discern from what God is doing in the world what they themselves should do; or, in language that those hostile to the change often quote: "The world sets the agenda." This type of Life and Work ecumenism had considerable momentum in the heyday of liberation theology, but since the end of the cold war, it has joined Faith and Order ecumenism in the doldrums. The survival of the ecumenism we have known seems doubtful.

The doubts are widespread even among those who are professionally involved in ecumenism and are all in favor of its continuance, though in new forms. Consider, for example, the report of a participant in a weeklong meeting of directors of ecumenical institutes from around the world held in July 2003 at Bossey, the study institute of the WCC. There was, he writes, "nearly unanimous and almost immediate resistance" to the "traditionalist" notion

> that the ecumenical movement has a single nature and a single goal. . . . Negotiating doctrines is giving way to . . . ecumenical spirituality. . . . Most people don't believe unity is the goal anymore; now it's dialogue, the sharing of stories. At Bossey it became clear . . . that the nature of the ecumenical movement is to have many goals, and the goal of the ecumenical movement is to let its many natures flourish and interact. . . . Nearly everyone in the seminar, including those who have devoted careers of many decades to the movement, responded positively to this new focus.[20]

The new focus includes the so-called "wider ecumenism," which is concerned with interreligious rather than intra-Christian relations and is greatly outstripping the latter in popular interest.[21] What is problematic about this focus is not interfaith dialogue but the failure to realize that this dialogue differs categorically from the search for Christian unity: the first is a matter of learning how to communicate with strangers, and the second, of overcoming estrangement within the family.[22] Once the two efforts are equated, favoring foreigners over family is perhaps

20. These remarks are pieced together from Patrick Henry, "Ecumenism's Nature and Goals," and his "Annual Report of the Executive Director," in *Ecumenical People, Programs, Papers* (Collegeville, Minn.: Institute for Ecumenical and Cultural Research, 2003), esp. 1–2 and 14–15. This is an occasional publication, and quotations from it should be read as part of a report, and not as statements of either Patrick Henry's own position or that of the institute, of which he has been a longtime and highly successful executive director. According to its mission statement, the institute "seeks to discern the meaning of Christian identity and unity in a religiously and culturally diverse nation and world, and to communicate that meaning for the mission of the church and the renewal of human community."

21. Already a decade ago, for example, most interfaith organizations in Massachusetts were former councils of churches, and when this transition occurs, as Diane Kessler, at that time director of the Massachusetts Council of Churches, reports: "All efforts to heal the still considerable divisions among the Christian churches are lost." The experience of Michael Kinnamon, formerly with the WCC in Geneva and now professor of ecumenics at Eden Theological Seminary, is a common one: "Many of my seminary students . . . regard Christian ecumenism as exclusivist and passé." *The Vision of the Ecumenical Movement and How It Has Been Impoverished by Its Friends* (St. Louis, Mo.: Chalice, 2003), 105.

22. Judaism does not fit neatly into either category from Christian perspectives. Jews and Christians may be viewed either as estranged members of the same family or as constituting separate families of strangers. Thus Vatican II, for example, first treated relations to the Jews as a part of *Unitatis redintegratio* (Decree on Ecumenism) but later

inevitable if for no other reason than that there are many families of foreigners and only one family that is one's own. Moreover, the turn from domestic to foreign affairs fits the now-dominant God–world–church paradigm, for to the extent the world sets the agenda, the problems of religious pluralism will in our day seem more pressing than those of Christian disunity. New external pressures will no doubt arise, but if it is these rather than the church's own compass and rudder that determine direction, the demise of the ecumenism that flourished briefly in the twentieth century is a certainty. That demise is what the directors of ecumenical institutes gathered at Bossey under WCC auspices expect, and that is what will occur if, to repeat, the world sets the agenda for the church.

If this happens, however, it will not be the first time in postbiblical history that the Zeitgeist has overridden concern for the unity of God's chosen people. Already in the second century, Gentile Christians expropriated even the name Israel from the Jews and proclaimed themselves the New Israel. Then in 1054 came the break between East and West, to be followed five hundred years later by the Reformation that sundered Catholics and Protestants and greatly weakened concern for unity. With the loosening in recent centuries of the Constantinian symbiosis of church and state, space opened for further fragmentation, especially among Protestants but also for unitive countercurrents in the nineteenth century that led to the modern ecumenical movement in the twentieth. During the cold war, the spirit of the age actively encouraged ecumenism. Western nations led by the United States favored a united church front to protect a purportedly Christian civilization from the communist threat (think, for example, of the ecumenical activities of John Foster Dulles, secretary of state under Eisenhower), while countries under Soviet control supported the participation of their chiefly Orthodox churches in the ecumenical movement as an Eastern counterpoise. It is a testimony to the Christian integrity of the ecumenical leaders of this period that they for the most part sought (and partially succeeded in) resisting both Western and Eastern pressures. Even the Orthodox ecumenical delegations, infiltrated with KGB agents though they were, were by no means always pushovers.[23]

Now, however, the winds of the world have shifted once again. Church unity may be needed more than ever, even for worldly reasons, in view

---

moved this section, reportedly because of pressure from Arab Catholics, to *Nostra aetate* (Declaration on the Relation of the Church to Non-Christian Religions).

23. The history of this resistance will perhaps never be written because its clandestine character left it undocumentable. I know of it only through personal contacts and word-of-mouth reports.

of the tensions generated by the simultaneous growth of pluralism and globalism, but it is now in disrepute. None of the major social, cultural, and political trends favor such unity. Efforts to mobilize Christians for political ends may be unprecedentedly massive on the right, and are by no means lacking on the left; but as is illustrated by antiabortion alliances between Roman Catholics and conservative Evangelicals and by antiwar protests gathering together both Christian pacifists and nonpacifists, these groupings are indifferent to ecumenism because, among other things, it has no public influence. The historically ecumenical churches have for the most part become ciphers in this respect, and uniting them is a matter of joining weakness to weakness, while the Evangelicals and Pentecostals who do have political weight are unecumenical or antiecumenical. The renewal of unitive ecumenism will have to come from within Christian communities without the support of external pressure. The question to Hauerwasians is how this renewal might best be promoted, or, in other words: What kind of renewal-minded unitive ecumenism should they choose?

Possible Choices

There are many ideal possibilities from which to choose, but of real, actually existing ones, I know of only two at the time of writing. Two contrasting visions of a new future for unitive ecumenism are taking public shape on this continent and may well be in competition at the Second North American Faith and Order Conference now scheduled to take place in 2005.[24] Both visions protest the neglect of unitive ecumenism, but one does so from within the ecumenical establishment and aims to retrieve emphases that have been lost, while the other originates outside present ecumenical and denominational structures and is open to the possibility that new organizational forms may be needed either in whole or in part. I shall take Michael Kinnamon (MK) as spokesperson for the insider, or establishment, protesters and the so-called "Princeton Proposal" (PP), with which I was involved, as representative of the outsiders.[25]

---

24. Notices of this conference are to be found in *Ecumenical Trends,* January 2003, and *America,* June 9–16, 2003, 11, but fuller and more recent information will be available by the time this essay is published.

25. For Kinnamon's position, see *Vision of the Ecumenical Movement.* For the Princeton Proposal, see *In One Body through the Cross: The Princeton Proposal for Christian Unity; A Call to the Churches from an Ecumenical Study Group,* ed. Carl E. Braaten and Robert W. Jenson (Grand Rapids, Mich.: Eerdmans, 2003). This is a "so-called" Princeton Proposal because the only reason for the name is that the study group happened to meet there; it

For both groups the fundamental conviction is one that Hauerwas shares. Michael Kinnamon's formulation comes out of an "unstructured" meeting on the future of ecumenism attended by thirty veterans of the movement a half dozen years ago. Many participants were surprised that the major topic came to be what a Catholic participant called "the erosion of the [theological] basis." As Kinnamon puts it: "If you don't believe that God has acted in Christ for the salvation of the world, then the idea that God has created a new community in Christ of Jew and Gentile as a sign and instrument of God's mission, will seem like pure idealism—impossible and ultimately irrelevant. In the absence of such conviction, ecumenism will become simply another arena for pursuing political agendas."[26] The Princeton Proposal presupposes the same conviction.

On the hypothesis that ecumenism is worth pursuing even in the present disintegrating state of the churches, Hauerwas would also agree with MK and PP that the church's unity is an end in itself. An inseparable part of the ecumenical task is to move the churches toward visible unity in, as the New Delhi statement put it (I abbreviate), "one baptism, one gospel, breaking the one bread, joining in common prayer, a corporate life reaching out in witness and service to all, a ministry and membership accepted by all, and the ability to act and speak together as occasion requires" (PP, 21).

Unanimity disappears, however, when one turns to the relation between this unitive part of the ecumenical task and its other aspects. For Kinnamon, the "most significant" failure of the Princeton Proposal is that it

> doesn't adequately link the concern for Christian unity to the church's ministry of justice. . . . The authors highlight Faith and Order while paying little attention to Life and Work. . . . [The PP] operates out of a God–church–world paradigm: the church must get its act together in order to carry the message of wholeness and reconciliation to the world. Many contemporary Christians . . . think more in terms of God–world–church: the church participates in God's reconciling mission in the world and thereby discovers something of its own unity. The movement has got to

---

has no connection with either the university or the seminary. The sponsoring Center for Catholic and Evangelical Theology is independent of all existing denominational, ecumenical, and educational institutions and models its project "on the *Groupe des Dombes*, founded in 1937, which pioneered many of the insights and formulations that enabled the successes of the post-Vatican II dialogues" (5). The membership of the study group spanned the confessional spectrum from the Eastern Orthodox to Pentecostal. Full disclosure requires that I admit to being one of the signers of the PP.

26. Kinnamon, *Vision of the Ecumenical Movement*, 7.

insist that these are not an either–or. . . . There is one ecumenical movement, committed because of the gospel to both unity and justice.[27]

There are other omissions in PP that Kinnamon complains of, but the downplaying of Life and Work and the related absence of the God–world–church paradigm are the main ones, as we have just seen. The remedy for him is a synthesis of the new and the old.

As I understand the disagreement, the MK hold that Faith and Order (the cooperative search for unity) and Life and Work (the cooperative service of, e.g., justice) are coequal ends in themselves, for they issue from distinct paradigms. And yet they are inseparable because they reciprocally reinforce each other: the more unified the church, the better it serves "wholeness and reconciliation" (which are inseparable from justice). And the more it serves the cause of justice, the better it "discovers something of its own unity." For the PP, in contrast, the God–church–world paradigm is the only one, and Faith and Order therefore takes precedence over Life and Work in somewhat the same way that faith takes precedence over works in Reformation teaching. Just as faith in God is an end in itself, so also church unity is an end in itself; and just as good works are the indispensable fruit and sign of true faith but not its end or its cause, so also cooperation "in witness and service to all," as New Delhi put it, is a necessary fruit and sign of church unity but not its end or cause. Without Life and Work, Faith and Order is dead, but without the primacy of Faith and Order, Life and Work is deadly; it becomes a countersign of the church, "simply another arena for pursuing political agendas," to use Kinnamon's own words. Kinnamon, however, writes as if that disaster threatens only when Faith and Order is forgotten, but an unspoken premise of the Princeton Proposal (with which I assume Hauerwas agrees) is that the marginalization of Faith and Order that has occurred in the ecumenical movement is inescapable once Life and Work is legitimized by the world-sets-the-agenda-for-the-church paradigm. From this perspective, the MK synthesis is wishful thinking, and PP must be chosen if a choice is to be made.

As usual, however, there is a practical side to the theological conflict that complicates the choice. The conflicting ecumenical visions are designed for different constituencies. Kinnamon speaks especially to the ecumenically interested in the mainstream denominations that were originally and, now joined by the Roman Catholic Church, remain the

27. Michael Kinnamon, review of *In One Body through the Cross: The Princeton Proposal for Christian Unity; A Call to the Churches from an Ecumenical Study Group*, ed. Carl E. Braaten and Robert W. Jenson, *Christian Century*, September 6, 2003, 36–39. The quotations are from 37–39.

mainstays of organized ecumenism. He does so as a member, a dissatisfied member, of the current establishment, but he seeks to retrieve lost
emphases without abandoning more recent ones in order to formulate
a synthesis as attractive as possible to all who are ecumenically interested. It is for practical reasons and not only theological ones that he
stresses the importance for ecumenism of the Life and Work programs
for justice, peace, and the integrity of creation (as well as, to mention
other topics of importance to him and his audience, the "celebration
of diversity," and the need for an "ecumenical hermeneutic" to satisfy
doubters that there is such a thing as the "apostolic tradition" to which
ecumenism must be faithful). Even if one does not think his synthesis
is viable, one can respect his motives. He is trying, it may be suggested,
to make room in the ecumenical tent for the weaker brothers and sisters
of whom Scripture tells us we should take special care. Moreover, it is
not only these sisters and brothers but also the ecumenical cause that
would suffer if JPIC concerns were simply excised. Indeed, would not
Kinnamon betray his duty to the largely liberal mainstream traditions
that have nourished him in the faith and to which ecumenism is heavily
indebted if he did not seek to correct what he sees as their ecumenical
failures from within? Might he not, despite theological differences, be
in practice engaged in a Hauerwasian project of building the church as
a contrast society to the surrounding culture in that part of the ecclesia
where God has placed him?[28]

The audience that the Princeton Proposal has in mind is very different. It is chiefly Evangelical and Pentecostal, on the one hand, and
Roman Catholic and Orthodox on the other. While the majority of the
(now disbanded) study group are members of Episcopalian, Lutheran,
Methodist, and Presbyterian churches, they believe that the future of
the kind of ecumenism that originated from these and other mainline
Protestant denominations now lies outside of them. It is among Evangelicals, Pentecostals, Roman Catholics, and the Orthodox, polar opposites though they seem, that there is a measure of agreement on where
and how the apostolic tradition is to be located and retrieved. They do
not find it necessary to invent a special "ecumenical hermeneutic" in
order to legitimate their search for the tradition in Scripture, under the
guidance of the affirmations regarding God the Father, Son, and Holy
Spirit confessed, for example, in the Nicene Creed. Even professedly
creedless Evangelicals and Pentecostals do not deny the Trinity nor that
Jesus Christ is true God and true man. Without ever having heard of
the catholic creeds in many cases, Evangelicals and Pentecostals seek

---

28. My understanding of a Hauerwasian notion of contrast society is dependent on
Rasmusson, *Church as Polis*, 370–74.

to read their Bibles in accordance with them, which makes theological convergence possible. Proof of this possibility is evident in recent conversations between prominent Roman Catholics and Evangelicals, but the main hope for bringing the fastest growing (and most fissiparous) portions of the Christian flock into the ecumenical enterprise probably lies in other ways of publicly witnessing to unity in Christ, of which the Princeton Proposal suggests a few. The sparseness of reference to Life and Work issues in the PP is regrettable, but these issues are so easily politicized when the audience is as varied as the one we thought of ourselves as addressing that no one actually proposed additional treatment of them. There is ample room (and fewer problems than in the case of MK) for those with Hauerwasian sympathies to locate themselves in the spectrum of possibilities suggested by the Princeton Proposal.

To return to my starting point, ecumenicity is imperative for Christians, but this imperative does not necessarily demand that all Christians enter into the ecumenical fray. This entrance occurs when the call to discipleship and witness coincides with visible participation in one's own community's search for the fullness of ecclesial unity. That call came to John Paul II and John Howard Yoder in a way it has not come to Stanley Hauerwas, and that may be all to the good: division of labor is a biblical principle. Yet I for one cannot but hope that the call comes, not only to those who have influenced Stanley, but also to many of those whom he has influenced. Ecumenism needs them.

12

What's Going On in the Church in South Africa?

Neville Richardson

In the month of extravagant national celebrations to mark ten years since the end of apartheid, the Christian church in South Africa celebrated Easter. Does the church in South Africa understand its great annual festival in relation to its social context? Can it be proud of its record under apartheid and in the decade since? How is the performance of the church to be evaluated—by whom and by what criteria?

Seeing through the Eyes of Outsiders

Visitors to churches far from home can offer a fascinating perspective. They can function as "flies on the wall," not knowing the history or social dynamics of a community and seeing only what is before their eyes. From the vantage point of outsiders, things are apparent that have become perhaps too commonplace for the regular members to see. A British visitor recently pointed out to me the scarcity of black people in my local congregation in the suburbs of a South African city—the few black faces in a sea of white that I, a regular worshipper, had blithely seen as a sign of real progress. He rightly reminded me that a whole decade had passed since the inauguration of the new democratic South Africa. I felt chastened, for even in the bad old days of apartheid, it was surely incumbent upon the church to witness, by its racially varied membership, to such basics of the faith as the unity of all humanity in God's creation and the availability to all of Christ as Savior and Lord. It took an outsider to see clearly what a local did not and to remind me of what I already knew.

In a similar vein, a South African friend told me of attending morning worship in a small town in Scotland. The congregation was fairly small, composed almost entirely of elderly people. Nothing unusual about that; it was the message of the sermon that puzzled him. The theme was "What's going on?"—and there seemed to be no clear answer. There had been some rearrangements between the three churches that make up the parish, and a new minister had joined the ministerial team. The preacher, apparently the senior minister, felt that the people were confused and needed to know why the changes had been made. His strange answer was that nobody really knew what was going on. The people might ask the kirk session; the session might inquire of the presbytery; the ministers might inquire of the moderator; and they might all together ask the general assembly; but he reckoned that no clear answers would be forthcoming. Seeing that it was the season of Pentecost, my friend anticipated a final punch line about the Holy Spirit speaking a word of clarity and truth into this obfuscated institutional situation. But no such punch line came. The service ended with what amounted to a shrug of the shoulders—a case of "who knows?" After the service the congregation moved into the adjoining hall for a sit-down tea. They all seemed perfectly content, and the hanging question, "What's going on?" seemed to fade away in the convivial atmosphere. The visitor left wondering if the minister and people would ever find an answer.

Observations and insights from the outside are potentially valuable and important to those trying to understand their situation from within. When the attempt is to understand the church and its theology in a particular national context, the writings of foreign theologians may be of great assistance. In South Africa this has certainly been the case, and in this regard, the work of Stanley Hauerwas now seems to merit special consideration.

Personal Theological Formation in Apartheid Society

Growing up in South Africa and becoming a Methodist minister in the late 1960s, I formed the strong conviction that the mission of the church must be closely allied to the struggle against apartheid. In 1970 Enda McDonagh, coleading a series of theology seminars for South African Catholics, saw the issue clearly: "As this was my first visit and my first exposure to the apartheid system I saw it as South Africa's primary moral challenge."[1] McDonagh registered his surprise at the muted nature of the seminar discussions on racial justice and contrasted this with the animated discussions of personal and especially sexual morality. Rather kindly, he granted that *Humanae Vitae,* published two years earlier, had brought questions such as contraception to the forefront of Catholic minds. Even more generously, he granted, in what became the main thrust of his argument, that the church needs both the sharpness of the "prophetic tradition" and the "more lenient and accommodating . . . Wisdom tradition."[2] While that point may be true in general, does it therefore imply that we should always seek a balance between the two approaches? It seems that in certain urgent cases the wisdom approach may be inadequate and the sharpness of the prophetic approach more appropriate. At that time and in that context, I was among those Christians who stood unreservedly on the prophetic side against what we perceived to be the obvious and gross social injustice of apartheid.

As the *Kairos Document* was later to bring into sharp focus, the church under apartheid was polarized between "the church of the oppressor" and "the church of the oppressed."[3] Either you were for apartheid or you were against it; there was no neutral ground. Given the heavy-handed domination of the minority white government, those who imagined themselves to be neutral were, unwittingly perhaps, on the side of apartheid. This complicity was especially true of those Christians who piously "avoided politics" yet enjoyed the social and economic benefits of the apartheid system. Clear opponents of apartheid were rare in white congregations. Given the glaring and pervasive evil of apartheid all around, I found myself struggling to take seriously much that passed for worship in

---

1. Enda McDonagh, "Prophecy or Politics? The Role of the Churches in Society," in *Faithfulness and Fortitude: In Conversation with the Theological Ethics of Stanley Hauerwas,* ed. Mark T. Nation and Samuel Wells (Edinburgh: T. & T. Clark, 2000), 302.
2. Ibid., 303.
3. *The Kairos Document: Challenge to the Church,* rev. 2nd ed. (Grand Rapids, Mich.: Eerdmans, 1986). The document cuts across denominational and doctrinal lines in its account of "the church of the oppressor" and "the church of the oppressed." It identifies three lines of theological development in South Africa: state theology, church theology, and prophetic theology. It is critical of all but prophetic theology.

those churches. Having a musical ear, I rather enjoyed the hymns, but the singing in white congregations, in contrast to the resonance of that in African worship, seemed hollow and of little "real value." The ringing denunciation of Israel's worship by the prophet seemed apt:

> When you come to appear before me, who asked this from your hand? . . . Wash yourselves; make yourselves clean; remove the evil of your doings from before my eyes; cease to do evil, learn to do good; seek justice, rescue the oppressed, defend the orphan, plead for the widow. (Isa. 1:12–17 NRSV)

During graduate study, bearing the freight of logical positivism, linguistic analysis, and secular theology, I found it increasingly difficult to believe that God was not dead. Under the weight of historical–critical scholarship, even the Bible began to sink in terms of significance. Only a few selected passages seemed defensible and worth retaining in the face of the pervasive moral injustice of our society: the exodus from Egyptian slavery; the social critics among the prophets (Amos 5, Isaiah 1, Micah 6); Jesus's "manifesto" in Luke 4; and the social concern of Matthew 25. This was the canon-within-the-canon of many white anti-apartheid Christians. This was the biblical flotsam to which our drowning faith clung. Surely the God of justice (or was it the justice that we assumed to be of God?) would not let apartheid triumph in the end. At the same time, the mainline churches seemed to continue their business as usual, as though nothing, or nothing much, was wrong. Although the black and white church leadership met at regional and national levels, local congregations were almost entirely monochrome. As the political climate began to heat up both inside the country and on the Namibian and Angolan borders, the population became more militarized. While young white men were conscripted into the South African Defence Force, many young black people fled the country to join the outlawed liberation movements that had their headquarters and training camps abroad. What could the church do in this revolutionary climate? And what should Christian theology now say?

It was in search of answers that I engaged in study in Oxford and Geneva, examining the ecumenical response to racial problems.[4] I carefully researched the development of ethical thinking and the institutional measures taken by the World Council of Churches with respect to racial injustice in South Africa, in particular the shift from a policy of changing hearts and minds through "contact, consultation, and statement" to

---

4. See Neville Richardson, *The World Council of Churches and Race Relations: 1960–1969* (Frankfurt: Peter Lang, 1977).

one of changing social structures through "confrontation and conflict" by providing financial support for liberation movements. I found that while I was largely in sympathy with those ecumenical efforts, I could not be confident of their theological rationale. If the people following this line of ethical reasoning were to find themselves in court in South Africa on a serious charge of subversive, antistate activity, could their defense be based on anything other than pragmatic political grounds or a general sense of social justice—to which the defenders of apartheid could also appeal? Their arguments could not be substantively Christian, and if there seemed to be nothing particularly theological in their rationale for the "crime," such a trial could hardly be a Christian witness. Ironically, it seemed that in the ethical reasoning of the World Council of Churches the church was relegated to the sidelines. The emphasis was described in the slogan "the world writes the agenda for the church," and the church's role became that of a platform for discussion of secular issues and a conduit for funds to approved secular causes. Paul Ramsey questioned this trend in his important book *Who Speaks for the Church?*[5] It was in my subsequent search for a substantively theological account of social ethics that I discovered the work of Stanley Hauerwas.[6] Before I say more about this discovery, and what it meant for me as a theologian living and working in South Africa, let me speak more generally about what is at stake in the transfer of theology from one cultural context to another.

Seeing through Foreign Eyes: Lessons of Reading Barth in South Africa

The 1980s saw the publication of at least two books in which major European Protestant theologians of the twentieth century were considered in terms of the South African context.[7] In his *Bonhoeffer in South*

5. Paul Ramsey, *Who Speaks for the Church?* (Edinburgh: St. Andrew, 1967).

6. Victor Bredenkamp, a senior colleague on sabbatical at Princeton in the early 1980s, kindly agreed to pose specific questions on Christian ethics to Paul Ramsey on my behalf. The answer I received: "Read Stanley Hauerwas." I am deeply grateful to both Vic Bredenkamp and the late Paul Ramsey for this advice.

7. The importance of Bonhoeffer and Barth is unmistakable, but there are other theologians who may equally have had books written about their influence in this country. Some earlier, pre-apartheid figures also to have had significant influence in South Africa are, in the Calvinist tradition, John Calvin himself, Andrew Murray, and Abraham Kuyper—all distorted through powerfully racist lenses—and, in the Anglican tradition, F. D. Maurice, who deeply influenced John William Colenso, the first Anglican Bishop of Natal. For a recent work on Colenso, see J. A. Draper, ed., *The Eye of the Storm* (Pietermaritzburg: Cluster, 2003). It must be said, however, that it was the struggle against apartheid and

Africa, John de Gruchy explains that although Dietrich Bonhoeffer never set foot on South African soil, his response as a Christian theologian to the growing Nazi oppression that would eventually kill him in 1945 is of particular relevance to theology and Christian witness in South Africa.[8] In his editor's introduction to the collection of essays titled *On Reading Karl Barth in South Africa,* Charles Villa-Vicencio emphasizes the importance of reading Barth's theology in context.[9] To display the importance of placing theology in context, let us briefly contextualize Barth, keeping in mind that a contextual reading entails, of course, a double imperative. First, we must read a theological text with an eye to the particular circumstances out of which the text emerged. Not to do this is to abstract that text and thereby incline it strongly toward the possibility of misunderstanding and misappropriation. Second, we must read with an eye to our own context.

The pressure of the particular context within which Barth's theology was forged is dramatically evoked by Duncan Forrester in his reflection on the juxtaposition of a quaint eighteenth-century church building and the fence of the notorious Dachau concentration camp.[10] Forrester speculates as to what went on in that little church. To continue with religious business as usual in such a situation would be highly questionable. He rightly asks: "Did its existence raise a question mark against the existence of the camp? Or was it a sign to the prisoners of sheer irrelevance?"[11] He grants that what a church stands for in theory may not find expression in its actions. Given human weakness, not unfamiliar among Christians, it is when the gap between the church's profession and its social location is too great that "there is often a jarring dissonance between the ethic

---

the perception of Bonhoeffer and Barth as theological allies in that struggle that provided the particular creative spark for such books to be written on them.

8. John W. de Gruchy, *Bonhoeffer in South Africa* (Grand Rapids, Mich.: Eerdmans, 1984).

9. Charles Villa-Vicencio, ed., *On Reading Karl Barth in South Africa* (Grand Rapids, Mich.: Eerdmans, 1988). The editor explains that the book was written during the centenary year of Barth's birth and was intended as a protest against the ways in which Barth had been misused in South Africa. He asserts that this misuse arose largely out of reading Barth noncontextually, that is, "without due concern for the central place he occupied in the resistance of the Confessing Church against Hitler in the 1930s" (11). Villa-Vicencio also points out that in both Afrikaner and English seminaries and universities there had been a conspicuous avoidance of Barth's theology.

10. Duncan Forrester, "The Church and the Concentration Camp," in Nation and Wells, *Faithfulness and Fortitude,* 189–207. These points by a Scots theologian about a German scenario in World War II raise a sharp challenge for the social ethics of the American Stanley Hauerwas. They also confront the South African church, especially with respect to its witness, not from the fence, but in the midst of a society profoundly damaged by apartheid.

11. Ibid., 195.

that the Church proclaims and what the Church in a particular context actually stands for and how Christians behave."[12]

Barth's best-known response to the social evils signified by Forrester in his reference to Dachau is probably the Barmen Declaration. There can be no doubt that Barth's theology and indeed his personal identity were shaped by his historical context. As Hauerwas notes in his Gifford Lectures:

> Barth's life was as dramatic as his theology; but he did not describe either his life or his work in terms of the risk both manifest. Barth thought that he was simply doing what he had to do. Yet most theologians in Germany did not think that they had to oppose Hitler or that they had to write the Barmen Declaration. Barth did both of these things, and that he did so cannot be incidental to any account of his theology.[13]

Similarly, Barth categorically condemned the capitalist economic system that was integral to his context. He regarded it as being against the will of God. He was not quite as unequivocal as to what God might have commanded as an alternative system. He did, however, point the church emphatically in the general direction of socialism and was a supporter of socialist causes all his adult life, even if, as Robin Petersen argues, his support for socialism was always set within the larger frame of his theological work:

> Barth's socialism was never dogmatic or doctrinaire; he could never take the internal arguments and discussions about its nature with the same seriousness as he would the theological task. This did not in any way undermine its importance for him, but it preserved the crucial eschatological proviso between the kingdom of God and "actually existing socialism" and secured the task of theology as theology, not disguised sociology or political science.[14]

In the light of the above pointers to the shaping effect of context on theology and church, three important principles emerge. First, context matters and cannot be ignored. Precisely what role context plays is a question for debate.[15] What seems clear in the case of Barth (not usu-

12. Ibid., 199.

13. Stanley Hauerwas, *With the Grain of the Universe: The Church's Witness and Natural Theology* (Grand Rapids, Mich.: Brazos Press, 2001), 147.

14. Robin Petersen, "Theology and Socialism," in Villa-Vicencio, *On Reading Karl Barth in South Africa*, 66.

15. For an account of this debate concerning theological education in South Africa, see Megan Walker and James Cochrane, eds., *The Contextualisation of Theological Education: Report of a National Workshop Held in Pietermaritzburg, 11–13 June, 1996* (Pietermaritzburg: School of Theology, 1996), esp. 6–13.

ally noted as being on the front line of "contextualization") is that concerns arose for him especially in the face of particular cases of human suffering and poverty. Such concerns suggest that the contextualization of theology is not merely a matter of awareness of the location of the theologian and the church. It seems that given the sources of theological knowledge that loom large for the theologian—for Barth, the witness of Scripture and faith in Jesus Christ—some contextual factors are more challenging than others. Second, there are limits to the influence of context on theology and church. However strong and consistent Barth's commitment to socialism may have been, however intense his fight against the Nazification of theology and church, for him the task of theology remained theological. This is the case at both the epistemological and the practical level. For Barth, theology never became "disguised sociology or political science." Third, contextual similarities strengthen the transferability of theology from one context to another. These similarities explain how Barth and Bonhoeffer, both European theologians, can speak to theology and church in South Africa decades later. Villa-Vicencio expresses this point in a particularly helpful way by noting two key requirements for the transferability of theologians' work from their location in time and space to our own. First, these theologians must have faced "crises similar to ours," and second, they must be "predecessors of the tradition within which we stand."[16] Although contextual theology lays emphasis on the first requirement, it often overlooks the second. Like "context," "tradition" can mean many things. It must mean, minimally, that such theologians share and give expression to the Christian faith and, maximally, that they belong to the same confessional family. Perhaps an even more powerful factor in the transferability of theology, however, is suggested in the pronouns "our" and "we," which would indicate a common experience of belonging in the community of faith and of struggling together as the people who witness to the lordship of Jesus Christ in a hostile world.

Judged by Villa-Vicencio's criteria, the work of Stanley Hauerwas might appear to be unsuited to or unhelpful in a South African context. Like Barth and Bonhoeffer, Stanley Hauerwas has not, to my knowledge, set foot in South Africa. But whereas Germany in the 1930s under a growing totalitarianism bore a resemblance to apartheid South Africa, it would be difficult to argue that Hauerwas's formative experience in the United States was significantly similar to that of South African

16. "When these people have been compelled by accidents of history to face crises similar to ours, and happen to be predecessors of the tradition within which we stand, then the importance of their journey through life takes on added significance for our own." Villa-Vicencio, *On Reading Karl Barth in South Africa*, 8.

Christians. It is not clear that he has faced "crises similar to ours." Two points of similarity might be the civil rights struggle for racial justice in the 1950s and 1960s and the protest movement against the war in Vietnam. While there are references to both of these movements in Hauerwas's writings, it is difficult to speculate on the degree to which they formed his thinking. Nonetheless, I want to show how the work of Stanley Hauerwas makes a significant difference to an attempt to see clearly the nature and role of the church in South Africa.

Transferring Hauerwas: An Autobiographical Review

Hauerwas's work is characterized by a growing antiliberal thrust, which provides an access point for those critics who would see Hauerwas as inclined, wittingly or unwittingly, toward conservative causes.[17] Such thinking misses Hauerwas's point, not only, as we will see, because his work does not necessarily align itself with "conservative" causes, but also because the decisions and dilemmas of supporting this or that particular cause are not Hauerwas's main concern. Indeed, it is because decisions and dilemmas are assumed to be precisely the work of the "ethicist" that he dislikes being labeled with that term.[18] His focus is primarily theological—on the truthful living of the Christian life in terms of character rather than on specific causes, on dispositions rather than on episodes. His social and political concern is primarily about the community life of the church. His complaint against liberalism is a theological complaint with two main aspects. First, Hauerwas condemns the liberal theology that arose out of the European Enlightenment that regards the autonomous individual as the only locus of morality and assimilates Christian theology to general assumptions in favor of de-

17. See, for instance, Jeffrey Stout, "Not of This World: Stanley Hauerwas and the Fate of Democracy," *Commonweal*, October 10, 2003, 14–20. Apart from some food for thought, such as the apparent arbitrariness of Hauerwas's selection of nonviolence as the primary moral requirement among the others in the New Testament, Stout's criticism is made from his own liberal presuppositions and takes little account of Hauerwas's philosophical and theological building blocks. The general impression of the criticisms, then, is similar to that of a cricketer judging a baseball batter to be, in cricketing terms, a bad player.

Critics who think Hauerwas's work lends support to conservative (as opposed to liberal) causes might think it inappropriate to relate his work to the South African experience, since his antiliberal positions might set him against the struggle for racial justice and therefore, in that sharply polarized context, on the side of apartheid. As should be evident in what follows, such critics would be mistaken.

18. See, for example, Stanley Hauerwas, "Christians in the Hands of Flaccid Secularists: Theology and 'Moral Inquiry' in the Modern University," in *Sanctify Them in the Truth: Holiness Exemplified* (Nashville: Abingdon, 1998), 201.

mocracy and human rights.[19] Second, he is particularly critical of the American form of liberal theology that sees its main task as making a better America. It is his conviction that Christian theology is distinct from this dominant way of thinking and that Christian social ethics must concern itself primarily with the community of faith and not the civil community.[20] Hauerwas sees the central task of the church not as aligning itself with political parties and causes but as witnessing to society at large.

When I first read Hauerwas's work in the early 1980s, I discovered an account of Christian ethics that addressed many of the questions for which previously I had found no satisfactory answers. Here was a theological ethic that was substantively theological—and distinctively and forcefully Christian. Here faith in God and a certain way of living were not separate and tenuously linked but were united as two versions of the same thing. This faith and life were not primarily individual but shared, in a historic community of faith. Any members of such a community finding themselves in court on a charge of subversion against the apartheid state could offer a distinctive rationale for their actions, markedly different from other prevalent justifications. Instead of appealing to political practicalities or the endlessly debatable application of general ethical principles, as in the "just revolution" concept, they could now appeal to the life of their community. That community, of course, is the church, the community of faith: a particular community, easily identifiable by its Christian character, that stands, by necessity in a non-Christian world, as an alternative community whose social counterstance is its witness.

Just as Hauerwas sees the church standing against the civil religion of the dominant liberal democracy in his native United States, so in South Africa before 1990 the church, in his terms, would be envisioned as standing against the civil religion of apartheid and for the truth of God's kingdom.[21] It would be intentionally multiracial in a strictly seg-

19. The force of Hauerwas's rejection of theological liberalism is seen in his critique of Gustavo Gutiérrez for making liberation the central metaphor of Christian existence. His complaint is that this metaphor and the way Gutiérrez articulates it evoke the autonomous individual of Kant and the Enlightenment to the detriment of the church. Stanley Hauerwas, *After Christendom: How the Church Is to Behave if Freedom, Justice, and a Christian Nation Are Bad Ideas* (Nashville: Abingdon, 1991), 55.

20. See, for instance, Stanley Hauerwas, *Against the Nations: War and Survival in a Liberal Society* (Minneapolis: Winston Press, 1985), 29–36; and "A Christian Critique of America," in *Christian Existence Today* (1988; repr., Grand Rapids, Mich.: Brazos Press, 2001), 171–90.

21. The apartheid policy received explicit theological support in the official statement of the Dutch Reformed Church, *Human Relations and the South African Scene in the Light*

regated society. Further, in a country with the highest Gini coefficient in the world, there would be active concern for the poor and a challenge to existing economic structures.[22] The rationale for these emphases would not be to score political points or even to effect economic and racial justice but to witness to the inclusive nature of God's creation and the gospel of Jesus Christ. In Hauerwas's terms, it would be a community that grows by means of its hospitality to the stranger, not because compassion is admirable, but because it is a noticeable feature of the biblical picture of the people of God.[23]

Is not this counterchurch likely to be unpopular and small? Yes indeed, but so it must be for those who stand faithfully for the gospel, who point to and embody God's kingdom in the face of the kingdoms of human power of all kinds.[24] Hauerwas levels his sharpest criticism at the church that collaborates with secular power. In South Africa, it was the apartheid-supporting church for which the sharpest criticism seemed appropriate. Hauerwas singles out as the most visible characteristic of the counterchurch its nonviolence in a violent world. While human political power, including that of liberal democracies, is gained and secured by violence, the business of the church is to develop nonviolent alternatives. This emphasis of Hauerwas resonated with the costly struggles of many young white men against the military conscription demanded of them by the apartheid system.[25]

---

of Scripture (Cape Town: NG Kerk Boekhandel, 1976). The "false gospel" of apartheid ideology was earlier condemned in The Message to the People of South Africa issued by the South African Council of Churches in 1968 and finally declared heretical in the 1982 Ottawa declaration of the World Alliance of Reformed Churches. For a full discussion on the heresy declaration, see J. W. de Gruchy and C. Villa-Vicencio, eds., Apartheid Is a Heresy (Cape Town: David Philip, 1983). The best accounts of the ideological underpinnings of apartheid may be found in W. A. de Klerk, The Puritans in Africa: A History of Afrikanerdom (Harmondsworth: Penguin, 1976), and T. Dunbar Moodie, The Rise of Afrikanerdom: Power, Apartheid, and the Afrikaner Civil Religion (Berkeley: University of California Press, 1975).

22. The Gini coefficient measures the gap between levels of wealth and poverty in a given economy. Under apartheid, South Africa had the highest Gini coefficient in the world.

23. Stanley Hauerwas, The Peaceable Kingdom (Notre Dame, Ind.: University of Notre Dame Press, 1983), 108–9.

24. The minority status of the church is a major tenet of Hauerwas's thinking. See, for instance, Hauerwas, Against the Nations, 9; and Christian Existence Today, 189 n. 33.

25. One of the countrywide organizations against conscription and in support of conscientious objectors was the End Conscription Campaign (ECC). The ECC received little support from the mainline churches, although some Christian NGOs and a few individual ministers were supportive. The only recognized category of conscientious objectors was the "religious objector." To be granted this status was a tedious and difficult process via a specially constituted legal tribunal. The great reward of success in this process was to be placed in menial employment by the state for six years. The alternatives were a six-

The communality of Hauerwas's ethic is not arbitrarily introduced but springs from his theological anthropology. Persons are not the autonomous, isolated, lonely heroes of Enlightenment anthropology but are persons-in-community. Nor is community merely a good idea for the increase of human security and productivity, although it is that too. Rather, community is necessary for persons to exist as persons. Language is an essentially communal enterprise, and moral language springs from moral community. Concepts and reasons must be locatable and describable within a particular community in order to be coherent.[26] Here again is an emphasis that resonates well with Africa, where traditional ways are being swamped by the global tidal wave of market capitalism and liberal democracy. I have pointed elsewhere to the need both for Christian ethics in Africa to hear this communal alternative from the West and for modern Western Christian ethics to take serious note of the communal emphasis that is common to Africa but rapidly disappearing.[27]

Like Christian faith, ethics in this account concerns the whole person. It is not, as the dominant ethics of the post-Enlightenment Western world would have it, a matter of dealing occasionally with moral dilemmas as isolated episodes. For Hauerwas, the focus in ethics is not on the right act but on the good person, and what constitutes a good person is more than just a certain number of right actions. The development of a good person is a matter of ongoing disposition, the development of moral character. Moral character, in turn, restores the virtues to the center of moral discourse, in place of values, which tend to be disembodied, ahistorical abstractions.[28] Virtues always have their place in particular human lives. Thus embodied in the lives of persons-in-community, ethics takes on flesh or, better, becomes expressive of historical existence, and thereby becomes descriptive and interesting. Novels, plays, biographies, movies, and historical narratives are all grist for the mill of this lively approach to ethics.

---

year criminal sentence in prison or illegal voluntary exile. For a related discussion, see my "How Can Theology Contribute to Peace in South Africa?" *Journal of Theology for Southern Africa* 111 (2001): 41–56.

26. Hauerwas focuses on the connection between community and language and, in particular, Christian community and Christian moral language in "The Church as God's New Language," in *Christian Existence Today,* 47–65.

27. See Neville Richardson, "Can Christian Ethics Find Its Way, and Itself, in Africa?" *Journal of Theology for Southern Africa* 95 (1996): 37–54, and "Community in Christian Ethics and African Culture," *Scriptura* 62 (1997): 373–85.

28. For a South African response to the resurgence of virtue ethics, see Robert Vosloo's carefully nuanced "Back to Virtue? Some Remarks on the Reappraisal of Virtue in Ethics," *Scriptura* 62 (1997): 299–310.

In addition to these features of Hauerwas's theological ethics, together with his emphasis on theological truth and a Christian faith that matters, my introduction to his work yielded several points of rich bonus. The first arises out of the necessary connection between community and narrative. Given the understanding of God's people as "a storied people," the Bible is rescued from imprisonment at the hands of the experts of the historical–critical method. Analogous to Luther's desire to tear the Bible from the proprietary grasp of the Latin-educated priests and place it in the hands of ordinary Germans, Hauerwas wrenches Scripture from the clutches of expert linguists and scientific historians and places it back in the hands of ordinary people of faith. It is for all the members of the believing community to debate among themselves, in matters great and small, the Bible's significance for them. This is autonomy, but a communal autonomy that is a far cry from the sovereign autonomy of Kant's individual moral agent. Of course, the community for which the Bible is authoritative is the church, and its authority is neither absolute nor sovereign but derivative from the sovereign authority of God. Implied in the sovereignty of God is the authority of the Bible for God's people. This close connection between church, ethics, and Scripture is evident in Hauerwas's most thought-provoking description of the church as an "extended argument over time" concerning the significance of the story of Jesus Christ in the world.[29] That story is vast in scope, starting with the narratives of the ancient Israelites, continuing with the stories of Jesus and the earliest communities of Christian faith, developing throughout church history, and still unfolding today in the experiences of the church in the modern world. Far from the sterility of historical criticism, yet learning from its findings, this is a fertile, lively understanding of the Bible. It is a view that embraces the whole canon of Scripture and sees that canon as engaging the life of Christians today. The whole of the written word that points to the divine Word is restored to the whole people of God. The unifying, community-creating potential of Scripture is highly significant in a society as divided as South Africa.

Understanding the necessary connection between narrative and community not only restores the whole biblical canon to its rightful place but also points to the importance of ecclesiology. While the predominant pattern in modern theological textbooks is to deal with the church in one of the closing chapters, in this approach the community of faith is a primary consideration. In contrast to the ecumenical approach of the 1970s, which was largely an expression of mainstream modern ethical reasoning in which the church became marginal as a theological factor, this approach is essentially ecclesial. The church is central to Christian

29. Hauerwas, *The Peaceable Kingdom*, 107.

ethics. This is not to claim that the church is some kind of moral paragon
or the dispenser of unfailingly sound moral advice—a glance into church
history or at contemporary newspapers shows the sadly flawed nature
of the institutional church. The claim here is rather that unless there
is a community of people who witness to their faith and who embody
their faith in their life together, albeit partially and imperfectly, there
cannot be Christian theology and ethics.

What, precisely, happens in the Christian community that makes
it moral community? The answer can only be that the entire life of
the church, to the extent that it is intentionally responding to God as
known in Jesus Christ, not only has a bearing on ethics but in fact is its
own ethics. Perhaps Hauerwas's most well-known declaration of this
view is: "The church does not *have* a social ethic; the church *is* a social
ethic."[30] Entailed in this ethic are mundane aspects of its communal
life such as "parking lots and potluck dinners."[31] More distinctive of the
church's activity is its worship. At least since Kant, worship has been
considered at best incidental to morality. In sharp contrast, for Hauerwas the worshipping activities of the church are preeminently ethical,
and not only as a source of inspiration or motivation to "be good."[32]
In its worship, and especially its sacraments, the church remembers
and faithfully participates in the story of Jesus, and the worshippers,
in turn, are morally transformed over time according to that story. Its
sacraments are its politics, for they give the worshipping community
its particular moral shape.[33] The hymns of the church are vehicles of
memory, communication, and celebration of the gospel.[34] Its preaching

---

30. Ibid., 99 (my emphasis).

31. Ibid., 107.

32. Although Hauerwas makes no attempt to indicate what may or may not be normative for Christian worship, it must be said that not all that passes for worship is worthy of
the name. There needs to be discretion and critical reflection on all parts of the church's
worship. Dirkie Smit rightly warns of the pitfalls of careless worship that takes no account of its particular context; see Dirkie Smit, "Liturgy and Life? On the Importance of
Worship for Christian Ethics," *Scriptura* 62 (1997): 259–80, esp. 272–74. Alertness to the
ever-changing context in which worship must be expressed and sensitivity to currently
pressing issues such as race, poverty, and gender should have a shaping influence on the
style and content of worship. More determinative than political correctness, however, is
faithfulness to the Christian story.

33. Stanley Hauerwas, *In Good Company: The Church as Polis* (Notre Dame, Ind.:
University of Notre Dame Press, 1995), 153–68, and *The Peaceable Kingdom*, 108.

34. As noted earlier, in the apartheid era the music of worship in white churches seemed
to ring hollow when judged by liberal criteria. With my introduction to the community-
narrative paradigm I could now account for my enjoyment of hymns and could recognize
their clear ethical function in the moral formation of Christians. The claim of my own
Wesleyan heritage that "Methodism was born in song" now resonated well with my theology
and ethics. Of course, the power of communal singing to unite people into groups is well

is a reaching out to the strangers in its midst, thereby both welcoming them and propagating itself. Being open to strangers in a racially segregated society makes for revolutionary possibilities![35]

This autobiographical reflection centers on my discovery of the work of Hauerwas in the fourth and final decade of apartheid in South Africa—the 1980s. That context and my experience as a Christian seeking an adequate theological ethic in it is the lens through which I read and understand his work. Just as news and other information were distorted in that anomalous situation, however, it is quite possible that my reading of Hauerwas is idiosyncratic. I have explained what drew me to his approach: it provided nothing less than a restatement and reinstatement of Christian faith and a moral understanding of life in the church. Further, I saw it as providing a way forward for Christian theology in the new post-apartheid era. It is that way forward that I now want to pursue.

The Truth and Reconciliation Commission: A Theological Window

What is now going on in the church in South Africa, and what theological guidance is there for life on the boundary between church and society? Where are we to look for answers?

A unique window onto the role of the church in South Africa was the Truth and Reconciliation Commission (TRC), which operated from 1996 to 1998 and was charged with confronting the pernicious effects of apartheid and the pain it inflicted on large parts of the population. The TRC, established by government legislation, was headed by the retired Anglican archbishop Desmond Tutu and was markedly Christian in its concept and ethos. The part played by the Christian churches in the

---

attested in spheres of life other than the church—from political rallies to sports crowds. This is in no way to signal approval of all such activity. The communal singing of the mesmerized Hitler-supporting crowds at rallies in the Third Reich and sometimes the tribal chanting of sports fans on popular sporting occasions is open to serious moral question. Clearly, the object of the singing, the content of the words, and the intention of the singers are of vital importance to the moral significance of a particular song. In this regard, some Christian hymns are more worthy than others, more central to the whole memory of the church. These worthy hymns of worship can be seen to have powerful moral significance in the worshipping community.

35. The importance of the stranger for Christian ethics is evident in Stanley Hauerwas, *A Community of Character: Toward a Constructive Christian Social Ethic* (Notre Dame, Ind.: University of Notre Dame Press, 1981), 10 (thesis 4), 26. The connection between preaching and the stranger is made in *The Peaceable Kingdom*, 108.

TRC process, however, was very small: "Given the scope of the TRC's mandate, the faith community hearings were but a small dab on a much larger canvas."[36] In general, the mainline churches acknowledged, in one form or another, their complicity in apartheid.[37] By their own admission, they had not been countercommunities. In his reflection on both the small scale of their submissions to the TRC and the somewhat abject nature of their testimony, Carl Niehaus writes in a somber vein of the churches' social witness and is decidedly pessimistic about any significant contribution they may be able to make in the future.[38] It is clear that the mainline churches have been judged in terms of their performance with respect to apartheid and have been found, at worst, guilty of willing collaboration or, at best, seriously lacking in their resolve to stand against it. The finding of the commission is depressing:

> The failure by religious communities to give adequate expression to the ethical teaching of their respective traditions, all of which stand in direct contradiction to apartheid, contributed to a climate within which apartheid was able to survive. Religious communities need to accept moral and religious culpability for their failure as institutions to resist the impact of apartheid on the nation with sufficient rigour. The failure of the churches in this regard contributed not only to the survival of apartheid but also to the perpetuation of the myth, prevalent in certain circles, that apartheid was both a moral and Christian initiative in a hostile and ungodly world.[39]

A different kind of response to the TRC was offered by the group of churches known collectively as the African Initiated Churches (AICs).[40]

36. James Cochrane, John de Gruchy, and Stephen Martin, eds., *Facing the Truth: South African Faith Communities and the Truth and Reconciliation Commission* (Cape Town: David Philip; Athens: Ohio University Press, 1999), 5. The report on the faith-community hearings, at which forty-one institutions were represented, numbers only 34 pages out of the total report of 2,739 pages—and this in a country often characterized as "very religious."

37. The term "mainline churches" refers to those Christian denominations that were introduced to South Africa from Europe, mainly through the work of missionaries, and would include, for example, the Anglican, Baptist, Congregational, Lutheran, Methodist, Presbyterian, and Roman Catholic churches. Also to be included are the racially constituted Dutch Reformed churches, the largest of which, the Nederduitse Gereformeerde Kerk, was openly supportive of the apartheid government.

38. Carl Niehaus, "Reconciliation in South Africa: Is Religion Relevant?" in Cochrane et al., *Facing the Truth*, 81–90.

39. *Truth and Reconciliation Commission of South Africa Report* (Cape Town: TRC, 1998), par. 121, 91.

40. There has been much debate over the most appropriate collective name for the many hundreds of Christian denominations gathered under the acronym AIC. The *A* indicates African and the *C* stands for church, but the *I* is variously held to mean Indepen-

These churches are often regarded as insignificant by the mainline churches. They were dismissed by the so-called prophetic churches and contextual and black theologians as being irrelevant to the struggle against apartheid, as more interested in cultural than political issues.[41] They were reckoned to be quietist and politically disengaged. They seemed to be self-absorbed, "inward looking and disinterested in political participation."[42] The AICs' activities center on dynamic, exuberant worship—characterized by singing, movement, and dance—on healing ceremonies, and on the interpretation of dreams. Their interpretation of Christianity in terms of their African traditions seems to resonate more with the Old Testament than the New.

Three AIC groups testified before the TRC: the Zion Christian Church (ZCC), the largest of the AICs;[43] Ibandla lamaNazaretha, otherwise known as the Shembe Church after their founder, Isaiah Shembe; and the Council of African Instituted Churches (CAIC). The submission of the CAIC followed the pattern of the mainline churches in acknowledging that they had not done enough in the struggle against apartheid. Invoking the dominant categories of political resistance, they judged themselves to have been cowards. The submissions of the ZCC and the amaNazaretha, however, were of a different order, and it is these that Robin Petersen

---

dent, Indigenous, Initiated, or Instituted. The TRC report uses the term "African Initiated Churches." These African churches collectively have the largest membership of all Christian communities in South Africa. They originated at the end of the nineteenth century in protest against the reluctance of the white-led missionary churches to open leadership positions to Africans. They grew spectacularly in membership through the twentieth century to the extent that it may be appropriate to ask if the term "mainstream" should not be applied to them rather than to the denominations of European origin. While they exist in many hundreds of denominational fragments, some groups are relatively large, the largest being one of those noted here, the Zion Christian Church. The other, the Ibandla lamaNazaretha, has a significant presence in KwaZulu-Natal.

41. The fact that the *Kairos Document* makes no mention of the AICs is an indication of the preconceptions of the document's authors, which, together with the preconceptions of black theology, were not indigenous to Africa but were Western imports.

42. The official TRC report states: "The African Initiated Churches have, at times, been regarded as inward looking and disinterested in political participation. This is not, however, always the case. The Council of African Initiated Churches unites across a number of bodies and has been politically engaged. It is also connected to other churches through its membership of the SACC" (*Truth and Reconciliation Commission of South Africa Report*, par. 14, 62). In its attempt to signal its approval of the AICs, the TRC report shows that it cannot imagine politics that differ from the mainstream Western paradigm. An "approval" of this kind would face rejection by the AICs.

43. The ZCC had drawn the wrath of anti-apartheid activists by inviting one of the apartheid presidents, P. W. Botha, to be the speaker at their major annual Easter rally in 1985. As a result of this apparent affirmation, some even suspected the ZCC of favoring the apartheid government.

surely has in mind when he claims that the AIC submissions force us
"to rethink notions of resistance and struggle." Petersen's incisive account continues:

> For the amaNazaretha and the ZCC in particular, their perceived lack of
> active resistance to apartheid is contested by them on a different terrain.
> They refuse to be trapped in a modernist logic that seeks to understand
> these terms solely within the framework of self-conscious political action.
> In answer to the probing on this point, they respond by contesting the
> categories in which the questions are posed.[44]

In response to a direct question as to their programs against apartheid, the ZCC spokesperson, Immanuel Lothola, replied: "As a church,
the Zion Christian Church did not lead people into a mode of resistance
against apartheid. But as a church the ZCC taught its people to love
themselves more than ever, to stand upright and face the future, to defy
the laws of apartheid; . . . not to hurt others, but to refuse to be hurt
by others." Petersen points to the irony around the term "resistance"
and exclaims:

> "Refusing to be hurt by others." What a statement of profound resistance.
> For apartheid's intent (along with that of its colonial predecessors) was
> to colonise the hearts and minds of its black subjects, to make them be-
> lieve that they were not fully human, not capable of full citizenship, that
> they were inferior and deserved their subjugation. To this domination,
> such a philosophy of self-love and self-reliance, of refusing to allow the
> dominator to "hurt," is supremely resistant, albeit at another level to that
> of direct political action.[45]

These churches bewildered the TRC by the form of their submissions,
thereby providing a display of the subtlety of their previous resistance
to apartheid. Mr. Mpanza, the amaNazaretha representative, reported
that although his submission was prepared in English (the language of
the commission), he would speak in Zulu because most of the people in
his congregation could not speak English. He was acknowledging that
he had the ability to cooperate with the terms of the commission but
declaring that he chose not to. Perhaps most telling of all was the witness of the authoritative and widely respected leader of the ZCC, Bishop
Lekganyane. In response to Chairperson Tutu's invitation to address
the commission, Bishop Lekganyane, with a benign smile, remained

---

44. Robin M. Petersen, "The AICs and the TRC: Resistance Redefined," in Cochrane
et al., *Facing the Truth*, 117–18.
45. Ibid., 118.

seated as two spokesmen instead took the stand. After some confusion and embarrassment, the chairperson allowed them to speak. Petersen comments:

> The power of silence. In a commission constituted by words (submissions and testimonies), it is silence that is ultimately the most dramatic. It unsettles and disconcerts even the usually unflappable Tutu. It is a gesture of refusal that frames the testimony of the ZCC in a powerful way. It is a statement which says, "I will not be reduced to your categories, even to your language. I do not have to justify myself to you in your terms." It is an act of resistance, of "independency" at its most dramatic.[46]

In these ways, both verbal and nonverbal, the AICs demonstrated their stance. They used the TRC hearings, which were nationally televised, to make known their role in resisting apartheid. They also sought to explain their kind of resistance, which was not readily acknowledged as such—either by liberation movements during the apartheid era, or later by the post-apartheid TRC. Petersen's article argues strongly for the recognition and appreciation of the distinctive resistance and Christian witness of the AICs. In effect, they were saying, "You ask us whether we resisted apartheid. Let us show you in the way we also resist your government-appointed commission with its modern Western categories of political resistance." This was the nimble-footed tactic of the poor and disadvantaged rather than the well-reasoned strategy of those with power and wealth. Petersen holds it up as a demonstration of what James Scott describes as "the weapons of the weak."[47] Petersen points to the extent of the cultural and moral counterstance of the AICs, far beyond the political purview of the TRC:

> Simplicity and self-reliance: hardly notions of extraordinary moment. But in a context marked by the market, shaped by the incessant production of consumptive desire through the commodification and reification of life under the domination of capital, and constituted by the extension of its capillaries of power in the making and shaping of the construction of the self as consumer and as dominated object, simplicity is a resistant moment.
>
> The solid core of this simplicity is seen in the moral codes which mark the AICs as different. For the amaNazaretha, the code is linked . . . to the simplicity of life, and includes prohibitions on alcohol, smoking of any

---

46. Ibid., 120.

47. Scott's key concept is the "hidden transcript" that the dominated employ as a means of coping with and subtly undermining those who have power over them. James Scott, *Domination and the Arts of Resistance: Hidden Transcripts* (New Haven: Yale University Press, 1990).

kind, pre-marital sexual intercourse and the use of medicine for healing.[48]

Two factors characterize the submissions of the AICs. First, these
churches stood against the dominant Western culture, which they clearly
saw in the TRC itself. Hence, they were conscious of sharp differences
between themselves and the TRC. They did not regard the TRC as a
natural ally in the kind of resistance they mounted against apartheid.
That is why they found it appropriate to employ tactics that questioned
the dominance of the TRC and to assert their autonomy in terms of what
they said and how they said it. Their unusual approach declared that
their submission was to be on their own terms. Second, and closely connected, the moral logic they followed was their own. The reasons they
gave for both the nature of their erstwhile resistance against apartheid
and their manner of presentation to the TRC (the bishop's silence and
the deliberate choice of a different language) were in terms of their own
communal life as African churches. Had they been asked to account for
their unusual response, the answer implicit in their submissions was
clear: "That's who we are, and that's what we do." Their answer was to
describe the life they required of their members. Their church was their
social ethic. This would also be their confident response to our question,
What's going on in the church in South Africa?

Unlike the mainline denominations that would try to answer the
question in terms of their attempts to apply abstract moral concepts
and to adapt their programs to the dramatically different political and
social context of the past ten years, the AICs would argue that they are
continuing to do what they have always done. Quite explicitly, they are
going about the business of being the church in Africa. In that task, they
are self-consciously different from, yet a responsible part of, the rest
of society. They are also self-consciously different from the mainline
churches that are rooted in European culture.

Levels of Questioning

Petersen listens intently to the submissions of the AICs, observes
carefully, reports with precision, and offers a brilliant account of the
interaction between the AICs and the TRC. He explains and defends the
methods of resistance of the AICs, methods that he clearly admires, but
he stops short of judging the extent to which the AICs are succeeding in
being the church. In other words, he stops short of theological evaluation.

48. Petersen, "The AICs and the TRC," 121–22.

To be fair, his question is not "What's going on in the church in South Africa?" but "What was the nature of the AICs' resistance to apartheid?" These are not only different questions; they function at different levels. The latter question must be answered according to political criteria, while the former must be answered ultimately in theological terms. Yet the two questions are held together inextricably in one historical nexus.

Careful scrutiny is called for with respect to levels of questions and the corresponding levels of answers. The question "What's going on in the church?" may be asked most basically at the level of mere curiosity. In this case, the answer will be purely *descriptive;* it will contain empirical information about activities and statistics, of the sort provided by outside observers such as historians and sociologists. A second level of question and answer, which builds on the first, aspires to be evaluative in terms of nontheological criteria. Petersen's analysis is a case in point. At this level, the church is characteristically understood in terms of its usefulness to certain interests and causes—social, political, economic, and cultural. The purpose of the church is identified with some external program or agenda, and the church is evaluated in terms of those external criteria. The work of the church is seen as *instrumental* to a cause that is wholly accounted for in terms other than the gospel or the kingdom of God. This level of question and answer uncovers a point of crisis for contextual theology, whose very name indicates an attempt to hold together the theological and the political;[49] its usual approach is precisely to see the church as instrumental to a nontheological end. Its concern, like that of Marx, is with the "use" of the church and not with the church per se.[50] It is *about* theology, but it is not theology. A danger here is that such studies are sometimes taken to be theology, or to lay down the primary criteria by which theology and church are to be judged.[51]

At a third level, the question may concern the nature of the church. At this level the answer must be *typological,* that is to say, it must be framed in terms of one or another of the various possible understandings of the church. The focus here may be on the institution and its programs, and

---

49. This tension is discussed in Segundo's account of the "two trajectories"—that of the educated theologian and biblical scholar and that of the poor and marginalized local community; see J. L. Segundo, "The Shift within Latin American Theology," *Journal of Theology for Southern Africa* 52 (1985): 17–29.

50. See Walker and Cochrane, *Contextualisation of Theological Education,* 17, and Robin M. Petersen, "Articulating the Prophetic and the Popular: Proposals for a Neomodernist Liberation Theology," *Bulletin for Contextual Theology* 5 (1998): 38.

51. See Neville Richardson, "On Keeping Theological Ethics Theological in Africa: The Quest for a (Southern) African Theological Ethics," *Annual of the Society of Christian Ethics* 21 (2001): 361–78.

these are open to external scrutiny. Typologies of the church, such as those of Ernst Troeltsch and Avery Dulles (and similar studies of theology, such as H. Richard Niebuhr's *Christ and Culture*), make it possible for this level of scrutiny to be open to those both inside and outside the church, and to both faith and nonfaith perspectives.[52]

A fourth level of question and answer seeks to evaluate the church in terms of its faithful Christian witness alone. This level is *theological*, involving an understanding of God and the gospel of Jesus Christ that is available only to those who live according to that understanding and that gospel and whose lives are transformed thereby. Clearly, at this level the question "What's going on in the church?" can be answered only by the church itself. Two landmark statements of the church in response to serious social and political challenges in South Africa and Germany, respectively, are the *Kairos Document* and the Barmen Declaration. These statements were similarly necessitated by context but are very different from each other. *Kairos* moves at the second, instrumental level, while Barmen moves at the fourth, theological level. *Kairos* is an attempt to render the church instrumental to the cause of liberation from apartheid. Barmen is a theological defense against an attempt to render the church instrumental to an external program—the Nazification of theology and church. That which is the primary consideration in the Barmen Declaration, the truth and self-sufficiency of the gospel of Jesus Christ, is in *Kairos* secondary to, or reduced to, the programs of the people in their struggle for liberation. The point of this distinction is emphatically not to demean the struggle against apartheid. It was an urgent requirement calling for the active support of the church at that historical moment. The rationale of *Kairos*, however, is political, while the rationale of the church for such support must be theological. The political struggle, however noble, heroic, and necessary, is not theology—the demise of apartheid is not the fulfillment of the gospel of Jesus Christ, and "the people" are not the church.

Wise as Serpents and Innocent as Doves

Despair in the face of totalitarian politics as experienced by the church in Nazi Germany and apartheid South Africa may encourage an apocalyptic tendency to think of church as entirely separate from politics. The distinction of levels of questioning in the previous section may

---

52. Ernst Troeltsch, *The Social Teaching of the Christian Churches* (London: George Allen and Unwin, 1931), Avery Dulles, *Models of the Church* (Dublin: Gill and Macmillan, 1976), and H. R. Niebuhr, *Christ and Culture* (New York: Harper & Row, 1951).

also suggest such a dichotomy. That perception would be incorrect. To claim that the question "What's going on in the church?" requires a theological answer is not to imply that politics has no part in the church and the church no part in politics. It is unavoidable for the church to be involved in politics in one way or another, for the political process is part of human society. Furthermore, and of central importance to Hauerwas, the church itself is a political process. Theology cannot be reduced without remainder to social science, nor the task of the church to a secular political agenda. Yet precisely because the community of faith belongs in the world, it cannot ignore its historical–social context. The church overlooks the findings of social analysts like James Scott and Jean and John Comaroff at its peril, especially in societies characterized by gross imbalances of power.[53] Such works not only alert the church to problems in secular society, but also indicate sensitivities to be navigated in mission policy and practice as well as in power relations within the church community. To disregard what social analysts are saying in these areas is to be less than responsible, potentially naïve, and guilty of violating Jesus's injunction to the disciples to be "wise as serpents and innocent as doves" (Matt. 10:16).

Karl Barth's alertness to his context gave rise to the Barmen Declaration, a policy statement of the church in a context that Barth saw as threatening not only the activities of the church but its very nature and existence. Barth was convinced that socialism was the kind of politics to support in his context. The unequivocal terms of the Barmen Declaration and Barth's socialist response to the needs of civil society were expressions of his Christian faith.[54] Can we develop a theology that is both similarly sensitive to its context and open to the findings of social analysts, yet one that holds as its primary concern its faithful embodi-

53. The works of James Scott on "hidden transcripts" and Jean and John Comaroff on ideology and hegemony provide theologians with vital tools both for understanding the social effects of their present work and for warning against the mistakes of church and missions in the past, especially where the context is the interface of different cultures and an imbalance of power. Serious difficulties arise for theologians, however, when the theoretical assumptions of such social scientific studies, which are methodologically atheistic and/or Marxist, are taken to be normative for theology; see Scott, *Domination and the Arts of Resistance*, and Jean and John Comaroff, *Of Revelation and Revolution: Christianity, Colonialism, and Consciousness in South Africa*, vol. 1 (Chicago: University of Chicago Press, 1991).

54. Dirkie Smit points out helpfully that Barth saw the Gospel miracles as demonstrating clearly that Jesus's actions were always for the poor, the suffering, and the miserable, those in extremis. This is not to claim Jesus as a social activist, confirming the ethical proclivities of the modern Western church. What Jesus did was simply to reveal the heart of God for poor, suffering humanity; see Dirkie Smit, "Paradigms of Radical Grace," in Villa-Vicencio, *On Reading Karl Barth in South Africa*, 27–32.

ment of and witness to the gospel of Jesus Christ? Such faithfulness must always remain primary, be it at the fence of Dachau or in the struggle against apartheid, be it swimming against the tide of secular humanism and global free-market capitalism or facing the HIV/AIDS plague.[55] Here, surely, is not a distraction from social concern, nor a diversion from political activism, but a calling to incarnational ministry and service. Forrester refers to an early work by Hauerwas in which he points out that the church "exists only as a mission to the world" and that the calling of the church may therefore differ in various contexts.[56] Then Forrester shifts the emphasis with a sleight of hand—barely noticeable, yet the difference is vital. In the very next paragraph, with which his article concludes, Forrester states:

> The Church is called to be the Church in different ways in different contexts. We attend to the Dachau concentration camp and the little church outside, and to the complex and often terrible story of the Church down the ages, and above all to Scripture, not to find there some universally valid pattern of being the Church, but rather to learn from the failures and the triumphs of the past how God is calling us to be the Church, a fellowship of disciples, today, and in relation to today's opportunities and problems. And in this conversation we are seeking above all to attend to the Church's Lord who calls the Church to be a manifestation not so much of goodness as of grace, of achievement as of faithfulness.[57]

From an emphasis on what the church does, the ever-changing activity (mission) that constitutes its existence, there is a subtle shift to an emphasis on what the church is—a change from the language of doing to the language of being. The article culminates with a descriptive account of that continuity through time known as church. The focus is not on the changing contexts that render God's call different with

---

55. HIV/AIDS is probably the next great social–ethical challenge for the church in South Africa. Recent statistics show that South Africa is one of the countries worst affected by the disease. In some areas up to one-third of women presenting at prenatal clinics are HIV positive, and AIDS is the cause of about 40 percent of all deaths in the 15–49 age group. Official figures, probably conservative, give the number of AIDS-related deaths in South Africa in the past six years as 457,000. Certainly this is a matter of life and death on a vast scale, in which the churches ought to be deeply engaged. See Ronald Nicolson, *God in AIDS? A Theological Enquiry* (London: SCM, 1996), and Stuart C. Bate, ed., *Responsibility in a Time of AIDS: A Pastoral Response by Catholic Theologians in Southern Africa* (Pietermaritzburg: Cluster, 2003).

56. Forrester, "The Church and the Concentration Camp," 206, citing Stanley Hauerwas, *Vision and Virtue: Essays in Christian Ethical Reflection* (Notre Dame, Ind.: University of Notre Dame Press, 1974), 216.

57. Forrester, "The Church and the Concentration Camp," 207.

respect to time and place but on the church that is called in different contexts to be a manifestation of grace and faithfulness. Yes, different contexts call for different ways of being the church, but in the end it is the church's life and the church's Lord that are central. This is the realm of theology and not of sociology, for our primary object is not human experience but God. What now constitutes the church as an ongoing continuity through time is not activity, however meritorious, noble, or sacrificial, but those virtues that are the communal embodiments of Christian convictions. Whatever the context, and however much the church may need to take account of contextual sensitivities, pressures, and demands, the decisive answer to the question "What's going on in the church?" can only be theological.

As we saw earlier, one church in South Africa explained to the TRC that in the face of suffering under apartheid—and of scorn from certain mainline churches, anti-apartheid activists, and contextual theologians—their members were taught "to love themselves more than ever, to stand upright and face the future, to defy the laws of apartheid; . . . not to hurt others, but to refuse to be hurt by others." Here we see an example of what Hauerwas refers to as "the politics that supports the practices necessary 'to fix the meaning of the community's most central beliefs.'"[58] That church was not asked by the TRC to set out the entire heart of its faith and community life. It offered no disembodied doctrine or abstract ethical principles. What it did was to outline its social boundaries that once bordered on apartheid oppression and now bordered on a threat of another kind—Western modernity that is increasingly secular in nature. Theirs was no abstract rationale or justification but a brief account of their communal existence, which, together with the shrewd manner of their presentation, displayed their faith in Jesus Christ for Africa.

Whatever is going on or not going on in the church in South Africa, here is a clear instance of one community being "as wise as serpents and as innocent as doves." We would do well to heed this example, for it warns against naïveté in social, political, economic, and cultural matters, and on that count may well be seen as a kind of contextual theology. More important, it follows the advice of Jesus Christ about how to live as his disciples, then and now. To live in this manner as a community in South Africa is to witness to the truthfulness of Christian convictions. It is not to dance to the tune of social science or of political expediency. It is rather to dance—as the AICs do in their worship with such characteristic vigor—before the Lord.

58. Hauerwas, *With the Grain of the Universe*, 213.

Part 4

Practicing Theology . . . and Learning from the Other

13

"An Immense Darkness" and the Tasks of Theology

Nicholas Lash

Prologue

Before the fourteenth century, Christians believed that, with Christ's coming, the daylight of eternity had dawned, conquering the darkness of the times before. (Admittedly, this confident periodization was counterpointed by the recognition—celebrated every Christmas and at every Easter Vigil—that the dispelling of the darkness, in which we always live and suffer, by the daylight of Christ's coming is ever fresh, astonishing, expected yet miraculous pure gift.)

But it was Petrarch, whom the present displeased, and who would have much preferred to live in ancient Rome, who first "reversed the traditional Christian distinction between 'ages of darkness' and 'ages of light.'" I wonder whether Joseph Conrad knew that it was, above all, in his epic *Africa* that Petrarch took "darkness" as symbol not of primitive beginning but of subsequent decline?[1]

The Confusion of Religion and the Disappearance of God

In his magisterial study, *Conrad in the Nineteenth Century*, Ian Watt took "one of the ideological lessons of *Heart of Darkness*" to be that "nothing is more dangerous than man's delusions of autonomy and omnipotence." "In *Heart of Darkness*," he said, "Conrad affirmed the need, as Camus put it, 'in order to be a man, to refuse to be a God.'"[2]

This seems to me exactly right in its implication that theological issues are central to Conrad's story. And yet, so far as I can see, this possibility is rarely even *mentioned*, let alone seriously considered, in the literature.[3] The novel has been variously described as an adventure story, as political—descriptions here range from claims that the novel was the first courageous indictment of the savage rapacity of imperialism in Leopold II's Congo to its being "bloody racist"—as psychological, or existential, or as "a symbolic presentation of moral and ideological problems," even as metaphysical, in the somewhat vague and gestural sense of being about "the nature of mankind." But almost never are its central themes construed as theological.[4]

1. Louis Dupré, *Passage to Modernity: An Essay in the Hermeneutics of Nature and Culture* (New Haven: Yale University Press, 1993), 148. Dupré drew upon Theodore Mommsen, "Petrarch's Conception of the 'Dark Ages,'" *Speculum* 17 (1942): 226–42.

2. Ian Watt, *Conrad in the Nineteenth Century* (London: Chatto and Windus, 1980), 168, citing Albert Camus, *L'homme revolté*.

3. One text may count as a partial, rare exception: Stanley Renner, "Kurtz, Christ, and the Darkness of *Heart of Darkness*," *Renascence* 28, no. 2 (Winter, 1976): 95–104. Renner explores "the parallelism between Kurtz and Christ." Reading Kurtz as a parable of "the historical Jesus stripped of what Conrad called 'the Bethlehem legend'" (101), Renner interprets the lie to the Intended as exemplifying the "reserve" with which those who have seen through the illusions of religious belief protect the simple faithful from the truth they are not strong enough to bear. Renner described this theme as "one of the few underdeveloped areas in the voluminous scholarship surrounding *Heart of Darkness*" (95). He found only one previous treatment of the theme: William Leigh Godshalk, "Kurtz as Diabolical Christ," *Discourse* 12, no. 1 (Winter, 1969): 100–107.

4. This possibility is not even mentioned in a special issue of *Conradiana* devoted to discussion of different ways in which *Heart of Darkness* had been, and might be, taught in the classroom: see *Conradiana* 24, no. 3 (1992). Conrad himself tended to present his book as "a story of the Congo," as "experience pushed a little (and only a little) beyond the actual facts of the case" (from a letter of July 22, 1906, and a note of 1917); see Joseph Conrad, *Heart of Darkness: An Authoritative Text; Backgrounds and Sources; Criticism*, ed. Robert Kimbrough, 3rd ed. (New York: W. W. Norton, 1988), 199, 197. (Henceforward, the text of *Heart of Darkness* from this edition will be cited as *HD*, and other material

According to Garrett Stewart, Marlow himself, who is portrayed, at the beginning and the end, as adopting "the pose of a meditating Buddha," and thereby "resembl[ing] an idol,"[5] "partially incarnates that idolatry masquerading as an almost religious truth . . . which is the monitory center of his tale."[6] It is the "almost" that is interesting. To put it with misleading brevity: my hunch is that the failure to read the story theologically is due, at least in part, to the assumption that the subject matter of theology is religion, rather than all things whatsoever in relation to the mystery of God, their origin and end.[7] Moreover, notwithstanding the profusion of religious imagery in *Heart of Darkness*—from the "pilgrims" to "inconceivable ceremonies of some devilish initiation"[8]—it would seem very odd to classify it as a "religious" novel: *Loss and Gain*

---

as *Norton*.) Ian Watt called the novel "an early expression of what was to become a worldwide revulsion from the horrors of Leopold's exploitation of the Congo" *(Conrad in the Nineteenth Century*, 139). According to Ross Murfin, Thomas Moser took it to be "a work critical of racist European imperialism"; see *Joseph Conrad, Heart of Darkness: Case Studies in Contemporary Criticism*, ed. Ross C. Murfin, 2nd ed. (Boston: Bedford Books of St. Martin's Press, 1996), 104, commenting on Thomas Moser, *Joseph Conrad: Achievement and Decline* (Cambridge, Mass.: Harvard University Press, 1957). "Bloody racist" was Chinua Achebe's famous verdict in the original version of his 1975 Chancellor's Lecture at the University of Massachusetts, later amended to "thoroughgoing racist" (see *Norton*, 251, 257; Peter J. Rabinowitz, "Reader Response, Reader Responsibility: *Heart of Darkness* and the Politics of Displacement," in Murfin, *Case Studies*, 131). According to Albert Guerard, Marlow "is recounting a spiritual voyage of self-discovery"; see Albert J. Guerard, *Conrad the Novelist* (Cambridge, Mass.: Harvard University Press, 1958), 39, whereas Frederick Crews read the story as an expression of the Oedipus complex: Frederick Crews, *Out of My System: Psychoanalysis, Ideology, and Critical Method* (Oxford: Oxford University Press, 1975), discussed, with other psychological readings of the text, by Murfin in *Case Studies*, 106–8. For soberly critical comments on the contributions of Guerard and Crews, see Ian Watt, *Conrad in the Nineteenth Century*, 238–40. Michael Levenson made the interesting suggestion that Conrad shifted his aim in the course of writing, from the primarily political focus of the first section to the primarily psychological of the third; see Michael Levenson, "The Value of Facts in the *Heart of Darkness*," *Nineteenth-Century Fiction* 40 (1985): 261–80, reprinted in *Norton*, 391–405. In his edition of Conrad's *Congo Diary and Other Uncollected Pieces* (New York: Doubleday, 1978), Zdzislaw Najder warned that using the *Diary* as an aid to reading *Heart of Darkness* "may distract us from seeing what it essentially is: not a relation about places and events, but a symbolic presentation of moral and ideological problems" (cited from *Norton*, 156). On what he calls "Nature of Man" interpretations, see Peter J. Rabinowitz, in Murfin, *Case Studies*, 137–38.

    5. *HD*, 76 (cf. 10), 7.
    6. Garrett Stewart, "Lying as Dying in *Heart of Darkness*," *PMLA* 95 (1980): 319–31; cited from *Norton*, 370. John Lester curiously describes Marlow's final pose as "a reminder of the misguided idolatry revealed in Marlow's story"; see John Lester, *Conrad and Religion* (Basingstoke: Macmillan, 1988), 63, as if there were versions of idolatry on offer that were *not* misguided.
    7. See Thomas Aquinas, *Summa Theologiae*, Ia, 1, 7.
    8. *HD*, 49; the "faithless pilgrims" make their first appearance, 26.

in Africa, perhaps! Accordingly, before turning to the text, some brief remarks about the confusion of "religion" and the disappearance of God would seem to be in order.[9]

In 1996, surveying the methodological confusion attending the study of religion, especially in the United States, with warring schools and tendencies often having little more in common than antagonism to theology, Professor Catherine Bell of Santa Clara University remarked: "That we construct 'religion' and 'science' is not the main problem; that we forget that we have constructed them in our own image—that is a problem."[10] I take this remark to be, in part, a warning against the dangerous illusion that "religion" and "society" are the names of natural kinds.

"Words matter," as John Bossy remarked in his 1981 Inaugural Lecture in the University of York, and "without a sense of their history they become manipulable in the cause of obfuscation."[11] Religion, in its modern sense, as a "social institution" with its own constitutive "beliefs and practices"[12] (which will, of course, vary from one "religion" to another), was invented, or constructed, in the seventeenth century, in the interests of political control.[13] As an example of the kind of obfuscation that Bossy had in mind, I offer Samuel Preus's definition of "explanation" in matters of religion: "the proposal of alternatives to the explanations that the *religious* offer for religion."[14]

For much of the twentieth century, Weberian views of religion as in irreversible decline before the rising tide of "rationality" (whether this erosion be seen as matter for celebration or lament) existed in tension with Durkheimian accounts according to which "something eternal in religion"—namely, worship and faith—is destined to outlast the replace-

9. For two very different attempts on my part to show how this confusion went and to suggest how it might be unscrambled, see my review, in the *Journal of Theological Studies*, n.s., 37 (1986): 654–62, of *Nineteenth Century Religious Thought in the West*, ed. Ninian Smart, John Clayton, Patrick Sherry, and Steven T. Katz, 3 vols. (Cambridge: Cambridge University Press, 1985), and my 1986 Richard Lectures at the University of Virginia: Nicholas Lash, *Easter in Ordinary: Reflections on Human Experience and the Knowledge of God* (Charlottesville: University Press of Virginia, 1988).

10. Catherine Bell, "Modernism and Postmodernism in the Study of Religion," *Religious Studies Review* 22 (1996): 179–90, 188.

11. John Bossy, "Some Elementary Forms of Durkheim," *Past and Present* 95 (1982): 3–18, 17.

12. Robert Towler, *The Need for Certainty: A Sociological Study of Conventional Religion* (London: Routledge and Kegan Paul, 1984), 2, 5.

13. See William T. Cavanaugh, "'A Fire Strong Enough to Consume the House': The Wars of Religion and the Rise of the State," *Modern Theology* 11 (1995): 397–420.

14. J. Samuel Preus, *Explaining Religion: Criticism and Theory from Bodin to Freud* (New Haven: Yale University Press, 1987), cited from Bell, "Modernism and Postmodernism," 181.

ment of "religious thought" by the "scientific thought" that is its "more perfected form."[15]

According to Robert Towler, however, Thomas Luckmann's *The Invisible Religion,* first published in 1963, was "the last major contribution to the sociology of religion to use the word 'religion' to denote beliefs and ideas with no super-empirical or supernatural reference, as Durkheim had done."[16]

For most of Jewish and Christian history, "gods" have been what people worshipped; that is to say, the grammar of the word "god" is similar to that of "treasure." A treasure is what you value; a god is what you worship. Only in the seventeenth century did the term "god" become, instead, the name of a natural kind: a kind of which (some people thought) there were no instances or, at least, no instances that could not be shown to be, in fact, instances of some other kind. Then, once it had been shown that the class of "gods" was empty, the word "god" had no further use (except, of course, by anthropologists patronizing cultures deemed less adult than their own): hence what Michael Buckley called "the massive shadow that Nietzsche and Newman watched descending upon Europe" in the nineteenth century, the shadow of God's eclipse, or disappearance.[17]

The world's great traditions of devotion and reflection, discipline and worship, memory and hope, are best understood not as "religions," in the modern sense, but as schools: schools "whose pedagogy has the twofold purpose—however differently conceived and executed in the different traditions—of weaning us from our idolatry and purifying our desire. All human beings have their hearts set somewhere, hold something sacred, worship at some shrine."[18] Insofar as what we worship is some fact or feature of the world, some object or ideal, commodity or dream or theory, nation, place or thing (and most of us include ourselves among the things we worship), then we are idolaters. To learn to worship only God, only the holy and unmasterable mystery that is not the world nor any part of it, is an unending task.

15. Émile Durkheim, *The Elementary Forms of the Religious Life,* trans. and intro. Karen E. Fields (New York: Free Press, 1995), 432, 431.

16. Towler, *Need for Certainty,* 3. Unfortunately, Towler, as is customary these days, uses the term "supernatural" in the degenerate modern sense of entities and forces "outside" what we take to be the "natural" world. One bizarre consequence of this shift is to make it commonplace to speak of God as "a supernatural being." Bizarre because it used to be supposed that *only* God could *not* act supernaturally, for what grace could elevate or heal God's nature?

17. Michael J. Buckley, *At the Origins of Modern Atheism* (New Haven: Yale University Press, 1987), 322.

18. Nicholas Lash, *The Beginning and the End of "Religion"* (Cambridge: Cambridge University Press, 1996), 21.

Sacredness, for Durkheim, is a quality acquired by objects when they are "set apart and forbidden" by some social group.[19] Thus, although his account goes with the grain of modern usage in denying to religion independent cognitive capacity, it goes against the grain in its admirable emphasis upon the *relational* character of the "holy" or the "sacred," of what were once called "gods."

Durkheim was born in 1858, the year after Joseph Conrad. *Heart of Darkness*, I propose to argue, is "about idolatry" in a sense that the author of the *Elementary Forms* might have appreciated. And, insofar as it is about idolatry, its concerns are (on my understanding of the tasks of theology) theological, notwithstanding the fact that neither Durkheim nor Conrad were, in any conventional sense, "religious believers."

Those who made the shift, during the nineteenth century, from talk of "God" to talk of "the Absolute," supposed themselves to be changing the subject. But God's disappearance did not mark the end of worship. Ceasing to call the object of one's worship "God" does not stop the worship being worship (and hence, by definition, the worship of *some* "god"), nor does it stop reflection on it being still theology, even if theology that supposes itself not to be theology is likely to be bad theology.[20] (There is far more theology around these days than most people appreciate, even if most of it is rather odd. This essay is offered in gratitude for Stanley Hauerwas's friendship, and in celebration of his work, in the belief that my understanding of what does and does not count as good—and bad—theology goes "with the grain" of his.)

"In the older Durkheimian tradition," says Towler, "there are those who have continued to identify such things as communism, psychoanalysis, and humanism as surrogate religion."[21] But, whatever the conventions of current sociological orthodoxy, there are—where the grammar of "god" is concerned—good reasons for continuing to prefer an account, closer to Durkheim's, according to which the rituals of the Soviet state, or American veneration of the flag, are, as forms of public worship, no

---

19. Durkheim's famous definition, at the end of the first chapter of *Elementary Forms*, was: "A religion is a unified system of beliefs and practices relative to sacred things, that is to say, things set apart and forbidden—beliefs and practices which unite into one single moral community called a Church, all those who adhere to them," 44.

20. See John Milbank, *Theology and Social Theory: Beyond Secular Reason* (Oxford: Basil Blackwell, 1990): "I hope to make it apparent that 'scientific' social theories are themselves theologies or anti-theologies in disguise" (3). See also Fergus Kerr, *Immortal Longings: Versions of Transcending Humanity* (London: SPCK, 1997).

21. Towler, *Need for Certainty*, 4, where the notion of "surrogacy" is taken from Roland Robertson, *The Sociological Interpretation of Religion* (Oxford: Blackwell, 1970). Robertson employs it in pursuit of a strategy that "tends strongly towards the exclusivist type of definitional approach," 39.

more "surrogate" than devotion to the Blessed Sacrament or the cult of Kali in Calcutta.

John Lester, in his study of *Conrad and Religion,* says that there are, in a *"figurative* sense, several deities clamouring for worship" in Conrad's tale.[22] But this is arbitrarily to suppose that "gods" are not what people worship but only what (some) people *call* "gods." As I read *Heart of Darkness,* however, the theme of worship that is so central to the story has to do with *real,* not "figurative," worship and, in that sense, treats of real, not "surrogate," religion.

Echoes of Scripture

In 1970, deploring the extent to which "a whole school of criticism has succeeded in emptying *The Heart of Darkness* of its social and historical content . . . through the endless reduction of deliberately created realities to analogues, symbolic circumstances, abstract situations," Raymond Williams insisted that "there is all the difference in the world between discovering a general truth in a particular situation and making an abstract truth out of a contingent situation."[23] Similarly, Peter Rabinowitz complains of the way in which what he calls "the Rule of Abstract Displacement," according to which "good literature is always treated as if it were about something else" than it appears to be, "has almost completely colonized writing about Conrad's novel."[24]

In arguing that *Heart of Darkness* is about idolatry, then, I am not denying that it is "about" the Belgian Congo, or the perils of fanaticism, or the devastation wrought by our rapacious egotism. It is about all these things—as aspects and instances of idolatry. The point is plain enough: Kurtz is really worshipped, and so is ivory; both Kurtz and ivory are gods.

In much of the literature, however, the issue is obscured by thick mists of confusion generated by modern notions of "religion." I have in mind, for instance, John Lester's reference to "the secular use of religious terminology in the novels," or Dwight Purdy's assertion that "in Conrad theophany is secularized."[25]

22. Lester, *Conrad and Religion,* 169, my stress.

23. Raymond Williams, *The English Novel from Dickens to Lawrence* (St. Alban's: Paladin, 1974), 118, 119.

24. Rabinowitz, "Reader Response," 139, 141. Ian Watt describes "the modern critical tendency to decompose literary works into a series of more or less cryptic references to a system of non-literal unifying meanings" as "a misguided response to a very real problem" (*Conrad in the Nineteenth Century,* 195).

25. Lester, *Conrad and Religion,* 171; Dwight H. Purdy, *Joseph Conrad's Bible* (Norman: University of Oklahoma Press, 1984), 19.

Matters are further complicated by the increasing extent to which the critics are becoming biblically illiterate. Yet *Heart of Darkness* is heavy with echoes of the Bible, not because Conrad was a Christian, but because he was a Pole who, in order to steep himself in English idioms and imaginative resources, "read and reread the King James Bible with great care."[26]

It may be useful, therefore, before addressing the central issue of the place of worship in *Heart of Darkness*—which I propose to do with reference to the interruptions to Marlow's story, the theme of speech and silence, and Kurtz's death—if I briefly indicate some of the biblical allusions that are too often overlooked.

Marlow's journey begins with his visit to "the Company's offices" in "a city that always makes me think of a whited sepulchre."[27] (And it is to this "sepulchral city" that, after Kurtz's death, he will return.)[28] The allusion to Matthew 23 sets off two associated trails that run right through the story: on the one hand, hypocrisy and "hollowness," the whitewashed tombs of imperial adventure and, on the other, the bleached dead bones of men and elephants that are its purpose and the price that is paid.[29]

On arrival at the Central Station, Marlow meets the Manager and a foppish fellow, a "young aristocrat" with "a forked little beard." "The business entrusted to this fellow was the making of bricks—so I had been informed; but there wasn't a fragment of a brick anywhere in the station, and he had been there more than a year—waiting. It seemed he could not make bricks without something, I don't know what—straw maybe."[30] This light allusion to the savagery and sadism of slavery, to Pharaoh and his taskmasters,[31] is quite lost on Richard Adams, who

---

26. Purdy, *Conrad's Bible*, 8. Although nominally a Catholic, Conrad was not, apparently, familiar with the Douay version (see Purdy, *Conrad's Bible*, 145–46).

27. *HD*, 13.

28. *HD*, 70.

29. On hypocrisy and hollowness, consider, for example: the chief accountant's "appearance was certainly that of a hairdresser's dummy, but in the great demoralisation of the land he kept up his appearance. That's backbone. His starched collars and got-up shirt-fronts were achievements of character" (*HD*, 21); "Once when various tropical diseases had laid low almost every 'agent' in the station [the Manager] was heard to say, 'Men who come out here should have no entrails.' He sealed the utterance with that smile of his as though it had been a door opening into a darkness he had in his keeping" (*HD*, 25); "I let [the brickmaker] run on, this papier–mâché Mephistopheles, and it seemed to me that if I tried I could poke my forefinger through him and would find nothing inside but a little loose dirt, maybe" (*HD*, 29); "the whisper" of "the wilderness . . . echoed loudly within [Kurtz] because he was hollow at the core" (*HD*, 57–58)—a thought that comes to Marlow while he is looking, through his spyglass, at one of the hollow skulls that decorate the posts round "the long decaying building" that was Kurtz's bungalow.

30. *HD*, 26, 27.

31. See Exod. 5.

makes no reference to it, while, in another Penguin edition, Robert Hampson adds a solemn one-word note: "Proverbial."[32]

In addition to the many such allusions to particular passages of Scripture, there are a number of places in which religious imagery and terminology are clustered to particular effect. Here, to give just one example, is Marlow, early on, wondering what he will find up river, in the heart of darkness: "What was in there? I could see a little ivory coming out from there and I had heard Mr. Kurtz was in there. I had heard enough about it too—God knows! Yet somehow it didn't bring any image with it—no more than if I had been told an angel or a fiend was in there."[33]

Finally, and of particular importance, there are passages that require what I can only call a *christological* reading of Kurtz (even if, as I shall suggest when considering his death, it is an inverse or parodied Christology). "I seemed," says Marlow, early in the journey up river, "to see Kurtz for the first time . . . *setting his face* towards the depth of the wilderness, towards his empty and desolate station. . . . His name, you understand, had not been pronounced once. He was: 'that man.'"[34] *Ecce homo*!

When the dying Kurtz has been brought on board the steamer: "I heard Kurtz's deep voice behind the curtain: 'Save me—save the ivory, you mean. Don't tell me! Save *me*! Why, I've had to save you. You are interrupting my plans now. . . . Never mind. I'll carry my ideas out yet—I will return.'"[35]

It is several pages later that Marlow recounts the struggle he had had with Kurtz, before he succeeded in bringing him to the boat:

> I had to deal with a being to whom I could not appeal in the name of anything high or low. . . . There was nothing above or below him—and I knew it. . . . Soul! If anybody had ever struggled with a soul I am the man. And I wasn't arguing with a lunatic either. Believe me or not, his intelligence was perfectly clear. . . . But his soul was mad. . . . No eloquence could have been so withering to one's belief in mankind as his final burst

32. See Richard Adams, *Joseph Conrad: Heart of Darkness*, Penguin Critical Studies (London: Penguin Books, 1991); Joseph Conrad, *Heart of Darkness with The Congo Diary*, ed. and intro. Robert Hampson (London: Penguin Books, 1995), 134. At the other extreme, Dwight Purdy suggests that "we can revise Marlow's line [that "All Europe contributed to the making of Kurtz," *HD*, 50] to say that everyone in Exodus contributes to the making of Kurtz" (*Conrad's Bible*, 69).

33. *HD*, 29.

34. *HD*, 34, my stress; cf. Luke 9:51; John 19:5. I do not think it is too fanciful to see—in the arrival of the "devoted band" that "called itself the Eldorado Exploring Expedition," "each section headed by a donkey carrying a white man in new clothes and tan shoes bowing from that elevation right and left to the impressed pilgrims" (*HD*, 32)—a parody of Palm Sunday.

35. *HD*, 61.

of sincerity. . . . When I had him at last stretched on the couch, I wiped my forehead while my legs shook under me as though I had carried half a ton on my back down that hill. And yet . . . he was not much heavier than a child.[36]

Interrupting the Story

At the beginning and the end of *Heart of Darkness*, Marlow, as I have already mentioned, is described as "adopting the pose of a meditating Buddha" and thereby resembling "an idol."[37] Much has been written about Conrad's interest in Buddhism and on the theme of Marlow's journey leading, if not to enlightenment, at least towards self-knowledge.[38] (It is worth noticing that, just before he finally meets Kurtz, Marlow—who has made it clear to Kurtz's Russian admirer that he wants to hear no more about the rituals of which his master was the object—remarks: "I suppose it did not occur to him that Mr. Kurtz was no idol of mine.")[39]

Thus it is that, appearing as "a Buddha preaching in European clothes and without a lotus-flower," Marlow prefaces his tale with a contrast between the colonization of Britain by ancient Rome: "just robbery with violence, aggravated murder on a great scale, and men going at it blind—as is very proper for those who tackle a darkness"; and contemporary British imperialism: "What redeems it is the idea only. An idea at the back of it, not a sentimental pretence but an idea; and an unselfish belief in the idea—something you can set up, and bow down before, and offer a sacrifice to."[40]

With that, the stage is set and, as the frame narrator puts it: "We knew we were fated, before the ebb began to run, to hear about one of

36. *HD*, 65–66. Purdy sees in that "struggle" an echo of Gen. 32, and Adams describes the end of the passage as "a grotesque parody of the St. Christopher story" (*Heart of Darkness*, 82).

37. *HD*, 76, 7.

38. See Lester, *Conrad and Religion*, 59–67.

39. *HD*, 58.

40. *HD*, 10. There is a disappointing and misleading discussion of this passage, with too little close reading of the text, in Patrick Brantlinger, "*Heart of Darkness:* Anti-Imperialism, Racism, or Impressionism?" in Murfin, *Case Studies*, 284–85. With the qualification that I indicated earlier (see page 259), Garrett Stewart is nearer the mark: "Idealism degrades itself to idol worship, as we know from the perverse exultation and adoration of Kurtz in the jungle, his ascent to godhead. . . . In line with the imagery of adoration, Marlow himself is twice described in the prologue as an inscrutable effigy. . . . His own person partially incarnates that idolatry masquerading as an almost religious truth . . . which is the monitory center of his tale" (cited from *Norton*, 370).

Marlow's inconclusive experiences."[41] There are, however, several inter-ruptions to Marlow's tale, interruptions that constitute "one of the most noticeable formal characteristics of Conrad's narrative," and that have the effect of preventing readers from simply continuing to go with the flow of the story, alerting us to "something that resists narrativization": what Brook Thomas calls "the glimpse of the truth we have forgotten to ask."[42] The point I want to emphasize, however, is that each of these interruptions—at least three of which express some tension or resistance on the part of Marlow's listeners—is prefaced by what one might call an intensification of theological allusion.

The first of these interruptions occurs shortly after the first mention of Kurtz, identified by the brickmaker as "the chief of the Inner Station," which tells Marlow virtually nothing![43] While "the great river . . . flowed broadly by without a murmur . . . the man jabbered on about himself. I wondered whether the stillness on the face of the immensity looking at us were meant as an appeal or a menace. What were we who had strayed in here? Could we handle that dumb thing, or would it handle us?"[44]

Marlow cannot, at this stage, *envisage* Kurtz: "He was just a word for me. I did not see the man in the name any more than you do. Do you see him? Do you see the story? Do you see anything? It seems to me I am trying to tell you a dream." Shortly after which Marlow was "silent for a while." Then: "'No, it is impossible. . . . We live, as we dream—alone. . . .' He paused again as if reflecting, then added: 'Of course in this you fel-lows see more than I could then. You see me, whom you know. . . .'" But, of course, they don't because: "It had become so pitch dark that we listeners could hardly see one another. For a long time already he, sitting apart, had been no more to us than a voice."[45]

Lest anyone suspect that to find this passage rich in Johannine para-dox of sight and blindness is to read too much into it, Conrad drives home the gospel overtones by evoking Gethsemane in this darkness in which Marlow is set "apart": "There was not a word from anybody," says the frame narrator; "The others might have been asleep, but I was awake."[46]

Introduced by the contrast between the stillness of the forest and the brickmaker's "jabbering," this whole passage is also the first full

---

41. *HD*, 11.

42. Brook Thomas, "Preserving and Keeping Order by Killing Time in *Heart of Dark-ness*," in Murfin, *Case Studies*, 250, 251.

43. *HD*, 28. "'Much obliged,' I said laughing. 'And you are the brickmaker of the Central Station. Everyone knows that.'"

44. *HD*, 29.

45. *HD*, 29–30.

46. *HD*, 30; cf. John 9; Matt. 26:36–46.

statement of the central theme of speech and silence on which I shall comment in more detail later on. Here, the ironies, as we would expect from Conrad, are multiple. Kurtz, whom at this stage he cannot visualize, who is "just a *word* for me," will, when Marlow does come closer to him and to understanding his significance, be "little more than a *voice*."[47]

A few pages later, Marlow, in his mind's eye, "seemed to see Kurtz for the first time . . . setting his face towards the depth of the wilderness."[48] There follows another detailed description of the dark, "impenetrable" stillness of the forest, "ominous" in its patience, "inscrutable" in its intention. After a while, Marlow almost ceases to notice this stillness, being preoccupied with more mundane matters concerning the navigation of the shallow river, picking a course between "hidden banks" and "sudden stones." In such circumstances, he says, "'reality . . . fades. The inner truth is hidden—luckily, luckily. But I felt it all the same; I felt often its mysterious stillness watching me at my monkey tricks, just as it watches you fellows performing on your respective tight-ropes for—what is it? half a crown a tumble. . . .' 'Try to be civil, Marlow,' growled a voice, and I knew [says the frame narrator] there was at least one listener awake besides myself."[49] Even the City and the Stock Exchange, it seems, are silently attended by something like divine judgment.

There follows a passage in which Marlow is confronted by the energy and sheer *otherness* of black Africa: "a glimpse . . . of peaked grass-roofs, a burst of yells, a whirl of black limbs, a mass of hands clapping. . . . The steamer toiled along slowly on the edge of a black and incomprehensible frenzy. The prehistoric man was cursing us, praying to us, welcoming us—who could tell? We were cut off from the comprehension of our surroundings."[50] By now, the reader is becoming familiar with the fact that Marlow regularly misreads, or fails to read, what is going on. The steamer's journey into Africa is a journey through retrospectively parted veils of misconstrual.

Now, no sooner has he accounted for his incomprehension by the fact that "we were travelling in the night of first ages, of those ages that are gone," than, with "truth stripped of its cloak of time," some recognition of the common humanity that he shares with the strange figures on the bank begins to dawn on him. This is too much for his listeners (and, perhaps, for many of the readers of *Blackwood's Magazine*): "Who's that

---

47. *HD*, 29, 48 (my emphases).
48. *HD*, 34 (see note 34, above).
49. *HD*, 35, 36.
50. *HD*, 37.

grunting? You wonder I didn't go ashore for a howl and a dance? Well, no—I didn't. Fine sentiments, you say? Fine sentiments be hanged! I had no time."[51]

An attack on the steamer, originally attributed by Marlow to unprovoked aggression (in due course, he discovers that the Africans were trying to save Kurtz from being "saved" by him),[52] results in the death of his African helmsman. "And by the way," says Marlow to one of the "pilgrims" who brings a message from the Manager, "I suppose Mr. Kurtz is dead as well by this time."[53] There follows an extraordinary passage, the theological richness of which I shall indicate later on, in which Marlow mourns the fact that

> "now I will never hear him. . . . I will never hear that chap speak after all—and my sorrow had a startling extravagance of emotion," [as if he had] "missed my destiny in life. . . . Why do you sigh in this beastly way, somebody? Absurd? Well, absurd. . . . Here, give me some tobacco." There was a pause of profound stillness, then a match flared, and Marlow's lean face appeared worn, hollow. . . . "Absurd!" he cried. "This is the worst of trying to tell. . . . Here you all are each moored with two good addresses like a hulk with two anchors, a butcher round one corner, a policeman round another. . . . And you say, Absurd!"[54]

Finally, if I am justified in insisting on the extent to which interruptions to the narrative signal passages of heightened theological significance, then we would surely expect some such interruption after Kurtz's death—the climax of all the main threads to the story.[55] However, Cedric Watts, who notes that "twice previously, Marlow's narrative had been interrupted by sceptical, disgruntled sounds from his audience"—thereby establishing a critical distance between Marlow's voice and Conrad's—denies that there is, at this point, "a further sceptical

---

51. *HD*, 37, 38.

52. "Save *me!* Why, I've had to save you," says Kurtz (*HD*, 61). "They don't want him to go," explained the Russian (*HD*, 54).

53. *HD*, 47.

54. *HD*, 48.

55. "All the main threads" may be a little too strong; some critics would defer the climax until Marlow's lie to "the Intended": his inability to confront her with the truth of Kurtz's last words. "'Repeat them,' she murmured in a heart-broken tone. 'I want—I want—something—something—to—to live with.' I was on the point of crying at her, 'Don't you hear them.' The dusk was repeating them in a persistent whisper all around us, in a whisper that seemed to swell menacingly like the first whisper of a rising wind. 'The horror! The horror!' 'His last word—to live with,' she insisted. 'Don't you understand I loved him—I loved him—I loved him.' I pulled myself together and spoke slowly. 'The last word he pronounced was—your name'" (*HD*, 75).

interruption from Marlow's hearers." Watts takes this lack of interruption to be an indication that "Marlow's confusion is largely shared by Conrad."[56]

I am not so sure. After Kurtz's death, Marlow falls ill, apparently delirious:

> The voice was gone. What else had there been? But I am of course aware that next day the pilgrims buried something in a muddy hole. And then they very nearly buried me. However, as you see, I did not go to join Kurtz there and then. I did not. I remained to dream the nightmare out to the end and to show my loyalty to Kurtz once more.[57]

However discreetly, that "as you see" establishes some distance between Marlow and his audience (and Conrad's readership), *enough* distance, perhaps, to invite us to clarify the confusion in which he remains.

Silence and Speech

"What the study of literature does, particularly that of nineteenth-century literature," according to John Coulson, "is to reveal the *form* of the questions which *should* have concerned theologians," but that (with the exception of Newman) for the most part "did not."[58] The "form" that Coulson had in mind is nowhere better expressed than in a passage from an unpublished notebook of Newman's on "faith and certainty"—a passage that Coulson set as epigraph for his study of *Religion and Imagination:* "We can only speak of Him . . . in the terms of our experience," therefore *"We can only set right one error of expression by another. By this method of antagonism we steady our minds,* not so as to reach their object, but to point them in the right direction . . . *by saying and unsaying, to a positive result."*[59]

What Newman was doing was recovering, for the nineteenth century, the recognition—central to the Christian imagination from the

56. Cedric Watts, *A Preface to Conrad,* 2nd ed. (London and New York: Longman, 1993), 137.

57. *HD,* 69. Marlow's final reference is to the lie to "the Intended": see above, note 55.

58. John Coulson, *Religion and Imagination: "In aid of a grammar of assent"* (Oxford: Clarendon Press, 1981), 4.

59. *The Theological Papers of John Henry Newman on Faith and Certainty,* partly prepared for publication by Hugo M. de Achaval; ed. J. Derek Holmes; intro. Charles Stephen Dessain (Oxford: Clarendon Press, 1976), 102. The passage is dated December 1, 1863; the italicized words in the quotation are those that Coulson took as epigraph: cf. Coulson, *Religion and Imagination,* ii.

fifth century to the fifteenth—that "a theological language subjected to the *twin* pressures of affirmation and negation" works in permanent tension between what Denys Turner calls "its wordiness and its astringency . . . its desire to speak and its knowledge of when to stop."[60]

A great deal, perhaps too much, has been written on the endlessly subversive patterns of paradox woven by Conrad on the theme of light and darkness, black and white, ivory and evil. Far less attention has been paid to the no less central theme of speech and silence: the silence of the African forest and the "wordiness" of Kurtz. I know no better route towards appreciation of the theological density and richness of *Heart of Darkness* than through reading Conrad's treatment of this theme in terms of Newman's "method of antagonism."

F. R. Leavis was notoriously scornful of Conrad's application of "the same adjectival insistence upon inexpressible and incomprehensible mystery" to "the evocation of human profundity and spiritual horrors." Had he been more attentive to the role played, in larger contexts of discourse and imagination, by negation and "unsaying," he might not have so pompously concluded that Conrad "is intent on making a virtue out of not knowing what he means."[61]

As Marlow sets off on the two-week trek towards the Central Station, there is "a great silence around and above." On arrival, he finds the white men wandering

> here and there with their absurd long staves in their hands like a lot of faithless pilgrims bewitched inside a rotten fence. The word "ivory" rang in the air, was whispered, was sighed. You would think they were praying to it. A taint of imbecile rapacity blew through it all like a whiff from some corpse. . . . And outside, the silent wilderness surrounding this cleared speck on the earth struck me as something great and invincible, like evil or truth.[62]

Cedric Watts has referred to "the 'demonisation' of the jungle in *Heart of Darkness*."[63] But this will not do: the "silent wilderness" is not demonic; it is *inscrutable*. "Evil" or "truth"? We cannot tell; it will not deliver up its sense: "the silence of the land went home to one's very

---

60. Denys Turner, *The Darkness of God: Negativity in Christian Mysticism* (Cambridge: Cambridge University Press, 1995), 22 (his emphasis), 21. For indications that Newman *knew* what he was doing, see, for example, Coulson, *Religion and Imagination*, 64.

61. F. R. Leavis, *The Great Tradition: George Eliot, Henry James, Joseph Conrad* (1948; repr., London: Penguin Books, 1972), 204, 207.

62. *HD*, 23, 26.

63. Watts, *Preface*, 63–64.

heart—its mystery, its greatness, the amazing reality of its concealed life."[64]

Marlow is at pains to emphasize that the "great silence" of the "impenetrable forest," the "stillness" that confronts the brickmaker and the Manager "with its ominous patience," "did not in the least resemble a peace. It was the stillness of an implacable force brooding over an inscrutable intention."[65] As I hinted earlier, the threat with which the silent wilderness is pregnant is the threat of *judgment*. Hence Marlow's heightening sense (of which, as an Englishman, he is somewhat ashamed: "You know the foolish notions that come to one sometimes") that, from this dark stillness, with its "air of hidden knowledge, of patient expectation, of unapproachable silence," will come speech.[66]

"You should have heard [Kurtz] say, 'My ivory.' Oh, yes, I heard him. 'My Intended, my ivory, my station, my river, my . . .' everything belonged to him. It made me hold my breath in expectation of hearing the wilderness burst into a prodigious peal of laughter that would shake the fixed stars in their places."[67] Contrast this passage (which occurs in the lengthy description of Kurtz's character that Marlow inserts into the narrative at the moment of the helmsman's death) with that which follows the Russian's account of Kurtz's influence upon him: "'We talked of everything,' he said quite transported at the recollection. . . . I looked around, and I don't know why, but I assure you that never, never before did this land, this river, this jungle, the very arch of this blazing sky appear to me so hopeless and so dark, so impenetrable to human thought, so pitiless to human weakness."[68]

Thus the tension that drives the story forward, the tension between "unsaying" and "saying," lies between the impenetrable, perhaps doom-laden "astringency" of the forest's silence and the "wordiness" of Kurtz's egotism.

As I mentioned earlier, when Marlow sets off from the Central Station, he still has only the haziest idea of who Kurtz is: "At the time . . . he was just a word for me" (and Marlow himself, as darkness now falls upon the Thames, becomes "no more . . . than a voice" to his audience aboard the *Nellie*).[69]

On the occasion of the helmsman's death, Marlow, whose unexplained but "dominant thought" is that Kurtz himself is also dead, makes "the

64. *HD*, 28.
65. *HD*, 35, 36.
66. *HD*, 35, 56.
67. *HD*, 49.
68. *HD*, 55.
69. *HD*, 29, 30.

strange discovery that I had never imagined him as doing, you know, but as discoursing. I didn't say to myself, 'Now I will never see him,' or 'Now I will never shake him by the hand,' but, 'Now I will never hear him.' The man presented himself as a voice."[70] And, although the impression that Kurtz is already dead proves mistaken—at least in the sense that Marlow finds him *physically* alive—yet, he adds a little later, "I was right, too. A voice. He was very little more than a voice."[71]

In the beginning was the word: "Going up that river was like travelling back to the earliest beginnings of the world. . . . An empty stream, a great silence."[72] But, at the heart of this still darkness, a voice resounds, a word is uttered. It was Kurtz's "eloquence" that gave him the power to elicit adoration from the Africans: "'Kurtz got the tribe to follow him, did he?' I suggested. [The Russian] fidgeted a little. 'They adored him,' he said."[73] After Kurtz's death, Marlow will read the draft report to the International Society for the Suppression of Savage Customs, in the opening paragraph of which Kurtz explained that "we whites, from the point of view of development we had arrived at, 'must necessarily appear to them [savages] in the nature of supernatural beings—we approach them with the might as of a deity.'" Marlow found Kurtz's "peroration . . . magnificent. . . . It gave me the notion of an exotic Immensity ruled by an august Benevolence. It made me tingle with enthusiasm. This was the unbounded power of eloquence—of words—of burning noble words." Then he came to the note "at the foot of the last page, scrawled evidently much later in an unsteady hand. . . . 'Exterminate all the brutes!'"[74]

Until almost the last moment of his life, the power of Kurtz's eloquence is undimmed. Borne towards the steamer on a stretcher, he is still "A voice! a voice! It was grave, profound, vibrating, while the man did not seem capable of a whisper. . . . No eloquence could have been so withering to one's belief in mankind as his final burst of sincerity." Even as the "brown current ran swiftly out of the heart of darkness bearing us down towards the sea . . . Kurtz discoursed. A voice! a voice! It rang deep to the very last."[75] When, at last, "the voice was gone,"

---

70. *HD*, 47, 48. As Ian Watt says: "Even at this stage Kurtz's power is a verbal one" (*Conrad in the Nineteenth Century*, 230).

71. *HD*, 48.

72. *HD*, 35. A comparison between this passage and the studied ambiguity of the passages in the "frame" of the story, considering the darkness of the Thames (cf. *HD*, 7–10, 76), leaves the reader uncertain as to whether this is a journey "back" because Africans are "primitive," or because Kurtz is "that man" (*HD*, 34), Adam, losing paradise.

73. *HD*, 56.

74. *HD*, 50, 51.

75. *HD*, 60, 65–66, 67.

Marlow reflects that, finding himself so close to death a little later, "I found with humiliation that probably I would have nothing to say. This is the reason why I affirm that Kurtz was a remarkable man. He had something to say. He said it."[76]

"Heaven and earth shall pass away, but my words will not pass away." Back in the "sepulchral city," Kurtz's "Intended" unintentionally nudges Marlow towards the lie with which his story ends: "It is impossible that all this should be lost. . . . Something must remain. His words at least have not died. 'His words will remain,' I said."[77]

Cries and Whispers

"He was very little more than a voice." But the voice of Kurtz, into whose making "all Europe contributed," is, as it were, the vortex of all the voices in the darkness of the world: "And I heard—him—it—this voice—other voices—all of them were so little more than voices—and the memory of that time itself lingers around me, impalpable, like a dying vibration of one immense jabber, silly, atrocious, sordid, savage, or simply mean without any kind of sense."[78]

This is, of course, remembering with hindsight. At the time, the voice was so *strong* that "the man did not seem capable of a whisper." And yet, it is exactly in that form that Kurtz's darkest utterance comes forth: "He cried in a whisper at some image, at some vision—he cried out twice, a cry that was no more than a breath: 'The horror! The horror!'" And this expiring whisper echoes "the whisper [that] had proved irresistibly fascinating," with which the silent wilderness had "whispered things about himself which he did not know."[79]

Moreover, just as Kurtz's voice was remembered as the center of the "dying vibration of one immense jabber," so the "low voice" of the Intended "seemed to have the accompaniment of all the other sounds full of mystery, desolation, and sorrow I had ever heard . . . the whisper of a voice speaking from beyond the threshold of an eternal darkness." And finally, at the moment of the lie, this dark "whisper . . . seemed to swell menacingly like the first whisper of a rising wind. 'The horror! The horror!'"[80]

---

76. *HD*, 69.
77. Matt. 24:35; *HD*, 70, 74, 75.
78. *HD*, 48, 50, 48–49.
79. *HD*, 60, 68, 57.
80. *HD*, 48, 74, 75.

"Some commentators," says Cedric Watts, find Kurtz's last words "affirmative, others find them nihilistic, others find them obscure."[81] It is, of course, possible to find them all of these, a view the plausibility of which is strengthened by the lengths to which Conrad goes to emphasize Marlow's own uncertainty as to how these last words are best read.[82]

One thing, at least, is clear, and that is the care with which Conrad presents Kurtz's death as an inversion of the death of Christ.[83] Here is Matthew's Gospel: "Now from the sixth hour there was darkness over all the land unto the ninth hour. And about the ninth hour Jesus cried with a loud voice, saying, 'Eli, Eli, lama sabachthani?' that is to say, 'My God, my God, why hast thou forsaken me?' . . . Jesus, when he had cried again with a loud voice, yielded up the ghost. And behold the veil of the temple was rent in twain, from the top to the bottom; and the earth did quake, and the rocks rent."[84]

Notice five features: darkness, the voice, the repeated cry—seemingly of despair—the rending of the veil and expiration of the spirit, surrender of the breath of God:[85]

> One evening coming in with a candle I was startled to hear him say a little tremulously, "I am lying here in the dark waiting for death." The light was within a foot of his eyes. I forced myself to murmur, "Oh, nonsense!" and stood over him as if transfixed. Anything approaching the change that came over his features I have never seen before and hope never to see again. . . . It was as though a veil had been rent. I saw on that ivory face

81. Watts, *Preface*, 136.

82. "Marlow suggests the following meanings for 'The horror! The horror!': (1) Kurtz condemns as horrible his corrupt actions, and this 'judgement upon the adventures of his soul' is 'an affirmation, a moral victory.' (2) Kurtz deems hateful but also *desirable* the temptations to which he had succumbed: the whisper has 'the strange commingling of desire and hate,' and therefore is not a moral victory after all, it seems. (3) Kurtz deems horrible the inner natures of all humans: 'no eloquence could have been so withering to one's belief in mankind as his final burst of sincerity,' when his stare 'penetrate[d] all the hearts that beat in the darkness.' (4) Kurtz deems horrible the whole universe: 'that wide and immense stare embracing, condemning, loathing all the universe. . . . 'The horror!'" (Watts, *Preface*, 136; cf. *HD*, 70, 69, 65–66, 72).

83. According to John Lester, "To regard Jim as archetypal Christ or Kurtz as diabolic Christ is, in many ways, to cease regarding them as individual characters" (*Conrad and Religion*, xxiii). But any theologian knows that Christology goes off the rails when it loses sight of the fact that "the Christ" is a particular Jewish individual. Indeed, the sustaining of the tension between these two acknowledgments could almost be said to be constitutive of competent Christology.

84. Matt. 27:45–46, 50–51 (AV).

85. Most of the critics miss some or all of these allusions. Dwight Purdy—whose suggestion that the passage also carries overtones of Gen. 15 I find ingenious but not persuasive—misses only the reference to the breathing of the spirit; see Purdy, *Conrad's Bible*, 47, 105.

the expression of sombre pride, of ruthless power, of craven terror—of an intense and hopeless despair. . . . He cried in a whisper at some image, at some vision, he cried out twice, a cry that was no more than a breath: "The horror! The horror!"[86]

The Place of Restraint

The centurion in Matthew's Gospel, who "feared greatly," says: "Truly this was the Son of God."[87] At the heart of Christianity is the recognition that the Crucifixion was a kind of victory—which is, in fact, what Marlow proclaims the death of Kurtz to be.[88] But victory for what? According to one critic: "The great moral center of *Heart of Darkness*" consists in Kurtz's ability, "without external religious sanctions of any sort," to judge himself condemned.[89] If this be victory, for Kurtz or humankind, what would defeat be like?

At the opposite extreme, there are critics who see Kurtz as "fellow-artist," with his creator, "of that nihilism that Conrad . . . found so attractive."[90] "Attractive" surely misdescribes the kind of drawing power exercised by the darkness with which the failure of the Promethean project may confront us. "Marlow," says Ian Watt, "is horrified, and so, just before his end, is Kurtz, to understand what happens to a man who discovers his existential freedom under circumstances which enable him to pervert the ultimate direction of nineteenth-century thought: not the disappearance but the replacement of God."[91]

In the end, however, "neither Conrad nor Marlow" finds darkness "irresistible."[92] And the source of their resistance lies in what Conrad calls "restraint." Against an individualist Romanticism that had established "the ideal of absolute liberation from religious, social, and ethical norms," Conrad—Polish aristocrat and English gentleman—grounded his ethic in "the Victorian trinity of work, duty, and restraint."[93]

---

86. *HD*, 68.

87. Matt. 27:54 (AV).

88. His dying cry is said to be "an affirmation, a moral victory paid for by innumerable defeats, by abominable terrors, by abominable satisfactions. But it was a victory" (*HD*, 70).

89. Juliet McLauchlan, "The 'Value' and 'Significance' of *Heart of Darkness*," *Conradiana* 15 (1983): 3–21; cited from *Norton*, 383, 382.

90. Brantlinger, *"Heart of Darkness,"* 295. A little earlier, he says: "For Conrad, Kurtz's heroism consists in staring into an abyss of nihilism so total that the issues of imperialism and racism pale into insignificance," 293.

91. Watt, *Conrad in the Nineteenth Century*, 166.

92. Ibid., 253.

93. Ibid., 228, 167.

On the journey up river, Marlow, knowing how much easier it is "to face bereavement, dishonour, and the perdition of one's soul—than this kind of prolonged hunger," is amazed at the restraint displayed by the starving African crew, outnumbering the whites by thirty to five: "Restraint! I would just as soon have expected restraint from a hyena prowling amongst the corpses of a battlefield. But there was the fact facing me . . . like a ripple on an unfathomable enigma."[94]

In contrast, it is lack of restraint that brings about the helmsman's death: "Poor fool! If he had only left that shutter alone. He had no restraint, no restraint—just like Kurtz." In circumstances lacking the external restraints of what we think of as "civilization," the wilderness "found [Kurtz] out early." Lack of restraint "in the gratification of his various lusts" caused his downfall.[95] Lacking restraint, he made himself the worshipped center of the world and, in so doing, disclosed the subhuman animality of post-Darwinian nightmare.[96]

Human beings, in order to be human, must refuse to be divine, to be objects of other people's worship (or their own!). If Conrad was not alone in seeing this, he was unusual in clear-sighted recognition of the idolatrous character of Leopold II's African adventure.

But, if we may not be worshipped, may we worship? Or is all worship, at its heart, idolatrous? Partly for temperamental reasons, and partly because of the narrow range of options available to him in the 1890s, so far as the "grammar" of the concept of God is concerned,[97] Conrad was undoubtedly drawn towards the latter view.

"He had the faith—don't you see—he had the faith," says the journalist to whom, back in the "sepulchral city," Marlow hands over Kurtz's report: "He could get himself to believe anything—anything. He would have been a splendid leader of an extreme party."[98]

Conrad rejected as "distasteful" the Catholic Christianity in which he was brought up, partly because he found ritual uncongenial and "the absurd oriental fable from which it starts irritates me," and partly on account of what Cedric Watts called "an Augustan distaste for fanaticism."[99]

94. *HD*, 43.

95. *HD*, 51, 57.

96. See E. N. Dorall, "Conrad and Coppola: Different Centres of Darkness," *Southeast Asian Review of English* 1 (1980): 19–26, in *Norton*, 305; cf. Watt, *Conrad in the Nineteenth Century*, 227.

97. For a brief view of these options, see my review of *Nineteenth Century Religious Thought in the West*, mentioned above in note 9.

98. *HD*, 71.

99. Joseph Conrad, *Letters from Conrad, 1895 to 1924*, ed. Edward Garnett (London: Nonesuch Press, 1928), 265; cited from Watts, *Preface*, 48.

And yet, the power of *Heart of Darkness* arises, in part, from the unspoken recognition that Conrad has so little to put in place of the idolatry that he deplored. Only the cannibals display the "restraint" that, for Conrad as for his contemporaries, epitomized the virtues of the English gentleman,[100] and the "efficiency" that he supposed the saving grace of *British* imperialism makes only marginal appearance.[101] Moreover, the passage in which Marlow insists that it is efficiency that "redeems" and "saves *us*" describes even this ideal as idolatry: "something you can set up, and bow down before, and offer a sacrifice to."[102]

Human beings, in order to be human, must refuse to be divine. Yet all the forms of this refusal seem threatened by their subversion as idolatry. "'We have lost the first of the ebb,' said the Director suddenly." *All* rivers seem "to lead into the heart of an immense darkness."[103] Nowhere, perhaps, did Conrad more prophetically articulate the crisis of Western culture as the nineteenth century ended than in his inability to consider the possibility that, in the twofold struggle against self-divinization and idolatry, human beings might, through disciplined acceptance of contingency, once again learn what it is to be a *creature* and, in that discovery, find forms of worship that are not idolatrous. The tasks of theology, as I understand them, are set at the service of such education.

"The burden of my argument in this last lecture, and the overarching ambition of all my lectures, is to show that Christian practice and theology are neither self-referential nor self-justifying."[104] The nightmare of modernity was the fear that, unless "we" ordered things, they would fall apart, be meaningless. The terror of postmodernism lies in the recognition that the quest for meaning is a waste of time. The duty of the reasonable remnant is to insist, against both hubris and despair, that "we" do not have either the first word or the last, and that in this discovery may be found our given peace.

---

100. "Restraint" was "the key defining quality of that increasingly vague figure—the English gentleman" (Professor Tony Tanner, personal communication). It is impossible not to be reminded of Newman's brilliantly ironic portrayal, sketched nearly half a century earlier, of "the ethical character, which the cultivated intellect will form, apart from religious principle"; see John Henry Newman, *The Idea of a University*, ed. and intro. I. T. Ker (Oxford: Clarendon Press, 1976), 180–81.

101. "What saves us is efficiency" (*HD*, 10). It is Marlow, the only Englishman in his story, who knows that rivets are what was "really wanted" to get the steamer under way again, and who is exasperated by the *in*efficiency of the failure to provide them (see *HD*, 30).

102. *HD*, 10.

103. *HD*, 76.

104. Stanley Hauerwas, *With the Grain of the Universe: The Church's Witness and Natural Theology* (Grand Rapids, Mich.: Brazos Press, 2001; London: SCM Press, 2002), 207.

Epilogue: In Search of Bones

"The Accountant had brought out already a box of dominoes and was toying architecturally with the bones."[105] It is, of course, in search of venerated bones that pilgrims journey. Nor should we forget that "bones and ivory were for centuries mistakenly believed to be the same substance."[106] "The word 'ivory' rang in the air. . . . You would think" that they, who wandered "like a lot of faithless pilgrims," were "praying to it."[107]

"Ivory! I should think so. Heaps of it, stacks of it. The old mud shanty was bursting with it," bursting with what Kurtz called "My ivory." In the same passage, Marlow describes the emergence of Kurtz, when at last they reach the Inner Station, as the disinterment of a corpse: "You should have heard the disinterred body of Mr. Kurtz saying, 'My Intended' . . . and the lofty frontal bone of Mr. Kurtz! . . . The wilderness had patted him on the head, and behold, it was like a ball—an ivory ball."[108] It is as a venerated relic, then, that Kurtz appears. The dying Kurtz, borne towards the steamer, resembles "an animated image of death carved out of old ivory." And, as Kurtz dies, Marlow sees "on that ivory face . . . intense and hopeless despair."[109]

Thomas à Becket, Mr. Kurtz, the elephants of Africa: variations woven, with Conrad's mastery of irony, on the theme of pilgrimage in quest of ivory, of dead white bones, the venerated skeletons of forms of faith. The final twist to Conrad's story, beyond authorial control, has his bones, like Becket's, laid to rest in Canterbury,[110] thereby opening up fresh dangerous possibilities of pilgrimage.

---

105. *HD*, 7.
106. Adams, *Heart of Darkness*, 8.
107. *HD*, 26; on "ivory," see 29, 33, 36, 44, 55.
108. *HD*, 49.
109. *HD*, 59, 68.
110. After a Requiem celebrated (as, some decades later, would be those of my father- and mother-in-law) in the Catholic church of St. Thomas of Canterbury. See Watts, *Preface*, 38.

14

Learning Made Strange

Can a University Be Christian?

Harry Huebner

There are many reasons for the inability of Christians to articulate what makes them Christian, but surely one of the most important reasons is the failure to maintain universities that are recognizably Christian.

—Stanley Hauerwas[1]

[That Jesus is Lord] is what we celebrate, as we participate in his priestly role and his kingly rule by watching our words.

—John Howard Yoder[2]

1. Stanley Hauerwas, *With the Grain of the Universe: The Church's Witness and Natural Theology* (Grand Rapids, Mich.: Brazos Press, 2001), 231–32.
2. John Howard Yoder, "To Serve Our God and to Rule Our World," in *The Royal Priesthood: Essays Ecclesiological and Ecumenical,* ed. Michael G. Cartwright (Grand Rapids, Mich.: Eerdmans, 1994), 140.

Introduction

The allusion in the title to John Milbank's book *The Word Made Strange* and his essay "Can Morality Be Christian?" can hardly go unnoticed.[3] Like Milbank in his answer to the morality question, I hold suspect easy positive answers to the pedagogy question. I end, of course, with an emphatic "Yes, universities can be Christian," yet not before questioning, in ways not unlike Milbank, the Christian enterprise itself. The claim of this essay recognizes that how the matter of Christian education is put—not only with respect to nouns and verbs but, more importantly, in regard to grammar itself—already decides much and therefore is in danger of precluding truthful outcomes. In other words, the qualifier "Christian" in the phrase "Christian university" does serve a function.

There are, characteristically, two dominant ways of presenting the matter. One way tends to make the chasm between "Christian" and "university" unbridgeable in principle. In this view the notion of a *Christian university* is an oxymoron. Universities think freely; Christians do not. The other approach puts forward all too easy "integrative" solutions. Integration language usually assumes two things: first, that knowledge and faith are largely independent entities that can be "brought together," and second, that all truth is one and whether you get there via the Christian faith or the standard disciplines of study is relatively unimportant, the point being that reason will get you there no matter which route you take. This essay wishes to avoid framing the issue in ways that oblige one to choose between these two options. But how else to begin?

Consider current practices. There are many examples, especially in North America, of thriving Christian universities. They are doing it! There is a newfound freedom, perhaps derived from a postmodern respect for particularity, that makes the notion of a university with a qualifier less repugnant than it used to be. Despite the damning prophecies of inevitable secularization[4]—perhaps themselves rooted in a modernist fear that particularity cannot survive—there is a rebirth of interest in how universities can be Christian. It is a hopeful sign that there are well-trained Christian scholars in several universities engaging precisely the question before us.[5]

---

3. See John Milbank, *The Word Made Strange: Theology, Language, Culture* (Oxford: Blackwell, 1997).

4. See, for example, James Tunstead Burtchaell, *The Dying of the Light: The Disengagement of Colleges and Universities from Their Christian Churches* (Grand Rapids, Mich.: Eerdmans, 1998).

5. An interesting example of such engagement is that undertaken by Messiah College faculty. See *Scholarship and Christian Faith: Enlarging the Conversation,* ed. Douglas Jacobsen and Rhonda Hustedt Jacobsen (New York: Oxford University Press, 2004).

And these scholars come from a variety of disciplines drawn from the entire university.

Yet all too often Christian pedagogy is shallow and misguided. For example, it is common to suggest a "Christian-values" overlay on an otherwise standard university curriculum. This approach abstracts the faith to an attitude or a disposition and leaves it void of content to be filled by any scholar who claims the Christian appellation. Such efforts do little to help students articulate what makes them Christian.

What is needed is a fresh look at the possibility of rooting the university curriculum in the content of the Christian story, not in its separation from psychology, philosophy, sociology, physics, and chemistry as something to be integrated with, but inclusively, asking what thinking Christians see as worthy agenda in the challenge to be faithful in a complex world. That is, what should Christians be saying about such notions as self, community, other, technology, body, suffering, nature, management, sin, violence, lying, change, money, land, gift, love, and kindness? This approach is different from the way it is commonly put in two respects: first, it is holistic in the way it begins. It assumes that Christian life touches all aspects of human existence. Hence every part of the university curriculum, including even the institutional structures, should express Christian convictions. Second, it begins the analysis from the standpoint of what the Christian story is instead of with what we already "know" education to be.

Instead of beginning with the terrain of contemporary pedagogy, epistemology, and reason, derived as it normally is from an analysis of how the mind works in general, and then asking how the Christian faith can meld into that fabric (thereby relegating Christian faith to subservience), we will ask what difference the content of the Christian story makes in the formation of our youth. What difference does it make with respect to how we speak about our entire life? In other words, unless learning itself is first of all made strange by gospel speech, which is something quite different from the speech of dominant culture, the likelihood of education taking place under the Lordship of Christ is not high.

Making Strange Speech: List 1

The first list of strange-sounding Christian speech is presented without comment and analysis. In a culture that is shaped by the operating assumptions that human activity drives history forward and that God, if there be God, is largely irrelevant, the very notion that God is at work in this world sounds at worst terrifying—a violation of our freedom—and at best superstitious. Its odd ring should therefore not be surprising. The second list will come after my characterization of what lies at the bottom of much of what passes for today's imagination out of which we teach, namely, a vacillating dis-ease with the metaphor of history. It is perhaps only after my reflections on this dis-ease that the strangeness of Christian learning will become truly evident.

1. Christians believe, *against the evidence,* that Creator God is actively bringing the darkness of this world to its ultimate demise, or to put it positively, to its brightest light. Empirical evidence fails to support at least progressive movement in this direction. So why would anyone believe such a thing? On what grounds can it be taught? Christians believe it on the basis of the stories that form the sacred texts of their faith, through which they learn to see the world differently to the extent that they might well see God at work even in the analyses of those who assume there is no God. Christians are the kind of people who see the world through stories of past lives that they then claim as their own. They have authoritative texts. They do not start from scratch, for they believe there is no scratch to start from. Some people may believe that the notion of authoritative texts itself sets Christians apart from others, but it is hard to think of a single intellectual tradition that does not do so as well. Even those who profess an antitradition stance will rely on a body of literature to support their claims.

2. The Christian imagination does not find it illogical that *change of heart* and *change of mind* are often in reverse continuity from what is ordinarily assumed. Christian conviction affirms that how we live often determines how we think (in this we agree with Karl Marx) but also that how we think undergirds how we live. Hence, as the Christian text puts it, "presenting our bodies as living sacrifices" and being "transformed by the renewing of our minds" are utterable in congruous sequence (Rom. 12:1–2). Since the ultimate goal of Christian education is to make disciples, it teaches with the aim of forming people whose hearts are so filled with the passion of life-giving God that they cannot help but subvert the very culture of death that their intellectually trained minds heretofore were able to rationalize. In other words, their culture-shaped goals have been transformed. But whether this (re-)learning happens with a practicum in the inner city, or in a classroom in sociology, political studies, or peace theology is determined by the contingency of the student's makeup and is not narrowly prescribed by pedagogical or epistemological theory. Theory is not that important to Christian education; what is important is to ensure that the story gets told right. We can, for example, know ourselves and our world as created, redeemed, and transformed only if we tell the story of faith properly. No theory can assure us of that.

3. Christians know that often what convinces is not simply *logical demonstration*, as if pedagogy *is* epistemology, but rather consistent and credible *witness*. This does not mean that epistemology is irrelevant to pedagogy; pedagogy just cannot be reduced to epistemology. That is why a martyr, who is perhaps unable to express the logical foundations—if there be any—of her resolute convictions, is often more convincing in her death than an articulate philosopher in a classroom. Yet "witness" should not be seen as opposed to philosophy or to argument. "Witness" rather precedes epistemology, or as Hauerwas says, "'Witness' names the condition necessary to begin argument."[6] To put the matter this way is significant, for while witness is a form of argument, to name it thus is to draw attention to and to counter the tendency to use coercive arguments to make convictions credible. Witness is not without its persuasive powers, yet the positions it advances are susceptible to refutation or confirmation with other arguments. Christians should be as persuasive as possible in their witness, but never without the awareness that it is the work of the Spirit that truly teaches. And even in "losing the argument" the Spirit may do a lot of teaching since it matters how the argument is lost. Human beings are so much more than mere minds. As bodies with passion and spirit, we participate in a power beyond ourselves; we find convincing those imaginations that represent to us a passion and zest for human existence, a truth that may initially or even ultimately transcend explanation.

4. Christians believe in the bodily *resurrection* of Jesus, and indeed in their own *resurrection*, not because our Western materialistic assumptions can make such beliefs compelling, for they cannot, but because of witnesses and because we refuse to give commonly held materialistic assumptions the pedagogical supremacy they normally enjoy. The import of this belief is not only the assent afforded a mere strange idea, but its coloring of the entire Christian imagination. It entails the notion that God is an active agent in this material world, meaning that how we get from here to there morally, politically, and even epistemologically is through the givenness of God's gracious and sometime wrathful presence, and not only through the implementation of strategies derived from universal sense-making logic, most often gleaned from available models of the social sciences and humanities. This belief therefore affords the opportunity for some profoundly strange-making questions. It likewise destabilizes today's obsession to manage outcome. Both of these things are disquieting prospects for teachers.

5. Christian teachers believe in the *importance of texts*—biblical, literary, historical, philosophical, political, scientific—but they know that

6. Hauerwas, *With the Grain of the Universe*, 204.

when they "teach the faith" they teach more than the content of texts, even biblical texts. They are engaged in more than the demonstration of the accuracy (or inaccuracy) of the written account. They are involved in a process of wanting students (and themselves) to "own" truthful convictions about life and God. Jim McClendon speaks for Christian teachers when he says that he wants his students to be just like him, each in his or her own way.[7] Christian teachers are much more than neutral presenters of facts, interpretations, and stories, for they participate in the very stories they are attempting to make credible. Their argument is witness, for they teach as disciples. Interestingly, in this respect, Christian teachers are probably not that different from other teachers. They are perhaps only more conscious of their commitments and hence more aware of their pedagogy.

For Christian learning to happen, not only explanation but complexification and subversion must take place. All need to be lodged in the Christian story, and we should note that unlearning often precedes insight. Yet this essay does not wish to propose a new theory or system of learning. It merely intends to expose the tension between the dominant pedagogical imaginations and gospel speech. It seeks to show, that is, bear witness to, how learning to see the world and our own lives on the basis of the Christian narrative is a strange-making enterprise.

Two Historicisms

The imagination that underwrites much current pedagogical practice could be called historicism. Unfortunately this term does not name anything very precisely. It is perhaps ironic that whereas the nineteenth-century scholar Ernst Troeltsch made historicism fashionable by deriding the tradition-based authority of European dogmatism, three-quarters of a century later the philosopher Alasdair MacIntyre characterizes his own "historicism" as a tradition-based rationality intended as an alternative to Enlightenment universality on the one hand and Nietzschean perspectivism on the other. Perhaps this shift only serves to demonstrate that historicism is like a mysterious disease, not easily located and even harder to overcome. In any case, we do well to attend to this shift. It is one way to locate the debate regarding the notion of a Christian university, since the two historicisms produce profoundly differing accounts of the university. MacIntyre understood the impact of this shift on the

7. This quote is attributed to McClendon by Michael Goldberg in his essay in *Theology without Foundations: Religious Practice and the Future of Theological Truth*, ed. Stanley Hauerwas, Nancey Murphy, and Mark Nation (Nashville: Abingdon, 1994), 289.

nature of the university and saw fit to reconceive the university from his perspective in his Gifford Lectures.[8] Troeltsch does not oblige us similarly. It is important to recognize, however, that Troeltsch champions a particular way of thinking that begins and ends with history and that has for almost a century been a powerful influence in shaping how we understand ourselves and our pedagogical practices. This section begins with Troeltsch and then presents MacIntyre's counterhistoricism, showing how it requires a reconception of the university. The next section examines how another scholar, John Howard Yoder, moves beyond both Troeltsch and MacIntyre.

Troeltsch has been called a historian, sociologist, philosopher, and theologian, a consummate interdisciplinary scholar! His primary adversary was dogmatism, which he also, with some variation of meaning, referred to as "supernaturalism" and "orthodoxy." In this respect he remains thoroughly Kantian. *Sapere aude* was as much a clarion call for Troeltsch as it was for Kant,[9] albeit Troeltsch historicized reason. Although on occasion Troeltsch combines both the dogmatic and the "evolutionary school of thought" as targets of his criticism—by charging, for example, that both place "Christianity, as a matter of principle, in a unique position"[10]—nevertheless, the evolutionary approach, according to Troeltsch, requires adjustment, whereas the dogmatic approach must be rejected. In his 1898 article "Uber historische und dogmatische Methode in der Theologie," he presents the difference between the two methods as one of principle and hence as irreconcilable.[11] The historical method begins, he contends, with the relativity of historical scholarship; the dogmatic approach begins beyond history with revelation, something given to and not itself the product of the human mind, nor subject to critique by historical reason.

Troeltsch's commitment to neo-Kantianism forbids association with dogmatism. The conclusions of the historical method are always relative, tentative, and particular, whereas the conclusions of the dogmatic method are presented as absolute, certain, and general. The historical

8. See "Reconceiving the University as an Institution and the Lecture as a Genre," in *Three Rival Versions of Moral Enquiry: Encyclopaedia, Genealogy, and Tradition* (Notre Dame, Ind.: University of Notre Dame Press, 1990), 216–36.

9. See Immanuel Kant, "Was Ist Aufklaerung?" in Michel Foucault, *The Politics of Truth* (New York: Semiotext, 1997), 7–20.

10. Ernst Troeltsch, *The Absoluteness of Christianity and the History of Religions*, trans. David Reid (Richmond: John Knox, 1971), 51.

11. Ernst Troeltsch, "Historical and Dogmatic Method in Theology," in *Religion in History*, trans. James Luther Adams and Walter Bense (Minneapolis: Fortress Press, 1991), 11–32. Troeltsch says, for example, "My concern . . . is not to detail the particular problems of each [method], but only . . . to insist on their incompatibility" (25).

method views history as a realm of the creative interplay between God and humanity, a realm produced and narrated by resourceful historical reason; the dogmatic method begins with what is given from outside the mind, namely, divine revelation in Christ. In the former method, human imagination produces knowledge; in the latter, Christ produces the imagination. The dogmatic approach sees humans as sinful all the way down (even to the depths of their imagination), and hence the products of the mind are unreliable. The historical approach claims even such a rendition of humanity as the product of human thinking. The historical method anticipates ever new and better ways of understanding; the dogmatic method is skeptical of progressivism and is more interested in dogma based on revelation intended to help humans see God within the givenness of the revelation of Jesus Christ.

Troeltsch sees historicism as a theory of truth, knowledge, and value. It is a new (twentieth-century) way of thinking about the world of being and value, and consequently it demands a new way of teaching, so that reality as a whole can be understood differently. Historicism is "in principle a new mode of thought that gained its orientation from history itself."[12] Troeltsch knows very well that the consequences of embracing historicism are immense:

> It relativizes everything, not in the sense that it eliminates every standard of judgement and necessarily ends in a nihilistic skepticism, but rather in the sense that every historical structure and moment can be understood only in relation to others and ultimately to the total context, and that standards of values cannot be derived from isolated events but only from an overview of the historical totality. This relativism and respect for the historical totality belong together, as indeed they are always cojoined in the practical application of the method.[13]

For Troeltsch everything becomes history: Christianity becomes history; the social sciences and humanities become history; education becomes history; truth becomes history. The primary consideration of understanding and learning is one of historical origin and development, or genealogy, as Nietzsche would say. There is no justification apart from explanation.

Troeltsch really has no way of measuring or evaluating what Christianity should be. All he can do is appeal to historical reason itself, namely, to what serious-thinking Christians make of Christianity by integrating their faith with the givens of culture. On this basis he is

12. Troeltsch, *Absoluteness*, 46.
13. Troeltsch, "Historical and Dogmatic Method," 18.

able to show only that Christianity has become something other than it was. His version of historicism does not permit him to do more. In fact, for Troeltsch, discourse ceased to be theological. This is perhaps why he was compelled to leave his chair in theology at Heidelberg for one in philosophy at Berlin. This "uncomfortable contentment" with truth working its way out in history caused him to place enormous faith in the human spirit, or perhaps he would say, the Holy Spirit.

If there was one concern that motivated Troeltsch it was to make the Christian faith credible so that its "cultured despisers"—to use a phrase from Schleiermacher, whose project he admired—would need to sit up and take note. For Troeltsch, Christianity was a sociology and not an ideology; as such, its social expression is what should interest educators and scholars. The Christian faith is best understood by observing the kind of people it produces, or if you like, it is best understood by its social teachings, which, in every age, get reshaped by the new cultural agenda. The Christian faith is contingent, and its credibility belongs within the larger debate of history, not merely with metaphysically minded theologians and philosophers, and certainly not with the dogmatists.

Troeltsch was compelled to start in the middle of historical relativity primarily because there was no reliable norm in history to start from. The message of Jesus did not provide a reliable reference for the *social teachings* of the churches. For Troeltsch it was

> clear that the message of Jesus is not a programme of social reform. It is rather the summons to prepare for the coming of the Kingdom of God; this preparation, however, is to take place quietly within the framework of the present world-order, in a purely religious fellowship of love, with an earnest endeavour to conquer self and to cultivate the Christian virtues. Even the Kingdom of God itself is not (for its part at least) the new social order founded by God. It creates a new order upon earth, but it is an order which is not concerned with the state, with society, or with the family at all. How this will work out in detail is God's affair; man's duty is simply to prepare for it. . . . The centre of His message was the glory of God's final victory, and the conquest of demons.[14]

For Troeltsch the fundamental idea of the gospel "was solely that of the salvation of souls,"[15] and that is why there could be no *sociological* or *ethical* grounding for the church in the gospel. When reading Troeltsch it sometimes seems that he would want Jesus to be socially and politically normative, but this is not so as a matter of historical fact. So in order for

14. Ernst Troeltsch, *The Social Teaching of the Christian Churches,* trans. Olive Wyon (Chicago: University of Chicago Press, 1976), 61.
15. Ibid., 63.

the church to be socially involved at all, the content of such involvement must be conceived outside of the gospel. Such involvement therefore necessarily entails a form of social accommodation and assimilation—he calls it compromise—to cultural practices and structures. The forms of the church that refuse cultural accommodations (which Troeltsch called sects) and that "take the Sermon on the Mount as their ideal" and "lay stress on the simple but radical opposition of the Kingdom of God to all secular interests and institutions" are therefore by definition immaterial to the social expression of the gospel.[16] Such groups have correctly appropriated the gospel and have by their withdrawal from society shown its apolitical nature.

When Troeltsch examines the socially embodied church in history, he sees it as it ought to be, fully integrated into the cultural and political mainstream. Hence Troeltsch is able to say: "The church only reached her full development . . . when, in the days of Constantine, she became a State Church. Only then was it possible for her to realize her universal and absolute unity and supremacy, which, during the time of the Holy Roman Empire, then enabled her to subdue the State itself."[17] Although Troeltsch does not commit himself on whether the church in history has exercised its integrating task responsibly—in some ways I suspect he would say that it has not—it did nevertheless find its proper place, namely, not outside the political and cultural mainstream, but fully within it. And what is the church to do there? Exercise influence and control. But alas, because the gospel itself contains "no programme of social reform," it can give no guidance on such influence and control. Ironically, then, it is the domestication of the church—its integration with culture—that becomes the sign of faithfulness for Troeltsch, while the otherness of the church is not only its irrelevance but also its apostasy.

We can now summarize what Troeltsch's analysis suggests about Christian pedagogy. It seems, given his approach, that the serious student is one who is thoroughly schooled in the cultural and political dynamics of history, bringing to bear the principles of historical reason, which Troeltsch identifies as criticism, analogy, and correlation, all of which

16. Ibid., 332.

17. Ibid., 463.

18. In "Historical and Dogmatic Method," Troeltsch suggests these three principles, which are to do the job of keeping his historicism from degenerating into a vicious relativism. He says: "The historical method itself, by its use of criticism, analogy and correlation, produces with irresistible necessity a web of mutually interacting activities of the human spirit, which are never independent and absolute but always interrelated, and therefore understandable only within the context of the most comprehensive whole" (15). How do these principles function? First, the *principle of historical criticism* "indicates that in

are completely formal principles.[18] Hence Christian pedagogy is the blending of the horizons of culture and personal (somewhat content-less) faith, a dichotomy later picked up by H. Richard Niebuhr. But there can be no criteria for the guidance of this blending other than historical reason itself.

This view of historicism contrasts sharply with Alasdair MacIntyre's precisely at the point of a universal, historical reason. MacIntyre rejects the notion of rationality as such. Whereas Troeltsch's historicism abstracts reason from particular traditions, MacIntyre's proposes that we can only engage in rational inquiry from within particular traditions. In other words, MacIntyre rejects the modern antithesis between tradition and rationality. He is no less committed to historicism than Troeltsch, but to a historicism not bound to a *universal,* historical reason. This means that the skills of rational inquiry are not derived from rationality as such but from a particular tradition, or more precisely, from those persons within a particular tradition who have mastered the linguistic, intellectual, and moral habits of that tradition. Notice that for MacIntyre it is not reason that determines which tradition or religion to embrace, since reason and tradition are in principle inseparable.

---

the realm of history there are only judgments of probability, varying from the highest to the lowest degree, and that consequently an estimate must be made of the degree of probability attaching to any tradition" (13). What Troeltsch is suggesting is that we must apply a critical attitude to all our historical judgments and to all our already-accumulated historical data. This means that through the process of historical criticism, historical conclusions are always in the process of analysis, correction, and transformation, in such a way that at no particular time is it possible to formulate an absolute conclusion; that is, one will always need to review previous conclusions in light of current knowledge and new experiences. A further implication is that no historical encounter is a priori excluded as a relevant base for the evaluation of historical judgments. Historical criticism "signifies above all the definitive inclusion of the religious tradition with all traditions that require preliminary critical treatment" (13). Second, the *principle of analogy* makes the notion of knowledge possible: "The illusions, distortions, deceptions, myths, and partisanships we see with our own eyes enable us to recognize similar features in the materials of tradition" (13). It is because of the recognized similarity between present and past events that it is possible for us to impute probability to historical events in the first place. It is by reference to the knowable in the one, that we can disclose the as yet unknown in the other. "The analogical method always presupposes a common core of similarity that makes the differences comprehensible and empathy possible" (14). Third, *the principle of correlation:* The principle of analogy shows that in order to have historical knowledge we must assume that there is a basic consistency to the human spirit and to its historical manifestation, which means that there is constant interaction of all phenomena within history. This assumption implies further "that there can be no change at one point without some preceding or consequent change elsewhere, so that all historical happening is knit together in a permanent relationship of correlation" (14). All historical events must be seen as relating to all other historical events. And a reinterpretation of one event has implications for all other events.

For MacIntyre rational inquiry is akin to a craft, by which he means that there are skills to be acquired and developed in order to attain the perfection inherent in the telos of a particular practice. Hence, to learn to become "good at it" one must become a particular kind of person who has acquired the intellectual and moral skills necessary to embody the goals of a rational tradition. Responding to the apparent Platonic paradox of how we are to learn at all if learning from the beginning requires certain skills, MacIntyre says:

> We also need a teacher . . . and we shall have to learn from that teacher and initially accept on the basis of his or her authority within the community of a craft precisely what intellectual and moral habits it is which we must cultivate and acquire if we are to become effective self-moved participants in such enquiry. Hence there emerges a conception of rational teaching authority internal to the practice of the craft of moral enquiry, as indeed such conceptions emerge in such other crafts as furniture making and fishing, where, just as in moral enquiry, they partially define the relationship of master-craftsman to apprentice.[19]

The student is therefore an apprentice learning the practices that embody the "best-so-far" standards of a particular tradition. The student begins by accepting on authority the nature of particular intellectual and moral habits, but the student eventually owns what was taught and then learns the skills of being self-critical. As MacIntyre recognizes, this understanding of rational inquiry as craft requires a reconception of the modern university itself. Contemporary universities do not teach this way. They assume, like Troeltsch, that reason stands outside of all tradition as the adjudicator among competing traditions. Learning to think generally is the primary goal for a Troeltsch-like university, whereas for MacIntyre this goal is the illusion of modernity. Learning the intellectual and moral skills of a particular rational tradition is, for MacIntyre, the more truthful option.

In his essay "Reconceiving the University as an Institution and the Lecture as a Genre,"[20] MacIntyre distinguishes three kinds of universities—the preliberal, the liberal, and "a twentieth-century version of the thirteenth-century university":

> The preliberal modern university was a university of enforced and constrained agreements. The liberal university aspired to be a university of unconstrained agreements and hence its abolition of religious and moral tests and exclusions, and hence also, so I have argued, its present endan-

19. MacIntyre, *Three Rival Versions*, 63.
20. Ibid., 216–36.

gered state. . . . What then is possible? The answer is: the university as a place of constrained disagreement, of imposed participation in conflict, in which a central responsibility of higher education would be to initiate students into conflict.[21]

Notice first of all that MacIntyre speaks about epistemic conflicts: in other words, profound and fundamental disagreements, for example, the disagreements between the liberals, the genealogists, and the tradition-based advocates that are the focus of MacIntyre's Gifford Lectures—or, generally the differences among rival traditions. These conflicts are in principle not resolvable in a liberal university because the arguments establishing the credibility of competing traditions are not admissible. More important, however, students are not initiated into such conflicts because the conflicts themselves are camouflaged, since by nature they are only apparent and in principle resolvable through universal reason. In MacIntyre's reconceived university the process of learning and teaching take on a different form:

> In such a university those engaged in teaching and enquiry would each have to play a double role. For, on the one hand, each of us would be participating in conflict as a protagonist of a particular point of view, engaged thereby in two distinct but related tasks. The first of these would be to advance enquiry from within that particular point of view . . . and so articulating through moral and theological enquiry a framework within which the parts of the curriculum might once again become parts of a whole. The second task would be to enter into controversy with other rival standpoints doing so *both* in order to exhibit what is mistaken in that rival standpoint in the light of the understanding afforded by one's own point of view *and* in order to test and retest the central theses advanced from one's point of view against the strongest possible objections to them to be derived from one's opponents.[22]

In other words, how students are initiated into both inquiry *and* controversy is fundamental to the educational task within MacIntyre's reconceived university. It is odd to have to emphasize this point since it seems self-evident; yet training how to conduct oneself in controversy is not the kind of training that is available at most typical universities. Even conflict resolution studies programs rarely recognize pedagogical or epistemological conflicts as part of the purview of their analysis.

21. Ibid., 230–32.
22. Ibid., 231.

There is a distinct difference between a Troeltsch-type university and the one envisioned by MacIntyre. For Troeltsch, differences must in principle be resolvable by a single, universal, historical reason, and hence whatever does not fit, like religion and moral training, must be rejected. MacIntyre's university of "constrained disagreements" acknowledges rival rationalities and, thereby, the real conflicts between competing, and indeed incompatible, interpretations of the world. In such a university competing rationalities are not only acknowledged but studied, and communication and debate between rival traditions are a primary goal. Education as "constrained disagreement" may take place within a single university, or it may lead to the establishment of rival universities. In this manner, the university teaches its students, and indeed the wider society, two things: first, that there are different ways of reading and seeing the world and not all of them are equally good at giving account of phenomena; and second, that the task of the university is to set the tone for debate and for the possibility of understanding and disagreement between competing views of the world. The task of MacIntyre's university is to create the kind of people who become fluent in both their own rationality and that of others, and who know how to conduct the discussion so that there can be real engagement and mutual learning.

MacIntyre's reconceived university sets the stage for the possibility of a Christian university, and MacIntyre goes a long way in developing the idea of this possibility. For Troeltsch, such a university would at best be misguided, because he would most likely see it as grounded in a dogmatism he wished to reject; or he might, at worst, see it as irrelevant and a product of sectarian idealism. On the other hand, there are those, like John Howard Yoder, who would question whether MacIntyre's alternative goes far enough. Although Yoder would affirm MacIntyre's critique of Troeltsch's universal historicism, he would consider it more significant to point to what MacIntyre and Troeltsch share: an impoverished ecclesiology, eschatology, and Christology, resulting from an inadequate critique of Constantinianism and an insufficient embrace of the normativity of Jesus.[23] These deficiencies are explicit for Troeltsch, whereas they remain largely implicit for MacIntyre. To spell out the implications of these shortcomings, I now turn to Yoder, the third mutant historicist.

---

23. See Chris K. Huebner, "Unhandling History: Anti-Theory, Ethics, and the Practice of Witness" (PhD diss., Duke University, 2001), for a helpful engagement of MacIntyre and Yoder on Constantinianism and ecclesiology.

Non-Constantinian Pedagogy

There are those who want to reject historicism altogether and argue for its replacement with another paradigm of learning.[24] Yet Yoder is not one of them. Why not? Yoder simply refuses to tarry long with methodology, not because it is unimportant, but because no single method can do the total job of disclosing truth to us.[25] He considers the disclosure

24. I have in mind here scholars like the Canadian philosopher George Grant; see his *Time as History* (Toronto: Canadian Broadcasting Corp., 1969). Grant, advocating a return to philosophical orthodoxy, especially Plato, laments: "Every literate high-school student would take a simple statement of . . . historicism for granted. We are taught early to use the language of values, to say that our values are dependent on our historical situation, and that this generalization proceeds from any objective study of the past. Civilizations and individuals have lived by different values. As there is no way of judging between the values of these values, we are taught early a very simple historical relativism. As we go farther in our education, we are taught to express that historicism with greater sophistication. However, the almost universal acceptance of this relativism by even the semi-literate in our society is very recent. The belief that men are enfolded in their historicity, and the consequent historical relativism with its use of the word 'values,' only began to be popular vocabulary in this century. Nietzsche is the first thinker who shows how this historicity is to be recognized in the full light of its consequences, in every realm of existence" (26). See also C. S. Lewis, *The Screwtape Letters* (London: Collins–Fantana, 1964). Screwtape, the devil's sage in Lewis's text, speaks similarly, if perhaps somewhat more popularly: "Only the learned read old books and we [the united spirits of hell] have now so dwelt with the learning that they are of all men the least likely to acquire wisdom by doing so. We have done this by inculcating The Historical Point of View. The Historical Point of View, put briefly, means that when a learned man is presented with any statement in an ancient author, the one question he never asks is whether it is true. He asks who influenced the ancient writer, and how far the statement is consistent with what he said in other books, and what phase in the writer's development, or in the general history of thought, it illustrates, and how it affected later writers, and how often it has been misunderstood (especially by the learned man's own colleagues)" (139–40).

Some may argue that Karl Barth, too, was among those who wanted to overthrow historicism. But I suspect that Barth was far too interested in history for that. Clearly this is not the place to sort out the intricacies of Barth's theological relation to Troeltsch, but it is important to note that it was Barth's struggle with early twentieth-century Protestant Liberalism that cost him his teaching position in Bonn. Moreover, he recognized its failure to be able to resist the Nazi machine because accommodation and assimilation had worked all too well. Says Hauerwas: "The discovery of the Christological center in theology [was] of a piece with his opposition to Hitler. . . . Barth has surely earned the right to ask us all to see why his discovery of the strange new world of the Bible is necessary for us to name as well as to resist the demons unleashed in the name of humanity" (*With the Grain of the Universe*, 270–71).

25. "'Patience' as Method in Moral Reasoning: Is an Ethic of Discipleship 'Absolute'?" in *The Wisdom of the Cross: Essays in Honor of John Howard Yoder*, ed. Stanley Hauerwas et al. (Grand Rapids, Mich.: Eerdmans, 1999), 24–42. See also my essay, "The Christian Life as Gift and Patience: Why Yoder Has Trouble with Method," in *A Mind Patient and Untamed: Assessing John Howard Yoder's Contributions to Theology, Ethics, and Peacemaking*, ed. Ben C. Ollenburger and Gayle Gerber Koontz (Telford, Pa.: Cascadia, 2004), 23–38.

of the truth to be the task of the scholar. Yoder is not often called a historicist, but the appellation may well be apt as long as that is not a doctrinaire assertion. The following caricature comes to mind: Troeltsch is a universal historicist, MacIntyre a tradition-based historicist, and Yoder a "Jesus-is-Lord" historicist, one who appeals to the normativity of Jesus, dislikes the term "absolute," and prefers more "contexualizing" language.[26]

Yoder never critiques Troeltsch's fundamental affirmation that the Christian faith is a sociology, but he does reject Troeltsch's Constantinian account of that claim. The ecclesiological shift that took place in the fourth century, and reverberates through history even to this day, profoundly changed the social meaning of Christianity. Troeltsch and Yoder both recognized that fact. Yet when Christianity became the official religion of the state, Troeltsch calls it "full development," whereas Yoder suggests that it moves away from a biblical ecclesiology and "stands for a new era in the history of Christianity,"[27] which he refers to as "disavowal and apostasy."[28] Troeltsch would not disagree with Yoder's claim about the new era, but he would argue against Yoder's evaluation of that era. Troeltsch believed that the changes Yoder calls "disavowal and apostasy" were simply the way the church sought to engage the world, and the church's quest to gain "supremacy" and to "subdue the state" was but the church being socially responsible. Yoder sees this "responsibility" as yielding to the temptation of "seizing godlikeness," which in the biblical tradition is called idolatry.[29]

The issue is ostensibly over the place of the church in history, but more importantly it is about how that place is determined. For Yoder, the church is not simply what the church does. For the church to be the church it must measure itself by Jesus Christ, who called it into existence. In other words, the ecclesiological difference between Yoder and Troeltsch is rooted in another, namely, a difference in reading the biblical account on who Jesus is. Troeltsch assumes that there is not within the biblical narrative a clear *social* and *political* critique, program, and strategy; Yoder argues that there is. This difference leaves Troeltsch with no other recourse but to uncritically accept the Constantinian synthesis, and it leads Yoder to say that "what the churches accepted in the Constantinian shift is what Jesus rejected, seizing godlikeness, moving

26. See, for example, Yoder, "'Patience' as Method," 25.

27. John Howard Yoder, *The Priestly Kingdom: Social Ethics as Gospel* (Notre Dame, Ind.: University of Notre Dame Press, 1984), 135.

28. Ibid., 144.

29. Ibid., 145. See also Alex Sider, "To See History Doxologically: History and Holiness in John Howard Yoder's Ecclesiology" (PhD diss., Duke University, 2004), for an engaging treatment of the interrelationship between Yoder and Troeltsch.

in hoc signo from Golgotha to the battlefield."[30] The issue is not over "compromise" or even accommodation, for both men advocate that. The issue is over good and bad compromises.[31] Yoder would point out that, if not Troeltsch himself, then at least his disciples, the Niebuhrs, in discussing the social relevance of Jesus, make compromises that are not faithful to the character of Jesus; and the Niebuhrs would point out that Yoder's form of compromise is unrealistic since he believes that the rule of Christ can be embodied on earth.

For Yoder the new "Christian" era inaugurated in the fourth century is characterized by a new ecclesiology, a new eschatology, a new universality, and a new metaphysic. In other words, it is so all-pervading that even today attempts at disavowal often remain captive to the very system they mean to critique. So much changed with Constantine that disentanglement is virtually impossible. We all remain thoroughly Constantinian![32]

Yoder points out that after Constantine one could no longer speak of the church without doctrinal refinement; that is to say, Augustine's doctrine of *ecclesia invisibilis* was essential to making theological sense of the church. But this doctrine meant that the visible church, which was the socially embodied church, was not the *true* church and the *true* church was invisible and so not socially embodied. Augustine knew that. But Troeltsch's discourse, bereft of the social normativity of Jesus, suggested that the "sect-type," which came closest to Augustine's notion of the true church, was sociologically irrelevant because it was invisible, and the "church-type," which was sociologically relevant, was not the true church. Moreover, eschatologically speaking, Christendom and empire became synonymous. Christians had inherited the divinely imparted duty to rule over the world through empire power. This meant, as the Crusades gruesomely attest, that the outsider now becomes the infidel, "the incarnation of anti-faith." And "to destroy him, or to give one's life in the attempt, has become a positively virtuous undertaking."[33] God's rule and the emperor's rule have become one.

---

30. Yoder, *Priestly Kingdom*, 145.

31. See Yoder, "'Patience' as Method," where he identifies the challenge as follows: "Being careful about the difference between good and bad kinds of 'compromises' or good and bad kinds of 'absolutes'" (24).

32. As Peter Dula has pointed out, it is important not to restrict, as Yoder does, the term "Constantinianism" to a dynamic that names only the problematic relationship between church and state, but to broaden it to include other powers like that of "global capital." When we do that, of course, the entanglement is only increased. See Peter Dula, "The 'Disavowal of Constantine' in the Age of Global Capital," in *Seeking Cultures of Peace: A Peace Church Conversation*, ed. Fernando Enns et al. (Telford, Pa.: Cascadia, 2004), 62–77.

33. Yoder, *Priestly Kingdom*, 138.

With Constantine also comes a new universality. Ethical agency and discourse are now general. Two important questions must now be asked in order to determine moral justification: "Can you ask such behaviour of everyone?" and "What would happen if everyone did it?"[34] For example, if everyone loved their enemies, who would ward off the terrorists? Can you really expect the New Testament love ethic of everyone? The rhetorical negative, of course, implies the unrealism and irrelevance of the biblical demands. Hence, moral discourse turns quickly from faithfulness, covenant, and revelation, to realism and effectiveness. Whatever does not promise results cannot be right, and the nature of the desired results has been defined by the concept of power.[35] Hence, a new Neoplatonism flourishes, with its functional ordering of powers: love governs the inward and the personal dimensions of life, while the ethics of power derived from beyond the biblical tradition governs the outward world of structures.[36]

It is important to note that Yoder's alternative, non-Constantinian reading of history is not dogmatic in the sense that Troeltsch has defined. It does not begin with an ahistorical point, but with Jesus, an event in history. This event is, however, a special historical event; it is normative, not absolutely, in that those who reject it are irrational, but rather only for those who claim the name Christian. Hence the quest for Christians is to gain a christological reading of history, church, and world, and the educational task consists in learning to see the world through Christ.

For Yoder, Christianity is itself a way of knowing and thinking—a way of seeing the world. Kant, Hegel, and Troeltsch are wrong in their claim that only universal reason can disclose truth to us. Much of what Troeltsch says about historicism may still be true, but not its universal underpinnings. Here MacIntyre's critique of a Troeltschean universal, historical reason is apt. But Yoder goes much further. He pushes for a more thorough christological reading of history than either MacIntyre or Troeltsch provides; for if Christianity is a way of thinking, then it is reason grounded in the revelation of Jesus Christ that is the key to understanding the faith. And if Jesus Christ is Lord of history and the cosmos, and if there is any social and political content for this assertion to be found in his teachings, then we must fundamentally recast our eschatology.

From a Yoderian standpoint institutions of learning should be reconceived on the basis of a biblical ecclesiology and Christology. In Christ

---

34. Ibid., 139.
35. Ibid., 140.
36. Ibid., 141.

we are invited to open our minds (to "renew" them, as Paul says in Rom. 12:2) to contemplate the mind and body of Jesus Christ in order to see the world differently. We must ask how disciplines of learning such as English, psychology, philosophy, physics, theology, and political studies can help us see the world through Christ. In other words, the adjudicator of truth is not historical reason or the disciplines, but the Word become flesh. The challenge is to learn to be disciples both in our learning and in our teaching: to engage the quest of learning to see, think, read, live, and feel from the perspective that Jesus is Lord.

Making Strange Speech: List 2

I turn now to a second list of strange-making discourse for Christian learning. Here we will ask specifically what a university might look like that is driven by the passion to train students to be disciples and shaped by disciples as teachers, administrators, and scholars. But first, what such a university would not look like. It would not be any less academically rigorous; it would be no less thorough in reading texts read at other universities and participating in debates with other colleagues in the field outside the Christian university. While it would expose students to distinctively Christian texts, it would also study the literature and debates of other universities. Its goal would be to train students to think deeply, to read profoundly, to articulate clearly, and to embody discerningly. It would invite students to discipleship. The faculty, but not necessarily the students, would be Christian and would be committed to learning what it means that Jesus is Lord over their disciplines of study and their teaching practice.

It is tempting to launch into a conception of new approaches to and structures of education. I wish to resist this temptation, rooted as it is in the assumption of the value of the quest for total perspective and mastery. Such an approach is driven by a desire for control and dominance more at home in a Constantinian context than in one where truth is embodied in a person—Jesus Christ—and in the body that constitutes his followers. Learning the faith can find expression in a variety of different ways within very different theories of education, and even in universities that are not Christian.[37] The character of the university envisioned here is defined by invitation and gift exchange—an invitation

---

37. I want to be quite clear that although in this essay I am speaking explicitly about a university that wishes to call itself Christian, much of what I say could be adjusted to apply to Christian professors who teach at secular universities. Granted, the interaction and discourse would be somewhat different, but the teaching itself might be quite similar.

that faculty members in dialogue and debate with others will work at the task of envisioning their subject matter through the conviction that Jesus is Lord, and then in turn gift students, fellow scholars, and the institution with their insights. Together faculty will in an ongoing way envision the curriculum to ensure that it embodies Christian convictions. Likewise, administrators in dialogue and debate with colleagues will reconceive their office from the standpoint of the politics of Jesus and then gift the institution with suggestions on how to make the administration Christian. Together administrators will in an ongoing way ask the question of how administration can best embody Christian convictions. In other words, what is suggested here is an ongoing *process* and not a specified *product* to be produced—a process that is open to answers we do not yet have, recognizing that the task is new and unusual, not something that any of us have received much explicit training in as we have prepared for our work. At the same time, this process embraces an important practice of the church, namely, that by working together under the Lordship of Christ answers we do not even have the questions for yet can emerge.

The list below attempts to flesh out markings that might make university education Christian. The list is obviously incomplete and could well be supplemented with other important Christian qualities.

1. *Jesus is the norm.* It may be surprising to think that beginning with Jesus as norm could produce anything like a university. Perhaps a seminary or a Bible college, but a university? Jesus is often thought of as irrelevant even in many Christian universities and colleges. It is commonly assumed that Jesus was a simple rural figure, hardly a basis for a contemporary university; that he was not about education but about personal salvation, and hence to draw pedagogical conclusions from what he said and how he lived is misguided; that he was unrealistic in his demands about discipleship because he assumed the imminence of the coming kingdom, affording him a radicalism that could not possibly ground an institution like a university; that he conceived of himself as unimportant and deflected importance to God, implying that while Creator God might ground a university, Jesus could not; that his radical prophetic pronouncements left him bereft of a concept of responsibility that those who run institutions in a democratic society must have; that he was uninterested in the establishment of an institution in principle

---

It is also possible that a Christian university might second some of its faculty to teach in other universities, or indeed invite non-Christian faculty to teach in its curriculum. In any case, it would be a ludicrous assumption to think that Christians can teach (or learn) only in the context of other Christians. In fact, this assumption would undercut the inherent evangelistic nature of the gospel.

because he was much more interested in tearing down than building up. Against these odds it may not be easy to make Jesus the norm for a Christian university. Yet within biblical scholarship there is today no question about the sociological and political relevance of Jesus. Jesus spoke to those kinds of matters that are pertinent for the pedagogical enterprise. It is the ethicists and administrators who have found it difficult to make the connections.

Stanley Hauerwas gives us a start on this project in a recent sermon entitled "On Milk and Jesus."[38] He argues that to be a Christian university does not mean being just another university with a Christian difference, for that is not yet to have caught the difference being Christian makes. That difference is appreciated only when it is acknowledged that Jesus makes a difference for how one teaches history, physics, English, and economics, a difference in how we organize scholarship to begin with. He suggests that the disciplines that enjoy autonomy in contemporary universities should in a Christian university be ordered under the one whom we really trust—Jesus—not pure reason, nor the guild. This ordering of the disciplines may, for example, initiate new teaching practices, such as team teaching across the disciplines, or teaching topical courses on forgiveness, war, revenge, evil, or happiness, with professors from a variety of disciplines. These and other ventures could communicate that such notions are not the jurisdiction of a single department or of narrow academic interest, but are central to the human experience. To bring the various perspectives into engagement with one another under the Lordship of Christ may well uncover new insights for Christian living.

2. *Jesus as teacher.* We should be careful how we speak about Jesus as a model teacher. In one way it matters little *how* Jesus taught, that he never taught at a university, that he spoke in parables, that he spoke the language of the commoner, that he never published. But it does matter that he worked at *retelling* the story of Israel, for knowing the story and telling it right are important if we wish to make it our story.[39] It matters

---

38. "On Milk and Jesus," a sermon preached at the installation of Dr. Gerald Gerbrandt as president of Canadian Mennonite University, Winnipeg, Canada, September 28, 2003. Forthcoming in *Disrupting Time: Sermons, Prayers, and Sundries* (Eugene, Ore.: Cascade Books, 2005).

39. See Kenneth E. Bailey, *Jacob and the Prodigal: How Jesus Retold Israel's Story* (Downers Grove, Ill.: InterVarsity, 2003). In this fascinating book, Bailey argues that Jesus took great care in retelling the story of God at work in this world, inviting people to become part of the story: "The story first creates a world and then invites the listener to live in that world, to take it on as part of who he or she is. Biblical stories invite the reader to accept them as *his* or *her* story. . . . The Bible is read to rediscover who we are and what we must yet become, because the biblical story of sin and salvation, law and grace, is *our* story" (51–52).

also that he concentrated on drawing his hearers into an imagination where God is at work in this world and cares about the individual and about structures and powers. It matters that he both problematized and clarified issues of social and religious position and power, that he proclaimed forgiveness of sins and invited disciples to learn on the job, and that he held united believing and doing. In other words, it matters less *how* he taught and much more *what* he taught. We should therefore avoid deriving a pedagogical theory from his teaching, but if Jesus is to be *our* teacher we must give attention to what he taught.

Jesus was not afraid to summarize and schematize. He did not hesitate to affirm love of God and neighbor as a way of summarizing the story of Israel. But at the same time he was far more interested in what the hearers understood that to mean than merely that they knew it to be so.[40] Even trick questions provided opportunity for Jesus to teach, although in the process he would demonstrate that the questions needed to be changed in order for the good news to be heard. What seems to have motivated Jesus above all was to teach and train disciples—to have them imagine a world in which God was the principal actor and into which they were invited, because they too mattered as participants in God's story. And part of this imagination included the fact that there are forces at work that distort, destroy, and are pitted against the work of God's redemption. These subtle forces may therefore be deeply within us, in our thinking, our living, and our feeling. Hence, when Jesus confronts his hearers with the reality of God, it is for both judgment and salvation.

It is interesting to ask how theological the teaching of Jesus really was. At one level he taught about economics (poverty and wealth); about politics (religious, social, and political power structures that kept people in places and roles that God did not intend); about psychology (how people could be freed from powers that bind them, how people could relate to each other doing the things that make for peace); about philosophy (wisdom, knowledge, and truth); and so on. And he gave many illustrations of everyday relationships that reminded people of how they could improve their quality of life. None of this is explicitly theological, and yet it is deeply theological in that it makes sense only within the framework that God is at work, bringing the world to redemption. It is also important to note that Jesus taught with his life. Not only did he proclaim salvation; he saved people. The many accounts of healing bodies, forgiving sins, of refusing to retaliate, of breaking cultural barriers and taboos, all speak of how the message he preached was also practiced.

---

40. See especially Luke 10:25–42, where Jesus illustrates what it means to love God and neighbor.

3. *Ecclesiology precedes pedagogy.* As we have seen, Constantinianism emphasizes the sameness of the church; non-Constantinianism emphasizes its strangeness. One of the main differences non-Constantinianism makes for teaching is that it suggests that ecclesiology precedes pedagogy. It answers the question "What does a Christian university educate for?" in a particular way—the church. What does this mean?

A Christian university begins with the notion that our convictions are embodied in the lives we live. In other words, the shaping of a political–social body of believers—the church—becomes a primary objective of the university, even if it may not be its only task. We need to acknowledge that this is also a rather contentious claim since it goes against the grain of so much in modern pedagogy, even though the postmodern critique has forced honest universities to recognize that they too produce certain kinds of people.[41] Perhaps this admission makes the *Christian* university's task even more challenging. Given the contemporary university's participation in underwriting the diversity inherent in a democratic social order it is easy to see that "Christian presence has been relegated to the realm of 'values' associated with courses in ethics or involved with issues in 'student life.' It has simply become unthinkable that Christian convictions might have something to do with the actual content of the curriculum and with pedagogical practice."[42]

The church has cradled, nurtured, and sustained the university for centuries. The church has always held that truth and knowledge lie firmly within its jurisdiction and that universities are needed for their explication. It is only in the last century that many universities, especially in North America, have shed their association with the church. This is not the place to rehearse the reasons for this disassociation, but surely one of the most profound factors is that the universities have succeeded in educating themselves *as well as the church* in the belief that the university is able to give account of itself quite apart from the church.[43] That is why Hauerwas is able to put the question in terms not

---

41. For example, this claim runs directly counter to what social philosophers like Max Weber have attempted to teach us, but which has come to be questioned by most universities. Weber argued that teaching has to do only with the dispensing of facts: "Politics is out of place in the lecture-room. It does not belong there on the part of the students. . . . Neither does politics belong in the lecture-room on the part on the docents. . . . The true teacher will beware of imposing from the platform any political position upon the student, whether it is expressed or suggested." Taken from Max Weber, "Science as a Vocation," in *From Max Weber: Essays in Sociology,* ed. H. H. Gerth and C. Wright Mills (New York: Oxford University Press, 1946), 145–46.

42. Hauerwas, *With the Grain of the Universe,* 232.

43. Examples of studies that address the issues related to the separation of church and university are: George M. Marsden, *The Soul of the American University: From Protestant*

of whether a university can be Christian but of whether a church exists that can sustain a Christian university.[44] And of course he is quite right. In other words, the hope for a Christian university lies with the people who realize that the rigor necessary to sustain their faith and the faith of their children cannot itself be sustained without such a university. The need for this institution becomes urgent when we recognize that God is there not to supply what is lacking in knowledge generally, which universities assume is a void they will be able to fill, but that God is the source, sustainer, and end of truth and knowledge. Those who worship God, therefore, cannot survive without a university.

The church needs to place on the university's agenda the claim that the faith of its members can be sustained only when its people are trained to negotiate the economics, politics, science, sociology, and philosophy of the biblical faith in a world that has strongly competing views on such matters. The request of the church is for the Christian university to participate in shaping a people who are literate and fluent in a language that is able to disclose what God is doing in this world. The church needs an educated people to present a more complexified view of human nature—of violence, sin, peace, and love—than most people have, given their somewhat distorted view of things learned from popular culture. The church needs an educated people to present alternative answers to questions of justice, international relations, and power; to present alternative models for how people can live together in ways that liberate and heal brokenness. The church needs an educated people to promote structures that foster the art of welcoming the stranger in a culture of protectionism; to promote that truth is not a possession but a gift in an age of capitalism; to promote that forgiveness is a viable strategy of social reconstruction in a culture of fear.

The claim that the church sets the agenda for the Christian university should, of course, not be taken to mean that only the immediate issues of the church are debated and clarified in the university. It should be understood in the larger sense that the church mandates the university to educate its youth to be the kinds of people who as Jews and Greeks, men and women, slave and free can live together in peace. In this sense, the university is a place where the walls of hostility can be broken down

Establishment to Established Nonbelief (New York: Oxford University Press, 1994); George M. Marsden and Bradley J. Longfield, ed., *The Secularization of the Academy* (New York: Oxford University Press, 1992); Burtchaell, *Dying of the Light;* Julie Reuben, *The Making of the Modern University: Intellectual Transformation and the Marginalization of Morality* (Chicago: University of Chicago Press, 1996); and Robert Benne, *Quality with Soul: How Six Premier Colleges Keep Faith with Their Religious Traditions* (Grand Rapids, Mich.: Eerdmans, 2001).

44. Hauerwas, *With the Grain of the Universe*, 233.

and the art of reconciliation can heal and restore. The university should address issues of poverty, wealth, power and impotence, forgiveness, sin, failure, revenge, war, structures, history, truth, praise, and gift—all traditional and current themes within any university and in the larger public. Ecclesiology precedes pedagogy because pedagogy must ask what teaching is for. The answer is given in terms of training people to see and read the world as the arena of God's redemptive activities and of training people to become particular kinds of people capable of bearing witness to such activities.

4. *Pedagogical humility/patience/nonviolence.* The Apostle Paul, in his First Letter to the Corinthians, makes the comment that "knowledge puffs up, but love builds up" (1 Cor. 8:1).[45] The Bible is replete with general admonitions about pride: "God opposes the proud, but gives grace to the humble" (James 4:6, drawing on Prov. 3:34). Evidently the biblical witnesses were concerned that those who overestimate their self-importance tend to underestimate God's. While salvation, history, truth, and knowledge all belong to God, we should beware not to see these first and foremost as human possessions, but as gifts that we may receive graciously and tenderly. Perhaps Jesus knew something of the power of knowledge and saw it as he saw wealth, namely, as an impediment to faith; both knowledge and wealth get in the way of being open to God. It is not an accident that Foucault's work on knowledge and power, for example, is sometimes seen as illuminating the gospel message.

The Apostle also says: "It is to peace that God has called you" (1 Cor. 7:15). Several contemporary scholars argue that violence is not merely an overt act, but also an organizing principle for how we think and act, a principle deeply rooted in our pedagogies and our epistemologies. It is therefore important that a Christian university examine how its way of teaching can be faithful to the call of peace.

The practices of patience and humility help to guard against violent pedagogies because these pedagogies are supported by practices like mastery, dominance, and speed.[46] There are several aspects to this claim. The pedagogical practice of most universities is rooted in an interest to control the outcome of things; thus we teach to understand, to change things for the better, to analyze what is wrong, and to train our students

---

45. All biblical quotations are from the NRSV.

46. It may not be evident how speed belongs to the list of items that fuel violence. I am drawing here on the work of the French writer Paul Virilio, who argues that the logic of speed characterizes "Pure War," which is not necessarily the kind of war that a nation declares. For an interesting study of Yoder and Virilio, see Chris K. Huebner, "Patience, Witness, and the Scattered Body of Christ: Yoder and Virilio on Knowledge, Politics, and Speed," in *A Mind Patient and Untamed,* 56–74.

and ourselves as teachers to fix things. But this pedagogy assumes a level of control that we do not have and is part of the imagination one might call pedagogical Constantinianism. A pedagogy that is based in Jesus Christ must be more humble and more patient. What Yoder has taught us about Christian pacifism might also apply to Christian pedagogy:

> That Christian pacifism which has its theological basis in the character of God and the work of Jesus Christ is one in which the calculating link between our obedience and ultimate efficacy has been broken, since the triumph of God comes through resurrection and not through effective sovereignty or assured survival.[47]

Applying this logic to the teaching enterprise suggests a double reference: first, to the impact one believes teaching has on society at large; and second, to the impact teaching has on individual students. In both cases, the logic suggests that the relationship is one of *bearing witness in the hope that God will bring redemption and new life,* rather than of cause and effect.

I suggest four specific characteristics that follow from this view of education. First, patience: Christians should know something about patience since they are people who are waiting for the coming of God's rule, knowing that they cannot produce it on their own. Nevertheless, they expect it to come. Teaching is similar. The desired results of having students, colleagues, and even oneself come to full insight and discipleship are often not swift in coming. Jesus understood this well. Discipleship training is like that. Yoder identifies nineteen elements of patience related to the pedagogical enterprise. Among them are: human learning happens in "sequences and stages" and not all at once; valid arguments have histories and take time to develop and to be understood; matters of trust and healing make it impossible for some arguments to be made in certain settings; patience requires respect for others; ecumenical patience is necessary to hear the depth of other traditions; there is a patience of the minority speaking to the majority, and a patience of subordination, of waiting to be heard; and so on.[48] To teach without patience is to teach violently and without proper attention to the fact that learning requires forgiveness, love, compassion, and mercy.

Second, humility: It may be a cliché but the truth is that although we have PhDs we know very little. Let us not teach about peace, for example, as though we know fully what peace is. Peace names a state of being

47. Yoder, *The Politics of Jesus:* Vicit Agnus Noster (Grand Rapids, Mich.: Eerdmans, 1972), 239.

48. Yoder, "'Patience' as Method," 24–42.

that is deeply complex, and its oversimplification does it injustice. The same could be said for truth, knowledge, evil, and the good. A natural human tendency is to claim to know more than we do. Although Christians may see Jesus, as the writer of Hebrews reminds us (Heb. 2:8–9), the task of knowing how to embody Jesus in our settings requires an ongoing corrective challenge of simplification and complexification, construction and subversion. Perhaps most important is learning the art of knowing when to pick up which challenge. That requires insight and humility.

Third, love of enemies: Teaching is a dialogue with enemies and friends. None of us can teach only what we know, perhaps because we know so little, but perhaps also because what we know is insignificant in the larger scheme of things. We therefore teach best when we are able to help students to read and understand texts, all kinds of texts, texts we agree with and texts we do not agree with, texts that are supportive of the Christian view of the world and texts that are not. It is perhaps even more important that we teach well those texts we do not agree with, and that we teach them with empathy. For in so doing we teach students to love enemies.

Fourth, witness: It is especially important for a Christian university to remember that truth is not a possession. Even though the Christian university as a whole puts forward a distinct argument that it holds to be true, we should be well aware of the limitations of such a claim. We are fallible scholars; we are sinful beings; we have not yet seen everything that is relevant for certain issues to be settled; not all matters have answers; and we do not always have the patience to wait until we have something to say. It is not our role to out-narrate our competitors in the debates, but it is our role to bear witness, to give the best account that can be given so far of the Christian perspective on things.

5. *The Mystery of God.* John the seer reminds us that Christians need to read and see the world doxologically. I am suggesting that we train ourselves to see Christian education in that light as well; that is, that in our disciplines of study, in the curriculum, and in the structures of the university, we express the Word become flesh. When we do this to the best of our abilities we sing praises to God for whatever fruits may follow; for God remains mystery and is not ours to domesticate. The wind blows where it wills; it is not ours to direct.

My English colleague Paul Dyck has introduced me to the short stories of Canadian author Gloria Sawai. One such story is entitled "The Day I Sat with Jesus on My Sundeck, and the Wind Blew My Kimono Open and He Saw My Breasts."[49] The title pretty much tells

49. See Gloria Sawai, *A Song for Nettie Johnson* (Regina, SK: Coteau, 2003), 277–96.

the story, except that when Jesus was asked what he thought, he said he liked them. This is a wonderfully unsettling story because it assumes unabashedly that Jesus is not ashamed of body or of the wind uncovering things we try to keep hidden. Whatever naughtiness there may be in this story, we should not forget that Jesus's body too hung uncovered on the cross. And our thoughtful response to this encounter is profoundly important. The story of how the one who died and was raised saves the world by exposing to us what we prefer to cover up surely must continue to scandalize and surprise. We do well to remember that when the unexpected mysterious forces uncover strange new vistas for us to see we are asked to give account. Learning to see what the wind blows open may yet prove to be one of the most basic Christian pedagogical practices. There are many times when we cannot know in advance, for life is contingent and it comes to us as gift and as mystery. And for students, faculty, and administrators to learn the meaning of life as gift in a capitalist culture remains an enormous challenge.

Conclusion: Making Strange Is Only the Beginning

I have perhaps overworked the strange-making metaphor. It is clearly not intended to project an isolationist university that hides from its sister academic institutions and narrowly serves only the church. A Christian university should serve the church in the broad sense and also invite robust interaction with other scholars and other institutions of learning. The reason for the emphasis on strangeness is to communicate the importance of identity and difference. For a university to be and remain Christian is hard work. Strong temptations exist to make it otherwise. But even here our example can be Jesus. The real options Jesus faced in his own life were to withdraw into the desert, on the one hand, and, on the other, to embrace one of the establishment religions, especially the insurrectionists—the Zealots—who were interested in change and justice. But Jesus rejected both options in favor of a third way characterized by and ending with the cross and resurrection. This was the option of presenting to the world around him the truth of God's loving presence and accepting whatever consequences came. Jesus could pursue this option because he knew that the real work was God's. There is perhaps no more fitting challenge to a university that chooses to use his name than to seek to do likewise—bear witness to the one who redeems all things, for we know the real work to be God's.

The role of the intellectual is to say the truth to power, to address the central authority in every society without hypocrisy, and to choose the method, the style, the critique best suited for these purposes.

—Edward Said[50]

It is established then that: a) nothing is taught without signs, b) knowledge should be more precious to us than the signs by means of which we acquire it; though c) possibly not all things which are signified are better than the signs which indicate them.

—Augustine[51]

50. Edward Said, *Peace and Its Discontents: Essays on Palestine in the Middle East Peace Process* (New York: Vintage, 1996), 184.

51. Augustine, *De Magistro* (The Teacher), in *Augustine: Earlier Writings*, vol. 6, trans. John H. S. Burleigh, Library of Christian Classics (Philadelphia: Westminster, 1953), 91.

15

Abrahamic Hauerwas

Theological Conditions for Justifying Inter-Abrahamic Study

Peter Ochs

Radical Traditions

Our radical theologian Stanley Hauerwas may have spent most of his days stirring up the pot of Christian faith and obedience to the living Christ. But now some of the pot has spilled over, and he has also taken to stirring up the pot of Abrahamic faith, and with it obedience to the scriptural word in its three indigenous forms. With this stirring has come Radical Traditions, a book series conceived and coedited by Stanley, in which Christian, Jewish, and Muslim theologians are called to affirm their traditional discourses unapologetically, while also acknowledging each other's efforts to serve the One God, Creator of heaven and earth. Surprisingly, it is Scripture that enables this vision of the three traditions that are one in their affirmation of the unity and holiness of God. This unifying role of Scripture is surprising, on the one hand, because those who reject theological dialogue among the Abrahamic faiths often do so in the name of the utter incomparability of one of the three Scriptures—Tanakh, Gospel (or also the entire canon of Old and New Testaments), Qur'an—with either of the other two. It is surprising, on the other hand, because those who champion interreligious dialogue often do so at the expense of Scripture, claiming that dialogue comes when the three faith communities discuss common ethical issues, apart from the divisive theological doctrines presented in the scriptural canons. Stanley's third alternative is to say that these three faiths have their unity in God alone, not in the idea of God, nor in any doctrines about God, and surely not in any ethical claims or constructions. God calls each community to serve him, and God alone can call all three communities to serve him also by way of their conversation with one another about him. Scripture alone offers each of the Abrahamic faiths words through which to speak about him and directives about how to speak with one another. Scripture alone therefore introduces conditions for the theological dialogue that underlies Radical Traditions.

Following Stanley's vision, contributors to Radical Traditions are joined in one additional way: they make use of at least one of the Western academy's theoretical discourses—philosophy, logic, social science, natural science, and so on. Unlike "modernist" or "conceptualist" theologians, they practice these discourses in service to the divine Word. Unlike antimodern theologians, however, they do not denigrate the instrumental value of academic theory, provided it is ultimately constrained by service to God as Creator, Revealer, and Redeemer. Unlike most premodern theologians, moreover, Radical Traditions scholars find that their own confessional service is strengthened—not weakened—by close collegial relations with scholars in the other Abrahamic confessions. As we have noted, these relations enable them to pursue a nonliberal path to inter-Abrahamic understanding and peace. As used here, "nonliberal" does not mean nonbenevolent, noncompassionate, or even nonrespectful of the modern political goals of democracy and human rights. It refers to a refusal to buy into modern secular presumptions that humanity can redeem itself: that it can construct instruments for observing universal truth and engineering universal peace, or even that it is graced with feelings or intuitions or habits that serve as instruments of this kind.[1] "Nonliberal" refers, equally, to a refusal to accept the resignation or despair that follows when humanistic visions fail.

---

1. We label the modern vision "conceptualist" when these instruments are taken to be concepts constructed by human individuals or human societies. Nonconceptualist forms of modernism are variously labeled "emotivism," "relativism," "skepticism," and so on.

The nonliberal No! applies also to what Hans Frei dubbed "mediating" efforts to accommodate the premises of scriptural religion itself to the terms of a humanistic vision. Radical Traditions scholars acknowledge the benevolent—and often scripturally based—motivations of modern humanists and the power of humanist feelings and cognitions as *instruments* of the scriptural word. For this reason, these scholars are not antimodern or antiliberal. But they are nonliberal, because they argue that the divine Word, alone, is author of "universal" truth and that the divine Redeemer, alone, is agent of universal peace. I know of no theologian or thinker who is as jealous of both sides of this nonliberalism as Stanley Hauerwas—or who so energetically defends it against both religious and secular challengers. Particularly in his more recent work, Stanley therefore argues not only against "the liberals" but also against recent movements in antiliberal theology. Comparable in this way only to Robert Jenson or just a few others, Stanley argues that proponents of unreformed premodern religion are often moved by universalizing epistemologies that are, in logical form, indistinguishable from their modern, secular descendants.[2] If, for example, antimodern Christian (*or* Jewish or Muslim) theologians promote *concepts* of God's "triune form" (or of "his Law" or of "his ineluctable simplicity") as utterly true and universal, then Stanley would argue that they are in effect reducing the divine Word to the terms of humanly constructed projects of reason.

"Universality" is a modality of propositions constructed by humans and applied to projects of reasoning in accordance with socially adopted systems of logic. It is not an attribute of the Creator, Revealer, Redeemer, which means that the only route to universal salvation is *by way of the divine presence* or, for Stanley, by way of the divine Word. Since this Word makes itself known only in its concrete relation to embodied communities of believers, the route to the universal is strictly by way of the concrete lives, languages, histories, and actions of these particular communities. Liberal humanists and religionists tend to fear this route through the particular as a dangerous or even damning detour, as if God and particularity were (God forbid) logical contraries, the way "universal" and "particular" appear to be in propositional logics. For Stanley, however, this is no less than the "detour" of incarnation. A dangerous and painful detour, indeed: as painful as death, since the cross is its marker. But it is the only path to take, since the alternative would be to take a detour around and away from God's creation; and that would be to shun humanity rather than to seek its redemption. If

2. See, for example, Jenson's critique of substantialist notions of Trinity in Robert Jenson, *Systematic Theology*, vol. 1, *The Triune God* (New York: Oxford University Press, 2001), passim.

this is so, does it not mean that seeking salvation is only for those who share in the incarnate Word, and are these not Christians alone? The liberal-and-antiliberal challenge to Stanley would be to offer him only these mutually exclusive alternatives: either to acknowledge the election of the church alone *or* to consent to the humanist choice of universal reason versus radical skepticism.

In this essay, we celebrate Stanley's fathering of Radical Traditions as a collective No! and No! to the liberal-and-antiliberal challenge: No, when God elects the church it is not like a human who elects a candidate! No, we need not accept these alternatives, for Yes, God elects the church, and God elects Israel; Yes, God's Word is incarnate in the particularities of this world, and Yes, his appearance amidst those particularities affirms God's power to redeem all creation; Yes, God is known only here and here and here, but Yes, this is the means through which he will be known everywhere; Yes, Stanley affirms "the unsubstitutability of Christ," but Yes, God is known not only to the Jews but to the Muslims as well. Yes, this is all possible. But how it is possible is not something we can argue out a priori.

We argue, to begin with, from *out* of the particular communities where God meets us, so we do not *begin* with an argument that could be addressed directly to others. The argument begins within a confessional community and is for that reason nonliberal. The argument leads its proponents, however, both toward an eschaton that implicates other communities and up to points of encounter with particular communities this side of the eschaton. Stanley's eschatology relaxes his intracommunal resistance to Christian–Jewish–Muslim encounter. But the possibility of this encounter is to be reasoned only regressively: from the fact of the encounter back toward the Christian bases for his theological reasoning. This rule of regression means that Stanley must imagine at least three paths of reasoning, as Christians, Jews, and Muslims reason back from their encounter toward the bases of Christian, Jewish, and Muslim reasonings. The liberal-and-antiliberal anxiety is that this plurality of reasonings would preclude the possibility of a rational *or* theological warrant for inter-Abrahamic inquiry. The author of *With the Grain of the Universe* lacks this anxiety because he has more faith that God can handle this little challenge.[3] This is a reasonable faith, moreover, not fideism, at least for those who believe that Kant is reasonable, whether or not he is right. For Stanley's reasoning on this matter is comparable to a christocentrically transcendental regress: from the fact of Abrahamic encounter to its transcendental possibility *in* the life of God incarnate

---

3. Stanley Hauerwas, *With the Grain of the Universe: The Church's Witness and Natural Theology* (Grand Rapids, Mich.: Brazos Press, 2001).

(where any egocentric unity of apperception is reduced to its source in Christ, which means to its source in the triune dynamic of the divine life, rather than in any static principle of identity I = I).

As a Jewish reasoner, to be sure, *I* do not reason this way, but *With the Grain of the Universe* suggests to me that Stanley does. I reason, instead, from the fact of Abrahamic encounter to its transcendental possibility in the Torah as the living Word of God (disclosed to Israel in and for her life among the nations). Now this is a different reasoning, but neither this nor Stanley's reasoning recognizes any principle of excluded middle according to which one of these reasonings precludes the logical possibility of the other. Logical possibility is what the Logos makes possible. Stanley's community observes this possibility in the life of Christ and tests its meaning through the study of Gospel and of Old and New Testament. My community observes this possibility in the life of Torah and tests its meaning through the study of Tanakh and early rabbinic literature. When each of our communities hears that the other undertakes tests of this kind, we find that each reapplies its scriptural study, now as a means of testing what we think of what the other is doing. Then, when we see that our modes of testing are so parallel yet different, we are moved to try this strange experiment: to conduct some of our testing at the same time, around the same table, looking back and forth at each other's Scriptures and at how they are being read and why. Then we find that some Muslim colleagues are engaged in comparably parallel yet different modes of scriptural testings. We get a bigger table, and we label the resulting activity scriptural reasoning: an experiment in allowing the God who speaks to us by way of our intracommunal studies to do what he would do with us when we study, at times, side by side.

I report here about these strange doings because they offer one illustration of how a theologian like Stanley could offer *reasoned warrants* for encouraging more than strictly intra-Christian scriptural study. The reasoning would have to come *after* the experimental *fact* of such study; this reasoning would have to be Christian for the Christians, Jewish for the Jews, Muslim for the Muslims; and any reason for this plurality of reasonings would have to come from the fact of inter-Abrahamic scriptural reasoning and from whatever we, within each of the three subcommunities, hear the word of Scripture to say about this scriptural reasoning. In other words, Stanley's reasoning on this topic would be at once intra-Christian and christocentric *and* influenced and moved by his subcommunity's encounters with these other Abrahamic subcommunities of scriptural study.

Stanley's Radical Traditions book series is not, per se, about such interactive studies. It promotes the published work of members of each of the subcommunities. *But* a theological justification for this kind of publishing would, it seems to me, have to include some sort of inter-Abrahamic activity like this. While grounded in some intracommunal argument, such justification would at some point have to leave the safety of such argumentation and, kenotically, allow itself to be both judged and articulated through the fruits of some inter-Abrahamic conduct. As far as I know, Stanley has not self-consciously attempted such a justification. As a token of love for him—and as my contribution to this Festschrift—I therefore want to do it for him. Or, more accurately—since I cannot share in his Christian reasoning per se—I want to offer a hypothesis that he or his students could test. It is that three of his actions have already defined the conditions for offering such a justification.

Three Theological Conditions for Justifying Inter-Abrahamic Study

1. Hearing Abraham's Call; or, The Call Stirs the Pot

Lech lecha: *"Go forth from your father's house to a land I will show you."*

—Genesis 12:1

The first condition is no more and no less than to have heard the voice that calls one to intracommunal confession call one now, as well, to a certain encounter with other Abrahamic confessions. Stanley's fathering of Radical Traditions is sufficient proof of this call.

2. Going Forth Is an Argument; or, How to Reason like Abraham

The second condition is to offer an intracommunal argument that releases an individual to "Go Forth" in this way, at least to scout out the inter-Abrahamic environment and report back one's findings. Stanley did indeed not write *With the Grain of the Universe* for this purpose, but I find that, inter alia, his great argument for what we might call Barthian pragmatism also serves as a warrant for inter-Abrahamic scouting. In this section, I will lay out my finding in the form of a commentary on Genesis 12:1.

Lech lecha: "Go forth from your father's house to a land I will show you."

Abraham went forth,[4] leaving the comforts of his earthborn city for the sake of this God who "speaks and it is" (*amar vayehi*). He exchanged a piece of the natural order, we might say, for a Word from the One who created the natural order but who also recreates it each day (*hu mechadesh b'kol yom maaseh breshit*).[5] Or, we might say, he exchanged the natural order for the created one, and the creation, as he discovered, is not done.

Both the Qur'an and the rabbinic sages portray "Abraham Our Father" (in rabbinic parlance) as a prophet who did more than passively receive divine instruction. For both traditions, Abraham *observed, reasoned,* and *argued* his way out of his father's tradition and toward this new faith in the One God. Two features of these traditions are particularly significant for us.

A. ABRAHAM'S OBSERVATIONS OF NATURAL PHENOMENA LED HIM TO CHALLENGE HIS PEOPLE'S CONVENTIONAL THEOLOGY OF THE WORLD.

According to the Qur'anic account:

> 1. Abraham spoke to his father Azar, "Do you take idols for gods? Truly, I see that you and your people have obviously gone astray." Thus We gave Abraham insight into [God's] mighty dominion over the heavens and the earth. . . . When the night overshadowed him with its darkness, he beheld a star; he exclaimed, "This is my Sustainer!" But when it went down, he said, "I do not love the things that go down." . . . Then, when he beheld the sun rising, he said, "This is my Sustainer! This one is the greatest!" But when it [too] went down, he exclaimed, "O my people! Behold, far be it from me to ascribe divinity, as you do, to aught beside God." (6:74–79)

According to Moses Maimonides' scholastic version of the earlier, rabbinic tradition:

> 2. There arose among humanity false prophets who asserted that God had commanded and expressly told them, "Worship that particular star, or worship all the stars. . . ." The honored and revered Name of God was forgotten by humanity. . . . Save for a few solitary individuals (such as Enosh, Methuselah, Noah, Shem, and Eber), the world moved on in this fashion until that pillar of the world, the patriarch Abraham, was born. After Abraham was weaned, . . . his mind began to reflect. . . . "How is

---

4. To be precise, it is *Abram* who received the call, since he was not renamed Abra*ham* until he entered into direct covenant with God (Gen. 17).

5. From the traditional Jewish Daily Morning Prayer Service: "God daily renews the order of creation."

it possible that this [celestial] sphere should continuously be guiding the world and have no one to guide it and cause it to turn around, for it cannot be that it turns round of itself?" . . . He realized that humanity everywhere was in error and their error was occasioned by the fact that they worshiped the stars and images, so that truth perished from their minds. (*Mishneh Torah. Deah* [Knowledge]. *Dine Ovde Kochevim* [Laws Concerning Idolatry] 1:2)

B. HAVING CONCLUDED THAT GOD, ALONE, MUST RULE THIS CREATION, ABRAHAM SOUGHT TO CONVINCE HIS FATHER AND HIS PEOPLE OF THIS TRUTH.

According to the Qur'anic account:

3. And his people argued with him. He said, "Do you argue with me about God, when it is He who has guided me? But I do not fear anything to which you ascribe divinity side by side with Him, unless my Sustainer so wills." (6:80)

According to Maimonides:

4. Having attained this knowledge, he began to refute the inhabitants of Ur of the Chaldees. . . . He broke the images and began to instruct the people that it was not right to serve any one but the one God of the universe. (Ibid.)

Although neither this Muslim nor this Jewish account of Abraham's departure from his father's tradition reiterates the plain sense of Genesis 12:1, we need not conclude that either account contradicts the scriptural word. And although we need not, we *could* say of both accounts that they uncover questions and answers that are implicit in the plain sense. There are questions about Abram's relation to God, about the source of or reason for the call: Why did Abraham and his father choose to go to Haran even before the call of Genesis 12? (a question for any plain-sense reader of Genesis 11); Why did God choose Abraham? (a question for rationally minded medievals); and Why would Abraham trust that it is the One God who commanded him? (Kant's question). And there are questions about the consequences of the call for Abram's (and Abraham's) relation to his people and other peoples: Why would the nations be blessed through this prophet? (a question for readers of Gen. 12:2); Why would he become a father of multitudes? (a question for etymologists of the name that Abram will acquire: *av-r-ham:* "father of multitudes"?); Or a father of the three Abrahamic faiths? (a general question for this essay). The Qur'anic and rabbinic accounts suggest that any of "us" in one of the Abrahamic traditions may read something like the following line of answers as implicit in Genesis 12:1: Abram did not act like a knight of faith alone, but also like an active leader. He did not act only as a self-referring creature, working independently of his Creator, but as one entering, stage by stage, into the active service of God. If observed and described atemporally, at any one stage, this movement from mere creaturehood to divine service would, like any change of state, display apparently contradictory features. Many of the questions raised above reflect atemporal readings of the plain-sense narrative, according to which Abram is *either* a mere creature passively obeying his God *or* a figure of the Active Intellect, self-animating his way to truth. Read in light of its eschatology, however, the narrative of Abram becomes the narrative of a third-someone: a creature of and not of this world, bound to this place and bound for a greater glory. If this Abram-who-will-be-Abraham is led by God—or even, initially, the idea of God—away from his city of origin, then he is being led, as well, from mere creaturehood to something more. It is not mere eisegesis that leads us to say that Abram is in transit from someone who serves the things of this world to someone who serves the Creator alone. If we do not posit this transformation, we cannot answer questions we believe are implicit in the plain-sense narrative. To read the narrative in this way does not mean that our answers expose *the* meaning of the narrative: the narrative is Scripture, and our answers are *abductions,* or speculative reasonings prompted by Scripture. Scripture can prompt several "legitimate" reasonings, which does not, at the same time, mean that our reasonings are mere creaturely constructions, as arbitrary as the *signifié* in de Saussure's semiology. Like Abram's narrative, our reasonings are themselves journeyings from what we are as plain-sense readers of the scriptural word to what we become as servants of the Word *as* Scripture—as Torah, Gospel, Qur'an—directing and transforming our lives in this world into lives in and for the eschaton. Our various journeys are different, however, since they begin in the different places and states of our creaturehood and since *they do not abandon that creaturehood but transform it into these various agencies for divine service.* Both our lives and our scriptural reasonings belong to this creaturehood-in-transit: there is therefore One Word but many journeyings; we pray that there is one eschaton, but we are bound to pray for and envision this eschaton in more than one way.

We are therefore comfortable with the rabbinic and Qur'anic readings of Abraham's narrative, because we cannot imagine better ways to articulate how Abram would have moved from creaturehood to divine service. We read Genesis 12:1 as entailing a critique of nature worship, because we cannot imagine Abram's leaving his father's house and his people's worship without his believing that the call comes from beyond the natural world *as* his people conceive it. At the same time, we believe that his journey can remain this-worldly, because the story implies that God makes and remakes worlds; the God who is not of nature will lead Abram to another nature, that is, another land and another social world. We envision Abram's debating with his people, finally, because we cannot imagine their not protesting his move and his not responding, as a leader would, with a strong argument for this new life with God. Within his own context of belief, finally, we envision his argument to be analogous to what we would call postliberal challenges to naturalism and naturalist theologies.

This is where Stanley comes in. In *With the Grain of the Universe,* he offers an argument against naturalism and naturalist theology that serves as a postliberal antitype of Abraham's argument. While he argues explicitly only on behalf of a Christian theology of creation, Stanley makes his case in a way that prepares Christians for theological meetings with the other children of Abraham as well. I read *With the Grain of the Universe* as refiguring the following four steps in the Abrahamic argument:[6]

1. *Leaving one's father's house presupposes leaving the "natural attitude": A pragmatic argument against foundationalist empiricism.*[7] Stanley offers a Jamesian critique of modern natural philosophy: there *is* reason for natural philosophy, but "nature" speaks to us (pace J. S. Mill) only by answering questions we ask of it, and, thus, we know the world only by way of the presuppositions we bring to it. To know the world in this way is, in the vocabulary of our scriptural heritage, to know the world as *creation.* Stanley argues that this sort of *creation* is the most, rather than the least, consistent with the goals of contemporary science. Truth is not a predicate of our immediate intuitions of the world, but only of our behavioral relation to the world, that is, of the "personality" we achieve in the world and, accordingly, of the attributes of this personality, which are our "virtues." Stanley's pragmatic theory of truth is that to test the veracity of our claims about the world is to test the veracity of virtues.

---

6. The following is adapted from my review, "On Hauerwas' *With the Grain of the Universe,*" *Modern Theology* 19, no. 1 (January 2003): 77–88. Page references to Stanley's text will appear parenthetically in the body of the essay.

7. I use the Husserlian term, "natural attitude," but adapting it as a reference to naïve realism, or the belief that we see the things of nature as they are rather than as they are for us. According to the rabbinic and Qur'anic accounts, the call announces a variety of idealism—one we might label "objective" or "pragmatic" idealism, as in Bishop Berkeley or Charles Peirce.

2. *To bring others on the journey is to argue for the God who calls: The philosophic reasonableness of "natural" (qua creation) theology.* For James, our knowledge of the world is inseparable from the particular way we act in it: inseparable, that is, from our will to believe. This understanding should lead James to argue that our knowledge of the world is "traditioned" and that a Christian tradition for knowing-and-acting in-the-world has no less validity, a priori, than another tradition. Stanley shows clearly, however, how James's cultural prejudices led him, for no good philosophical reason, to dismiss specifically *Christian* presuppositions. Leaving James behind as inadequately pragmatic, Stanley turns to his central argument: that Christianity is a reasonable source for our presuppositions about the natural world *and* that pragmatic philosophy ought to be a reasonable dialogue partner for both Christianity and natural science. There is no a priori argument to be offered about the relative superiority of Christianity as the source of our presuppositions. Christianity is to be proven through its practical consequences rather than through any evidentiary apologetics. This is, in fact, close to Charles Peirce's argument, and it is precisely why Peirce claimed that his pragmatism was nothing other than "the logical corollary" to Jesus's injunction "that ye may know them by their fruit."[8] Peirce knew what he was saying: both *that pragmatism was nothing other than the logic of Jesus's Scripture,* and *that pragmatism represented Christianity's stake in the logic of scientific inquiry.* Peirce is, indeed, the pragmatist Stanley could adopt and love almost to the end of the argument, where Peirce fails to carry out the logic of Scripture that was implied in his citation of Matthew. But, in a stunning move, Stanley enlists Karl Barth as most of the source of his scriptural pragmatism.[9]

8. Peirce's most incisive remark comes in a note he added in 1893 to his classic statement of the "Pragmatic Maxim." The relevant part of the note is: "Before we undertake to apply this rule, let us reflect a little upon what it implies. It has been said to be a skeptical and materialistic principle. But it is only an application of the sole principle of logic which was recommended by Jesus: 'Ye may know them by their fruits,' and it is very intimately allied with the idea of the gospel." See *Collected Papers of Charles S. Peirce* (hereafter *CP*), 5.402 n. 2. See also Peirce's unpublished manuscript: "A Survey of Pragmaticism" (1905), reproduced in *CP*, 5.464–96, esp. 465. I take such references to signify Peirce's otherwise underdeveloped sense that Scripture discloses a logic of repair, or what one might also call a logic of redemption, and that this is the logic of pragmatism.

9. For want of space, I bypass Stanley's account of Reinhold Niebuhr, who provides the link between naturalist and Christian pragmatisms. To be sure, Niebuhr failed to sustain the linkage, since his witness to Christ was compromised by Stoicism: rather than enact revealed presuppositions, he sought to account for them, as well, through a universalist and naturalist apologetics. Niebuhr is thus corrected by Barth the way James is corrected by Peirce.

3. Journeying forth is an argument for journeying forth: Barth as "natural" (qua creation) theologian. For Stanley, Scripture's accounts of revelation offer unsurpassed records of the grammar of how we acquire the ultimate presuppositions of our knowledge of the world, and Barth offers this era's most powerful account of the presuppositional grammar of revelation. The grammar may be reduced to these elemental rules:

a. No! to the world. A presupposition of our knowledge of the world cannot itself belong to the world, lest we commit the naturalist or stoic fallacy (141). To study the grammar of Scripture in its own terms is to study the grammar of presupposition in its own terms.

b. Thus, Christian "'natural theology' simply names how Christian convictions work to describe all that is as God's good creation." The inner grammar of Scripture is the grammar of a habit of being in the world, and all natural knowledge participates in this being (142).

c. All *analogia fidei* emerge from out of the realm of presupposition—that is, Scripture—rather than out of nature. They cannot emerge out of "nature" itself without leading us into an infinite regress, since all knowledge of nature emerges out of our presuppositions.

d. In its own terms, Scripture presents itself as a story that gives witness to the life of God incarnate as the life of Christ, which life is to be imitated by those who would serve Christ in the world. This is strictly a nonidentical imitation, for God enters life only as God, and any imitation must represent a particular enactment of God's presence, or else it is not imitation: "We can only repeat ourselves" (173).

e. Adopted as the elemental presupposition for a Christian life in the world, this story becomes a *lived* argument against any behavior in the world and any reasoning about the world that is incompatible with God's life (182). *This is why Stanley, like Abram in the plain sense of Genesis 12, can argue for God's call without stooping to apologetics.* He describes life in the story of God as a *performed* argument.

A helpful explanation can be found in Peirce's pragmatic logic:[10] (1) As Aristotle recognized, the premises of axiological arguments

---

10. Peirce's study of the logic of hypothesis-making, or "abduction," is central to his entire logic of pragmatism. He makes the connection most explicit in his 1903 "Lectures on Pragmatism": specifically, Lecture 7, entitled "Pragmatism and Abduction" (reprinted in *CP*, 5.180–212). He says, for example: "If you carefully consider the question of pragmatism you will see that it is nothing else than the question of the logic of abduction" (that is, it concerns how we can admit hypotheses as reasonable and testable hypotheses about how to repair the problems of practice that our inquiry arises to repair; 5.196).

are not themselves conclusions of arguments. But they are not just givens. (2) There are warranted and unwarranted premises. Premises are warranted by a kind of hypothetical reasoning that is neither argument nor the mere acceptance of some given. (Abram is neither skeptic nor mere knight of faith.) This reasoning can be termed *abduction:* a reasoning that *if* some surprising fact, A is B, is true; and assuming our knowledge that C is B; then, A *may* be C! (3) Abductive premises have the truth only of probability: some will judge them "true" to the degree that they are empirically confirmed; others will judge them "strong or weak" depending on the strength or weakness of the conclusions to which they lead. (4) Since their premises are abductive, axiological arguments are probable: their truth or strength will be known according to their fruit, that is, the consequences to which their conclusions give rise. (5) The truth of axiological arguments is therefore of a social and eschatological nature. It is eschatological, because we cannot know a priori that we have seen all the consequences that are yet to be seen of a given conclusion. The truth is social, because its pursuit will most likely outlive any of us as individuals and because none of us is likely to be the sole author of our premises nor the sole judge of the conclusions to which we have been led.

In these terms, arguments for going forth have abductive premises and probable conclusions that are "known by their fruit." For Stanley, they are known by the lived consequences of the virtues of action to which they give rise: this knowledge is eschatological and social, or of the church (198, passim).

f. The lived argument per se is the embodied Logos: lives led in *imitatio Christi.* Stanley concludes *With the Grain of the Universe* with an account of how the lives of saints and martyrs, who live imitating Christ, display the virtues of action through which the world should be known. Beyond his exegesis of Barth's dogmatics, this account highlights Stanley's unique, performative theology, one which, to borrow Peirce's terminology, we might label scriptural "practics."[11] Beyond the limits of a theology of Scripture per se,

---

11. Peirce's preferred term for what others call "ethics." See Charles S. Peirce, "The Basis of Pragmatism" (1906), in *CP,* 1.573 and 5.551.

12. "Sapiental pneumatology" is a term that has been used to characterize the work of both Daniel Hardy and David Ford. See Daniel Hardy, *God's Ways with the World* (Edinburgh: T. & T. Clark, 1996), chap. 14; *Finding the Church* (London: SCM Press, 2001), chaps. 3, 6; and "The God Who Is with the World," in *Science Meets Faith* (London: SPCK, 1998), chap. 9. In each case, his references to the Holy Spirit and Christ illustrate this pneumatology. See also David Ford, "Holy Spirit and Christian Spirituality," in *The Cambridge Companion to Postmodern Theology,* ed. Kevin J. Vanhoozer (Cambridge: Cambridge

this is a practical and sapiental pneumatology:[12] a Spirit-filled account of how Logos can be embodied in social and political lives, worldly vocations, and empirical sciences, as well as in ecclesial and liturgical activity. To look for and learn from saints is to declare to Abraham: Yes, I recognize that your argument on behalf of God's call appears through a journey, but I must observe the journeying proximately, through lives led closer to where I live.

4. *To a land I will show you: the argument is abductive, and Stanley may be Abrahamic as well as Christian.* As represented here, the first three steps of Stanley's argument could contribute to a wholly intra-Christian account of what it means to hear God's call and abandon naturalism. But it is time for us to note how, without any move to universalism, his account also constitutes an intra-Christian argument for venturing toward inter-Abrahamic encounter. Most simply put, the "how" is God. Stanley has reasoned with us in *With the Grain of the Universe*, but he has not offered any particular reason as a substitute for the divine presence. The claim that God's call interrupts theological naturalism (and the societal conventionalism that corresponds to it) is true if God has called, and the proof of that, as we have seen, is in the lives that are led as a consequence of this call. The Christian reader may, indeed, assume that these are lives led by Christians, explicitly in *imitatio Christi.* But I do not see anything in the argument that precludes their also being the lives of Muslims or Jews. Since there is no universality as substitute for God, only God may judge where his presence may be known. According to *With the Grain of the Universe*, Christ is an imitable measure of this presence on earth, but we do not appear to know, before the fact, who will and will not stand up to that measure, for that "ye shall know by their fruit." For the same reason, we also cannot say, before the fact, that Muslims and Jews *will* stand up to the measure. There is no substitute for being there when they are measured, and this must mean being with them when they also stand before Christ. But what does this mean, practically? I cannot of course anticipate what Christian readers will take it to mean, but I know that it will not matter what Christians think if Jews and Muslims refuse to show up for the measurement. And what will get them to show up? We have already observed one answer in the Qur'anic and rabbinic accounts of Abraham. There are both Muslims and Jews who hear God's call in the reading of Scripture and who hear it in ways that display some significant homologies with the

---

University Press, 2003), 269–90; and Peter Ochs, "The Sapiental Pneumatology of Daniel Hardy and David Ford," in "Postliberal Christianity and the Jews" (unpublished MS).

argument of *With the Grain of the Universe*. It is through Scripture that these Muslims and Jews go forth and leave their father's house, and not Scripture alone, but Scripture as enacted in lives lived in *imitatio dei*. Reading Scripture as witness to God is therefore a way to get Muslims and Jews to show up. But which Scripture? Muslims come to Qur'an and Jews to Torah. Without Gospel, however, there is no adequate witness to Christ the Measure, and how would Christians bring Muslims and Jews to the reading of Gospel?

The answer offered by Stanley's Radical Traditions series complements that offered by the Society for Scriptural Reasoning (SSR): invite Christians, Muslims, and Jews to share the fruits of their scriptural reasoning with one another. One way is by reading each other's writings (as in Radical Traditions). Another way is by gathering around tables of fellowship to read and discuss all three Scriptures (the practice of SSR). Within this fellowship, no one (individual or subcommunity) measures the other, but standing together in the presence of God's Word, all stand to be measured by that Word. For Christians, to be measured by the Word is to be measured, per se, by Christ. Although Jews and Muslims will, of course, identify this measure differently, there is no need for the participants, together, to reduce the simultaneity of these measures to any single one.[13] When they return from the fellowship table to their own ecclesial communities, moreover, Christian participants may and should indeed speak of the encounter fully in christological terms. Only *then*, after having engaged in this shared study, can they measure it by the light of Christ and thereby prove Stanley's argument for inter-Abrahamic study.

If Abraham's argument for the call is abductive, so is Stanley's, and such abductions are known by their fruit. The "land I will show you" cannot be seen before one has journeyed there; before the journey's end many journeys show themselves, and one's identity as journeyer is not defined by the law of excluded middle.

3. The Argument Concludes in "a Land I Will Show You"; or, "Walk after Me," and You Will Be There

"The land I will show you" names the third condition for justifying inter-Abrahamic study. Stanley has met this condition through sharing in inter-Abrahamic study and, by the light of Christ, as we have said, reasoning to the christologically transcendental condition for such

---

13. David Ford uses the term "simultaneity" to characterize the irreducible copresence yet difference of these three measures. See David Ford, "Knowledge, Meaning, and the World's Great Challenges," *Scottish Journal of Theology* 57, no. 2 (2004): 182–202.

study. Here are brief excerpts from Stanley's participation in 2000 in a Jewish–Christian–Muslim discussion of the three scriptural accounts of "Pharaoh's Hardened Heart."[14]

A. "PHARAOH'S HARDENED HEART: CRUEL AND UNUSUAL PUNISHMENT AND COVENANTAL ETHICS"

The discussion began with a Jewish philosophic reading of Exodus 4–14 by Shaul Magid, then of the Jewish Theological Seminary:

> My assignment . . . is to offer a "Jewish" reading of the Bible's description of the hardening of Pharaoh's heart (Exod. 4–14).
> . . . The philosophical problem of God's hardening Pharaoh's heart requires two distinct presuppositions. (1) That the Bible be understood outside the orbit of its own literary and theological world-view . . . , [so that] the Bible speaks to every generation and contains wisdom for any readership. (2) That there be no absolute ontological distinction between the Israelite and non-Israelite in the Bible . . . , [so that] all human beings are created in the image of God with free-will, all have the capacity to repent for their errors, [and that] free-will is a necessary, perhaps central, part of covenantal ethics, including but not limited to the Sinai covenant. [In these terms,] God's hardening Pharaoh's heart and thus removing the possibility of repentance . . . raises the question of ethical reciprocity and just desserts . . . [and] raises the possibility that God may harden anyone's heart, nullifying the reciprocal nature of covenantal ethics and rupturing the foundation of God's relationship to humanity.
> . . . My analysis is based on three medieval Jewish commentators. The first, Rashi, . . . avoids the ethical problem by viewing Pharaoh as an inadequate covenantal partner. The second, Moses ben Nahman (Nahmanides), draws this episode into the orbit of covenantal ethics and interprets God's actions as just in light of Pharaoh's sinful behavior. The third, Moses ben Maimon (Maimonides), goes farther than Nahmanides by viewing this episode as integral to God's covenantal relationship with humankind and more specifically, Israel. . . . For both these philosophically-inclined exegetes, covenantal ethics includes the loss of free-will resulting from continued unremorseful sin, after which the individual loses the right of partnership with God and can be used as a tool for teaching others of the limits of covenantal ethics. For Maimonides, at least, this does not mean that one is excised from the covenant. Rather, the covenant includes, in extreme cases, the justification for such cruel and unusual punishment . . . in order to administer retribution for previous behavior, especially in

---

14. The 2000 Annual Meeting of the Society for Scriptural Reasoning, published as *Journal of Scriptural Reasoning* 2, no. 2 (September 2002). Available on-line at www.etext. virginia.edu/journals/ssr/issues/volume2/number2.

cases (such as this) when such punishment can be a public display for others.

. . . When Israel enters into its covenant with God, it needs to know that the power [it is] given is not [its] own but still the property of God. The abuse of power will result in the loss of power. But, the loss of power does not negate the covenantal relationship. . . . Losing free-will is the result of abusing free-will. Abusing free-will is the calculated effort to deny the "image of God" in other human beings (Exod. 1:11). The punishment is to lose the "image of God." I would suggest that taking away one's free-will is an example of cruel and unusual punishment in that it dis-empowers the covenantal partner while still holding that partner covenantally responsible. In that sense alone, the story remains problematic.

B. "PHARAOH'S HARDENED HEART: SOME CHRISTIAN READINGS"

Stanley responded with this Christian reading:

Like Pharaoh I have a hard heart that only responds by having the shit kicked out of it. Yet if Shaul's account of the reading of the hardening of Pharaoh's heart by Jewish sources is correct, my lack of concern about free will may indicate that I represent the habits of Christian readers.

It is not for me to question Shaul's account of Jewish readings of this text as representing a "philosophical problem" concerning free will, but I would like to know more about why God's covenant with Israel requires the presumption that "all human beings are created in the image of God with free will." Shaul notes, for example, that Nahmanides recognizes the need to justify God's action in a way Rashi does not, but Nahmanides does not see the need to justify God's action outside this particular narrative. But I should have thought that is the whole point—why would you ever be led as a reader of Scripture to think the creature can assume a stance that puts God in the dock? Surely that is why, as Shaul teaches us, Maimonides saw that freedom is never absolute. "To be in a covenantal relationship with God is to live knowing that retribution of willful acts may include the loss of the will to act. In this, Pharaoh is our teacher."

Origen, I think, has a position quite like Maimonides. He begins (*Exodus Homily IV*) noting that in the first five plagues Pharaoh is said to have hardened his heart, but in the last plagues God is said to have "hardened Pharaoh's heart." Origen is also quite well aware of Exodus 4:21. Origen observes that we should not regard the divine spirit so lowly as to suppose this distinction was made by chance. Yet he notes that he is "not fit or able in such difference to pry into the secrets of divine wisdom," but he thinks Paul is. Appealing to Romans 9:14ff, Origen quotes Paul's claim that "it depends not on human will or exertion, but on God who . . . has mercy on whomever he chooses, and he hardens the heart of whomever he chooses."

. . . [Origen and Augustine] read the narrative in relation to other stories in the Scripture, which allows them to weave the stories of Scripture into an ongoing narrative. We should not be surprised, therefore, that the "rule of faith," which we now call the Apostles' Creed, was the outline the church discovered for testing the many readings they knew Scripture required.

Christians would, therefore, deny that such readings are "imposed" on the Scripture. Rather they simply are following the mode of reading exemplified in Scripture itself. For example, in Deuteronomy 28:27—surely some of the most chilling warnings we can find in the Bible—Israel is threatened "with the boils of Egypt" if she does not obey the commandments. Does this mean that Israel can become like Egypt in her unfaithfulness? I would be fascinated to know if and how the Rabbis commented on this text. Can Israel's heart, like the heart of Pharaoh, be hardened? Christians could, I believe, learn a great deal from such readings particularly if you believe as I do that Christian reading of Scripture has for too long been shaped by Christian political power not unlike that of the Pharaoh.

I should like to end on that note, but I feel I need to raise one last issue that cannot help but be painful to Christian and Jew alike. The last and most horrible plague, the death of the firstborn, which finally it seems got Pharaoh's attention, cannot help but haunt us. Of course God is to harden Pharaoh's heart one more time, but nonetheless we cannot help after the Shoah to feel the horror of the last plague. A Christian reading of the last plague is made even more difficult by our Scripture. "When Herod saw that he had been tricked by the wise men, he was infuriated, and he sent and killed all the children in and around Bethlehem who were two years old or under, according to the time that he had learned from the wise men" (Matt. 2:16). If Jesus is the rod of Moses it seems those who have had to pay the price from the time of his birth are Jewish children. If I were Jewish I think I would find it very hard not to think of Christianity as one long plague.

Christians, of course, believe that Jesus is the blood that has been painted over the lintels and doorposts of the church. Yet as a homeless people desperate for security we have, I believe, far too often made Jewish children pay the price for our attempt to find a home in this world. Such a reading may be too "foreign" to questions surrounding the hardening of Pharaoh's heart, but in these times I do not believe Christians can afford not to raise them. If we Christians fail to recognize the way we have become Pharaoh to the Jews we risk not recognizing the hardness of our hearts—a recognition that seems unavoidable given God's gracious gift of plagues.

C. "'I AM YOUR LORD MOST HIGH': PHARAOH AND THE SIN OF HUBRIS IN THE QUR'AN"

The Muslim response was offered by Vincent Cornell, of the University of Arkansas:

In Islam, fundamental error consists in rejecting or misunderstanding the concept of *tawhid*—in holding that the Absolute is not absolute, or that it is relative, or that there is more than one Absolute, or that the relative itself is absolute. Sin consists in actualizing this error on the level of human behavior. In the Qur'an, Pharaoh personifies fundamental error and sin through his denial of the uniqueness of the Absolute and by his hubris in considering himself more than a mortal man.

It often comes as a surprise to the non-Muslim to discover that the most widely mentioned prophet in the Qur'an is Moses. . . . More than just the political liberator of his people, the Qur'anic Moses is a Messenger of the divine word and liberator of the human soul. In the course of the Qur'anic narrative he transforms the tribe of Israel *(Banu Isra'il)*, the oppressed and lowly slaves of the lordly Pharaoh, into a paradigmatic community of divine guidance *(umma)*—a community whose servitude now belongs only to God.

In the Qur'anic narrative, Pharaoh appears as Moses' foil: his grandeur, limitless worldly authority, and pretended divinity contrast sharply with Moses' simplicity, lack of rhetorical fluency . . . , and complete dependence on guidance from above. Yet despite his personal shortcomings, the Qur'an mentions time and again that Moses, not Pharaoh, is the one who possesses true authority *(sultan)*. . . . The most conclusive proof of Pharaoh's illegitimacy lies in his outrageous claim of divinity—an act of hubris unparalleled by any other in the Qur'anic narrative.

Concluding Note

Reasoning back from the fact of this discussion, the last step of our inquiry would be to ask: What are the christological conditions for Stanley's engagement in such an inter-Abrahamic study? Only Stanley's Christian community can answer this question, however. For now, I will close by suggesting features of this discussion that might prove particularly conducive to communal reflection:

- The reverence of all three discussants for the scriptural word and for the God who reveals it.
- The discussants' concerns (a) to read the plain sense; (b) to reread it in relation to the entire scriptural canon and (c) in relation to ancient and medieval commentaries; (d) to maintain and integrate all these levels of reading.
- The interscriptural character of the discussion, where some comparable issues arose across the three traditions and where some interpretive differences were most noticeable within a given tradition rather than between traditions.
- The way the discussants "go forth" across the borders of each other's commentary traditions, while also returning "home," while also going forth again in ways that lend the entire discussion its own movement toward an as yet undisclosed land.

Contributors

Robert N. Bellah is Elliott Professor Emeritus of Sociology at the University of California, Berkeley. His most recent book is *Imagining Japan: The Japanese Tradition and Its Modern Interpretation* (Berkeley: University of California Press, 2003).

David B. Burrell, CSC, is Hesburgh Professor of Philosophy and Theology at the University of Notre Dame. He most recently published *Faith and Freedom: An Interfaith Perspective* (Oxford: Blackwell, 2004).

H. Tristram Engelhardt, Jr., is Professor of Philosophy at Rice University and Professor Emeritus at Baylor College of Medicine. His most recent book is *The Foundations of Christian Bioethics* (Lisse: Swets & Zeitlinger, 2000).

C. Rosalee Velloso Ewell is Professor of Biblical Theology and Ethics at South American Theological Seminary in Londrina, Brazil. She is coeditor of *Baptist Roots: A Reader in the Theology of a Christian People* (Valley Forge: Judson, 1999).

Rowan A. Greer is Walter H. Gray Professor Emeritus of Anglican Studies at Yale University Divinity School. His most recent book is *Christian Life and Christian Hope: Raids on the Inarticulate* (New York: Crossroad, 2001).

Harry Huebner is currently Vice President and Academic Dean at Canadian Mennonite University, Winnipeg, Manitoba. He is author of *Mennonite Education in a Post-Christian World* (Winnipeg: CMBC, 1998).

Reinhard Hütter is Associate Professor of Christian Theology at Duke University Divinity School. He most recently published *Bound to Be Free: Evangelical Catholic Engagements in Ecclesiology, Ethics, and Ecumenism* (Grand Rapids: Eerdmans, 2004).

Robert W. Jenson is Senior Scholar for Research at the Center of Theological Inquiry in Princeton, New Jersey. His most recent book is *On Thinking the Human: Resolutions of Difficult Notions* (Grand Rapids: Eerdmans, 2003).

L. Gregory Jones is Dean and Professor of Theology at Duke University Divinity School. His most recent book is *Everyday Matters: Intersections of Life and Faith* (Nashville: Abingdon, 2003).

Emmanuel M. Katongole is Associate Research Professor of Theology and World Christianity at Duke University Divinity School. He is author of *Beyond Universal Reason: The Relation between Religion and Ethics in the Work of Stanley Hauerwas* (Notre Dame: University of Notre Dame Press, 2000).

Nicholas Lash is Norris-Hulse Professor Emeritus of Divinity at the University of Cambridge. He most recently published *Holiness, Speech, and Silence: Reflections on the Question of God* (Aldershot, England: Ashgate, 2004).

George Lindbeck is Pitkin Professor Emeritus of Historical Theology at Yale University Divinity School. His most recent book is *The Church in a Postliberal Age* (Grand Rapids: Eerdmans, 2003).

Peter Ochs is Edgar Bronfman Professor of Modern Judaic Studies at the University of Virginia. He recently coedited *The Jewish–Christian Schism Revisited* (Grand Rapids: Eerdmans, 2003) and *Textual Reasonings: Jewish Philosophy and Text Study at the End of the Twentieth Century* (London: SCM, 2002; Grand Rapids: Eerdmans, 2003).

Arne Rasmusson is Associate Professor in Theology and Ethics at Umeå University in Umeå, Sweden. His most recent book is *The Church as Polis: From Political Theology to Theological Politics as Exemplified by Jürgen Moltmann and Stanley Hauerwas*, rev. ed. (Notre Dame: University of Notre Dame Press, 1995).

Hans S. Reinders is Willem van den Bergh Professor of Ethics and Mental Disability at the Vrije Universiteit in Amsterdam. He is author of

The Future of the Disabled in Liberal Society: An Ethical Analysis (Notre Dame: University of Notre Dame Press, 2000).

Neville Richardson is Associate Professor of Theological Ethics in the School of Theology, University of KwaZulu-Natal, Pietermaritzburg, South Africa. His most recent publications include "On Keeping Theological Ethics Theological in Africa: The Quest for a (Southern) African Theological Ethics," *Annual of the Society of Christian Ethics* 21 (2001): 361–78; and "Nonviolence at Apartheid's End: A Theological Retrospect," *Journal of Theology for Southern Africa* 116 (2003): 81–100.

Bernd Wannenwetsch is University Lecturer in Ethics in the Theology Faculty, University of Oxford. His most recent book in English is *Political Worship: Ethics for Christian Citizens* (Oxford: Oxford University Press, 2004).

Robert Louis Wilken is William R. Kenan, Jr., Professor of the History of Christianity at the University of Virginia. He most recently published *The Spirit of Early Christian Thought: Seeking the Face of God* (New Haven: Yale University Press, 2003).

The publisher would like to thank David Toole for coming out of editorial retirement to copyedit this book—simply for the love of Stanley.

Index

Abraham, 315–17
Africa, 133, 136–37, 139, 145–52
African Initiated Churches, 244–48, 249, 253
Ambrose, 74–87, 196n5
America, 112, 114, 125–30
Anabaptists, 203n23, 215
Annas, Julia, 64n23
Antiochus of Ascalon, 16–17
apartheid, 229–39, 243–53
Aquinas, Thomas, 8, 14, 35, 36, 37, 41, 45
Arendt, Hannah, 109
Arians, 74, 80, 81, 82, 84
Aristotle, 8, 14, 37, 39, 40–41, 45, 63–67
Augustine, 42, 44, 78, 84, 154n1, 174, 195n3, 308, 325
    on the church, 27, 182, 296
    on heavenly city, 169, 179
    on Rome, 177n25, 178
    on truth, 13–34
    on wants and desires, 48–49
autonomy, 57, 124, 237, 241

Bailey, Kenneth E., 300n39
Baldovin, John F., 190
baptism, 27, 28–29, 108–9
Barmen Declaration, 96, 235, 250, 251
Barth, Karl, 89–103, 106–7, 110–11, 163, 168, 200, 204, 215n8, 233n7, 234–36, 251, 294n24, 319–20
Basil the Great, 200, 201, 208
Bauckham, Richard, 167, 168, 177, 181

Becket, Thomas à, 279
Bell, Catherine, 260
Berkeley, Bishop, 318n7
bishops, 73, 79–87, 153, 154
Blenkinsopp, Joseph, 36
Bonhoeffer, Dietrich, 182n37, 219, 233n7, 234, 236
Boniface VIII, 203
Bonnke, Reinhold, 149–50
Bossy, John, 260
Botha, P. W., 245n43
Bowman, Carl, 129
Boyarin, Daniel, 104n61
Boyarin, Jonathan, 104n61
Brantlinger, Patrick, 266n40, 276n90
Bredenkamp, Victor, 233n6
Brueggemann, Walter, 117
Buckley, Michael, 261
Burtchaell, James Tunstead, 35
Bush, George W., 125, 126–28

Calvin, John, 123, 233n7
Calvinism, 123, 124n23, 233n7
capitalism, 92, 143, 235, 240, 252
Cartwright, Michael, 104n61
Cavanaugh, William, 90
Chapman, Mark, 93
character, 8, 56, 58, 63–64, 136, 202, 240
Charlemagne, 157, 195n3, 197
China, 114, 116–17, 122
Chisholm, Roderick, 40
choice, 40, 42, 47, 50–51, 52, 54, 57

Christendom, 89, 95, 96, 110, 111, 155, 201, 213–14n3, 296
Christian civilization, 157–63
Christian education, 281–85
Christian life, 24–25, 27, 32
Christian university, 281, 293, 298, 302
Christology, 94, 102–3, 295–96
Chrysostom, John, 85, 200
church
    Augustine on, 27, 182, 296
    as body of Christ, 206
    as community, 134, 136, 200–201, 202
    as culture, 155, 157–62
    faithfulness, 251–53
    as instrument to nontheological end, 249
    marks of, 207
    minority status, 239n24
    and nation-state, 89
    pilgrimage, 182, 191
    and secular political agenda, 251
    typologies of, 249–50
    and world, 8, 125, 289
Cicero, 13, 79
city, 168–72, 177–78, 183–189, 192
civil religion, 113, 172, 174, 186, 189, 191, 192, 238
Clark, Mary, 41
Clement of Alexandria, 17n12, 31n40
Colenso, John William, 233n7
Comaroff, Jean and John, 251
community, 28, 217, 238–42
Congar, Yves, 220–21
Conrad, Joseph, 257–59, 262–79
Constantine, 73–74, 77, 78, 79, 122, 154–55, 156, 197, 198n9, 201, 289
Constantinianism, 74, 79, 122, 129, 130, 197–98n9, 223, 293, 295–97, 302, 305
Constantius II, 74, 80, 83
Cooper, John, 64
Cornell, Vincent, 326
Coulson, John, 270
Council of Nicea, 74, 80
creation, 44–45, 52, 101, 177, 318
creator, 38–40, 43, 44–46, 48
Cyprian, 76–77, 209n42

Davies, Brian, 45n21
Day, Dorothy, 138, 218, 219
de Gruchy, John W., 234

democracy, 48, 123, 127, 137, 240
Derrida, J., 161
Descartes, R., 40
De Wachter, Frans, 133, 134–35
disabled, 53, 58
    see also intellectual disability
Drake, Harold, 73
Dula, Peter, 296n32
Dulles, Avery, 250
Dulles, John Foster, 223
Dunne, Joseph, 39n10
Durkheim, E., 260-61, 262

ecclesiology, 94–96, 148, 241, 295–97, 302–4
education, 282, 284, 291–93, 298
Egypt, 114, 115–16, 117–18, 120
Eliot, T. S., 211
Elshtain, Jean Bethke, 178
empire, 115, 126–30
Enlightenment, 39, 113, 124, 194–96, 200, 237, 238n19, 240, 285
Epicurus, 16
eschatology, 168, 170n10, 317
ethics, 55–56, 107–8, 139, 238–42
Eucharist, 108, 109, 156, 208
Eusebius of Caesarea, 82
Evagrios the Solitary, 202
evangelicals, 128–30, 224, 227

Ford, David, 323n13
forgiveness, 89, 108, 109
Forrester, Duncan, 234–35, 252
Foucault, M., 304
foundationalism, 39, 318
Francis of Assisi, 219
Frankfurt, Harry, 132
free church, 89, 110
freedom, 35, 36, 37–38, 48–49, 148
Frei, Hans, 311
friendship, 8, 54–56, 59–63, 65–67, 69

Gadamer, Hans-Georg, 39
Gifford Lectures (Hauerwas), 9–10, 73, 89, 137, 217, 235
Gifford, Paul, 150–51
Girard, R., 176
God, 44–45, 177, 241, 261–62, 306
Gorski, Philip, 123
Grant, George, 294n24
Gratian, 81, 83

Greenfield, Liah, 93
Gregory Palamas, 200
Gregory the Theologian, 200
Gregory VII, 85
Guerard, Albert, 259n4
Gustafson, James, 134, 200
Gutiérrez, Gustavo, 238n19

Hampson, Robert, 265
Harink, Douglas, 107n73
Harnack, Adolf von, 90, 204n27
Hauerwas, Stanley
    on church, 200–201, 202–11, 251
    on Constantinianism, 197–98n9
    as contrarian and polemicist, 8
    ecumenicity, 214–20
    on Enlightenment, 194–95n3, 197n9
    on friendship, 67–70
    on marriage, 206
    political theology, 168
    on South Africa, 236–37
    on violence, 193
Hawthorne, Nathaniel, 47
Hays, Richard, 139
Healy, Nicholas, 102, 106
Heart of Darkness (Conrad), 258–59,
    262–79
heavenly city, 33, 169, 170
Hegel, G. W. F., 194n3, 297
Henry IV, 85
Henry, Patrick, 222n20
Herrmann, Wilhelm, 90, 91–93, 94, 97, 99
high culture, 155–56, 157–62, 163
historicism, 285–90, 293, 294–95, 297
Hitler, A., 95
HIV/AIDS, 252
Hobbes, T., 175
holiness, 98, 204, 208, 210
Hunsinger, George, 89–90n5, 99
Hussein, Saddam, 127
Husserl, Edmund, 318n7
Hütter, Reinhard, 215n8

idolatry, 26, 84, 95, 262, 263, 277–78, 295
Ignatius, 87, 209n41
illumination, 18, 23, 24, 25
image of God, 23, 25, 34
imagination, 90, 93, 111, 139, 152, 283,
    284–85, 287, 301, 305
intellectual disability, 54–57
interreligious dialogue, 310, 313–14

Jacobsen, Thorkild, 115
James, William, 318–19
Jefferson, Thomas, 124
Jenkins, Philip, 139–45, 152
Jenson, Robert, 311
Jerome, 30-31, 196n5
Jesus, 22, 24n23, 51–52, 68, 121–22, 130,
    199, 284, 299–301
John Paul II, Pope, 73, 88, 138, 217–19, 228
Johnson, Chalmers, 126n28
John the Theologian, 206n30
Judaism, 104–6, 107, 222n22
Julian, 77, 80
justice, 19–20, 64, 232, 237
Justina, 81
Justinian, 156
Justin Martyr, 155

Kant, Immanuel, 43–44, 46, 47, 134–35,
    194n3, 196n5, 238n19, 241, 242,
    286, 297, 312
Keegan, John, 93
Kessler, Diane, 222n21
Kierkegaard, S., 46
kingdom, 33, 89, 98, 100, 111, 121, 238–
    39, 249, 288
Kinnamon, Michael, 222n21, 224–28
knowledge, 19, 23, 24, 26, 304
Kovesi, Julius, 36
Kroeker, Travis, 109
Kuyper, Abraham, 233n7

Lash, Nicholas, 39n10
Leavis, F. R., 271
Lekganyane, Bishop, 246
Leo XIII, Pope, 36
Lester, John, 259n6, 263, 275n83
Levenson, Michael, 259n4
Levinas, Emmanuel, 50
Lewis, C. S., 294n24
liberal empire, 126–27
liberalism, 8, 48, 55, 113, 124n23, 237–38,
    292
liberal Protestantism, 124–25, 130, 204
liberation theology, 150, 221, 238n19
libertarian freedom, 38, 40–41, 42, 48,
    50, 52
Little, David, 125n24
liturgy, 155, 156, 190–91
Lohfink, Gerhard, 88
Lothola, Immanuel, 246

love, 22, 24, 25, 29, 297
    for enemies, 306
    for friend, 67
    for God, 19–20
    for neighbors, 19–20
    of self, 22, 26, 67, 169n9
Lubac, Henri de, 36
Luckmann, Thomas, 261
Luther, Martin, 47, 241

Machiavelli, 119n14
MacIntyre, Alasdair, 36, 41, 56, 196n4,
    199, 285–86, 290–93, 295
Magesa, Laurenti, 148n28
Magid, Shaul, 324–25
Maimonides, Moses, 315–16, 324, 325
Malo, David, 118
Mark of Ephesus, 200
Marshall, Bruce, 217
Marshall, George C., 127
Marx, Karl, 249, 283
Maurice, F. D., 233n7
Maximian, 75
Maxwell, David, 149
McCabe, Herbert, 139
McClendon, Jim, 285
McCormack, Bruce, 94
McDonagh, Enda, 231
Mennonites, 110, 123, 130, 203n23, 215
mentally handicapped, 55
    see also intellectual disability
Methodists, 124, 203n23, 242n34
Metropolitan Maximos, 207n37
Meyer, Birgit, 146–49
Milbank, John, 137, 262n20, 281
Milton, John, 44
modernity, 56, 58, 92, 113n3, 146–47,
    149–50, 170, 278, 291, 310–11
Moltmann, Jürgen, 216
Moses ben Nahman, 324
Mother Teresa, 216, 217, 219
Mugambi, Jessi, 148
Murfin, Ross, 259n4
Murray, Andrew, 233n7
Muslims, 44–45, 51, 313, 322–23

Najder, Zdzislaw, 259n4
nationalism, 92–93, 95–96, 110, 124–25
nation-state, 89, 91–93, 94–97, 100–101,
    110, 111, 123, 136–37, 139, 144,
    146, 149, 151

natural theology, 106, 137–38, 318–19, 320
Nero, 78, 154
Nevsky, Alexander, 210
Newman, John Henry, 39, 261, 270–71,
    278n100
Niebuhr, H. Richard, 250, 290, 296
Niebuhr, Reinhold, 130, 200, 296, 319n9
Niehaus, Carl, 244
Nietzsche, Friedrich, 183–89, 192, 261,
    285, 294n245

Ochs, Peter, 104n61
O'Donovan, Oliver, 170, 176
Origen, 74, 76, 79, 325

pacifism, 99, 105, 208–10, 224, 305
Paul VI, Pope, 221
peace, 8, 174, 305
Peirce, Charles, 318n7, 319, 320, 321
Pentecostals, 141, 145–51, 224, 227
Petersen, Robin, 235, 245–47, 248–49
Petrarch, 257–58
Philo, 74
Pieper, Josef, 38
Pinches, Charles, 60, 67–68
Plato, 14, 17–18, 20, 31, 34, 37, 41, 42, 45,
    294n24
Platonism, 15, 16, 19, 20, 33
Plotinus, 18, 25
politics, 121, 136–37, 139, 167–68
post-Christendom, 96–100
postliberalism, 318
postmodernism, 39, 40, 46, 278
power, 40, 42, 47, 92, 110, 304
Preller, Victor, 35
Preuss, Samuel, 260
prevenient grace, 21, 26, 27, 28–29
pride, 22, 24, 26, 304
Protestantism, 202–3
    and Enlightenment, 197n9
Prudentius, 83, 87, 155, 162
Purdy, Dwight, 263, 265n32, 275n85

Qur'an, 310, 315–16, 327

Rabinowitz, Peter, 263
Rade, Martin, 90, 91n10
Radical Reformation, 123
Radical Traditions, 309–14, 323
Radner, Ephraim, 217
Rahner, Karl, 111

Ramsey, Paul, 200, 233
Rashi, 324
Rasmusson, Arne, 215n8
Ratzinger, John Cardinal, 203, 207n37
Reformation, 123–24, 200, 223, 226
Renaissance, 196–97, 200
Renner, Stanley, 258n3
resident aliens, 33, 110, 189
resistance, 246–48, 249
Rhodes, Edward, 126–27
Robertson, Roland, 262n21
Roman Catholics, 111, 123, 130, 202–3,
    224, 227
Romanides, John S., 194n2
Rome, Roman Empire, 79–80, 87, 110,
    122, 177–78, 179, 189, 190
Rorty, Richard, 39
Rousseau, Jean-Jacques, 112
Rubens, Peter Paul, 85

sacraments, 155, 207–8, 242
Sadat, Anwar, 51
Said, Edward, 308
Sawai, Gloria, 306
Schleiermacher, Friedrich, 288
Scott, James, 110, 247, 251
sect, sectarianism, 33, 136, 154, 289, 296
Segundo, J. L., 249n49
Sergius of Radonezh, 210
Servetus, Michael, 123
Smit, Dirkie, 242n32, 251n54
socialism, 90, 93, 235–36, 251
Sokolowski, Robert, 45n23
South Africa, 229-39, 243-53
Spong, John, 141
Stern, Jessica, 125n24
Stewart, Garrett, 259, 266n40
Stout, Jeffrey, 215, 237n17
Stump, Eleonore, 37–38, 41
Symeon the New Theologian, 200
Symmachus, 83–84

Tacitus, 169n6
Tanakh, 310, 313
Taylor, Charles, 113n3
Temple, Placide, 133n3
Tertullian, 209n42
Theodosius, 81, 84–86, 87n31
theological realism, 57–59

Theresa of Avila, 219
Thessalonica, 85
Thomas, Brook, 267
Towler, Robert, 261, 262
tradition, 207n36, 236, 285, 290–92, 319
Trinity, 14, 94, 98, 160–61, 311n2
Troeltsch, Ernst, 90–93, 94, 97, 99, 106,
    249–50, 285–89, 291, 293, 294n24,
    295–96, 297
truth, 13–14, 16–19, 26, 30–32, 34, 60, 138
Truth and Reconciliation Commission
    (South Africa), 243–48, 253
Turner, Denys, 271
Tutu, Desmond, 243, 246–47

universality, 110, 310, 311–12, 322
university, 281, 291–93

Valentinian, 75, 81
Valentinian II, 81, 83, 84
Vatican II, 36, 80, 203, 219, 221, 222n22
Velázquez, 159
Villa-Vicencio, Charles, 234, 236
violence, 92, 125n24, 176, 193, 304
Virilio, Paul, 304n46
virtue, virtues, 8, 19–21, 23, 63–65, 67, 240

Walzer, Michael, 51, 118–19
war, 8, 33, 88, 96, 209–10n42
Watt, Ian, 258, 259n4, 263n24, 276
Watts, Cedric, 269, 271, 275, 277
Weber, Max, 115, 120, 260, 302n41
Webster, John, 99
Wilken, Robert, 36
Williams, George, 123
Williams, Raymond, 263
Willimon, William, 198n9
Wilson, Woodrow, 127
witness, 30–32, 60–61, 108, 284, 306
Wittgenstein, Ludwig, 35
World Council of Churches, 216, 222–23,
    232–33
worship, 180–83, 190, 204, 208, 242, 245,
    253, 261–63, 277

Yoder, John Howard, 36, 89, 96–100,
    103–11, 121, 123, 138, 200, 217–19,
    228, 280, 286, 293–97, 305